JPS GUIDE

THE
JEWISH
BIBLE

The JPS Project Team

JPS GUIDE

THE
JEWISH
BIBLE

2008 • 5768
Philadelphia
The Jewish Publication Society

The Jewish Publication Society
2100 Arch Street, 2nd floor
Philadelphia, PA 19103
www.jewishpub.org

Design and Composition by Masters Group Design

Manufactured in the United States of America

08 09 10 11 12   10 9 8 7 6 5 4 3 2 1

Library of Congress Cataloging-in-Publication Data

JPS guide : the Jewish Bible.
    p. cm.
    Includes bibliographical references and index.
    ISBN 978-0-8276-0851-1 (alk. paper)
    1. Bible. O.T.–Introductions.
    BS1140.3J67 2008
    221.6'1–dc22
                        2008010794

CONTENTS

Acknowledgments

This volume began with a simple idea: to create a concise companion to the Bible. But that led to a not-so-simple question: How does one develop a guide that is worthy of accompanying such a complex book and keep it short and uncomplicated? A book based on scholarship without being "scholarly"? For JPS, which prides itself on publishing scholarly books, especially ones about the Bible, this was a challenge.

Fortunately, we had some excellent resources right at JPS, and some fine people to call on to help. We invited scholars—those who wrote for the JPS Bible commentaries and for *Etz Hayim*, who advised on the JPS TANAKH, and who contributed to *The Contemporary Torah*—as well as educators and librarians, to tell us what they thought should be in such a guide. Some of these people also contributed chapters to complement the new pieces we commissioned. And we had a first-rate advisory board whose members read every word and made invaluable suggestions throughout the manuscript's development.

With such excellent help, *The Jewish Bible: A JPS Guide* is what it set out to be: an introduction and compact reference to the most fascinating and influential book of all time.

We very much want to thank JPS CEO and editor-in-chief Ellen Frankel, for supporting us each step of the way; she has been our cheerleader and guide, encouraging us to turn a promising idea into a real book and setting high standards for it.

And it was our three advisers who helped us strive to meet these standards. Thank you senior adviser Shalom Paul, and advisers Frederick Greenspahn and Ziony Zevit for your wise counsel and for generously giving us so much of your time in reviewing outlines and drafts, final manuscripts, map sketches, and more.

We are indebted to Marc Brettler, for giving us access to material from his book *How to Read the Bible.* And to all the others who contributed their knowledge and writings: Adele Berlin, Joyce Eisenberg, Michael Fishbane, Michael Fox, Leonard Greenspoon, Jill Hammer, Nahum Sarna, Stuart Kelman, Adriane Leveen, David Mandel, Lionel Moses, Adele Reinhartz, Benjamin Scolnic, Ellen Scolnic, David Stein, Jeffrey Tigay, Barry Walfish, and Andrea Weiss.

Thank you Cullen Schippe, Chuck Stetson, and the Pflaum Publishing Group, for permission to excerpt from *The Bible and Its Influence;* Don Kraus and Oxford University Press, for an excerpt from *The Jewish Study Bible;* and Keter Publishing House, for permission to adapt from "Poetry" in *Encyclopaedia Judaica.*

We are grateful to Sharon Liberman Mintz, the curator of Jewish art of the library of the Jewish Theological Seminary, for opening up JTS's extensive archives to us; to Paul LoBue and his design team for creating our maps; and to series designer Lisa Weinberger for her stylish layout and color scheme.

At the outset Julie Pelc helped us get this project jump-started, poring through her personal library and that of the American Jewish University, making suggestions, and writing early drafts.

Julia Oestreich picked up where Julie left off, researching so many topics, preparing boxes, finalizing charts and tables, directing map work, gathering art, and doing with great competence dozens of other tasks to prepare for production. JPS interns Robyn Weiss, Rachel Maimin, and Miriam Newman devoted part of their summer to this project. And Karen Schnitker took time out of her other JPS work to do research and writing as well.

Many thanks, too, to copyeditor Debra Corman, whose keen knowledge of judaica was such an asset; to sharp-eyed proofreader Candace Levy; and indexer Mark Lautman. And of course, to production manager Robin Norman and managing editor Janet Liss, who together oversaw the final, critical stages of quality control and kept us all on track and in good humor.

Carol Hupping

Abbreviations for the Books of the Bible

Amos	Amos
1 Chron.	1 Chronicles
2 Chron.	2 Chronicles
Dan.	Daniel
Deut.	Deuteronomy
Eccles.	Ecclesiastes
Esther	Esther
Exod.	Exodus
Ezek.	Ezekiel
Ezra	Ezra
Gen.	Genesis
Hab.	Habakkuk
Hag.	Haggai
Hosea	Hosea
Isa.	Isaiah
Jer.	Jeremiah
Job	Job
Joel	Joel
Jon.	Jonah
Josh.	Joshua
Judg.	Judges
1 Kings	1 Kings
2 Kings	2 Kings
Lam.	Lamentations
Lev.	Leviticus
Mal.	Malachi
Mic.	Micah
Nah.	Nahum
Neh.	Nehemiah
Num.	Numbers
Obad.	Obadiah
Prov.	Proverbs
Ps.	Psalms
Ruth	Ruth
1 Sam.	1 Samuel
2 Sam.	2 Samuel
Songs	Song of Songs
Zech.	Zechariah
Zeph.	Zephaniah

WHAT IS THE BIBLE?

The word "Bible" derives from the Greek *biblia*, meaning "books." By its very name, "the Bible" refers to "*the* collection of books"—that is, the one that is deemed to be authoritative, or canonical.

Different communities have different Bibles. For Christians, the Bible includes the New Testament; for Jews it does not. To distinguish the Jewish Bible from the Christian Bible, people have suggested a variety of names for it. Christians typically call it the Old Testament, where "testament" is an archaic way of referring to a contract ("covenant"). This name is based on a prophecy in Jeremiah that states: "See, a time is coming—declares the LORD—when I will make a *new covenant* with the House of Israel and the House of Judah. It will not be like the covenant I made with their fathers, when I took them by the hand to lead them out of the land of Egypt, a covenant which they broke, though I espoused them—declares the LORD" (31:31–32). Early Christian tradition understood this passage as a prophecy about a new covenant, centered around Jesus, which replaces the old Mosaic one. This led to the terms "New Testament" and "Old Testament."

Jews, however, view the original covenant as still operative. For this reason, Jews have tended to reject the term "Old Testament." Many simply call this body of literature "the Bible." For religious Jews, this name is by definition appropriate: these are "the books" that are authoritative.

Academic scholars, meanwhile, generally prefer not to take sides in the debate as to which covenant with God is in force. Therefore, in scholarly circles, the more neutral terms "Hebrew Bible" or "Jewish Scripture(s)" have gained currency. Admittedly, the first term is slightly imprecise, because some passages of the Bible are not in Hebrew but rather in Aramaic, a related Semitic language.

Other Jewish Names: A Historical Review

In the texts written during the biblical period itself—which lasted more than a thousand years—we know of no name given for this set of books. The Bible was then still in formation as an authoritative collection. It received its title only after it came into being—signaling the start of the postbiblical period.

In the 1st century C.E., Josephus (the great Jewish historian who wrote in Greek) knew of these texts. He called them *Ta Hiera Grammata* (The Holy Writings). He also called them *grammasi* (that which is written)—often translated as "Scripture," but better rendered uncapitalized, as "scripture."

In classical Rabbinic literature, the two most common terms for the Bible are *miqra* (literally "that which is read or recited aloud") and *Kitvei Hakodesh* (The Holy Writings). Sometimes, the Rabbis referred to the Bible as "Torah, Nevi'im, Kethuvim" (the Torah, the Prophets, and the Writings).

In the Middle Ages, perhaps in the late first millennium C.E., scribes shortened "Torah, Nevi'im, Kethuvim" into the acronym "TANAKH," and Jews today still commonly use that name for their Bible. As the title of The Jewish Publication Society's 1985 translation, the "TANAKH" makes a point that other names ("the Bible" or "Holy Scriptures,") do not. Namely, it underscores that the translators rendered directly from the Hebrew (not from an ancient Greek version, like some Christians translations) *and* drew on Jewish interpretive tradition.

Making an issue out of what to call these texts might seem pedantic, but it is not. The "Hebrew Bible" and the "Old Testament" differ in more than name only. They contain the same texts, but they are organized and ordered differently. (The ordering matters because it alters the context in which we understand the text; a book's meaning can shift depending on which books we read before and after it.) More significantly, the term "Hebrew Bible" suggests a corpus that is self-standing, whereas the "Old Testament" does not. (Using the word "old" implies that there is something "new" with which to contrast it.) The meaning of many passages in the "Old Testament" changes when one views them as part of a larger whole that includes the New Testament.

How the Bible Is Organized

The name "TANAKH" reflects a three-part (tripartite) organization of the Bible; for Jews, this is the standard division of the Bible. The name of each of its parts, however, warrants some explanation. The name of the first part, as we have said, is "Torah." Christians have often translated the term as "Law," but this is too restrictive; it misrepresents this collection of books, which also features nonlegal elements such as narrative and poetry. (It also misrepresents Judaism, which is far more than a "religion of law.") Rather, "Torah" is a broad term that means "Teaching" or "Instruction." (It is also sometimes called the Pentateuch, which is Greek for "five parts"; *humash,* which is Hebrew for "five"; or the Five Books of Moses).

The name of the second part, "Nevi'im," is called "Prophets" in English. However, many of its books are not actually prophetic works. Its first portion, often called the "Former Prophets," consists instead of narrative texts. They continue the story begun in the Torah. Although prophets play an important role in these narrative books, which include Joshua, Samuel, Isaiah, Ezekiel, Lamentations, Habakkuk, and Zechariah, these books dwell on far more than prophecies.

The name of the final part of the Bible, "Kethuvim," means "Writings." Of course, the rest of the Bible also consists of "writings." What therefore justifies giving the last set of books such a generic name? The answer is a matter of history. In this case, "Kethuvim" has come to serve as a catchall term. It is a mixed collection, and it contains such diverse works as Psalms (prayers), Chronicles (history), Daniel (prophecy), and Song of Songs (erotic poetry).

The Christians' Old Testament

The early Christians came to adopt the order of the Septuagint (the first Jewish translation of the Hebrew Bible, into Greek) for two main reasons. First, they spoke Greek (rather than Hebrew), so it was natural for them to rely on the

---

Teachings, Prophets, and Writings

Torah, the Hebrew word for "Teaching," does indeed contain the central teachings and laws of Judaism. But there is much more here: it also contains humanity's beginnings, the religious history of biblical Israel from the days of Abraham through the death of Moses, and instructions for conducting worship and celebrating the festivals of the Jewish calendar. And there are the genealogies—lists of humanity's and Israel's family trees, sometimes humorously referred to as "the begats" (from the King James Version's archaic English term for "was the ancestor of," as in Gen. 6:10, "And Noah begat three sons, Shem, Ham, and Japheth").

Nevi'im, "Prophets," includes both historical narratives and prophetic messages. The narratives continue the religious history of biblical Israel from the arrival in the Promised Land through the rise and fall of the kingdom of David and his descendants. Destructive conquests by the Assyrian empire drove most of Israel's ten tribes into exile. Then, conquests by the Babylonians led to exile for the people of Judah and to the destruction of Jerusalem and the Temple. The poetic messages are addressed to the People of Israel from their God, alternately reprimanding them for their misdeeds, comforting them in their afflictions, and predicting their future redemption. Linking these two very different literary forms is the presence of the prophets, individuals sent by God to guide the people.

Kethuvim, "Writings," contains books displaying a wide assortment of themes and literary forms, including prayers, poetry, wise sayings, short narratives, and the continuation of Israel's religious history during and after the Babylonian exile.

From Cullen Schippe and Chuck Stetson, *The Bible and Its Influence.*

3

The Books of the Hebrew Bible
Here is the standard arrangement of the books in the Hebrew Bible, as in the JPS TANAKH. Only in Jewish Bibles will you find the books grouped into three parts. This tripartite structure is found in all Hebrew manuscripts of the Bible, and all contemporary Jewish translations follow its outline.

Torah	Nevi'im (Prophets)	Kethuvim (Writings)
Genesis	Joshua	Zechariah
Exodus	Judges	Malachi
Leviticus	1 Samuel	Psalms
Numbers	2 Samuel	Proverbs
Deuteronomy	1 Kings	Job
	2 Kings	Song of Songs
	Isaiah	Ruth
	Jeremiah	Lamentations
	Ezekiel	Ecclesiastes
	Hosea	Esther
	Joel	Daniel
	Amos	Ezra
	Obadiah	Nehemiah
	Jonah	1 Chronicles
	Micah	2 Chronicles
	Nahum	
	Habakkuk	
	Zephaniah	
	Haggai	

Greek translation and adopt the Greek order. Second, that order—unlike some others—ended with the prophetic books. In the Christian canon (Old Testament + New Testament), this arrangement juxtaposed the Prophets (which, according to Christian tradition, predict the arrival of Jesus as messiah) with the Gospels (which describe that arrival, fulfilling the prediction). Thus, while the Christian Bible used an order of Old Testament books that predates the rise of Christianity, that order served Christian purposes well.

THE APOCRYPHA
The scope of many Christians' Old Testament is larger than that of the Jews' Bible. The former includes not only the books listed above, but also the Apocrypha (which is Greek for "hidden"). These are various writings of the

Second Temple period that the Catholic, Orthodox, Coptic, and other Christian Churches have held to be authoritative and sacred, but of lesser status than the other books of the Bible. These include books like the first and second books of the Maccabees (a historical text) and Ben Sira (called Ecclesiasticus in Greek, a Wisdom text similar to Proverbs). The Protestant Church later rejected the Apocrypha as part of the canon.

Divisions in the Bible

CHAPTERS

The chapter numbers now found in Bibles are not part of the traditional masoretic text, but rather date from 13th-century manuscripts of the Vulgate, the Latin translation of the Bible that the early church father Jerome wrote. By the mid-16th century, Jewish editors introduced chapters into printed Hebrew Bibles as well. Thus the chapter divisions are relatively recent, representing one particular understanding about how the Bible may be subdivided.

PARAGRAPHS

Torah scrolls divide the Pentateuch into the equivalent of paragraph units by placing blank space between units. These spaces are of two types: short ones called *setumah* (closed), where the next unit continues on the same line; and longer ones called *petuchah* (open), where the rest of the line is left open and the following unit continues only on the next line. This tradition of leaving spaces dates back at least to the Dead Sea Scrolls (mostly from the 3rd century B.C.E. to the 1st century C.E.). However, the Dead Sea Scrolls do not always agree with the divisions found in contemporary Torah scrolls, which the great medieval Jewish scholar Maimonides (1135–1204) established on the basis of a highly accurate 10th-century biblical manuscript that is now called the Aleppo Codex (see "The Crown of Aleppo," on p. 22). In other words, spaces or paragraph divisions—which vary somewhat even among medieval Hebrew manuscripts and printed editions of the Bible—have never been entirely uniform. They do, however, represent a significant early interpretive tradition.

Unfortunately, these divisions are not reflected in English Bible translations. Rather, each translator has independently decided where units begin and end, and the typesetters have set the type accordingly. Thus, for example, the paragraph breaks in the JPS translation represent the places where three committees working in the second part of the 20th century felt new units should be demarcated. As with any translation, their decisions deserve consideration but are not definitive.

VERSES

Various Rabbinic sources beginning with the Mishnah (approximately 200 C.E.) attest to the division of the Bible into *pesukim* (literally "dividing points")—what we would call verses. No early comprehensive list exists of where these divisions were perceived to be. However, some evidence suggests that they were largely the

How Bibles Differ

Jewish (JPS)	Protestant (NRSV)	Roman Catholic/ Orthodox (New American Bible)
Torah (Law)	*Pentateuch*	*Pentateuch*
Genesis	Genesis	Genesis
Exodus	Exodus	Exodus
Leviticus	Leviticus	Leviticus
Numbers	Numbers	Numbers
Deuteronomy	Deuteronomy	Deuteronomy
Nevi'im (Prophets)	*Histories*	*Histories*
Joshua	Joshua	Joshua
Judges	Judges	Judges
1 Samuel	Ruth	Ruth
2 Samuel	1 Samuel	1 Samuel
1 Kings	2 Samuel	2 Samuel
2 Kings	1 Kings	1 Kings
Isaiah	2 Kings	2 Kings
Jeremiah	1 Chronicles	1 Chronicles
Ezekiel	2 Chronicles	2 Chronicles
Hosea	Ezra	Ezra
Joel	Nehemiah	Nehemiah
Amos	Esther	Tobit
Obadiah		Judith
Jonah	*Poetical/Wisdom Books*	Esther
Micah	Job	1 Maccabees
Nahum	Psalms	2 Maccabees
Habakkuk	Proverbs	
Zephaniah	Ecclesiastes	*Poetical/Wisdom Books*
Haggai	Song of Solomon	Job
Zechariah		Psalms
Malachi	*Prophets*	Proverbs
	Isaiah	Ecclesiastes
Kethuvim (Writings)	Jeremiah	Song of Solomon
Psalms	Lamentations	Wisdom of Solomon
Proverbs	Ezekiel	Sirach
Job	Daniel	
Song of Songs	Hosea	

Jewish (JPS)	Protestant (NRSV)	Roman Catholic/ Orthodox (New American Bible)
Kethuvim (Writings)	*Prophets*	*Prophets*
Ruth	Joel	Isaiah
Lamentations	Amos	Jeremiah
Ecclesiastes	Obadiah	Lamentations
Esther	Jonah	Baruch
Daniel	Micah	Ezekiel
Ezra	Nahum	Daniel
Nehemiah	Habakkuk	Hosea
1 Chronicles	Zephaniah	Joel
2 Chronicles	Haggai	Amos
	Zechariah	Obadiah
	Malachi	Jonah
		Micah
	The Apocrypha	Nahum
	1 Esdras	Habakkuk
	2 Esdras	Zephaniah
	Tobit	Haggai
	Judith	Zechariah
	Esther (with additions)	Malachi
	Wisdom of Solomon	
	Wisdom of Jesus Son of Sirach (Ecclesiasticus)	
	Baruch	
	Letter of Jeremiah (Baruch)	
	Prayer of Azariah and Song of Three Children Susanna	
	Bel and the Dragon	**Most Orthodox include**
	Prayer of Manasseh	1 Esdras
	1 Maccabees	2 Edras
	2 Maccabees	Prayer of Manasseh
		Psalm 151
		3 Maccabees
		4 Maccabees

7

same as the later divisions found in medieval Hebrew manuscripts, which indicate verse endings by a musical note (called a *silluk*—a vertical line) under the final word, as well as what looks like a colon (*sof pasuk*) after each verse. Thus, of the three divisions noted in manuscripts—chapters, paragraphs, and verses—the last should be seen as the most ancient. Yet, there are sometimes differences in how the same words are divided into verses in different biblical contexts; some medieval manuscripts reflect these differences in their verse counts. Given the variants that we find, the verse divisions should not be seen as fully authoritative. Occasionally, weighty evidence suggests that a unit of thought really ends midverse while the second part of that verse starts a new unit or that a word at the end of one verse belongs at the beginning of the next.

Characteristics of Hebrew Language and Literature

To read and understand the Hebrew Scriptures we need to know a few things about Hebrew:

○ **The importance of the word.** The Hebrew alphabet is one of the oldest in the world, and its early development reflects the importance that ancient Hebrew-speaking peoples gave to spoken and written language. In the Hebrew account of creation, for example, the entire universe comes into being at God's spoken command.

○ **Symbolic word choices.** In many biblical passages, personal and place names have symbolic meanings drawn from Hebrew etymologies.·

○ **Parallelism and repetition.** Most of the Hebrew Scriptures originated in oral tradition, and they bear the marks of narratives told and retold, poetry chanted to musical rhythms, and laws memorized and recited by heart. Both parallelism (setting two accounts or ideas side by side for comparison or contrast) and repetition make it easier to commit oral material to memory and transmit it to new generations. These devices remain important even when the texts are set down in writing. Hebrew poetry, for example, relies almost entirely on parallelism for its structure, as it does not use rhyme or standardized meters.

○ **Figures of speech.** The Hebrew respect for language allows dazzling displays of creative wordplay. Pay particular attention to simile, metaphor, exaggeration, irony, and personification, all of which assist in capturing the ineffable experience of the divine within the limitations of human language.

From Cullen Schippe and Chuck Stetson, *The Bible and Its Influence.*

RECOGNIZING THE BIBLE'S DISTINCT LITERARY UNITS

The foregoing conclusions concerning chapter, paragraph, and verse divisions have significant implications for how we read the Bible. We have to discover and use textual clues other than these "late" formal markings to decide where units begin and end. Thus the Bible should be envisioned as a text punctuated only by word spaces—with nothing to indicate sections, paragraphs, or even verses. Our first step when reading *all* biblical texts must be to subdivide that biblical text into these kinds of units.

An analogy illustrates this procedure and why it matters. Let's imagine that a typesetter made a mistake in laying out the type of a collection of poems and printed them all as one long poem. Someone with modern or postmodern interests might enjoy reading the result as a unified work. But most of us would prefer to divide the long poem into separate poems. To do so, we would use stylistic and content-based criteria. If, for example, an e. e. cummings poem followed an Emily Dickinson poem, this would be easy because cummings' verse is distinct for the absence of upper-case letters; in other cases, it would be more difficult.

The Bible should be treated like this imaginary poetry book. Even though our printed version shows chapters and verses, these should be ignored. It must be imagined as a single, continuous text. Furthermore, we must develop a way to distinguish the different compositions embedded in it. Otherwise, we might do the equivalent of reading the first two lines of a cummings poem as the conclusion of the preceding Dickinson poem!

The criteria used for separating biblical sources are similar to those used to analyze poetry. We read carefully, attuned to changes in style and content, looking for contradictions between verses.

None of these criteria is airtight or *absolutely* objective. There is no consensus about how much variation a text may contain to be considered a unified work. Nor do scholars always agree on whether or not a larger text is self-contradictory. Thus in some cases we find real debate about where a unit begins and/or ends. In most cases, however, there is widespread agreement.

———— • + • ————

The Torah's Four Sources

Many scholars are of the opinion that the text of the Torah was collected from several sources and edited (or redacted) into the five biblical books we have today. When applied to the Torah as a whole, this type of analysis, called source criticism, suggests that the Torah comprises four main sources—four originally separate, (more or less) complete documents—that have been woven together. The date of these documents, called J, E, D, and P, has been the subject of much debate in biblical scholarship.

The oldest document may be J, which was given this name because in Genesis it typically uses the four-letter name of God, *YHWH,* which some Christian translators have transcribed as "Jehovah." The JPS translation represents this name as "the Lord," while other translations use "the Eternal," "Yahweh," or *YHWH.* Probably of Judean authorship, this source was written in the first half of the monarchic period.

Next is E, the Elohist document, so named because it typically refers to God in Genesis using the term *Elohim* (God). It probably originated in the Northern Kingdom and is likely slightly later than J. E is relatively short and it is unclear if it should be viewed as an originally separate document.

P refers to the Priestly source, which also uses *Elohim* and other divine names (but not *YHWH)* in Genesis. This document is shaped by Priestly concerns, including order, purity, and ensuring the Divine Presence among Israel. Its date has been an issue of great debate in biblical scholarship. Most likely, this source represents a school of thought that was active over a long period of time, both before and after the Babylonian exile of 586 B.C.E.

The D source stands for Deuteronomy, the final book of the Torah. With the exception of parts of the final chapters, which contain a diversity of material, most of Deuteronomy features a special vocabulary and particular theological concerns— especially the proper worship of a single God in the proper way in the proper place (Jerusalem), where God's "Name" resides. Like P, D is not a totally unified composition from a single time and place but represents a stream of tradition.

With the exception of the D source, which more or less makes up its own book, the Torah as it is now structured represents a careful combination of these sources.

Given the apparent existence of individual sources, they must have been edited together, or "redacted," at some point. Most likely this occurred in stages. Scholars call the final editor R, for "redactor". In this form, the work of the Priestly source has a particularly strong voice and even introduces the Torah. (Gen. 1:1–2:4a is P; Gen. 2:4b and verses following is J.) For this reason, some scholars equate R with the final voice of P.

Exactly why the sources were intertwined in this way is unclear. Exploring this issue really involves asking two questions: (1) Why were all of these sources retained, rather than just preserving the latest or most authoritative one? (2) Why were they combined in this odd way, rather than being left as complete documents that would be read side by side, much like the model of the four different and *separate* Gospels, which introduce the Christian Bible, or New Testament?

Because there is no direct evidence going back to the redaction of the Torah, these issues may be explored in only a most tentative fashion, with plausible rather than definitive answers. Probably the earlier documents had a certain prestige and authority in ancient Israel and could not simply be discarded. In addition, the redaction of the Torah from a variety of sources most likely represents an attempt to enfranchise those groups who held those particular sources as authoritative. Certainly, the Torah does not contain *all* of the early traditions of Israel. Yet, it does contain the traditions that the redactor felt were most important (most likely during the Babylonian exile).

Adapted from Marc Zvi Brettler, *How to Read the Bible.*

HOW THE BIBLE BECAME "THE BIBLE"

We know little about the Bible's origin—how so many books comprising so many diverse ideas became "the Bible." Clearly, the process happened in stages, over a long time. Nobody woke up one morning, decided to create the Bible, and arranged the next day for all Jews to adopt it as such.

The process was at least as much "bottom-up" as "top-down." That is, the wider population helped determine what the Bible included; it was not primarily an official (Rabbinic) decision. Indeed, the Bible likely came into being before the publication of the Mishnah, the first great Rabbinic work (about 200 C.E.). This is why few Rabbinic opinions describe the Bible's development. There is some Rabbinic evidence of the making of the Bible from Josephus, the 1st-century C.E. Jewish historian, and other Jewish writers of the same period Also the Dead Sea Scrolls shed light on the process, but that evidence is indirect and often ambiguous.

The Canon

Until recently, scholars addressed the questions of how the Bible became the Bible in terms of the "canon" of the Bible. Some scholars, however, have recently emphasized that this term (related to the Greek word *kanon*, a "reed" or a "measuring stick") may be anachronistic in reference to the Bible; it more properly refers to a collection of writings that defines a particular religious community. The early church first used this term with reference to lists of books that are part of the Christian Bible. It is not native to early Jewish literature concerning what is part of—or excluded from—the Bible. Applied to the Jewish Bible, "canon" has been used in many ways, making it an ambiguous and confusing term.

For these reasons, many scholars prefer to speak of "the development of scripture," rather than "the canonization of the Bible." Yet that is not much of an improvement, because "scripture" is a foreign term. Furthermore, because "scripture" means merely "that which is written," it is historically imprecise. Therefore, it is better to frame the question as follows: When and how did a central set of books with a particular name come into being within Judaism?

The process evolved gradually, partly because the books that now compose the Bible were written over a period of more than 1,000 years. Furthermore, the three-part (tripartite) structure of the Bible most likely reflects historical development: at first, the Torah alone was central; by the Hellenistic period, Jews treated other books as important and worthy of study as well.

The most important evidence that there was a group of sacred books beyond the Torah comes from Josephus, who noted: "Our books, those of which are just accredited, are but two and twenty, and contain the record for all time." He was employing the concept of a set number of authoritative books, which he called these "holy books." Josephus nowhere enumerated them. However, contemporary scholars widely agree that Josephus was referring to the 24 books that we now call the Bible, with Ruth being counted as part of Judges and Lamentations as part of Jeremiah.

However, even though Rabbinic literature often refers to "24" biblical books (the same number we have) over the more or less two centuries known as the Rabbinic period, the entire group of sages may not have shared the same Bible. Thus for this period it might be best to speak of a "*largely* closed" set of texts that composed the Bible—or several competing conceptions of it. Quite possibly another set of texts that composed the Bible, mostly identical to our current Bible, also existed among a Jewish sect that lived in the Judean desert, whose surviving library is what we now call the Dead Sea Scrolls. This community may not have had a notion of canon; at least, they had no special term for such a thing. However, in their interpretive literature they did tend to cite particular books. Furthermore, certain books still exist in many copies, indicating that they were especially important to the community.

Of the books that are part of the classical Rabbinic Bible, only the book of Esther is missing among the Dead Sea Scrolls that we have today (We have no remains of Nehemiah either, but it may have already been combined with Ezra); thus the community probably did not consider that book authoritative. In contrast, other Dead Sea Scroll texts cite the Temple Scroll and the book of Jubilees as authoritative. Furthermore, the community kept a large number of manuscripts of both works. Thus, our term "canonical" Bible seems anachronistic for this group in the pre-Rabbinic period. Nevertheless, it is safe to say that its set of authoritative books largely, but not completely, overlapped what would eventually become "the Bible" for the Rabbis.

The Order and the Ordering of Biblical Books

For the many centuries before Jewish scribes published books in codex form, they preserved books in the form of separate scrolls. In certain cases, the scribes put several books in a single scroll—and in a particular order. This was true of the Torah, which needed to be ordered because Jews read it ritually in order, as part of their worship. Similarly, the scribes grouped Joshua, Judges, Samuel, and Kings in sequence since they tell a more or less continuous story in chronologi-

The Dead Sea Scrolls

In 1947, seven ancient Jewish scrolls were discovered in a cave by the shore of the Dead Sea in Qumran, approximately nine miles south of Jericho and 13 miles east of Jerusalem. Over the next nine years more than 15,000 writings dating from the late Second Temple period (200 B.C.E. to 68 C.E.) were found in 11 nearby caves. Scholars generally agree that the Khirbat Qumran sect, identified as the Essenes, gathered the Dead Sea Scrolls from approximately 150 B.C.E. to 68 C.E., when the site was destroyed by the Romans during the Great Revolt of the Jews against Rome.

The documents themselves date from the mid-3rd century B.C.E. to the mid-1st century C.E.. A few fragments provide evidence of the Hebrew texts that were translated into the Septuagint, as well as those that formed the basis for the Samaritan Pentateuch. The texts included in the scrolls begin with the earliest works of the Hebrew Bible. Parts of every book except Esther can be found in the scrolls.

A second group of scrolls contains apocryphal or pseudepigraphic texts. The manuscripts were preserved in their original languages, so some of these texts are in Greek, Aramaic, and other languages, including a copper scroll that appears to be a list of hidden treasures from the ancient Temple in Jerusalem. A third group of scrolls contains sectarian texts. These texts establish a connection between the Dead Sea Scrolls and the Khirbat Qumran sect because they contain the rules and customs that governed the life of a self-contained Jewish community.

The scrolls are now housed in the Shrine of the Book, which was built in 1965 expressly for them, at the Israel Museum complex in Jerusalem.

cal order. However, for the rest of the Bible, even in Rabbinic times, there was a varying order of the Prophets (except for the "Minor Prophets") and the Writings.

Certain people and groups (especially professional scribes!) love order. Mesopotamian scribes often copied series of cuneiform tablets in standard orders. The resulting predictability made it easier for readers to find what they were looking for, no matter which copy they consulted. Similarly, perhaps ancient Israelite librarians may have kept biblical scrolls in ordered cubbyholes, so that they could locate the right text easily. This may be the original function of ordering the books of the Bible.

The Bible shows evidence of ordering at both the macro and the microlevel. On the microlevel, its text is divided into books—typically, what can fit on a scroll. (Thus the 12 Minor Prophets constitute a single book or scroll, even though it is made up of many books.)

On the macrolevel, this large collection comprises smaller collections. Exactly how and when this was done are subjects of intense current debate: How early is the three-part division of the Bible into Torah, Nevi'im, and Kethuvim? When and why did this tripartite division develop? Rabbinic sources—though not any of the earliest such sources—do attest to a three-part (what scholars call a "tripartite") Bible. Scholars have found allusions to this structure in the New Testament and among the Dead Sea Scrolls. However, these references do not decisively prove that the Bible was organized into three parts as early as the 1st century C.E. Indeed, Jews clearly employed a variety of orders and ordering schemes in the Second Temple period.

The tripartite ordering was likely one of the early ordering schemes, for its classifications are not obvious ones. Daniel properly belongs with the Latter Prophets; Ezra-Nehemiah, Chronicles, and perhaps some other books belong with the Former Prophets. Thus their present classification seems to reflect an evolution: by the time those later books were composed, the set of books known as Prophets had already been determined, so they could not be included in that section. That is, over time the Torah became authoritative first, then Nevi'im, and finally Kethuvim.

This hypothesis for the evolutionary development of the tripartite canon would also explain the stability—and lack of stability—of order within each section. The Torah—authoritative first—is fully stable: all manuscripts have the order as Genesis, Exodus, Leviticus, Numbers, Deuteronomy. (Of course, given the contents of these books, their order is not really flexible.) Within Nevi'im, the same is true for the Former Prophets. Concerning the order of the Latter Prophets, there is more flexibility; most manuscripts do not follow the talmudic order. Within Kethuvim, manuscripts show a tremendous variation in the order of its books. Quite surprisingly, the ancient sources do not indicate what the last—culminating—book of the Bible should be!

The Stabilization of the Biblical Text

A book may be authoritative even though it does not have a fixed text. The spelling of its words, certain whole words themselves—even whole verses—could and did vary from one written copy to another. Thus we should consider the issues of canonization and textual stabilization separately. Indeed, it is highly likely that the biblical text became stable only in the early Rabbinic period. By then, Jews already had a relatively clear idea as to which texts were "in" and which were "out," and they had devised certain methods of midrashic interpretation (namely, methods of interpretation that read the text carefully and may even be based on fine spelling variants). Functionally speaking, the latter development allowed for fluid meaning even as the text became fixed.

The Dead Sea Scrolls community considered authoritative a Bible of sorts, yet they did not have a single stable text for its books. That ancient desert community still proceeded to expound its texts—sometimes in versions that are quite different from those found in what later crystallized as the masoretic text. In fact, in at least one case it seemed to be interpreting two different versions of the same verse. In other words, just because the community believed a certain work to be holy and inspired did not imply that the text had to exist in a single version.

Based on the early texts available to us, we can say that the Bible's consonantal text (that is, the consonants only, without the vocalization—the vowels and cantillation marks) largely stabilized by the 2nd century C.E. We do not know exactly how this happened; perhaps someone made a master edition from which other scribes copied. Perhaps the destruction of the Second Temple in 70 C.E. and the failure of the revolt of 132–135 C.E. (the Bar Kokhba rebellion) created a crisis that served as an impetus for creating an authoritative text.

Considering the wider range of ancient versions (and the opportunities meanwhile for scribal errors in transmission), medieval biblical texts show remarkably few variants. However, even that era knew occasional, significant textual variants, including readings in the Babylonian Talmud that differ from most of our biblical manuscripts. The stabilization of the consonantal text continued until well after the advent of printing in the late 1400s. Even so, to this day, a few variant spellings remain.

Today, were we to open two texts of the Hebrew Bible, they would contain the same books, grouped into three major parts, appearing mostly in the same order, with a well over 99 percent agreement on the consonants and vocalization. This consistency was the result of a long and complicated process that took place largely behind the scenes, obscured from our view.

More than half a century later, guardians of the biblical text devised various systems of marking the proper vocalization of the consonantal text. The vocalization system associated with the Masorete Aaron Ben Moses Ben-Asher and with the city of Tiberias in the Galilee "won" over competing systems, giving us the Bible as we now have it. This means that in its current form (with vowels), the Bible is only a little more than 1,000 years old.

Adapted from Marc Zvi Brettler, *How to Read the Bible.*

THE ORIGINS OF THE HEBREW BIBLE TEXT

Acourt of law relies on witnesses to establish the facts of a case. But for those who seek the "facts" of the original biblical texts, no firsthand witnesses exist. We have only the testimony of various manuscripts, produced hundreds of years after the Bible's books were completed. And even if we had an autograph copy of, say, the book of Ezra, it would not answer all our questions, for it was created at a time (2,400 years ago) when writing was imprecise—even before the invention of punctuation. During each transmission of the books of the Bible from person to person, uncertainty has grown. Schools have sometimes disagreed on pronunciation. Handwriting has not always been legible. And every scribe has occasionally made mistakes in copying.

Witnesses testifying in court often disagree. Little surprise, then, that the Bible's textual "witnesses"—farther removed from the original "event"—differ from each other in a wide range of small ways: spelling, punctuation, layout of poetry, and so on. Sometimes entire verses appear in only a few manuscripts.

So which version is true?

The Unbroken Chain of Uncertainty

Accuracy has been ensured by means of side documentation—part of what is called *masorah*. This resulted in to a "masoretic text"—a Bible that accords with the *masorah*. But there were so many variances among the different manuscripts that the *masorah* couldn't address them all. And the masoretic notes have been

> **Masorah**
> The term *"masorah"* refers to everything transmitted with the biblical text. It includes vowel signs, accent signs, large and small letters, dots over consonants, arrangements of poetry, marginal notes, and endnotes, as well as separate treatises on the copying and use of manuscripts. The early medieval masters of the biblical text who developed this documentation are known in English as Masoretes. Many masoretic annotations seem designed to reduce loss or distortion in transmission of the text.

neglected through the ages; written in shorthand, they are often vague, and sometimes contradict one another.

Much *masorah* seems to have been created only after problems arose; in such cases, it could only reinforce the torn textual fabric, not mend the hole. Unable or unwilling to choose between variants, scribes sometimes preserved two versions of a word side by side—transmitting both. Furthermore, by nature the Bible is not predictable. Because of its spiritual subject matter, its choice of words is puzzling at times. So is a given puzzling phrase due to scribal error—or religious mystery? When are we to expect the text to follow rules of grammar— and when to allow for artistic expression?

Despite these pitfalls, Bible scholars have always refined the text as they found it. Each expert begins with a different set of available manuscripts, from scribes of varying (and uncertain) reliability. They each use different methods for resolving textual problems. So the experts come to different conclusions as to what is the "best" Bible text. Ironically, the result is a Bible whose text continually *evolves*—the changes being justified to preserve the accuracy of tradition. Thus, an early printed Bible edited in Italy by R. Jacob ben Hayyim ibn Adonijah (1525 C.E.) reconstructed the work of the Tiberian textual tradition from 600 years earlier. His effort was impressive enough that soon afterward owners of old manuscripts all across Europe altered their parchments to match his newly authoritative book.

As mistakes were corrected, new ones appeared. R. Meir Letteris of Austria edited a Hebrew Bible first published in 1852, based on lists of "corrections" by experts who perceived mistakes in earlier editions. It became the standard Hebrew text among many Jews to this day. Yet, like all prior printed Bibles, it contained hundreds of its own typographic errors.

Meanwhile, in the modern era, certain early medieval manuscripts—safeguarded in isolated Middle Eastern communities—were brought to the attention of Bible

---

The Masoretes—Preservers and Protectors of the Hebrew Bible
The Masoretes' main goal was to preserve the text of the Hebrew Bible with the utmost accuracy. To this end, they developed the system of vowel signs still in use today in the Hebrew Torah text to ensure that each word would always be read the same way. They also counted the number of words and letters in the Torah and compiled a list of even the most insignificant deviations from what they had established as the authentic text of the Hebrew Bible.

From Lionel Moses, "Torah Reading," in *Etz Hayim: Torah and Commentary.*

scholars. These have proved to be the oldest known witnesses of the now standard Tiberian tradition. Only recently has the wider, evolutionary, corrective process taken these unusually reliable texts into account. These manuscripts still contain inconsistencies and differ slightly from each other. But on the whole, they confirm the "received" (evolutionary European) traditions of the Bible text, especially for the Torah. Amazingly, manuscript differences are truly minor. More than 99.9 percent of the time, the masoretic Bible's witnesses give identical accounts. Rarely does the variation impact the meaning of a given verse.

Parchment Scrolls and Codex

For about 800 years before the invention of printing, Jewish books were written on parchment in two formats, scroll or codex. A codex was made of bound folios; it was easier to use for study, and it could hold far more information. In manuscripts, the entire Bible has appeared only as a codex, never as a scroll. Classical Hebrew terms for a codex are *mazor, mitzhaf,* and *keter.*

The History of the Hebrew Text

Since ancient times, Jews have traced the chain of transmission of Scripture: "Moses received Torah at Sinai and handed it on to Joshua, Joshua to the elders, and the elders to the prophets. And the prophets handed it on to the Great Assembly . . ." (*Mishnah Pirkei Avot* 1:1). For the Hebrew text found in the *JPS Hebrew-English* TANAKH the textual transmission history is as follows.

AARON BEN MOSES BEN-ASHER (TIBERIAS, CA. 930 C.E.)

An industrious family of Masoretes once lived in the Galilean town of Tiberias (an ancient center of Jewish scholarship). The last in their line of scholars was Aaron ben Moses Ben-Asher, who flourished circa 930 C.E. He authored a classic masoretic treatise. He is the first known scribe to complete a manuscript of the entire Bible (whose books had been preserved somewhat independently). An important part of his work included the proofreading of others' manuscripts, which is how he enters into our picture.

SAMUEL BEN JACOB (EGYPT, 1010 C.E.)

Two generations later, a scribe in Fostat (Egypt's thriving center of trade and learning) spent years composing a Bible codex. Noting its completion in 1010 C.E., he recorded that he copied from several manuscripts into this one volume: "Samuel ben Jacob wrote out the consonants, vowels, punctuation, accents, and annotations of this codex of Scripture from the texts checked and corrected by the late master Aaron ben Moses Ben-Asher; it has been checked and corrected per tradition."

The Crown of Aleppo

Also known as the Aleppo Codex, the "Crown of Aleppo" is believed to be the oldest existing and most accurate manuscript of the entire Hebrew Bible that contains vowels and cantillation signs. The scholar who added the vowels and accents was Rabbi Aaron Bar Asher, an expert in the masoretic system used both for maintaining the accuracy of the written, consonantal text of the Bible and for recording the vowels and accents (which had previously been handed down through oral memorization). Written in the 10th century in Palestine, the Aleppo Codex was then used by Maimonides when he formulated his regulations for writing Torah scrolls.

In the 16th century, the codex was stolen from Cairo; and when it ended up in the city of Aleppo, the local Jewish community held on to it, refusing even to lend it out to scholars. After Aleppo was attacked by anti-Jewish rioters, the manuscript was thought to have been destroyed. When that was revealed to be false, a concerted campaign of pressure and persuasion by the Israeli government, scholarly institutions, and Jewish organizations convinced Aleppo residents to move the codex to Jerusalem for safekeeping in 1958. However, approximately one third of the manuscript, which included most of the Torah up to Deuteronomy 28:17, remains missing. Some believe that this section was destroyed in the anti-Jewish riots in Aleppo. Others speculate that residents of Aleppo have continued to keep parts of that section for themselves.

Samuel's Bible contains 60,000 marginal notes on the text, including more than 1,000 divergences between consonantal text (*ketiv*) and reading tradition (*kerei*). In proofreading and correcting his work, Samuel ben Jacob missed (or let stand) hundreds of errors—which is actually an impressive result, given the millions of characters in a Hebrew Bible. As the contemporary scholar E. J. Revell comments, "This is a long way from perfection, but it is close to ideal when compared to the situation in most [later] medieval manuscripts."

RECENT EDITIONS OF THE LENINGRAD CODEX

Today, Samuel ben Jacob's work is the oldest-known complete Hebrew Bible, and the oldest complete representative of the Ben-Asher tradition. (Only for a few dozen characters is this codex not clearly legible—given some parchment stains, flaked ink, and ambiguous pen strokes.) For centuries, however, it was kept out of circulation, unknown to historians or Bible editors. Then in 1840, a manuscript collector announced possession of this Bible—which has since become known as the Leningrad Codex. Repeatedly since then, international teams of Christian and Jewish scholars (both religious and academic) have edited this codex for modern use. The first group, led by Rudolph Kittel and Paul Kahle, made it the base text for a critical edition, *Biblia Hebraica Kittel* (BHK, 1937). After World War II, another team revised BHK, producing *Biblia Hebraica Stuttgartensia* (BHS, 1967–77), upon which the Hebrew text in the *JPS Hebrew-English TANAKH* is based.

Adapted from David E. S. Stein, the preface of *JPS Hebrew-English TANAKH*.

THE TORAH SCROLL

In its earliest transmission, the words of the Torah were written on papyrus and animal skins. To maintain this sacred tradition, Jews observe the mitzvah of writing the words of the Torah on specially prepared parchment, which is sewn together and rolled onto two wooden rollers. When Torah is read publicly, it is read from a Torah scroll (*sefer Torah*). When the Torah text is studied, it is read from a book.

In Deuteronomy 31:19, it is written: "Therefore, write down this poem and teach it to the people of Israel." This verse, according to the sages, prescribes the responsibility of each Jew to write a Torah scroll. To fulfill this mitzvah, one can personally write a scroll, have it written by a professional scribe (*sofer*), or help purchase one for a community.

A *sofer* is a professional scribe, and the work of a *sofer* is considered holy. It requires the mastery of many halakhic (Jewish legal) details and is transmitted through an apprenticeship with a master *sofer*.

The *sofer*'s day begins with immersion in a *mikveh* (ritual bath), which is an act of spiritual purification that declares one's readiness to accept the obligation of the holy act of writing the scroll. (If a *sofer* is unable to attend the *mikveh* for the day, wherever God's name would be written, a space is left, postponing the writing of God's name for a day on which the *sofer* can immerse in a *mikveh*. On that day, a "God quill" and bottle of special ink may be used.)

The *sofer* commences work by writing the name of Amalek (the ancient enemy of the Jewish people) on a scrap of parchment. The name is then crossed out to fulfill the mitzvah of "blotting out the memory of Amalek from under the heaven" (Deut. 25:19). The *sofer* then writes a statement that translates, "I am writing this Torah in the name of its sanctity and the name of God's sanctity."

The *sofer*'s tools—parchment, pen, and inkwell—are referred to as "articles of honor." The parchment is made from specific sections of the hide of a kosher animal (not necessarily slaughtered according to Jewish ritual). The hide consists of three layers, but only the flesh side of the inner layer and the outer side of the hairy layer may be used for Torah parchment. The methods of cleaning and softening the hide have changed throughout the centuries. During talmudic times, salt and barley flour were sprinkled on the skins, which were then soaked in the juice of gallnuts. In modern times, the skins are softened by soaking them in clear water for two days, after which the hair is removed by soaking the hides in limewater for nine days. Finally, the skins are rinsed and dried and the creases ironed out with presses, in a process similar to the curing of leather. In keeping with the sanctity of processing material for a scroll, the person handling the skins must make a verbal declaration of intent, acknowledging that all actions are being performed for the holiness of the scroll.

Although reeds were used as pens in the days of the Talmud, quills are used today, and the sturdy, durable turkey feather is preferred. The *sofer* cuts the point of the feather to give it a flat surface, which is desirable for forming the square letters, and then slits it lengthwise.

The ink used in writing a Torah scroll must be black and durable, but not indelible. During talmudic times, a viscous ink was made by heating a vessel with the flame of burning olive oil; the soot thus produced on the sides of the vessel was scraped off and mixed with oil, honey, and gallnuts. Today, ink is produced from a mixture of gallnuts, gum arabic, and copper sulfate crystals. Some scribes also add vinegar and alcohol to render it glossy.

The actual printing of the letters follows one of three styles of script: The Ashkenazic resembles the script described in the Talmud. The Sephardic is identical with the printed letters of the Hebrew alphabet currently used in sacred texts. The Lurianic is the third style. The *sofer* must shape each letter precisely as pictured, and each must be written from left to right, with the initial stroke being (generally) a curved line produced by using just the point of the quill. Next, using the entire surface of the pen, the *sofer* draws the letter. The thickness of each letter varies, and it is often necessary for the *sofer* to make several strokes to form a letter.

Tagin (an Aramaic word meaning "crowns") are specific ornamental designs placed at the upper-left-hand corner of 7 of the 22 letters of the Hebrew alphabet. Composed of three strokes, these crowns and their letters form the source of many mystical interpretations found in the kabbalistic literature. There is a tradition that the crowns and the letters contain spiritual essences that emanate from God.

There are precise specifications concerning the number of columns a Torah must have on each piece of parchment, as well as the size of the columns, the space between individual letters, and the size of the gap between *parshiyot* (weekly reading portions). Although guidelines are incised for the top of a line of Torah text, there are none for the bottom of each letter. If a *sofer* makes a mistake in writing the scroll, the ink can be removed with a knife, pumice stone, or piece of broken glass. However, base metals are generally not used to correct or even touch a Torah scroll, as these metals are used to make weapons, which render them unfit to touch a scroll, which is an instrument of peace.

Any mistakes in the spelling of any of the names of God cannot be corrected, as the name of God cannot be erased. If a scroll has extensive corrections, it is considered unsightly and, therefore, invalid. When invalid or beyond repair, a scroll is stored in a *genizah*. In talmudic times, it was customary to bury such scrolls alongside the grave of a prominent rabbi.

Genizah

A *genizah* is a storage space for damaged or obsolete prayer books, Bibles, and other religious works. Jewish law considers anything on which God's name is written to be holy, and so strict halakhic law forbids the destruction of any paper—no matter how small, old, or damaged—that contains the name of God. As books become obsolete or too damaged to use, synagogues traditionally place them in a *genizah*, usually a small room or closet attached to the synagogue. In some communities, the *genizah* is emptied every seven years and the books taken to the cemetery and buried. In other communities, the *genizah* is emptied and its contents interred in times of drought or simply when it is full. In ancient and medieval times, nearly every synagogue had a *genizah*. Today most sizable traditional Jewish communities have one.

Not only holy works were stored in ancient and medieval *genizahs* (or *genizot*); rabbis classified many books they considered heretical or otherwise dangerous as *sefarim genuzim* (books to be hidden away) and stored them in a *genizah* to prevent them from being read. Purely secular or non-Jewish works are sometimes also stored in *genizahs*. The Cairo Genizah—the most famous *genizah* in the world, contained fragments of the Quran, the Islamic holy book, as well as legal writings and simple correspondence, much of it written in the local Arabic language in Hebrew letters.

The Cairo Genizah was not emptied, possibly for fear of attacks on Jewish funeral processions, from at least 882 C.E.. until 1896. The accumulated contents—more than 250,000 manuscripts—provide a wealth of information on medieval Jewish life. Its documents reveal day-to-day interactions of ordinary Jews with their Muslim and Christian neighbors. Its store of personal documents provides some of the only contemporary evidence of the Fatimid and Ayyubid rulers of Egypt and unique, firsthand accounts of the Jewish commentator Maimonides.

Once the writing of a Torah scroll is carefully checked and approved, the individual sheets of parchment are sewn together with a special thread made of tendon tissue taken from the foot muscles of a kosher animal. These sections of parchment are sewn on the outer side of the parchment, with one inch left unsewn both at the very top and bottom. To reinforce the thread, thin strips of parchment are often pasted on the top and bottom of the page. After connecting the sheets, the ends are tied to the wooden rollers that hold the scroll. Each roller consists of a center pole (*atz chayim*), with a handle of wood and flat circular rollers to support the rolled-up scroll. In addition to providing a means to roll the scroll, the rollers prevent people from touching the holy parchments with their hands. In many Sephardic communities, flat rollers are not employed, because Torah scrolls are kept in an upright ornamental wooden or metal case called a *tik*. When reading from a scroll one does not touch the Torah with one's hands but uses a *yad* (pointer; literally, "hand") to follow the letters.

Decorating the Torah Scroll

The reverence with which the Torah scroll is regarded is shown by its costly accessories and ornaments.

The two rolls of the Torah scroll are fastened together with a wimpel, a long band of material, usually two to three inches wide; then the Torah cover (*mappah*) is fitted over them. This decorative, embroidered cloth mantle used to protect and beautify the Torah has two openings at the top to accommodate the poles (*atzei chayim*) to which the Torah scroll is attached.

After the Torah has been covered, or dressed, the breastplate (*hoshen*) is attached to a chain and draped over the Torah poles. Usually made of silver, modern breastplates are reminiscent of the one worn by the High Priest in biblical times, which had 12 precious stones engraved with the names of the Twelve Tribes of Israel. Usually a small box (*tas*) is soldered to the plate; it contains silver nameplates for each holiday and special Sabbaths. Two small, decorative silver crowns (*rimonim*) are placed on the Torah poles. Finally, the pointer (*yad*) is attached to a chain or a string and hung from the Torah.

The scroll is housed in an ark, a cabinet, which in Ashkenazic synagogues is set into or against a wall that faces east toward Jerusalem. In Sephardic synagogues, the ark is often in the center of the sanctuary. An embroidered curtain (*parochet*) further shields the Torah scrolls inside the ark.

Adapted from Stuart Kelman, *Etz Hayim: Torah and Commentary.*

PUBLIC READING OF THE TORAH

The first public reading that involved "a prototype" of the Torah took place in the mid-5th century B.C.E., when Ezra undertook the initial reading on Rosh Hashanah, followed by a daily reading during the festival of Sukkot. By the time of the Second Temple, the public reading of Torah was a regular feature of the synagogue service, on Mondays, Thursdays, the Sabbath, and holidays.

The Reading Cycle

The custom of the Land of Israel was to complete the reading of the Torah once every three years; in Babylonia it was completed annually. The holiday Simchat Torah is a post-talmudic holiday that originated in Babylonia during the gaonic period. It is a celebration of the conclusion of the annual Torah reading, after which the cycle of reading begins again. In the three-year cycle, Simchat Torah was a moveable festival, occurring at various times during the year. However, by the 12th century C.E., the influence of Babylonian Jewry was virtually universal, and the annual cycle became the norm for most communities around the world, as it still is today.

It should be noted, however, that Reform Judaism and some Conservative synagogues have adopted the three-year cycle to shorten each week's Torah reading. Instead of reading the Torah consecutively, this cycle divides the weekly portions into three parts, and one part is read in each of three years of the cycle. Thus, while the reading of the entire Torah is not complete until the three-year cycle is complete, each year readers start with Genesis and finish, on Simchat Torah, with Deuteronomy.

Chanting the Torah

The Torah is not literally read; it is chanted in a musical mode according to a system of marks that are found in printed versions of the Hebrew Bible but not in the Torah scroll. Each of these marks designates a series of musical notes called masoretic accents, also called *ta'amim* and trope. The system of *ta'amim* was developed by biblical scholars known as Masoretes, who lived in Tiberias, in northern Israel, during the 9th and 10th centuries C.E. See "The Masoretes—Preservers and Protectors of the Hebrew Bible," on p. 20.

The Five Scrolls

The Five Scrolls, or Five *Megillot*, are part of the third part of the Bible, Writings (Kethuvim). These short books are customarily read aloud in synagogue on corresponding Jewish holy days.

In addition to the reading of the Five Scrolls on various holy days throughout the Jewish year, the book of Jonah is read aloud on Yom Kippur, when Jews atone for their sins. Jonah's story is one of atonement: the power of repentance and the mercy of God save Jonah from the belly of the whale.

Book	Holy Day	Explanation
Song of Songs	Passover	As the celebration of Passover is a marker of springtime, so is the Song of Songs, which focuses on the blossoming of nature, love, and beauty. The flowering of love that is described in the Song of Songs can also be connected to Passover in that it represents the flowering of love between the Israelites and God during the Exodus. Hence, the Song of Songs may stand as the courtship between God and Israel, which was consummated at Mount Sinai.
Ruth	Shavuot	Shavuot marks the Jews' receiving and accepting the Torah and all of its commandments, while Ruth is a convert who traditionally accepts the Torah and commandments to become a Jew. In addition, events recorded in Ruth took place at harvest time, and Shavuot is the harvest festival. And Ruth was the ancestor of David, who, according to tradition, died on Shavuo
Lamentations	Tisha b'Av	Lamentations mourns the destruction of Jerusalem and the First Temple, while describing the suffering of the Jewish people, just as Tisha b'Av marks a day of fasting in remembrance of the destruction of the Temple.
Ecclesiastes	Sukkot	Ecclesiastes is read during Sukkot, possibly because Kohelet, the author of the book, writes about the transience of life, like the temporary booth, the sukkah. The verse, "Distribute portions to seven or even to eight" (11:2) was applied by the Rabbis to the seven days of Sukkot and the eighth day. Also, Ecclesiastes encourages one to enjoy life, (9:7–9) fitting for the holiday which is called "the time of our rejoicing."
Esther	Purim	The book of Esther tells the story of Purim and the events that led up to it.

The *ta'amim* have three distinct functions: musical, syntactical, and grammatical. Primarily they indicate the musical motifs in which the biblical text is chanted. Each accent represents a group of notes, "tropes", that the reader fits to each word. The accents usually identify the stressed syllable in each word and are placed above or below the syllable that receives the stress. Knowing which syllable receives the stress helps provide meaning to the text, because often the only distinction between two words that sound the same but have different meanings is which syllable gets the emphasis. The musical motif of the accents produces a chant that adds an aesthetic dimension to the public reading, as recommended in the Talmud.

Today, there are five main musical modes, or melodies, for chanting the Torah: Yemenite, Ashkenazic, Middle Eastern and North African, Jerusalem Sephardic, and northern Mediterranean.

The Haftarah
The haftarah is a reading from one of the books of the Prophets (Nevi'im) selected to complement the weekly Torah reading or highlight the theme of a specific occasion. Of the 54 readings, 14 are from the book of Isaiah, eight from Jeremiah, six from Ezekiel, and nine from the books of the Minor Prophets.

The Torah text is divided into weekly readings, each known as a parashah (*parashot*, plural) and also as a *sidrah* (*sidrot*, plural), and each of these is accompanied by another reading, called a haftarah (*haftarot*, plural), taken from one of the books of the Prophets. There are 54 sets of these readings, so that the reading cycle can be completed in one year. This number of *parshiyot* exceeds the number of Sabbaths in the usual calendar and provides the needed flexibility for a Jewish leap year, which adds four weeks to the calendar, seven times in 19 years. In non-leap years, certain *parshiyot* are combined to ensure that the entire Torah is completed within the year. The extra *parshiyot* also allow for combining and separating them to accommodate the special readings for festivals when they occur on the Sabbath.

Adapted from Lionel Moses, *Etz Hayim: Torah and Commentary,* with additions.

The Name of God

In Hebrew tradition, names carry enormous power. The personal name of God, as revealed to Moses (Exod. 3:15) is the most powerful and sacred word of all. This name, which is known in Greek as the Tetragrammaton, consists of four Hebrew letters. Because the name of God could be spoken only within the Holy of Holies, the inner sanctuary of the Temple in Jerusalem, a substitution is made when reading the Hebrew Scripture aloud.

Most Jewish readers say *Adonai* (usually translated in English as "Lord") instead. The name "Jehovah," given by some Christian traditions as God's name, is based on a non-Hebrew-speaker's error, using the vowel sounds for *Adonai* with the consonants for "Yahweh."

In everyday practice, some Jews avoid even *Adonai,* preferring other euphemisms such as *ha-Shem* ("the Name"). Documents containing the name of God are treated with the utmost respect. English-speaking Orthodox and some Conservative Jews often use the formation "G-d" when writing, so as not to spell out—and possibly subject to desecration—the holy name.

Both Jewish and Christian printed Bibles often observe the custom of separating God's name from ordinary text by setting the words "God" or "Lord" in capitals or small capitals when the words refer to the one God of Israel.

Adapted from Cullen Schippe and Chuck Stetson, *The Bible and Its Influence.*

A Short History of Bible Translations

T he book of Genesis narrates two stories in which translation plays a role. The first, the well-known tower of Babel episode (Gen. 11), vividly describes the dangers that can occur when all nations and peoples speak the same language. To prevent evil from spreading among people, God divides the world into many tongues, which makes translation a necessary, but not a desirable, result. If all humanity could behave, the story implies, there could be one universal language, with no need for translators.

The other story is embedded in the lengthy account of the negotiations between Joseph, now second in command to Pharaoh, and his brothers. Although Joseph immediately recognizes his siblings, for quite some time they do not know his true identity. Since they are from a foreign land, we are told, "there was an interpreter between him [Joseph] and them [his brothers]" (Gen. 42:23). Here translation is understood as a practical necessity of life, something to be valued when communication among different peoples occurs.

Of course, neither of these two stories relates specifically to translation of the Bible. But in a sense, they can serve as paradigms for two of the different ways in which Bible translations were evaluated within Jewish communities over several millennia: grudgingly acknowledged or openly accepted. As we shall see, even within these two large groupings, there are gradations of acceptance and rejection. This is one of the themes explored in this chapter, as we examine how Jews have translated sacred writ for more than 2,000 years.

The Earliest Translation: Greek

The first Bible translation, the Septuagint (often abbreviated "LXX"), dates to approximately 275 B.C.E.; it was prepared in Alexandria, the Egyptian capital city. Ptolemy I, one of Alexander the Great's generals, had settled large numbers of Jews there a few decades earlier as part of his efforts to solidify his empire, which was centered on Egypt but stretched northward to Syria and Palestine. The *Letter of Aristeas*, which was composed at least a century later than this event, provides our earliest narrative account of the circumstances that produced this translation.

As recorded in the *Letter*, the second ruler of Hellenistic Egypt, Ptolemy II Philadephus, was persuaded by his librarian to initiate and support a Greek

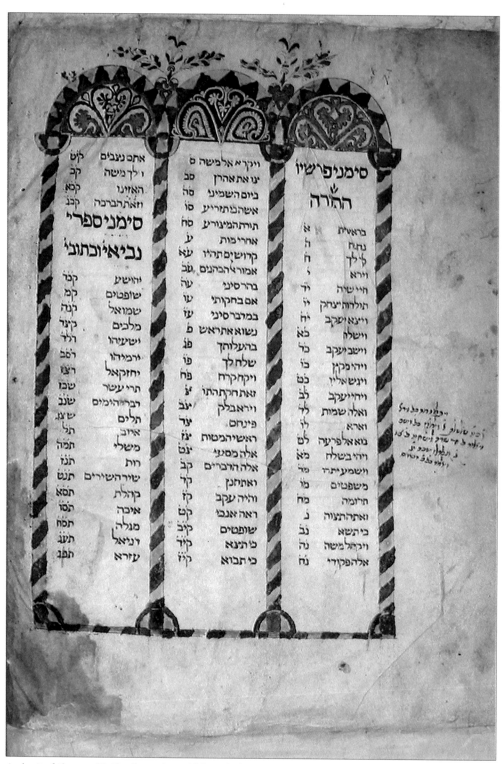

A chart of the weekly Torah portions, Bible, Toledo, 1492. This chart is part of a Bible that was copied by Abraham Kaliff a few months before the decree of expulsion was issued against the Jews of Spain. After the decree, it was then smuggled out of the country unfinished, then completed in Constantinople in 1497. It is one of the earliest published Hebrew texts to contain full accents and vocalization markings. (Courtesy of The Library of the Jewish Theological Seminary.)

translation of the Jewish law, or Torah. This text was to occupy a place of honor, along with a great many others, in the magnificent library that Ptolemy was assembling at Alexandria. He arranged with the High Priest in Jerusalem that 72 Jewish elders—each an experienced scholar exhibiting the highest moral standards—would be sent from Jerusalem to Alexandria. Ptolemy welcomed them with sumptuous meals and extended conversation, after which they set about their task in the palatial quarters the monarch provided them. They formed subcommittees to work on their renderings, and after 72 days of consultation and cooperation, they completed their Greek translation of the books of Genesis, Exodus, Leviticus, Numbers, and Deuteronomy.

The final section of the *Letter of Aristeas* describes a formal ceremony at which the Jews of Alexandria accepted this Greek translation of the Torah as sacred writ. The author of the *Letter* consciously shaped his narration of this ceremony to call to the reader's mind the account of Moses's giving of the Law in the book of Exodus. To give support to the high status accorded to this text, a curse was uttered against anyone who dared to make even the slightest alteration in the wording of this Greek version.

We cannot know for certain what factors led the author of the *Letter of Aristeas* to promote the Septuagint as a document with sanctity and authority equal to the original Hebrew. It may well be that he and his community were confronted with revisions of this earliest Greek version and that he felt obliged to attack such revisers with the strongest weapon in his arsenal: the assertion that their alternatives represented direct challenges to sacred writ. We find support for this view in the writings of the 1st-century-C.E. Jewish philosopher Philo, himself a native of Alexandria, who equated the Septuagint translators with biblical prophets, thus according their words—especially the differences between the Greek and the Hebrew texts—the status of inspired revelation. Philo, who wrote in Greek, did not know Hebrew; for him (and for many others like him), the Bible in Greek assumed preeminent importance.

Philo was certainly not the only Jew of this period to hold the work of the earliest translations in such high regard; nonetheless, this point of view is more characteristic of early Christians than Jews. Therefore, Christian, rather than Jewish, writers more frequently embellished the relatively sober account of *Aristeas* with an increasing array of miraculous occurrences: Each scholar was said to have worked alone (or in isolated pairs) to produce, under divine intervention, exactly the same text as his colleagues. Until Jerome (340–415 C.E.), there were hardly any church leaders who studied Hebrew and could read the Hebrew Bible in its original. The Greek text served that purpose, as it continues to do for Orthodox Christians to this very day. Jerome's Latin translation, the Vulgate, was indeed based largely on Hebrew rather than Greek texts, but its popularity also resulted in diminishing the need—for more than 1,000 years—for Christian theologians to consult the Old Testament in Hebrew.

Is the *Letter of Aristeas* correct in its contention that the primary impetus for the earliest Greek version was the intellectual curiosity of Ptolemy II and his librarian? Or is it more likely the result of internal concerns about the need for authoritative interpretation as understanding of the Hebrew language grew increasingly rare among the members of Alexandria's large Jewish community? As is so often the case, the response need not be either/or. Although not documented outside of the *Letter*, the activities it ascribes to Ptolemy II are wholly in keeping with what is known about him from many other sources. And it makes good sense that Alexandrian Jews would support, if not initiate, a translation into what was becoming their everyday language, Greek.

The initial translators of the Torah into Greek generally followed a reasonably literal approach to their Hebrew text. It can be observed that all translators have a dual allegiance: (1) to the text that they are translating (the base text) and (2) to the audience for whom they are translating (the target audience). If renderings remain too closely moored to the foreign-language original, audiences contemporary with the translator may not easily understand them. On the other hand, very free translations, while immediately accessible to readers, may end up changing significant meaning and nuance along with characteristic structure or grammar of the earlier text. If then we think of a continuum from literal to free, we can place the translators responsible for the Greek Pentateuch (the Old Greek version of the Torah) on the moderately literal side of the scale. We are able to affirm this at the same time we note that, against the evidence that the *Letter of Aristeas* provides, modern scholars have detected five, probably six, translators who were principally involved in producing this version (one for each book of the Pentateuch, with a second for the latter part of Exodus).

And what of the remainder of the Old Greek version of the Hebrew Bible? It is difficult to speak with certainty about the order in which other books were translated, where this took place, and under whose auspices or sponsorship. Nonetheless, some later translators (such as the translator of the book of Joshua) consciously modeled their renderings on the generally literal approach taken by the translators of the Torah, while others apparently felt free to modernize, harmonize, and otherwise modify the Hebrew they were rendering, presumably to meet what they perceived as the needs of their readers (see, for example, the books of Isaiah and Proverbs).

And what was the Hebrew text that the Greek translators worked with? It is certain that it often looked very much like the masoretic text (MT) that forms the basis of modern editions of the Hebrew Bible, although without the vowels and other markers that were not regularly inserted into manuscripts until approximately 900 C.E. But it is equally certain that some Greek translators had before them a Hebrew text that diverged, to greater or lesser extent, from the MT. This results from the fact, most clearly demonstrated in the Dead Sea Scrolls, that there was no "standard' text for "biblical" books at this time.

Modern scholars were not the first to note that there are divergences between the Septuagint and the MT. Even before the Common Era, readers observed such differences, which on occasion they sought to "remedy" by "correcting" the Greek on the basis of their Hebrew. In fact, this seems to be the primary motivation for the very revisers that the author of the *Letter of Aristeas* sought to combat. We do not know the names of any revisers as early as the mid-2nd century B.C.E; however, from the late 1st century B.C.E. through the early 3rd century C.E., we do have evidence of at least three Jewish revisers or re-translators: Theodotion, Aquila, and Symmachus. Widely divergent biographic accounts of these individuals circulated already in antiquity. We believe that all three were Jewish and motivated by theological as well as stylistic concerns. The writers of the New Testament knew the early layer or stratum of the text attributed to Theodotion; Symmachus may still have been active in the early 3rd century C.E. Greek-speaking Jews continued to use and further develop Aquila's extremely literal version well into the Byzantine period.

All of this evidence should lead us to be very cautious about oft-repeated statements that the Jews abandoned the Septuagint when early Christians adopted it. Although it is true that, except for the Greek speakers mentioned above, Jews did eventually stop using and studying the Septuagint (until the early 19th century, when Jewish scholars began to make major advances in Septuagint studies), the continuing revision of old(er) Greek manuscripts for several centuries shows how much interest and authority it managed to maintain for at least some Jewish communities.

The sources cited earlier give witness to differing views about the value of the Greek version, but none condemns translation per se. Rabbinic sources, on the other hand, do contain such condemnations, as well as positive statements, often specifically directed to the Greek text, about biblical versions in languages other than Hebrew. For example, there is *Soferim* 1:7:

> It happened once that five elders wrote the Torah for King Ptolemy in Greek, and that day was as ominous for Israel as the day on which the golden calf was made, since the Torah could not be accurately translated.

And there is in the Babylonian Talmud, *Megillah* 9a:

> It was related of King Ptolemy that he brought together 72 elders and placed them in 72 rooms, and he went into each one individually and ordered them, "Write for me the Torah of your Teacher Moses." The Holy One, blessed be He, put wisdom in the heart of each one so that they agreed with one accord and wrote for him, "God created in the beginning ...."

These widely divergent opinions likely reflect deep divisions among Rabbinic authorities, based on factors such as chronology (before or after the destruction

Octaplus psalterii, Augustini Iustiniani Genuensis, predicatorii ordinis, Episcopi Nebiensis, dentem hebree de verbo ad verbum, tertia latinam communem, quarta grecam, quinta ptam, septima latinam respondentem chaldee, vltima vero hoc est octaua, con

Hebrea.	Latina respondens hebree.	Latina communis.	Greca.
ספר תהלים א	Liber hymnorum .I.	Dauid prophetæ carmen, & regis Deo. Incipit Psalterium A. siue liber hymnoru siue psalmo rum siue soliloquiorum. Psalmus Dauid .I.	Δαϊβιδ Προφήτου και βα σιλεως μελος. Ψαλμος το Δαϊβιδ όπται γραφαι παρίβραϊς. α

שרי האיש אשר לא הלך בעצת	Eatus vir, B. qui non abiit, in consilium	Eatus vir qui non abiit n consilio	Ακριος ανηρ ος ουκ επορευθη εν βουλη
רשעים וב	impiorum,	impiorum	ασεβων,
ובדרך	& in via	& in via	η εν οδω,
חטאים לא עמד	peccatorum non stetit,	peccatorum non stetit,	αμαρτωλων ουκ εστη,
ובמושב לצים לא	& in sede derisorum, non	& in cathedra pestilentie non	η επι καθεδρα λοιμων ουκ εκαθισεν. ΑΛΛ η εν τω νομω
ישב כי אם בתורת	sedit. Sed in lege	sedit. Sed in lege	κυριου το θελημα αυτου,
יהוה חפצו	DEI voluntas eius,	domini voluntas eius,	η εν τω νομω αυτε μελετηση
ובתורתו יהגה	& in lege eius meditabitur	& in lege eius meditabitur	ημερας η νυκτος. Και εσαι
יומם ולילה והיה	die ac nocte. Et erit	die ac nocte. Et erit	ως το ξυλον το πεφυτευμενον παρα
כעץ שתול על	tanq arbor plantata super	tãq lignu qd platatu est secus	τας διεξοδους των υδατων, ο
פלגי מים אשר	riuulos aquarum, que	decursus aquarum, quod	καρπον αυτε δωσει εν καιρω αυτω.
פריו יתן בעתו	fructu suu dabit in tpe suo,	fructu suu dabit in tepore suo.	Και το φυλλον αυτε ουκ αποφρυησεται
ועלהו לא יבול	& folium eius non defluet,	Et folium eius non defluet,	η παντα οσα αν ποιη
וכל אשר יעשה	& omne quod faciet	& omnia quecuq faciet	κατευοδωθησεται. Ουχ ουτας
יצליח לא כן	prosperabitur. Non sic	prosperabuntur. Non sic	οι ασεβεις ουχ ουτας, αλλ η ωσει
הרשעים כי אם כמץ	impii, sed tanquam festuca	impii non sic, sed tanq puluis	ον εκριπτει ο ανεμος απο προσωπου
אשר תדפנו רוח	quam proiicit ventus.	que proiicit vetus a facie terre.	Δια τουτο ουκ αναστησοντ (της γης
על כן לא יקמו	Propterea non surgent	Ideo non resurgunt	ασεβεις εν κρισι,
רשעים במשפט	impii in iudicio,	impii in iudicio,	ουδε αμαρτωλοι εν βουλη
וחטאים בעדת	neq peccatores i ogregatoe	neq peccatores in consilio	δικαιων. Οτι γινωσκει
צדיקים כי יודע	iustorum. Quoniam nouit	iustorum. Quoniam nouit	κυριος οδον δικαιων,
יהוה דרך צדיקים	DEVS viam iustorum,	dominus viam iustorum,	η οδος ασεβων απωλειται
ודרך רשעים תאבד	& via impiorum peribit.	& iter impiorum peribit.	

psalteriu & Cithara hoc interesse, qd cithara deorsum percutitur, psalterius sursum hoc pluribus costare chordis .i. dece illa tn sem hoc superius habere concauitatem illa ueroinferius Augustinus uero psalterii sic dscripsit. Psalteriu est organu qd qde manibus per tatur pcutietis, & chordas distinctas h3 sed illu locu unde sonu accipiut corde, illa cociuu lignu qd pendet & tactu resonat, qa to

---

A two-page spread from Genoa Psalter (Psalterium Octaplum), Genoa, 1516. These pages from this book of Psalms demonstrate the typical layout of a biblical polyglot, where several languages of the same text sit side be side. This polyglot, however, is particularly impressive, as it was one of the first containing biblical material ever published, presenting the text of Psalms in seven languages, and providing the editor's references and notes in the final column on the right. (Courtesy of The Library of the Jewish Theological Seminary.)

oîus prima columnella habet hebream editionem, secunda latinam interpretationem, respon
arabicam, sexta paraphrasim, sermone quidem chaldeo, sed literis hebraicis conscri
tinet scholia idest annotationes sparsas & intercisas.

Arabica.	Paraphrasis chaldea.	Latina respondens chaldee.	Scholia.
		Interpretatio. .I.	A.

Arabica	Paraphrasis chaldea	Latina respondens chaldee
		Eatitudo viro, qui non ambulauit in consilium
		impiorum,
		& in via
		peccatorum non stetit,
		& cum societate derisorum non circumiuit. Sed in institutione
		DEI voluntas eius,
		& in lege eius, meditatur
		die ac nocte. Et erit
		tanq̃ arbor vite, que plantata est sup
		fonticulos aquarum, cuius fructus
		maturescit in tempore suo,
		& folia eius non defluunt,
		& omne germen quod germinat,
		granescit & proficit. Non sic
		impii, sed sicut quisquilie
		quas proiicit ventus.
		Propterea non surgent
		impii, in die iudicii magni,
		neq̃ peccatores in societates
		iustorum. Quoniam manifesta est
		ante DEVM, via iustorum,
		& via impiorum perdetur.

Scholia (right column):

Vt admodū dux prefati sumus i principio Mas thei nolumus nunc iustos condere cōmenta rios in psalterio sicut nec in reliquis sacre scripture libros. Cas sus siquidem & uanus existimari posset labor noster si post Didymū Origenē Eusebiumq̃ grecos, aut post nros Hilarium Augustinū: Hieronymus Ambro sium Cassiodorū, aut etiam post Salomonē Abraha Dauidem & multos alios hebreos, magnamq̃ iuniorum turbaq̃ aggrederemur. Atqui paucula quedā adducemus qbus neo terici hebrei redargui possint, nostri uero & delectari & in dogma te christiano cōfirma ri, quaquam que mar tyrū sanguine & roma noq̃ potificum aucto ritate roborata sunt confirmatione non idi gent. Itaq̃ psalteriū, ut ali libri nomie ordia mur, grecum uerbum est, quod latine lauda torium organum dici potest. Eie autem ut Hieronymus ad Dar danum scripsit, uas in modum qua arā ci ty pei cum decem cordis, secūdum quod scriptū est in psalterio decem chordarum psallire il li. In cōmentariis uero psalmorum idem Hie ronymus quid sit psal teriū num magis expri mit, dicens illud esse genus organi musici mehus sonantis qua ci thara, similitudineq̃ habere cithare sed nō esse Citharam, in eoq̃

pit aerē psalteriū in superiore pte h3. Cithara uero hoc genus ligni cauū & resonās, in inferiore pte h3. Itaq̃ in psalterio chorde desup
sonū accipiūt. In cithara chorde ex inferiore pte sonū accipiūt Hieronymo ex authoribus hebreoq̄ cōsensi ū plures, & in primis Si
meon q̃ ut refert cōmentator Salomon psalterium a cithara distinguit, quod psalterium plures q̃ cithara cōtineat chordas. Appellant

A
y

The translations from left to right are: Hebrew, the Latin translation of the Hebrew text, the Vulgate Latin version, the Greek Septuagint version, Arabic (one of the earliest examples of Arabic printing using movable type), Aramaic, and the Latin translation of the Aramaic text. This polyglot also contains the first printed reference to Christopher Columbus in any book, mentioning that the "ends of the earth" had been discovered by one of Genoa's native sons. (Courtesy of The Library of the Jewish Theological Seminary.)

of the Jerusalem Temple by the Romans in 70 C.E.), geography (in the Land of Israel or the Diaspora), and ideology. Although Christians disputed—sometimes heatedly, as in the case of Jerome and his contemporary Augustine—*which* text to translate, the question of whether or not to translate did not often arise.

In a formal sense, the Septuagint was the earliest recorded written version of scripture in a language other than Hebrew. But it is likely that the Hebrew Bible itself contains evidence of its translation or interpretation several centuries earlier than 275 B.C.E. Nehemiah 8 describes Ezra the scribe as standing before the people at Jerusalem's Water Gate, reading from the book of the Law (which many scholars identify with the Torah that we know to this day) in Hebrew, with others providing an explanation. This explanation or interpretation was almost certainly in Aramaic for the benefit of the populace, who were no longer fluent in Hebrew, for by then (the mid-5th century B.C.E.) Aramaic was the common language of the ancient Near East. In this scenario, interpreters were using Aramaic to supplement and explain, but not replace, the Hebrew wording of the Torah, and in an oral rather than written form.

The Aramaic *Targums*

At some point in the pre-Christian era, scribes began to write down Aramaic renderings of the Hebrew Bible; these texts are called *Targums* (or *Targumim*). Traditional Jewish sources identify the books of the Torah as the first to be translated into Aramaic. Indeed, among the Dead Sea Scrolls there are two small Leviticus fragments, but by far the longest Aramaic text among the Scrolls is the *Targum* of Job. The most important and well-preserved *Targums* date from the early centuries of the Common Era, although the material they incorporate is often much older. There are several important *Targums* for the Torah, the Former Prophets (roughly equivalent to the Historical Books in the Christian tradition), the Latter Prophets, and the Writings (or Kethuvim). The most influential *Targums* were composed in Babylonia.

These *Targums* were initially used as supplements to the Hebrew, and their translators stayed relatively close to that Hebrew text. When the translators did part company with it, they felt freer than most Septuagint translators to introduce considerable blocks of "nonbiblical" material into legal as well as narrative sections. Among the techniques they adopted were circumlocutions for references to God. Thus, for example, at Genesis 11:15, *Targum Neofiti* has "The Glory of the *Shekhinah* of the Lord was revealed to see the city and the tower," where the Hebrew reads, "The Lord came down to see the city and the tower." Another *Targum* to the Torah, *Pseudo-Jonathan*, presents this text at Genesis 26:3, "Sojourn in this land and My word will assist you," for the Hebrew, "Sojourn in this land and I will be with you." They also reshaped and updated the Hebrew to a considerable degree to conform to their perceptions of their readers' needs and to the oral tradition.

As part of Christian Scripture, the books of the Old Testament also circulated in Syriac (also called Eastern Aramaic), and Latin. As mentioned earlier, Jerome made a point of learning Hebrew to produce his Latin text, and he also consulted Jewish teachers. For these activities, he was roundly attacked on philological as well as theological grounds. Nonetheless, it is the case that almost all subsequent Christian translators (for example, Martin Luther) and translation committees (such as those responsible for the King James Version) made use, often extensive use, of Jewish sources.

An Arabic Translation

The Arabic language gained prominence with the rapid rise of Islam in the mid-7th century C.E. Jews living in the East and in North Africa quickly adopted the language, but several centuries passed before there was a major translation of the Hebrew Bible into Arabic. It was Saadiah ben Joseph, born and raised in Egypt, and a *ga'on* (head of a Babylonian rabbinic academy), who undertook this task in the early 10th century. His Arabic translation may have first appeared written in Hebrew characters, a procedure that several later translators also adopted when rendering the Bible into German and other languages. Saadiah Ga'on's version ultimately became the standard biblical text for Arabic-speaking Jews. In his translation, Saadiah was able to achieve his primary goal; namely, to produce a clear, unadorned Arabic rendering of what he understood to be the meaning of the Hebrew original. With primary emphasis on the needs of his contemporary readers, he was willing to simplify or omit distinctive features of Hebrew grammar and style if they were likely to confuse or intimidate his target audience of Arabic speakers.

German Bibles

As Jews settled or increased their presence throughout Europe, they did not typically produce Bible translations right away. The example of German-speaking Jews is instructive in this regard. Although Jews had arrived in Germany as early as the 4th century C.E., translation of the Hebrew Bible into any of the German dialects first appeared only in the 1200s. These early German versions were intended primarily for the home and school and tended to be very literal renderings of the Hebrew. The home and school (in this case, what might be termed "elementary school") were typically run by women, who were also an explicit audience for the *Teutsch Humash* of Jacob ben Isaac of Yarnow, who lived in the mid-1600s. This edition, better known as the *Tsena Urena*, or "Women's Bible," incorporated enormous amounts of material, largely aggadic, from outside of the Bible. This version, and many subsequent ones based on it, supported and maintained the view that only women and children needed the Bible in translation—and then only in a translation embellished with nice stories and easy-to-understand examples. Male children, of course, would outgrow

HESTER

themate excogitare · quibz verbis uti
potuit qui iniuriam passus est · uel ille
qui iniuriam fecit. Vos aut o paula et
eustochium quoniam ʒ bibliothecas
hebreoʒ studuistis intrare · et interpre=
tum certamina comprobastis · tenen=
tes hester hebraicum librum per singla
verba nostram translatione aspicite:
ut possitis agnoscere me nichil etiam
augmentasse addendo: sed fideli testi=
monio simpliciter sicut in hebreo ha=
betur · historiam hebraicam latine lin=
gue tradidisse. Nec affectamꝰ laudes
hominum nec vituperationes expauesci=
mus: deo eni placere curantes minas
hominum penitus non timemꝰ: quonia
deus dissipat ossa eoʒ qui hominibz
placere desiderat: et scdm apostolum
qui eiusmodi sunt serui cristi esse non
possunt. Cursum in libro hester alpha=
betum ex ninio usqʒ ad theta litteram
fecimꝰ diuersis i locis: volentes scilicet
septuagica interpretu ordine per hec in=
sinuare studioso lectori. Nos enim
iuxta more hebraicu ordinem prsequi
etiam in septuagica editione maluimꝰ.
Qui prologꝰ Incipit liber hester. c. j.

I diebz assueri qui regnauit ab india
usqʒ ethiopiam sup centumuigintiseptem
prouincias: quando sedit in solio re=
gni sui · susa ciuitas regni eius exordi=
um fuit. Tercio igitur ano imperij sui
fecerat grande conuiuium cunctis prin=
cipibus · et pueris suis fortissimis per=
sarum ʒ medoʒ inclitis et prefectis pro=
uinciarum coram se: ut ostenderet di=
uicias glorie regni sui ac magnitudi=
nem: atqʒ iactantia potentie sue multo
tempore: centu videlicet et octoginta
diebz. Cumqʒ implerentur dies conuiuij:
inuitauit omne populum qui inuentꝰ est
in susis a maximo usqʒ ad minimum:

et iussit septem diebus conuiuiu prepa=
rari in vestibulo orti et nemoris · qd
regio cultu et manu consitum erat. Et
pendebat ex omni parte tentoria aerei co=
loris et carbasini ac iacinctini · susten=
tata funibus byssinis atqʒ purpureis:
qui eburneis circulis inserti erant et co=
lumnis marmoreis fulciebantur. Le=
ctuli qʒ aurei et argentei sup pauimen=
tum smaragdino ʒ pario stratu lapi=
de dispositi erant · qd mira varietate
pictura decorabat. Bibebant aut qui
inuitati erant aureis poculis: et alijs
atqʒ alijs vasis cibi inferebantur. Vi=
num quoqʒ ut magnificencia regia di=
gnum erat habundans et precipuum po=
netabatur: nec erat qui nolentes cogeret
ad bibendu: sed sic rex statuerat prepo=
nens mensis singulos de principibz
suis: ut sumeret unusquisqʒ qd vellet.
Vasthi qʒ regina fecit conuiuiu femi=
narum in palacio ubi rex assuerꝰ ma=
nere consueuerat. Itaqʒ die septimo cu
rex esset hilarior et post nimiam potio=
nem incaluisset mero · precepit mauma
et bazatha et arbona et bagatha et
abgatha et zarath et carchas septem
eunuchis qui i cospectu eius ministra=
bant · ut introducerent vasthi regina
coram rege · posito sup caput eius diade=
mate: ut ostenderet cunctis populis et prin=
cipibus eius pulcritudinem. Erat eni
pulcra valde. Que renuit et ad regis
imperiu quod per eunuchos manda=
uerat venire contempsit. Vnde iratus
rex et nimio furore succensus · interroga=
uit sapientes qui ex more regio semp
ei adherebant et illoʒ facietat cuncta con=
silio · scientiu leges ac iura maiorum:
erant aut primi et proximi charsena et
zethar et admatha et tharsis ʒ mares
et marsana et mamucha septe duces

Beginning of book of Esther, Gutenberg Bible, Germany, 1455. This illuminated page is from one of, if not the, earliest books ever printed in Europe using movable type. Johannes Gutenberg printed between 160–180 Bibles, many with hand-painted decoration on them. Thus, these printed Bibles became like the manuscript Bibles that had preceded them, which had been written by scribes and adorned with hand-painted art. (Courtesy of The Library of the Jewish Theological Seminary.)

this need; as men, they would be entrusted with the sacred text in its Hebrew original.

Two and a half centuries later, in the late 1700s, the Jewish intellectual and Enlightenment leader Moses Mendelssohn turned his attention to remedying what he saw as the sorry state of Bible versions available to his fellow German-speaking Jews. The style and level of German in those texts were, in his opinion, thoroughly unacceptable for a Jewish community that should be seeking close cultural and social ties with the Christian elites of his day. So he chose to prepare a version in the High German used by such elites, making sure to exclude all specifically Christian renderings familiar from Martin Luther's classic translation and other previous renderings. In their stead, he introduced typically or traditionally Jewish interpretations. Like Saadiah's Arabic translation, the first editions of Mendelssohn's work were printed with Hebrew characters. The first complete translations of the Hebrew Bible into Judeo-German (as the dialect of German spoken by Jews of this period is known) came at the end of the 17th century. They resulted from the efforts of Isaac Blitz and Joseph Witzenhausen. Both Bibles were initially published in Amsterdam.

Subsequent editions of Mendelssohn's translation, printed with German characters, were evidence of a growing market that became increasingly diverse with the rise of Reform and neo-Orthodox communities among German-speaking Jews. Within the former, Bible translators and commentary writers—Leopold Zunz and Ludwig Philippson are well known in this regard—welcomed some of the critical, nontraditional scholarship then being developed by Protestant researchers. Among neo-Orthodox Jews, the versions of Samuel Raphael Hirsch and his son Mendel were widely read. Publishers also discovered that they could increase sales by packaging some editions as family Bibles.

The Jewish philosophers Martin Buber and Franz Rosenzweig were responsible for another German-language translation deserving mention. They began their work before World War I, but it was not until after World War II that Buber alone completed it (Rosenzweig had died in 1929). The version Buber-Rosenzweig created aimed to introduce modern readers to myriad linguistic and literary features (such as wordplays and repetitions) that up until then were accessible only to those who could read the Hebrew in the original. To achieve their goals, they stretched the German language to (and some might say, beyond) the breaking point.

Yiddish Bibles

For many centuries, Jews had been preparing Yiddish translations of the Hebrew Bible as well. In the late 19th century, Christians—more precisely Jews who had converted to Christianity—also became active in this area. They were primarily

43

supported by organizations like the British and Foreign Bible Society. Thus it is not surprising that the Yiddish-language Old Testaments they produced were compatible with Christian theology; together with Yiddish versions of the New Testament, such Yiddish Bibles were widely distributed by missionary societies in eastern Europe and later aboard ships, in harbors, and within communities throughout the West wherever Jews settled.

This period also witnessed the preparation of what is probably the best-known Jewish translation of the Bible into Yiddish. As was the case with Saadiah and Mendelssohn, this was the work of a single individual: Solomon Bloomgarden, who is generally known by his pen name, Yehoash. He began publishing his version, in serialized form, in 1910, in the United States, where he lived, and continued to revise it until his death in 1927. His work did not appear as a whole until a decade later, on the eve of World War II. By then, alas, Yiddish as a living language and large numbers of Yiddish speakers were already on the road to destruction.

Other European Language Bibles

Among other modern languages into which Jews translated the Bible are Spanish and Italian. Jews are responsible for two of the most famous Spanish Bibles: the Alba Bible, prepared in the early 15th century by Rabbi Moses Arragel; and the mid-16th-century Ferrara Bible, which formed the basis for many subsequent renderings. Italian translations by Jews go back to the medieval period, but probably the best-known Jewish versions in Italian are the work of the major 19th-century figure Samuel David Luzzatto, also known as Shadal.

The First English Translations, from Great Britain

The history of Jewish translations of the Bible into English has a number of features in common with Jewish versions in other modern languages. Its development is also marked by distinctive elements that reflect cultural, political, religious, and even economic forces at play in the United Kingdom and later in the United States.

For at least three centuries, the King James Version (KJV) of 1611 functioned for English speakers as Martin Luther's version had for those who spoke German. Although there were no Jewish members on the committees responsible for preparing the KJV, this translation is nonetheless deeply imbued with insights drawn from the Jewish Bible commentator David Kimchi; moreover, its word choice, cadence, and overall structure powerfully evoke the Hebrew original (but with Christian or Christianized renderings of several key passages). It is apparently for these reasons that England's growing Jewish community did not feel the need to produce its own translation until the closing decades of the 18th century.

The first Jewish versions of the Bible in English, which appeared in the 1780s, were limited to the first five books, the Torah. They were not, strictly speaking,

Translations Differ

Take a look at one verse, Genesis 2:18, as it appears in several different translations. Notice the subtle but interesting differences in the way it is rendered. For instance, more recent versions have exchanged the traditional "man" for less gendered language and "helper" for more egalitarian language. There is also variation in rendering the divine name.

Original Hebrew text	18 וַיֹּ֙אמֶר֙ יְהוָ֣ה אֱלֹהִ֔ים לֹא־ט֛וֹב הֱי֥וֹת הָֽאָדָ֖ם לְבַדּ֑וֹ אֶֽעֱשֶׂה־לּ֥וֹ עֵ֖זֶר כְּנֶגְדּֽוֹ׃
King James Version	"And the LORD God said, It is not good that the man should be alone; I will make him an help meet for him."
Old Jewish Publication Society (OJPS) TANAKH (1917)	"And the LORD God said: 'It is not good that the man should be alone; I will make him a help meet for him.' "
The Living Torah (1981)	"God said, 'It is not good for man to be alone. I will make a compatible helper for him.' "
New International Version (1984)	"The LORD God said, 'It is not good for the man to be alone. I will make a helper suitable for him.' "
New Revised Standard Version (1989)	"Then the LORD God said, 'It is not good that the man should be alone; I will make him a helper as his partner.' "
The New American Bible (1991)	"The LORD God said: 'It is not good for the man to be alone. I will make a suitable partner for him.' "
Holy Bible: Contemporary English Version (1995)	"The LORD God said, 'It isn't good for the man to live alone. I need to make a suitable partner for him.' "
The Five Books of Moses: The Schocken Bible, vol. 1 (1995)	"Now YHWH, God, said: It is not good for the human to be alone, I will make him a helper corresponding to him."
Tanach, Stone Edition (1996)	"HASHEM God said, 'It is not good that man be alone; I will make him a helper corresponding to him.' "
JPS TANAKH (NJPS, 1985)	"The LORD God said, 'It is not good for man to be alone; I will make a fitting helper for him.' "
Richard Elliott Friedman, Commentary on the Torah (2003)	"And YHWH God said, 'It's not good for the human to be by himself. I'll make for him a strength corresponding to him.' "
Robert Alter, The Five Books of Moses (2004)	"And the Lord God said, 'It is not good for the human to be alone, I shall make him a sustainer beside him.' "
The Contemporary Torah (2006)	"God יהוה said, 'It is not good for the Human to be alone; I will make a fitting counterpart for him.' "

new translations: A page of Hebrew text faced the corresponding English of the KJV, enhanced with a few explanatory notes taken from traditional Jewish sources such as that of the commentator Rashi. Such editions may have been in response to Hebrew-English texts published in the preceding decades under Protestant auspices. In context, these versions, which were consciously shaped for English-speaking Jews, represent an important step.

As was the case with the origins of the Septuagint over 2,000 years earlier, a number of concerns, both within and outside of the Jewish community, motivated such steps at the turn of the 19th century. By then, most Jews, whose families had fairly recently immigrated from Spanish-speaking lands as well as those from German and Yiddish backgrounds, were increasingly familiar and comfortable with English. Synagogues established by both German and Spanish communities were making use of prayer books with some English, and it was becoming common to hear at least a few sermons in English. Under such circumstances, the appearance of "Jewish Bibles" in English was not surprising.

External forces were also moving the Jewish community in the same direction. By the early 1800s, a growing number of missionary societies were focusing their efforts and resources on the conversion of Jews to Christianity. Aided by technological advances that allowed for the mass production of inexpensive Bibles, such Christian proselytizers became a frequent sight in the Jewish neighborhoods of London and other major cities (Yiddish Bibles of this sort were noted earlier). Producing its own English-language versions was one of the most effective responses the Jewish community could devise.

The few Jewish versions with pre-1800 copyright dates came not from the Jewish establishment, but from individuals on the periphery of the organized community or even at odds with it. By the mid-1800s, the preparation of English-language versions had passed squarely into the hands of those who were well connected with the community's leadership. This could be seen, in unmistakable terms, when the chief rabbi of the British Empire gave his official approval to two of these versions—pointedly not for the synagogue use but for use in schools and homes (thus harkening back to similar constraints imposed several centuries earlier in German-speaking lands).

By the end of the 19th century, the Jews of England had their choice of more than a dozen English-language versions specifically marketed to them. None of these translations differed markedly from the style and structure of the KJV, even as their editors and sponsors edited out Christian language, thereby restoring for Jews traditional biblical interpretation.

OJPS, NJPS, and Other American Translations

Unlike their Protestant or Catholic counterparts, British Jews did not form committees to translate scripture, but continued the long-standing practice of working as individuals. This was also the case in the United States in the 19th century, where one man, the energetic and resourceful Isaac Leeser, was responsible for a very well known English-language version. His translation of the Torah, which appeared in the 1840s, was followed a decade later by his rendering of the entire Hebrew Bible. Although his style may be criticized as wooden and devoid of literary distinction, it was his Bible that was most often found in American Jewish homes until the beginning of the 20th century.

At that time, the recently founded The Jewish Publication Society of America (JPS), in Philadelphia, sought out and organized a committee to produce a version that would replace Leeser's. JPS carefully chose members of the translation committee to represent the three major Jewish institutions of higher learning then in existence in the United States: Hebrew Union College in Cincinnati, affiliated with the Reform movement; the Jewish Theological Seminary in New York City, part of the Conservative movement; and Dropsie College in Philadelphia, which offered graduate-level instruction in a number of fields not easily accessible to Jews elsewhere.

Tanakh, Tanach
Tanakh (and its alternative spelling, "Tanach") is an acronym reflecting the traditional three-part Jewish division of the Hebrew Bible: **T**orah, **N**evi'im (Prophets), **K**ethuvim (Writings).

To chair this committee, JPS selected as editor-in-chief Max L. Margolis, a well-established scholar who was thoroughly grounded in traditional Jewish learning and equally knowledgeable in the classics and in the critical approaches to biblical study then in vogue. Margolis was also an immigrant to the United States; as such, he saw how often the progress of his fellow immigrants was impeded by their poor language skills. For Margolis, the KJV offered the best model of proper English. Shorn of its Christian interpretations, a "Judaized" KJV would be an ideal text to ease the passage from Jewish immigrant to Jewish American. In viewing his work in this manner, Margolis was modeling his efforts on the earlier work of Moses Mendelssohn.

Margolis's efforts were entirely consistent with the approach set out by JPS. The language of the KJV was largely retained; of course, Margolis and his committee took out overtly Christian language and introduced some traditional Jewish interpretation. The finished product (sometimes referred to as the OJPS or Old Jewish Publication Society translation)—first published in 1917 and reissued in numerous editions over the next half century or so—was a valued complement to the home of middle-class American Jews, in exactly the same way that the KJV found a place in the libraries of their Protestant neighbors.

In the mid-1950s, Jewish biblical scholar Harry M. Orlinsky began to call for a replacement of the 1917 version—not simply an updating, but an entirely new type of translation that would mark a clear departure from the KJV. For Orlinsky, the effectiveness of a Bible translation could be judged by how easily readers understood it. His contemporaries, he observed, were put off by antiquated or obscure words, and they were confused or bored by foreign-looking sentence structure and grammar. In Orlinsky's view, the key question for translators was this: What did the original authors intend to say to their audience, and how can we convey that meaning to our audience? In short, this approach to translation seeks to bring the text to the reader. Among his Jewish predecessors, Orlinsky's closest model in this regard was Saadiah Ga'on. More broadly, Orlinsky was allying himself with a number of Protestant scholars associated with the American Bible Society, who promoted and practiced a dynamic or functional equivalence approach to Bible translation. Formatting and typographic fonts were also updated in keeping with this approach.

Orlinsky carried out his task from what he understood to be a thoroughly Jewish stance. The resultant translation, the New Jewish Publication Society translation (or NJPS), was thus positioned to take its distinctive place among the more accessible and readable English Bibles of the middle to late 20th century.

Orlinsky served as editor-in-chief of the committee that prepared the Torah translation of the NJPS, which initially appeared in the mid-1960s; he was also part of the group that worked on the Prophets. Other scholars from North America and Israel composed the committee for the Writings. Each committee first published its efforts as separate volumes. In 1985, the entire TANAKH, or Hebrew Bible, appeared, incorporating in revised form the efforts of all three translation committees. It was not until 1999 that JPS was able to publish its first Hebrew-English language edition, thereby facilitating comparison between text and translation.

The post–World War II period has witnessed the proliferation of new, often competing English-language versions, especially among Protestants. By comparison, the corresponding market for Jewish versions is quite limited. Nonetheless, the NJPS is not the only modern translation for English-speaking Jews.

Among the most widely advertised and beautifully produced versions is ArtScroll's *Tanach*, which was first published by Mesorah Publications of Brooklyn, New York, in 1996. It is aimed primarily at more traditional or Orthodox segments of the Jewish community, but its appeal extends beyond that market. For the Torah, its translators relied on the interpretations of the medieval commentator Rashi; elsewhere, they are more eclectic—but they never range beyond traditional sources.

Another version intended primarily for Orthodox and other traditional Jews is the *Living Torah*, by Rabbi Aryeh Kaplan, and the *Living Nach*, three successive volumes covering the Prophets and the Writings, which were translated by

Kaplan's followers after his death. Kaplan, a prolific writer on Jewish topics, often emphasized mystical elements in Jewish thought and practice. The volumes influenced by Kaplan reflect traditional Jewish sources, especially the philosopher Maimonides for legal interpretation, and they also display a demonstrable interest in spiritual matters.

Working on his own, the Jewish scholar Everett Fox draws the contemporary reader into the world of antiquity through a modern-language version that incorporates many aspects of the ancient Hebrew text absent in most other English renderings. The effect Fox produced in English is reminiscent of the results Buber and Rosenzweig achieved in German. This imparts a distinctive flavor, as it were, to his *The Five Books of Moses: The Schocken Bible,* volume 1.

Two other renderings of the Torah by Jewish scholars have received notice: Richard Elliott Friedman, *Commentary on the Torah, With a New English Translation and the Hebrew Text;* and Robert Alter, *The Five Books of Moses: A Translation with Commentary.* Friedman is a scholar of the Bible; Alter, a professor of English. In both cases, as indicated by the titles of their works, the translation is accompanied by a substantial and substantive commentary. (For more on these works, "Commentaries on the Bible, on p. 121")

In 2005, the Union for Reform Judaism published a revised edition of its widely used *The Torah: A Modern Commentary.* Most recently, JPS itself introduced *The Contemporary Torah;* the subtitle, *A Gender-Sensitive Adaptation of the JPS Translation,* marks its most innovative feature. In addition to numerous changes with reference to humans, this Jewish version uses gender-neutral language for almost all references to God. These principles are in keeping with recent trends in Bible translation in general; even some conservative Protestant editions have been moving in this direction.

These are among the most important English-language Jewish versions on the market today. But there are others as well. Theological, literary, social, even fiscal forces have come to play a role in this phenomenon, which is as old as the Septuagint and as new as the latest version. For Jews, the questions that arise are ancient and perennial, modern and immediate: What is it that makes a Bible translation Jewish? Should a Jewish translation ever supplant, rather than supplement, the Hebrew original? Who, if anyone, should determine which mode of translation, or presentation, or annotation is best? Do differing versions serve to divide Jews, and, if so, should there be one version to unite? Whatever answers translators arrive at, it is possible to be optimistic that Jewish Bible translators will remain true to their distinctive task of finding and perfecting ways to link contemporary communities with the sacred texts that make up the Torah, the Prophets, and the Writings.

Leonard Greenspoon.

THE MATTER OF GENDER
IN THE JPS TORAH TRANSLATION

Harry Orlinsky, the editor-in-chief of the New Jewish Publication Society (NJPS) translation of the Torah (1962), lectured widely on what at that time was a new topic in translation: gender. He would point out that the best-known Bible versions have too often rendered certain Hebrew nouns as referring to men, thus making women appear relatively invisible. For example, the Decalogue (the Ten Commandments) in the classic King James Version (KJV) of 1611 has God "visiting the iniquity of the fathers [*avot*] upon the children" (Exod. 20:5) even though logic dictates—and other biblical passages indicate—that also in view were mothers and *their* sins. Orlinsky saw such customary renderings as misrepresenting the biblical text, and in his opinion, the solution lay in a contextual, idiomatic approach to translation—of which NJPS was the exemplar. (NJPS reads: "visiting the guilt of the parents upon the children.") He would reiterate that the NJPS approach has no inherent ideological bias but rather "seeks to determine within the context and in the light of pertinent data elsewhere in the Bible and in related extra-biblical societies what the author meant to convey."

Where the Torah's language suggests a neutral sense, NJPS avoids misleadingly ascribing gender, not only by rendering inclusively some "male" nouns but also by rendering masculine inflections and pronouns idiomatically rather than literally. Thus, for example, what KJV renders as "thou shalt not wrest the judgment of thy poor in *his* cause" appears in NJPS as "you shall not subvert the rights of your needy in *their* disputes" (Exod. 23:6). In short, NJPS led the way among contemporary translations in "gender-sensitive" rendering.

References to Human Beings

Like every translation, NJPS contains some internal inconsistencies. For example, NJPS renders *avot* in the same phrases and in similar contexts using terms with differing social-gender senses—NJPS reads "parents" in Exodus 20:5 (as noted earlier), yet "visiting the iniquity of *fathers* upon children" in Numbers 14:18.

Meanwhile, at times the NJPS translators rendered in unduly male terms. For example, the Hebrew wording in Numbers 14 is ambiguous as to who is to be punished for brazen faithlessness: the men or the people as a whole. Seeking the plain sense, the translators quite reasonably opted for the latter view. Yet to render two Hebrew phrases that do not themselves specify gender, they employed English idioms at odds with their overall interpretation. We read that Moses urges an incensed God not to "slay the people to a *man*" (14:15) and that God then condemns a generation of Israelites to die in the wilderness "to the last *man*" (14:35).

Ironically, in some other cases NJPS reads neutrally where a *non*inclusive rendering is actually called for. For example, NJPS could render *yeled* contextually as "lad, boy" (for example, Gen. 4:23, 37:30); yet it unconventionally casts the plural *yeladim* as "children" in Genesis 32:23 even though in that context the term can refer only to Jacob's sons (not to his daughter, Dinah). Similarly, NJPS renders the noun *edah* five different ways in the Torah; yet its rendering states that Moses was instructed to take a census of the Israelite "community" (*edah* [Num. 1:2]), although ancient censuses counted men only. And unlike prior translations, NJPS renders *banim* as "children" in Leviticus 10:13–15, although the topic is donations that are restricted to priests—that is, Aaron's "sons."

In a number of other instances, the NJPS translators appear to have based their rendering on an inaccurate understanding of social gender in the biblical setting. For example, where God refers to Abram's eventual death as going "to your *avot*" (Gen. 15:15; cf. 47:30), NJPS seems to have relied on a modern scholarly opinion that the Israelites counted only their male forebears ("fathers") as kin. Yet that view appears to be based on an etymological fallacy, meanwhile ignoring ample circumstantial evidence that suggests ancient Israelites also viewed their deceased mother and even her forebears as kin. The weight of the evidence argues for rendering *avot* inclusively here as "ancestors" or the like.

Last but not least, the NJPS translators employed the standard English style of using male nouns and pronouns where a neutral sense was meant, which closely correlates with Hebrew grammatical structure. Unfortunately, this has proven ambiguous with regard to gender: it can be difficult to tell whether "man," "kinsmen," "he," "his," or "him" connotes only male gender or an inclusive meaning. In a sense-for-sense translation like NJPS, the standard style can confuse readers. The very nature of NJPS as contextually precise argues against readers taking its male language as neutral; we would reasonably expect male terms to carry a male gender sense.

Contemporary readers make their way through a translation without the benefit of knowing the biblical setting. Many of us misconstrue that setting, perceiving the translated Bible as more male oriented than the original audience probably perceived the Hebrew text to be. We imagine the Israelite past as having been so "patriarchal" that, for example, in the context of ritual animal sacrifices and male-only priests, some of us infer that women were not part of the scene. Thus when NJPS relates that if someone eats sacrificial meat while ritually impure, "that *person* shall be cut off from *his* kin" (Lev. 7:20b), we may take the word "his" not as gender neutral but as referring to a male—discounting "person" as if it were a falsely generic term. That is, we may well understand NJPS to mean "that *man* shall be cut off from *his* kin." In such ways the standard English style has put a stumbling block before readers.

References to Divine Beings

To refer to God, the Torah uses grammatically masculine language; as was typical of English translations, NJPS employs corresponding masculine terms in its rendering. Given that a Jewish translation would have reflected the standard belief that God *transcends* human gender categories, the translators presumably meant their masculine wording in a gender-neutral sense.

Many of us are well aware that "Lord" is a male title by common usage; rendering God's personal name as "the LORD" can function like wearing male sunglasses to view the invisible Deity: "I'm not sure what I'm seeing—but it appears to be masculine." Furthermore, the translation's masculine pronouns may conjure up an image of a male deity, even though as a matter of logic or belief we could argue that God has no gender. In short, the NJPS style hinders some readers' appreciation of the Torah text.

At the same time, many scholars of Israelite history now believe that our ancient text's masculine inflections and occasional male imagery refer to what everyone at the time understood to be a *male* god—which would have gone without saying. If so, then the most *historically accurate* way to render the Torah's God-language today would be in masculine terms.

Yet it can be argued that the Torah promoted to its original audience a deity "beyond gender." Its text never ascribes to God anatomical sex features or sexual activity, in contrast to some ancient Near Eastern literature about high gods. Only in poetry and other clearly figurative passages does the text depict God in male social status terms. It meanwhile cautions against taking such images too literally—as if to say: the reality of God is beyond such terms. Further, grammatically masculine language would have been the only way to refer to a *non*-gendered deity. And contrary to conventional wisdom, the text seems to be written as if the audience were expecting definite signals before ascribing gender. In short, the Torah's silence about God's gender may well be a meaningful one, even when viewed in its original setting. Finally, although it's likely that few readers have considered the matter, the same question regarding the depiction of God's gender also applies to that of the Torah's other divine beings, namely angels. The NJPS translators appear to have presumed that in the ancient world all of God's divine agents were understood to be male, but there is reason to doubt that presumption. But to mention shortcomings of NJPS is not to censure what remains as the Jewish translation of choice for those who value contextual precision and modern idiom.

A Gender-Sensitive Adaptation of NJPS

In 2006, The Jewish Publication Society published a new, gender-sensitive version of the NJPS translation. *The Contemporary Torah* provides a new option for those interested in a historically based representation of social gender roles in the Bible, as well as for those who have become accustomed to gender-sensitive English in other aspects of their lives.

In preparing this work, the editors undertook a comprehensive analysis of the Torah's gender ascriptions, consulting both recent biblical scholarship as well as traditional Jewish sources. They selected language that portrays ancient gender roles to reflect a more sensitive understanding of the biblical world and its original audience.

In most cases, references to God are in gender-neutral language. The Tetragammaton, the unpronounceable four-letter name for the Divine, appears in this translation in unvocalized Hebrew to convey that the name is something totally "other"—beyond translation, gender, speech, and understanding. In some instances, however, male imagery depicting God is preserved because it reflects biblical society's view of gender roles.

Guided by principles set down by the original JPS translation committee, the editors found more inclusive ways of rendering "generic" terms—"humankind" for "mankind," "herders" for "herdsmen"—and replaced male pronouns in cases where gender was not germane or is now understood differently in light of new research about the biblical family, Israelite society, and neighboring cultures. A sampling of such language changes in *The Contemporary Torah* can be found in the table on p. 55, with comparisons of the same passages in the Old Jewish Publication Society (OJPS) and NJPS translations and in two Christian Bible translations.

Comparing Gender-Related Language in the Bible

	New Revised Standard Version (NRSV, 1989)	Today's New International Version (TNIV, 2005)	OJPS (1917)	NJPS (1985)	Contemporary Torah (2006)
Genesis 15:7					
וַיֹּאמֶר אֵלָיו אֲנִי יְהֹוָה	Then *he* said to him, "I am the LORD …"	Then *he* said to him, "I am the LORD …"	And *He* said unto him: "I am *the* LORD …"	Then *He* said to him, "I am *the* LORD …"	Then [*God*] said to him, "I am יהוה …"
Genesis 15:15					
וְאַתָּה תָּבוֹא אֶל־אֲבֹתֶיךָ בְּשָׁלוֹם תִּקָּבֵר בְּשֵׂיבָה טוֹבָה:	As for yourself, you shall go to your *ancestors* in peace; you shall be buried in a good old age.	You, however, will go to your *ancestors* in peace and be buried at a good old age.	But thou shalt go to thy *fathers* in peace; thou shalt be buried in a good old age.	As for you, / You shall go to your *fathers* in peace; / You shall be buried at a ripe old age.	As for you, / You shall go to your *ancestors* in peace; / You shall be buried at a ripe old age.
Exodus 21:7					
וְכִי־יִמְכֹּר אִישׁ אֶת־בִּתּוֹ	a *man* sells *his* daughter	a *man* sells *his* daughter	a *man* sells *his* daughter	a *man* sells *his* daughter	a *parent* sells a daughter
Deuteronomy 1:17					
לֹא תָגוּרוּ מִפְּנֵי־אִישׁ	you shall not be intimidated by *anyone*	do not be afraid of *anyone*	ye shall not be afraid of the face of any man	Fear no *man*	fear *no one*

Adapted from David E. S. Stein, *The Contemporary Torah.*

STORYTELLING IN THE BIBLE

Our brains seem uniquely adapted to making sense of experience through stories. We tell stories and listen to them not just in our daily conversation but on the news, in the movies, and in novels. Even a sacred text such as the Bible seeks to make sense of the world through stories. Thomas Hardy, the great English novelist, greatly admired biblical stories. "They are written with a watchful attention (though disguised) as to their effect on their reader," Hardy remarked in his diary on Easter Sunday, 1885. "Their so-called simplicity is, in fact, the simplicity of the highest cunning" (*The Mayor of Casterbridge*). Hardy is quite right. Biblical stories aim to have an effect on the reader, and we know they have succeeded when they stick with us. Eve chooses wisdom over Paradise and is expelled from the Garden of Eden. Cain kills Abel, whose blood cries out from the ground to accuse him. Abraham prepares to sacrifice his son at God's request. The Egyptian-raised Moses becomes the greatest prophet of ancient Israel.

As children, we're entertained by such biblical stories; returning to them as adults, we discover their power anew. They offer us a mirror into both a distant time and our own time. Perhaps even more than the stories we tell in our daily lives, a biblical story invites us to reflect on our deepest experiences, whether of God, of our families, of our community, or of the terrors and pleasures of life. In other words, these stories aim to make us think about important, even urgent matters. But rather than telling us how or what to think, they force us to find out what we think and how to respond. If we're lucky, we are rewarded with insight and perspective we would otherwise miss, engrossed as we usually are in more commonplace matters. Such stories, when studied together or chanted aloud, help join us to others and shape our identity as a community.

Of course some biblical stories might be based on events that "really happened." Many refer to historical events on a grand scale—the appointment of kings, victories and losses in battle, the destruction of the First Temple. But rather than give us an eyewitness account of a historical event, a biblical story reflects on an event and what it might mean for the People of Israel. Biblical stories are less concerned with facts and details than in the "truth" of experience, whether of a moral, spiritual, or psychological nature. They teach us about the human condition and the many ways in which human beings have encountered God. They teach us how we might best respond to God in our own lives.

Major Narratives in the Bible

The following are some of the most well-known stories in the Hebrew Bible, stories that have helped shape Jewish and Christian consciousness and ideas about God.

(Note: when a single verse in cited, it is the start of the narrative.)

The Beginning of the World

The creation of the world and Adam and Eve (Gen. 1:1)
The first murder (Gen. 4:1)
The great Flood (Gen. 6:9)
The tower of Babel (Gen. 11:1)

The First Jewish Family

Abraham and Sarah leave their native land (Gen. 11:27)
The birth of Ishmael (Gen. 16:1)
Sodom and Gomorrah (Gen. 18:16)
The birth of Isaac (Gen. 21:1)
The binding of Isaac (Gen. 22:1)
Jacob's dream of the ladder (Gen. 28:10)
Jacob marries Leah and Rachel (Gen. 29:1)
Jacob wrestles with the angel (Gen. 32:4)
Joseph and his brothers (Gen. 37:1)
Joseph in Egypt (Gen. 39:1)

Slaves in the Land of Egypt

The birth of Moses (Exod. 2:1)
The Burning Bush (Exod. 3:1)
The Ten Plagues and the first Passover (Exod. 7:14)
The splitting of the Sea of Reeds (Exod. 13:17)

Forty Years in the Wilderness

The giving of the Ten Commandments (Exod. 19–20)
The Golden Calf (Exod. 32:1)
Miriam and Aaron challenge Moses (Num. 12:1)
The scouting of the Land and the punishment of wandering (Num. 13–14)
Moses bids farewell (Deut. 31–32)

In the Promised Land

Joshua and the battle of Jericho (Josh. 1–4)
Deborah (Judg. 4–5)
Samson (Judg. 13–17)
Ruth and Naomi (Ruth 1–4)

The Founding of the Kingdom of Israel
Hannah and the birth of Samuel (1 Sam. 1:1)
Samuel appoints Saul king (1 Sam. 8)
Saul loses his kingdom (1 Sam. 15)
David and Goliath (1 Sam. 17)
The struggle between Saul and David (1 Sam. 24)
David conquers Jerusalem (2 Sam. 6)
David and Bathsheba (2 Sam. 11:1)
The judgment of Solomon (1 Kings 3)
Solomon and the Queen of Sheba (1 Kings 10:1)

Israel Splits in to Two Kingdoms
The kingdom divides (1 Kings 11)
Elijah and the priests of Baal (1 Kings 18)
Elijah ascends to heaven in a fiery chariot (2 Kings 2)

Exilic Period
The fall of Jerusalem and the First Temple (2 Kings 24)
Ezekiel and the valley of dry bones (Ezek. 37)

Post-Exilic
Jonah and the great fish (book of Jonah)
Esther saves her people (book of Esther)
Return from exile (Ezra 3)
Daniel in the lion's den (Dan. 6)

The Bible contains many kinds of writing besides stories. Biblical writing includes poetry, laws, family trees, wise sayings, and prophetic messages; and different kinds of writing interact with one another. For instance, a story might lead to a victory poem. A law might be made more concrete by a story in which an Israelite violates that law and is punished. Not only is there a variety of writing in the Bible with different purposes, but even within the category of "story" we find different stories that serve different purposes.

The Many Functions of a Story

A story may entertain or delight us. The lad David, equipped only with a slingshot, defeats the giant Goliath in 1 Samuel 17, in spite of the Philistine's threatening size, mighty armor, and weaponry. While entertaining us, this story also serves another, more political purpose, introducing us to David, the future king of Israel, in the best possible light. We have legends of mighty figures such as Samson, who in Judges 16 pulls the pillars of a whole temple down upon Philistine idolaters, killing himself at the same time.

We have stories that retell and transform the stories of other cultures. For instance, in the book of Genesis, Noah builds an ark and saves a remnant of the human race. The biblical story of the Flood draws on a Mesopotamian myth of a great flood, and while the two stories have many details in common, the biblical story has its own unique ending. Noah enters into a covenant with God, who introduces a law prohibiting murder, God's solution to the violent and troublesome behavior of human beings.

A biblical story may provide an explanation for pain or joy, such as the tale of Adam and Eve in Genesis 2. When things begin to go wrong after the couple eat the forbidden fruit, God informs Eve that she will experience suffering when giving birth. This punishment provides an explanation for the pains of labor. Adam will work the ground with great difficulty, providing the origin for a different kind of hard labor. Other stories explain why a place is named the way it is or why we avoid eating certain foods. Many tales teach us right from wrong, providing moral lessons or warning us against certain behavior. Adultery is punished, obedience rewarded.

Some stories demand to be remembered. The most important story that the ancient Israelites must remember is described in the book of Exodus, in which God frees the People of Israel from oppression in Egypt. This collective memory provides Israel with an explanation for its beginnings in slavery, how they managed to escape with God's help, and the motive for continued loyalty to God. It helps shape the community and strengthen it over time. In fact, the entire community of Israel participates in retelling the story of the Exodus year after year, and God even commands parents to tell the story to their children. Once they leave Egypt, the People of Israel accept God's offer of a covenant (a binding contract). The covenant obligates them to serve God, who in turn will care for them by giving them laws that will help them create a good and just community. A story told about the past demands actions in the present in order to build a better future.

The Bible also contains many stories about individuals who face the difficulties of life, leaving home to travel long distances alone to meet uncertain futures. Some flee to escape the murderous rage of brothers or the abuse of mistresses. Others are abandoned by lovers. These individuals are recognizably flawed, and we are meant to identify with them. How these characters handle the events of their lives and God's role in supporting them through such trials are among the key lessons of the story for the reader.

Finally, and perhaps most important, biblical stories describe encounters with God that are personal and private or public and communal. An entire people, Israel, witnesses God's presence on top of Mount Sinai, in thunder and smoke. An individual, Jacob, alone and frightened, is suddenly attacked by a mysterious wrestler; he manages to beat that wrestler, only to exclaim that he has seen none other than God, face to face. Such stories allow us to glimpse and be moved by the remarkable religious imaginations of the biblical storytellers.

How Biblical Stories Engage Us

The reader of a biblical story cannot remain passive; biblical stories demand their readers participate "in an unfolding conversation with the text" (Joel Rosenberg, in *Back to the Sources*, Barry W. Holtz, ed.). There are many reasons a reader gets involved. For one, biblical stories never give us enough details; our curiosity is constantly triggered, and we are left to supply the missing details ourselves. Not knowing until the very end of Genesis 32 who Jacob wrestles with throughout the night, we consider the possibilities. Is it a river demon? A messenger from God? Jacob's brother? His own guilty conscience confronting him in a dream? Only when Jacob announces that he has seen God face to face do we realize the identity of his opponent. We put aside our guesses and modify our view.

Sometimes we are certain what we think about an event or a character, but then we are proved wrong. In the opening chapters of 1 Samuel, Eli the priest fails to recognize real piety in front of him, mistaking Hannah's profound prayer for a drunken stupor. Soon after that encounter, a messenger from God informs this same priest that because he is too forgiving of his corrupt sons, they will be killed and a new priesthood established. By this point we have enough information about Eli to consider him in a strongly negative light. Yet in the midst of these problematic events, Eli continues to lovingly instruct his young protégé, the future prophet Samuel. He does so even after realizing that God has commanded Samuel to announce Eli's tragic fate to him. Eli's gentle response to the difficulties of his life forces us to reevaluate him, and we exchange contempt and scorn for pity and surprise. The process of adjustment keeps us involved.

Uncertainty also keeps us interested. Are we to consider the David of 2 Samuel 11 a solicitous king or a duplicitous adulterer as he deals with the husband of a woman David just got pregnant? The Bible does not tell us what to think or what moral we should carry away with us, instead forcing us to form our own opinion after reading its stories. Remarkably, we may reread a story at a different stage of our life and discover something that we never noticed before or perhaps never understood. That sense of discovery also invites us to reread biblical stories year after year.

Techniques of the Biblical Storytellers

If we learn to recognize the techniques of the biblical storytellers, we will better appreciate and understand their creations. For instance, as first proposed by Martin Buber and elaborated on by Robert Alter in *The Art of Biblical Narrative,* a key word may be chosen and repeated enough times for the reader to realize that it conveys the meaning of the larger story. For instance, in chapter 1 of Genesis the word "good" appears so often as to convince us that everything God creates is good. When God first speaks to Abraham in Genesis 12, God uses a form of "blessing" five times in just two verses, leading us to understand that Abraham will be a source of blessing in the world. In the concluding chapters of Numbers, the word "inheritance" appears frequently, reminding us that the tribes of Israel are about to leave behind the wilderness in which they have wandered for 40 years and indicating that they are ready to begin their new lives in the Promised Land. Years later the People of Israel approach the prophet Samuel to demand that he appoint a king over them, and he tries to warn them against such a plan by unmistakably repeating the word "take" to argue that a king will rob them of their children and much of their wealth.

Words may also allude to other stories. When that happens, we need to consider the connection between the two stories. For instance, Joseph brings his father "bad reports" of his brothers in Genesis 37. Events that follow eventually lead the entire family to settle in Egypt, where Pharaoh enslaves their descendants. Four hundred years later, having escaped with God's help, the Israelites fall under the spell of another "bad report," this time about the Promised Land (Num. 13). Even after suffering so much in Egypt, the descendants of Joseph immediately long to return to Egypt. Such a desire has disastrous results for their entire generation.

A great deal of repetition occurs in biblical stories, but we should not consider the writer who uses repetition as careless. The writer purposefully triggers our attention through repetition. We can spot small but very meaningful differences when a conversation or scene is repeated. (Robert Alter calls this type of repetition a "type-scene.") A man meets a woman at a well, and this leads to a proposal of marriage. Such an encounter at the well takes place in the tales of Rebekah and Isaac (Gen. 24), Jacob and Rachel (Gen. 29), and Moses and Zipporah (Exod. 2). Yet in each scene, in spite of the familiar pattern, subtle changes exist that convey a great deal about the characters involved. Isaac does not meet Rebekah himself, but a servant finds her and enters into negotiations on his behalf, suggesting the passivity that is part of Isaac's character. Unlike his father, Jacob exhibits superhuman strength in rolling the stone away from the well so that his beloved Rachel may water her herd. The stone provides an obstacle that he overcomes, but it also hints at the obstacles that lie in store for him before he can marry Rachel. Before Moses can water Zipporah's flock, he must fight off bandits, anticipating his future role as liberator. Through small variations, each scene illustrates some aspect of the character or of the character's future.

Repetition also occurs within the same story. For instance, in 1 Samuel 3, after God first calls to Samuel in the middle of the night, the young prophet fails to recognize God's voice. Instead he mistakenly goes to his mentor, Eli the priest, three times in a row! Each time Samuel announces, "Here I am, for you have called me." The repetition unifies the entire scene and communicates Samuel's utter obedience to his master Eli as well as his perplexity about who is calling him and for what reason. But there are also small differences in each encounter. The second time, instead of running, Samuel walks to his mentor, less eager to answer the call. When Eli sends him back to bed, he adds, "my son," acting like a parent who wants to calm Samuel, while revealing his own fondness for the young boy. In the third interaction, Eli finally realizes that it is God who has been calling Samuel and, instead of merely sending Samuel back to his bed, instructs him on how to respond to God's call. The change in the pattern highlights both Eli's selfless role as mentor and the momentousness of Samuel's new role as prophet. (See Uriel Simon, *Reading Prophetic Narratives*, on this particular scene.)

Repetition sometimes occurs in a phrase or even within a verse in a special structure called a "chiasm." God announces the prohibition against murder to Noah at the end of the Flood story in the following words: "Whosoever sheds the blood of man, by man shall his blood be shed" (Gen. 9:6). The structure is A, B, C and then reversed, C, B, A. Each letter represents a word: A = shed, B = blood, and C = man.

sheds   blood   man

man   blood   will be shed

The writer uses this special structure to communicate an important principle or message to the reader.

A different kind of repetition involves repeated images. For instance, "fire" haunts the story of Samson. The divine messenger who announces Samson's birth goes up in a flame from the altar. The name "Samson" includes the Hebrew word for the sun, a great fire in the sky. He is born near a place that includes "fire" in its name, Eshtaol. He has a fiery temperament, expressed in the destructive burning of Philistine fields (Judges 15:5), and he escapes from the Philistines when the cords that bind him melt away like fire (15:14). At the end of his life, he is buried in Eshtaol. The many uses of "fire" reinforce the destructive and unpredictable side of Samson.

Another way in which the biblical writer conveys meaning to the reader is through the use of dialogue. Often when characters speak to each other, or about each other to a third party, they repeat each other's words. Yet a second character might make a slight change in the words of the first speaker that often surprises the careful reader. Those changes may distort the original meaning or may add a twist that conveys something new. Sometimes the altered repetition lets us know that the second character is "on to" the first. In another use of dialogue, two characters may be defined by a contrast in tone, style, or substance. The panicked Saul can't think of what to bring the seer in the town up ahead as an offering and anxiously quizzes his servant. The servant calmly informs him that the situation is well in hand. Such a contrast in temperament highlights the emotional roller coaster that is Saul's personality, an instability that makes him less than suited to be king of a struggling new nation.

Naming speeches can also characterize a biblical figure. When a woman gives birth in the Bible, she often names the child and supplies a special meaning that usually involves a pun on the name. Not only are we introduced to a new character but we gain some insight into the experience of the mother in question.

Often the Bible will give us a seemingly extraneous detail that turns out to anticipate what will come. For instance, we learn in the very first chapter of 1 Samuel, in verse 3, that Eli has two sons, Hofni and Pinehas. They do not reappear in the story until 2:11. At that point they become very important to the story, as their corrupt behaviors lead to their deaths and to the death of their father, Eli. Repeatedly in the books of Samuel, sons gravely disappoint their fathers or lead them into catastrophe. In addition to the sons of Eli, we need only think of Jonathan's loyalty to David rather than to his father, Saul, or of Amnon, son of David who rapes his half-sister Tamar, David's daughter. In consequence, a second son of David, Absalom, rebels against his father in a civil war. Even the prophet Samuel, whose birth occurs in the very chapter that introduces us to the corrupt sons of Eli, must eventually face the fact that his own two sons are equally as corrupt.

Techniques That Convey Special Meaning
- Repetition of key words
- Words that connect one scene or story to another
- Repetition of events and encounters
- Repetition of images
- Careful use of dialogue
- The meaning of a name
- A detail that foreshadows, or anticipates, something to come

---

Putting Biblical Stories Together

In the Bible, not only does a story have a writer, but also an editor. The editor places different stories together and does so in a careful and creative way (Joel

Rosenberg suggests that we consider the editor an artist in his own right in *Back to the Sources*). On the surface, two stories may seem to contradict one another, but if the reader pays attention, one discovers that these stories have different points of view that complement each other. For instance, in chapter 1 of Genesis, God appears from the heavens to create the creatures of the world, including the human. In chapters 2 and 3 (considered to be written by a different author), God appears to have a much closer relationship with the human being, even sharing the Garden of Eden with the first woman and man. Thus we can appreciate God both as a transcendent being and as a figure who is quite close to the human. Later in the Bible, David is introduced to us in 1 Samuel 16 as a simple shepherd boy, chosen by God, and in the very next story David wins popular praise, thanks to his daring and skill with a slingshot. These stories also complement each other. David is chosen by God, who loves him, but at the same time he earns a reputation due to his exceptional gifts. (See Robert Alter, *The David Story*, for a translation and commentary on the relevant chapters.)

Sometimes different stories disagree. In Genesis 1, all that God creates is good. But in Genesis 2, God creates a tree of knowledge of good and bad. Is God the source only of good or of both good and bad? (See Israel Knohl, *The Divine Symphony*, for a fuller discussion of the differences between these stories.) In the book of Numbers, memory is seen as both positive and problematic. Chapter 10 reports that the priests designed specially hammered trumpets to be used first in the wilderness and later in the Temple. If blown in the Land, the trumpets will remind the people of that long-ago journey through the wilderness when God accompanied the people until they successfully arrived in the Promised Land. That memory unifies the people and reinforces their loyalty to God and to the priests. Yet in chapter 11, memory proves to be very destructive. The people are overcome with memories of Egyptian delicacies and want to abandon God and their leaders and immediately return to Egypt. In consequence, an entire generation will not enter the Land.

In each example, the editor has placed two stories next to one another to challenge us to think about such important matters as the nature of God, the origins of evil, the complex personality of King David, and the unreliability of memory. These stories represent different viewpoints, written by different authors in different times, and then placed together by yet another figure, the editor. The Bible does nothing less than preserve the collective wisdom and religious experiences not just of one writer but of generations of writers.

Moses and the Story of Israel

I conclude this chapter by looking at one story in some detail—the early life of Moses, found in Exodus 1:3. It is an example that illustrates many of the points made earlier. Though about an individual, Moses, the narrative anticipates and introduces the story about the community Israel. We can also glimpse the religious imagination of the writer in the depiction of the Burning Bush. (See Moshe Greenberg, *Understanding Exodus,* for more discussion about this.)

Every good story has a context that provides the reader with the needed background. Our context begins with the very beginning of Exodus, chapter 1, even before Moses is born. We are told: "But the Israelites were fertile and prolific; they multiplied and increased very greatly, so that the land was filled with them" (Exod. 1:7). Right away we have several allusions to chapter 1 of Genesis. The word "prolific" (often translated as "swarming") appears three times in two verses (Gen. 1:20–21). In 1:22, God creates the creatures of the planet and blesses them: "Be fertile and increase." In 1:28, God blesses the humans the same way, "Be fertile and increase," but then adds, "fill the earth." The first three terms come together in 9:7 (as they do in Exodus). At the end of the Flood story God announces to Noah, "And you, be fertile and increase and swarm [be prolific] all over the earth ..." (translation mine). Why does Exodus open with such clear allusions to the creation of the world and to the Flood's aftermath? Both of the earlier stories in Genesis are about beginnings, the very first beginning and then, after the Flood, a new beginning. At that time God offers humanity a second chance after the near destruction of the world. By using allusion, our writer in Exodus is proclaiming another beginning: the creation of the People of Israel. The birth of Moses and the birth of Israel as a people are connected to one another.

In fact, there are repeated references to birth in the opening chapters of Exodus. The Egyptian Pharaoh seeks to kill off newborn males, but heroic midwives thwart his plan. Then Moses is born, and part of the plot involves finding a nurse to suckle him. Eventually, the image of a birth canal is symbolically re-created in the narrow path that the Children of Israel must take through the waters of the Sea of Reeds. The opening chapters of Exodus also emphasize the crucial role of women in caring for the infant Moses. In addition to midwives, we read about Moses's mother and sister and even the daughter of the Pharaoh, who saves him from the Nile River. Moses is repeatedly saved by the actions of women.

Let us turn to the brief story of Moses's early years. We are told very specific details about Moses. After he is born, his mother sees that he is "good" (Exod. 2:1)—a clear echo of God's creation of heaven and earth in Genesis 1. When Moses is too old to be hidden from the Pharaoh, his mother places him in a little basket (*teivah*). This is the same term used for the ark of Noah, the only other time the term is used. The allusion suggests that just as the world's survival depended on Noah, now the survival of the Israelites depends on this one vulnerable infant, Moses. After the baby is saved by the Pharaoh's daughter, she names him in a speech that explains why she chose "Moses": "I drew him out of the water," in which the Hebrew verb for, "I drew him out" is a play on words (a homonym) on the name "Moses" in Hebrew (Exod. 2:10). In so doing, she has reversed her father's intention that all Israelite males be drowned in the river. Unknowingly, the Pharaoh's daughter also anticipates God's future saving of the people by means of water as they leave Egypt.

Time passes. The narrator zooms in on a particular event in Moses's early life in Exodus 2:11–15. As readers, we need to consider why the narrator focuses on this one event and no other. What does the event teach us about Moses? Moses leaves the Pharaoh's setting and discovers the suffering of his "brothers" the Israelites. It is not clear that Moses knows he is an Israelite, but he recognizes oppression when he sees it and stops an Egyptian from beating a Hebrew. He then has to run for his life. The story suggests that Moses has to leave the confines of the Egyptian royal court before he can confront injustice and cruelty in the world. It also suggests that Moses still identifies with the People of Israel, despite having been raised in the palace. Before long he leaves his Egyptian loyalties behind him.

After this episode Moses arrives in Midian. Once married to Zipporah (the Midianite he encounters at a well), he has a son. Moses names this son Gershom, literally "a stranger there." He proclaims, "I have been a stranger in a foreign land" (Exod. 2:22). In this way we learn that Moses has come to see himself as a stranger in Egypt. So concludes the early years of Moses.

The narrator temporarily interrupts the next chapter in the life of Moses to announce the main concern of Exodus, the story of the birth of the People of Israel. God hears the cries of the enslaved Israelites and remembers the covenant with the Patriarchs and Matriarchs. At this moment, the story of the individual, Moses, becomes completely involved in the story of the People of Israel. It is only after God decides to act on behalf of Israel that Moses encounters God (Exod. 3:1–6). The wilderness setting is very important, as Moses finds himself in a place far removed from his family, left to face God alone. The very wilderness, in its stark majesty, reinforces the vulnerability of this one single human being.

As he tends to his flock in the vast wilderness, Moses happens upon a miraculous sight. He sees a bush burning that is not consumed by the fire, and Moses turns aside. "Seeing" is a key word of the story of Moses. His mother sees that he is "good" when she gives birth to him. The daughter of Pharaoh sees him and rescues him. Moses sees the oppression of his brothers. Now Moses sees a vision of God. Only after Moses turns aside does God speak to him.

As readers of biblical stories, we must always pay careful attention to the details. For instance, why does God appear in a fire that does not consume the bush? Such a fire, especially in a wilderness, overturns the natural course of things. Fire is a substance that is both positive and negative. It can harm us, but it can also warm us and provide us with light. God can be destructive and out of control, and in those moments God's fire can burn us (Lev. 10, Num. 11). At other times, God offers us wisdom that can enlighten us and illuminate our lives. "Fire" identifies something profound in our experiences of God.

The name of the bush, *seneh*, in Hebrew, is another important detail. At first *seneh* creates a link through sound to Mount Sinai, but then God instructs Moses to bring the people to Sinai "to this mountain," and we realize that the two sites are identical (Exod. 3:12). God plans to appear to the entire people at Mount Sinai after having freed them from Egypt. It is at this moment in our story that God sends Moses away from the *seneh* back to Egypt on a mission to do just that. In other words, Moses will lead the people out of Egypt to this very site.

The story of the People of Israel, we realize, exactly parallels the story of Moses. They literally follow in his footsteps. Moses is rescued from death despite a royal decree, and so are the People of Israel, who escape certain death when the Egyptians chase them into the Sea of Reeds. Just as Moses is rescued from water, so too are the entire people as God miraculously parts the sea. Just as Moses flees to the wilderness and encounters God, so too do the people flee to the wilderness. They arrive at the very spot in which God first appears to Moses, the bush (*seneh*) that is Mount Sinai.

The people also share Moses's long journey to faith. It takes Moses quite some time to realize that he is an Israelite. He has to figure out who he is and what he is meant to do. Even after encountering God at the Burning Bush, Moses is reluctant to accept God's instructions. The people hesitate in the same way. Even after God reveals God's self at Mount Sinai, the people take quite some time to understand God's greatness and to implement God's plans for them. They complain and rebel. So it is that the story of the individual Moses and the story of the People of Israel are intertwined. The opening chapters of Exodus introduce us to the story of the birth of the People of Israel by helping us see their story reflected in the story of Moses in the most human and personal of terms.

Because Bible stories are timeless, they provide us with an ongoing source of strength. They help us make sense of our lives, connecting us to one another and to those who lived long ago. As biblical characters come to understand the truths that give their lives meaning, so, too, do we.

Adriane Leveen.

BIBLICAL LAW

A look at a society's legal system can give us insight into that society's values and beliefs. Mesopotamia is acknowledged to be the ultimate cradle of law, and law during Bible times was highly indebted to its Mesopotamian (Sumerian, Babylonian, and Assyrian) predecessors. These societies had a profound respect for law as the backbone of society, and many of their legal prescriptions, terminology, and formulations were adopted (and adapted) in the books of the Bible.

An enormous amount of Mesopotamian legal material exists on tablets, written in cuneiform, from the mid-third millennium to the end of the 1st century B.C.E., including deeds, dockets, lawsuits, loans, leases, contracts, marriage and adoption documents, real estate transactions, commercial sales, royal edicts, and—most significantly—several collections of laws. And in these tablets we can find many similarities between their topics and terminology and those in the Bible (with some exceptions, particularly in their penalty clauses; for example, sexual relations with one's stepmother, daughter-in-law, mother, or one's daughter; the rape of a betrothed woman; an assault causing a miscarriage; and homosexuality).

Despite this shared fundamental legal background, the basic concept of law in Israel differs radically from Mesopotamian law. Biblical law receives its validity from being a divine pronouncement, a revelation of the God of Israel. God alone is the ultimate source and sanction of law. In Mesopotamia, on the other hand, it was the king who composed the laws to impress upon the gods that he was a righteous and just ruler. The human authorship of Mesopotamian law clarifies many of the differences between these two legislative systems.

Biblical Collections

Biblical law is divided into several major collections:

- The book (or record) of the covenant, the name of which comes from Exodus 24:7: "Then he [Moses] took the record of the covenant and read it aloud to the people."

- The priestly rulings in the sacral and ritual spheres found in Exodus 25–40, Leviticus 1–16, and Numbers, which can be subdivided into two separate collections: the Priestly Torah, and the Holiness School (the latter primarily in Lev. 17–26). These two are distinguished by their linguistic and stylistic traits along with their differences in ritual, legal, and theological content.

○ Deuteronomy 12–26, which is marked by its injunctions regarding the destruction of cult places outside of Jerusalem and the centralization of ritual worship within Jerusalem and its humanitarian tone. This source is dated to about 622 B.C.E., the time of the reforms instituted by King Josiah of Judah, following the discovery of "the Scroll of the Teaching" (or "the book of the Law") in the Temple (2 Kings 22:11).

The fact that these are independent collections written at different times can be shown by their many repetitions referring, for example, to festival laws and the Sabbath. Compare, for instance, the prescription, "You shall not boil a kid in its mother's milk," appearing in three separate places: Exodus 23:19, Exodus 34:26, and Deuteronomy 14:21. One can cite specific differences between these collections in the laws concerning the Passover sacrifice. According to Exodus 12:9: "Do not eat it any of it raw, or cooked in any way with water, but roasted," yet according to Deuteronomy 16:7: "You shall cook [boil] and eat it." Nevertheless, all these collections are called *Torat Moshe,* "the Teaching of Moses," just as Israel's Wisdom Literature is ascribed to Solomon and its hymnic literature to David. The Hebrew word "Torah," literally meaning "teaching, instruction" and misleadingly translated as "law," came to be used to designate the Pentateuch, the Five Books of Moses.

613 Mitzvot

Many people mistakenly think that the 613 mitzvot are part of biblical law. But nowhere in the Bible is there a list of these commandments, nor is there any direct reference to them. It is only in the Talmud that we read of these 613 mitzvot.

According to talmudic tradition, the Torah describes 613 obligations, or commandments, required for living a good Jewish life. Many of these could be interpreted as good deeds, such as giving to charity; others have to do with Jewish rituals and ritual behavior, such as reciting prayers and keeping kosher. Some are moral obligations, such as the prohibition against incest. This last is also an example of a negative commandment, of which the sages say there are 365. The remaining 248 they consider positive commandments.

Since the sages of the Talmud did not list these mitzvot, there has been much discussion through the centuries about just what makes up the list of 613. Although others have compiled lists, the one most widely accepted is that by noted medieval scholar Maimonides, in his great work the *Mishneh Torah.*

To these collections one must add, in particular, the Ten Commandments (the Decalogue) that God gave to the people of Israel on Mount Sinai (Exod. 20:1–14; Deut. 5:6–18, with some variations between the two sets of commandments, such as the different justification for the observance of the Sabbath). (See the box "The Decalogue, or Ten Commandments" on p. 173 in "Summaries of the Books of the Bible.") The Ten Commandments, inscribed on "two tablets of stone" and eventually placed in Solomon's Temple, was modeled after the pattern of international vassal treaties between monarchs and their vassals at the time and became the underpinning for all Israelite legislation. Thus, Exodus 20:2 ("I the Lord am your God [the 'monarch'] who brought you [the 'vassal'] out of the land of Egypt"), similar to Hittite treaties, commences with the identification of the lawgiver and is followed by an historical prologue explaining why the people owe God their undivided loyalty. There then ensues the listing of laws that they are commanded to follow. Thus any breach of the commandments amounted to a breach in the treaty between the People of Israel and God. On the other hand, God as the sovereign has the obligation to protect people if they keep God's laws.

Unique Aspects of Biblical Law

In light of the basic difference between biblical law (divine authorship) and Mesopotamian law (human authorship), and the expressed goal of biblical law: "But you shall be to Me a kingdom of priests and a holy nation" (Exod. 19:6), it is possible to single out several of its distinctive traits:

1. Since law is an expression of divine will, all crimes are considered sins and certain offenses become absolute wrongs incapable of human forgiveness. This applies, for example, to the case of adultery: "If a man commits adultery with a married woman … , the adulterer and the adulteress shall be put to death" (Lev. 20:10; compare with Deut. 22:22). Unlike the Mesopotamian laws that permit the husband or the king to decide either to punish the wife and adulterer or to grant them pardon, adultery in the Bible is not merely an offense against the husband but also a sin against God that cannot be pardoned by a human agency.

2. The whole of one's life is directly related to the will of God. Only in Israel are all civil, moral-ethical, and religious obligations interwoven into a single body of legislation. In Mesopotamia, these three realms would be incorporated, respectively, in legal collections, wisdom compilations, and priestly handbooks, all composed by different human authors. Since God is Israel's sole legislator, the people are ultimately held solely responsible to God for all aspects of their existence.

3. Unlike in Mesopotamia, where the king alone was chosen by the gods to write the law, the God of Israel selects all the Children of Israel to be the recipients of the divine law. God's care and concern extend to all members of this community, not to one chosen individual. Thus everyone is held

personally responsible for the observance of the law. This, in turn, leads to the concept of individual and joint responsibility. No longer is it the sole concern of the leader of the community (as was for the king in Mesopotamia) to maintain justice and to protect the rights of the community; it is now the responsibility of every member of the society. Since the law was communicated to all, the obligation for its observance rests on the entire people. Each member of the community, then, has the dual responsibility to observe the law personally and collectively, as a group. Each must see that justice is executed and that all crimes are punished; otherwise the community and its members are threatened with dire consequences. Faithful observance of the law grants divine protection and reward to both the individual and the group. Law becomes the single most important factor in the life and destiny of Israel.

4. The law is proclaimed openly to the entire society and is not restricted to any professional class of jurists, lawyers, or judges. Exodus 21:1 makes this patently clear: "These are the rules that you shall set before them." Biblical law, publicly promulgated in advance, is to be contrasted with the epilogue of one of the Mesopotamian law collections (the laws of Hammurabi), where the offended party learns of the condition of the law pertaining to his case only after the crime has been committed. Though Mesopotamian law collections were copied in scribal circles, there is no mention in them of making the law public knowledge. In Israelite society, on the other hand, the law was proclaimed publicly at the very outset, at Mount Sinai. And Ezra, in a public ceremony that took place on the first day of the seventh month (Tishrei) read the Torah aloud before the entire population in Jerusalem (Neh. 8:1–12), and a public reading was held during the reign of King Josiah (2 Chron. 34:30–32).

5. Biblical law, then, was a body of teaching that served as an educational tool. Unlike the Mesopotamian collections (with very few exceptions), motive clauses, which gave reasons for observing the law, are occasionally appended to the biblical laws. See, for example, Exodus 22:2, "You shall not wrong a stranger or oppress him, for you were strangers in the land of Egypt"; and Exodus 22:25–26, "If you take your neighbor's garment in pledge, you must return it to him before the sun sets; it is his only clothing.... In what else shall he sleep?" Such explanatory, ethical, religious, and historical additions were intended to appeal to the people's conscience and motivate them to observe the law.

6. Since all human beings are conceived as being created in the divine image, the sanctity of human life is a primary concern of the law. Thus whoever destroys a human life must give a reckoning for it: "Whoever sheds the blood of man, by man shall his blood be shed. For in His image did God make man" (Gen. 9:6). The uniqueness of human life in the Bible does not allow it to be measured in terms of monetary or property compensation, as it does in Mesopotamian law; see Numbers 35:31, "You may not accept a

ransom for the life of a murderer who is guilty of a capital crime; he must be put to death."

7. Whereas biblical legislation demands "a life for a life," in Mesopotamia, the law of talion (the law of retaliation, wherein the punishment corresponds in kind and degree to the injury) pertaining to physical offenses committed by one person against a member of the same class or status was extended by analogy to all members of society (except for slaves; see point 8), thus applying the principle of equal justice for all. The punishment is limited to the exact measure of the injury and is restricted to the offender himself, thereby restricting the right of revenge.

8. The sole exception to the principle of equal justice is the slave. Nevertheless, all the laws pertaining to slaves are concerned with protecting them and preserving their human dignity. Their status is intended to be temporary and their physical being must be guarded against abuse.

9. Brutal punishments (primarily the mutilation of body limbs) and multiple punishments (monetary, mutilation, and bodily blows with a rod), though prevalent in Mesopotamian laws, are all but absent from Israelite law.

10. The principle of individual guilt predominates in biblical law. Punishment for secular offenses is meted out to the actual offender and not to someone who acts or serves as one's proxy ("vicarious punishment"), as, for example, when a son or a daughter is punished for the father, or when the wife of one who raped another woman is handed over to be a rape victim, as in Mesopotamian law.

11. Biblical legislation is primarily drawn up in a cause-and-effect ("casuistic") style. This legal formulation begins with an "if" clause (the statement of the case) and concludes with an implied "then" clause (the solution; that is, the penalty). This style of law, which is part and parcel of Israel's Mesopotamian legal heritage, is pragmatic and does not appeal to any religious postulates. However, biblical law contains another type of legal formulation that is imperative, obligatory, and nonconditional ("apodictic"): "You shall (not)," which commands what one must (or must not) do, prescribing rather than describing. No time limit is placed on its demands since it is always intended to be in force and there are no attached sanctions.

This direct-address formulation, unique to biblical law, is absent from Mesopotamian legal collections. Here, again, a unique aspect of a society can be clarified in terms of its basic constitution. The Israelite community was founded on a covenantal treaty agreement between God and God's Chosen People. Only in Israel is there a binding relationship between this covenant and the law, which combines impersonal legislation (casuistic law) and personal obligation and commandment (apodictic law). The future of the nation rests entirely on the observance of covenantal law.

Representative Legal Procedures and Legislation

Basic justice was administered by the local court of elders sitting at the city gate, while more difficult cases came before the king (1 Kings 3:16–28). Moses is said to have set up a hierarchical system of courts in the desert (Exod. 18:13–26), and King Jehoshaphat is credited with appointing royal judges in the cities of Judah (2 Chron. 19:5).

○ Property law deals with the ancestral estate. On the father's death, his sons divided the land into equal shares, the firstborn taking a double share. If one of the sons died childless before there was a division of the estate, either because the father was still alive or because after the father's death the brothers had continued to hold the land in a kind of partnership ("brothers dwelling together"), levirate law applied: the surviving brother had to marry the deceased's widow, and their offspring would take the place of the deceased, thereby preserving his share of the inheritance (Deut. 25:5–10).

○ If a man died leaving daughters but no sons, the daughters were allowed to inherit the family's estate (Num. 27:1–11, 36:1–12).

○ Various laws protected the family's ownership of their land. If poverty forced the owner to sell, he or a kinsman could redeem the land and thus bring it back into the family (Lev. 25:25–27). If redemption were not possible, the land would automatically return to its owner at the Jubilee, which occurred every 50 years (Lev. 25:28).

○ A person cultivating land bore social responsibilities. He had to set aside part of his crop for the poor and needy (Lev. 19:9–10; Deut. 24:19–21) and every 7th and 50th year leave his land fallow so that its produce could feed those in need (Exod. 23:10–11; Lev. 25:3–7).

○ The law made great efforts to alleviate debts. Interest was forbidden on loans to fellow-Israelites (Exod. 22:24). Although a creditor was entitled to foreclose a debtor's possessions, or even his family (2 Kings 4:1), certain items (such as a millstone) could not be taken in payment of debts (Deut. 24:6). Impoverished kinsmen, like land, could be redeemed (Lev. 25:47–53) and slaves could be set free automatically after a number of years' service (Exod. 21:1; Lev. 25:54; Deut. 15:12). It has often been suggested that such laws were merely utopian. In fact, it was common practice for the kings of the ancient Near East to declare a cancellation of debts and consequently emancipate slaves and land. This was regarded as one of the king's duties, although the timing was left to his discretion. The difference in the biblical law is its replacement of the king's role by an automatic cycle of 7 or 50 years, which would ensure the enforcement of these reform measures. King Zedekiah actually declared a freeing of slaves, but subsequently the officials and the people forced them into slavery again (Jer. 34:8–11).

○ Marriage was an alliance between families in which the bride was the object of the transaction. The first phase was an agreement between the groom (or his father) and the bride's father, who could demand a payment known as *mohar* for the hand of his daughter (Exod. 22:15–16). Payment would normally be in money, but could, as in the case of Jacob, be in services (Gen. 29). Once the *mohar* was paid, the girl was betrothed, and although the marriage was not yet consummated, the law already regarded her as married (Deut. 22:23–29). Divorce could be initiated by the husband alone. A special provision ruled that a wife, once divorced and remarried, could not return to her first husband if her second marriage ended (Deut. 24:1–4).

○ Polygamy was permitted, but it was forbidden to marry two sisters (Lev. 18:18). This had apparently not been the case in the time of the Patriarchs, for Jacob married Laban's two daughters, Leah and Rachel (Gen. 29).

The leading motifs of early biblical literature—election, redemption, covenant, and law—are closely interconnected: God elected the Children of Israel to be God's treasured possession. God's redemptive intervention into history liberated an enslaved people who became bound to God through a pact whose stipulations demand the utmost obedience. The continued existence of this religious community, according to the Bible, completely depends on the observance and performance of those principles and injunctions that constitute the charter of its covenant with God. The will of God expressed through law is the basis of the covenantal relationship between God and the nation of Israel.

Shalom M. Paul.

BIBLICAL POETRY

Although prose dominates, poetry permeates every part of the Bible. Indeed, about one third of the Bible is poetry. It can be found in almost every book—sometimes just a single line, but there are large blocks of poetry as well: all 150 psalms, the Song of Songs, the oracles of the prophets, and much of Proverbs, Job, Ecclesiastes, and Lamentations.

Explaining the nature of biblical poetry is not easy because there are no clear-cut distinguishing features to it and the differences between poetry and prose in the Bible are often quite subtle. Look, for example, at these two versions of the first plague on the Egyptians. The account in Exodus is commonly classified as prose, while the retellings in Psalms are categorized as poetry (and are set in line–verse format in the English translation of the Hebrew):

> Moses and Aaron did just as the LORD commanded: he lifted up the rod and struck the water in the Nile in the sight of Pharaoh and his courtiers, and all the water in the Nile was turned into blood and the fish in the Nile died. The Nile stank so that the Egyptians could not drink water from the Nile; and there was blood throughout the land of Egypt (Exod. 7:20–21).

> He turned their rivers into blood;
> He made their waters undrinkable (Ps. 78:44).

> He turned their waters into blood
> and killed their fish (Ps. 105:29).

What qualifies the Exodus passages as "prose" and the Psalms passages as "poetry"? Ask Bible scholars this question and you will get different and sometimes conflicting answers. Nevertheless, in spite of uncertainties in our understanding of this ancient, sacred literature, it is possible to delineate those sections of the Bible widely considered poetry and to outline their key stylistic features.

Searching for Signs That It Is Poetry

In the classical period, thinkers like Aristotle and Horace penned theories about the nature, mechanics, and effects of poetry. However, in the Bible we do not find definitions of poetry or discussions of how biblical poetry operates. In fact, biblical Hebrew does not have a general term for "poetry," though various terms do seem to signal the presence of a poetic passage. For instance, the passage known as the "Song of Moses" is introduced with the statement: "Then Moses and the Israelites sang this song [*shirah*]" (Exod. 15:1). David's eulogy for Saul and Jonathan is labeled as a "dirge" (*kinah*) (2 Sam. 1:17). Many compositions in Psalms begin with the word *mizmor*, which is translated as "psalm" and likely indicates a song accompanied by a stringed instrument. Such terms suggest that a number of labels were used to classify certain types of compositions; yet these titles are not used consistently throughout the Bible, nor are they affixed to every text that we would consider a poetic passage.

Since these internal indicators do not point conclusively or consistently to the presence of poetry, we might look to visual means to identify it. When opening selected Hebrew editions or translations of the Bible, one can determine the poetic sections by the distinctive layout of the verses. For example, in the JPS TANAKH, in Genesis 4:23–24, the prose format gives way to poetic verse, signaling a shift in language. Yet, in other editions of the Bible, no graphic distinction is made between poetry and prose.

The convention of visually distinguishing poetic passages, called "stichography," evolved over time. Bible fragments from the Dead Sea Scrolls show that the formatting of texts into verses was sporadic. In talmudic times, spacing was used widely in certain books, but it was not required. The Talmud established special writing for only five sections: Exodus 15:1–18, Deuteronomy 32, and Judges 5, which are poetic texts, as well as Joshua 12:9–24 and Esther 9:7–9, which are lists found in prose passages. Throughout the Middle Ages, Jewish scribes commonly incorporated some type of special spacing not only for the sections mentioned in talmudic sources but also for other parts of the Bible, such as Psalms, Proverbs, Job, Lamentations, the Song of Asaph (1 Chron. 16:8–35), and selected lists. After the advent of the printing press, most printed masoretic Bibles abandoned stichographic arrangement of all but those passages mandated by the Talmud. Most modern scholarly editions reverse this trend, employing stichography for everything considered poetry, including many of the prophetic books.

Poetry in the TANAKH

Though some scholars caution against drawing sharp distinctions between poetry and prose, most agree about which parts of the Bible contain poetry.

Writings (Kethuvim) contains the most poetic material, including Psalms, Proverbs, Job 3:3–42:6, Song of Songs, and Lamentations, along with scattered poetic selections in Ecclesiastes (for example, 1:2–9; 3:1–8) and other books (for example, 1 Chron. 16:8–35). Poetry overshadows prose in the Latter Prophets, for most of the prophetic books contain poetic verse exclusively or predominantly; Jonah and Ezekiel stand out as exceptions. In the Former Prophets, poems punctuate the narrative account of Israel's history in Judges 5

The beginning of the book of the Song of Songs, the Rothschild Mahzor, Florence, 1490. The Rothschild Mahzor is one of the most beautiful illuminated Hebrew texts still in existence today. It contains prayers for the entire year, as well as *piyyutim* (liturgical poems). It also contains seven penitential psalms, *"mizmorim penitenziali,"* that were used in Christian rituals for penance in times of anguish. Thus, the Mahzor represents the degree of Christian influence on at least upper-class Italian Jews during the Renaissance. This manuscript had been stolen from the Rothschild family by the Nazis, but was discovered after World War II in the possession of a Berlin book dealer. (Courtesy of The Library of the Jewish Theological Seminary.)

(Song of Deborah), 1 Samuel 2:1–10 (Hannah's Prayer), 2 Samuel 1:19–27 (David's eulogy for Saul and Jonathan), 2 Samuel 22 (David's Song), and 2 Samuel 23:1–7 (David's last words). Some of the smaller poetic passages include Jotham's fable (Josh. 10:12–13) and Solomon's declaration to God (1 Kings 8:12–13).

The Torah preserves several lengthy poems, including the Testament of Jacob (Gen. 49:2–27), the Song at the Sea (Exod. 15:1–18), the Song of Moses (Deut. 32:1–43), and Moses's Blessing (Deut. 33:2–29). We also find a number of shorter poetic compositions or fragments, such as the Song of Lamech (Gen. 4:23–24); Miriam's Song at the Sea (Exod. 15:21); the Song of the Ark (Num. 10:35–36); the Song at the Well (Num. 21:17–18); the Victory Song over Moab (Num. 21:27–30); and the Oracles of Balaam (Num. 23:7–10,18–24; 24:3–9,15–24). In some instances, often in the course of a dialogue, a few poetic verses interrupt the surrounding prose narrative, as when the man names the woman (Gen. 2:23), God speaks to Cain (Gen. 4:6–7), and Rebekah's family bids her farewell (Gen. 24:60).

In each part of the Bible, the poetic material displays a considerable degree of diversity in content. Note the range of poetic expression in Writings, with aphorisms in Proverbs, passionate diatribes on human suffering in Job, sensual love songs in the Song of Songs, and mournful laments for the destruction of Jerusalem in Lamentations. Within the book of Psalms itself, in certain texts the speaker joyfully sings God's praises, while in others the Psalmist cries out in pain and calls on God's help. Likewise, the poetry of Prophets contains many passages in which the prophets rail against the people for their moral and religious failings and others in which they exhort their listeners to repent or entice them with visions of a glorious future. The Torah contains a similar poetic panoply, with songs of victory, deathbed blessings, oracles, and other assorted passages. Nevertheless, for all this variety in genre and subject matter, the poetic sections of the Bible exhibit considerable stylistic similarities. Understanding biblical poetry requires a familiarity with the literary devices adeptly wielded by the writers of this poetry; namely parallelism, rhythm, terseness, imagery, metaphor, repetition, patterning, and other effects.

Parallelism

The identification of parallelism as a central defining feature of biblical poetry traces back to the *Lectures on the Sacred Poetry of the Hebrews*, delivered by Bishop Robert Lowth in 1753. Lowth defined parallelism as a certain "equality" or "resemblance" between the members of a poetic unit. He identified three types of poetic parallelism: synonymous, antithetic, and synthetic. In the most frequent variety, synonymous parallelism, the same sentiment is repeated in different, but equivalent terms, as in Isaiah 60:3:

> And nations shall walk by your light,
> Kings, by your shining radiance.

Antithetic parallelism pairs contrary or opposite terms, as seen in Proverbs 27:6:

> Wounds by a loved one are long lasting;
> The kisses of an enemy are profuse.

The third and rather amorphous category, called synthetic parallelism, consists of everything that does not fit in the other two classifications. Bishop Roberth Lowth cited Psalm 46:7 as an example:

> Nations rage, kingdoms topple;
> at the sound of His thunder the earth dissolves.

For over 200 years, Lowth's tripartite understanding of parallelism dominated the discussion of biblical poetry. Then, starting in the late 1970s and 1980s, a number of studies were published that challenged Lowth's perception of parallelism and expanded our understanding of the nuances and complexities of biblical verse. In the 1981 book *The Idea of Biblical Poetry: Parallelism and Its History,* James Kugel contended that the ways of parallelism are numerous and varied, far exceeding Lowth's limited three categories. He observed that the degree of connection between two parallel clauses may range anywhere from no perceivable correspondence to just short of a word-for-word repetition. He insisted that the second clause does not simply restate the first clause. Instead, the second line expands on the first in a multitude of different ways: reasserting, supporting, particularizing, defining, completing, or going beyond the first line. In his *The Art of Biblical Poetry,* Robert Alter highlighted what he termed the "impulse to intensification" in biblical poetry. He argued that even in lines that appear at first glance to be nearly synonymous, a closer reading often reveals a "dynamic progression" from one half of the line to the next.

81

In the 1985 study *The Dynamics of Biblical Parallelism,* Adele Berlin applied the study of linguistics to the topic of parallelism in a way that helps us uncover and appreciate the intricacies of biblical parallelism.

Isaiah 1:10 provides a good example of the dynamic nature of poetic parallelism:

> Hear the word of the LORD,
> You chieftains of Sodom;
> Give ear to our God's instruction,
> You folk of Gomorrah!

The two lines in this verse (separated by a semicolon), often called "cola," (colon, singular) certainly meet Lowth's definition of synonymous parallelism, for the same sentiment appears to be repeated in different, but equivalent terms. However, further investigation reveals varying degrees of equivalence and contrast. We find a number of word pairs that exhibit a high degree of similar meaning. The divine names "LORD" and "God" are more or less synonymous. The verbs "hear" and "give ear" both call on us to listen, though the first verb is more commonplace and the second more poetic. Similarly, the nouns "word" and "instruction" are both used to designate God's teaching, though the first term is more general and the second more specific. With the last two words in each colon, we see more contrast. The nouns "leaders" and "people" cannot be considered synonymous, for the first word refers specifically to the ruling class, whereas the second denotes the population as a whole. The place names "Sodom" and "Gomorrah" identify two different cities, though often they are often paired, as in "Sodom and Gomorrah"; the two cities symbolize a place of debauchery and sin.

In terms of content, the two lines mean pretty much the same thing: the second colon echoes the basic sentiment of the first. In both sentences, the prophet calls the intended audience to listen to God's message. By invoking the place names "Sodom" and "Gomorrah," Isaiah metaphorically maligns his listeners, a fitting prelude to the divine diatribe that follows.

When we look at the lines grammatically, we see similar equivalence and contrast. Both sentences contain a verb, followed by a direct object (a noun and divine name) and then the subject (a noun and place name). However, there are a number of contrasting elements. For instance, the masculine Hebrew noun translated as "word" contrasts with the feminine Hebrew word for "instruction," and the plural Hebrew word for "chieftains" contrasts with the singular "folk."

The interplay of equivalence and contrast on these different levels animates the verse. In addition, the grammar reinforces the prophet's message. By addressing both the leaders and the people as a whole, Isaiah implies that all strata of society are guilty and thus fitting recipients of his words. In a more subtle manner, the grammatical contrast reinforces this message: masculine and feminine, singular and plural, all need to heed God's charge to "cease to do evil; learn to do good" (Isa. 1:16–17).

Now let us compare the relationship between the two cola in Isaiah 1:10, repeated here:

> Hear the word of the LORD,
> You chieftains of Sodom;
> Give ear to our God's instruction,
> You folk of Gomorrah!

to the two cola in Hosea 14:2:

> Return, O Israel, to the LORD your God,
> For you have fallen because of your sin.

In this case, the two halves of the verse do not mirror each other in word pattern or echo each other in meaning. Instead, the second colon continues the topic introduced in the first colon, providing a justification for the prophet's call to return. Together the words in the two cola in Hosea 14:2 connect to one another and form a sequence, whereas the two parts of Isaiah 1:10 essentially repeat and reinforce the same meaning.

Often, the nature of the relationship is not as clear as in Isaiah 1:10 and Hosea 14:2 or a passage may combine various elements. In some cases, how one views the relationships between isolated words and the cola as a whole can influence how one interprets a given passage. For example, Hosea 14:3 reads:

> Take words with you
> And return to the LORD.

If we consider "take words" and "return to the LORD" as phrases that are basically synonymous, we can interpret this passage to mean that repentance involves a verbal confession or declaration of the sort provided by Hosea in the verses that follow this one. In contrast, if we understand the two phrases as two parts of a consecutive sequence, then the passage suggests that one must speak words of contrition *before* one can reconcile with God.

These examples show how analyzing the various aspects and levels of a poetic passage helps us gain a keener appreciation of the artistry and interpretative possibilities involved in biblical parallelism.

Meter and Rhythm

In many types of poetry, meter stands out as a defining feature. The word "meter" derives from the Greek term "measure" and refers to the counting and organization of various aspects of spoken discourse, such as syllables and accents. Over the centuries, scholars have scoured the poetic sections of the Bible, looking for signs of these various forms of meter. One factor that complicates the matter is that, unlike other ancient languages such as Akkadian and Greek, we are not certain just how biblical Hebrew was pronounced since the Hebrew script contained no vowels. Largely influenced by contemporary poetic aesthetics—be that Greek, Arabic, Renaissance, or other types of poetry—some ancient, medieval, and modern scholars have insisted on the existence of biblical meter. Others have maintained that meter does not exist in the poetry of the Bible, and today this is the prevailing opinion. Because biblical poetry does display a certain degree of symmetry and sound patterning, some have suggested shifting the focus of the discussion from meter to the broader notion of rhythm, which refers to various forms of sound repetition and regularity.

83

Many Types of Biblical Poetry

The Bible contains many different kinds of poems: those praising God, praising Israel, and asking for help or protection; poems of mourning or grief, and others of love. With their evocative, measured language, these poems provide a colorful tapestry of the ways ancient Israelites imagined themselves and their relationship to God. Here is a sampling:

Blessings
Seedtime and harvest (Gen. 8:22)
Hagar's blessing (Gen. 6:10–12)
Isaac and Jacob (Gen. 27:28–29)
Jacob's blessing (Gen. 35:9–12)

Prayers and Songs of Praise
Miriam's song (Exod. 15:21)
Refuge (Ps. 11)
A Song for the Sabbath (Ps. 92:2–16)
Hannah's prayer (1 Sam. 2:1–10)

Poetic Moments
Rebekah's family blesses her when she
    leaves to marry Issac (Gen. 24:60)
A vision of the Prophet Isaiah (Isa. 6:1–7)
The vision of Nebuchadnezzar
    (Dan. 4:7–14)

Testaments and Pronouncements
The last words of David, (2 Sam. 23:1–7)
Desert of the sea (Isa. 21:1–10)
Dumah (Isa. 21:11–12)
In the steppe (Isaiah 21:13–15)

Laments
Deliver me (Ps. 3)
I am weary (Ps. 6:2–11)
How long? (Ps. 13:2–6)
Protect me, O God (Ps. 16)

Judgment Oracles
The streets of Jerusalem (Jer. 5:1–9)
Howl, you shepherds (Jer. 25:34–38)
Wail (Ezek. 30:2–6)
Lofty Egypt (Ezek. 31:2–9)

Prophecies of Salvation and Consolation
Swords into plowshares (Isa. 2:2–4)
I will espouse you (Hosea 2:16–25)
Paternal love (Hosea 11)
Joy to Jerusalem (Zeph. 3:14–20)

Wisdom Writings
Happy is the Man (Ps. 1)
In praise of wisdom (Prov. 1:2–7)
The way of the good (Prov. 2:20–22)
Tree of Life (Prov. 3:13–18)

Love Songs
Song of Songs

Terseness

The rhythm of biblical poetry results in part from the terseness of parallel lines, the fact that the lines of biblical poetry tend to be short and comprise about the same number of words and stresses. Several trends contribute to the terseness of biblical poetry. First, poetic verses frequently omit certain grammatical particles, such as the Hebrew definite article (*h*), the accusative marker (*et*), and the relative pronoun (*asher*). Second, there often are no conjunctions joining cola. In prose, dependent clauses are usually linked with conjunctions—such as "and," "but," and "for"—that specify how one clause relates to the other. Frequently, as in the above example from Hosea 14:3, two cola appear one after another, merely connected by the conjunction *vav*, which carries a range of meanings but is translated in Hosea 14:3 as "and." The vague nature of this conjunction can produce ambiguity, requiring the reader to determine the meaning of the connection. Does the conjunction indicate that the second line repeats the basic idea of the first: "Take with you words and *thus* return to the LORD?" Or does it imply a sequence of actions: "Take with you words and *then* return to the LORD?" In many other cases, two poetic lines are juxtaposed with no grammatical marker specifying the relationship between the statements, as seen in the following passages:

> You turned my lament into dancing,
> you undid my sackcloth and girded me with joy (Ps. 30:12).

> A garden locked
> Is my own, my bride,
> A fountain locked,
> A sealed-up spring (Songs 4:12).

Imagery, Metaphor, and Simile

The quotes from Psalms 30 and Song of Songs 4 highlight another defining feature of biblical poetry: the abundant use of imagery. The term "imagery" is complicated and often is used to speak about figurative language in general—imagery—or the more specific figure of speech—metaphor. In Psalms 30:12, the speaker paints a visual picture of a person in mourning who breaks out in dancing—imagery. In Song of Songs 4:12, the speaker also evokes a mental image, but in this case the images of the garden, fountain, and spring function as part of a comparison—the key component of a metaphor.

Imagery creates a mental image, which can involve sight, hearing, smell, or other senses. For instance, the prophet Joel depicts a future time of judgment, "the day of the LORD" (Joel 1:15), when "the beasts groan" and "the watercourses are dried up" (Joel 1:18, 20). The first comment involves an auditory element, while the second is primarily visual. Amos also speaks about the day of the LORD, warning that "it shall be darkness, not light" (Amos 5:18). When Isaiah speaks about a very different future, he likewise relies on imagery, creating a vision of a wolf dwelling with a lamb and a leopard stretching out alongside a young goat (Isa. 11:6).

In these examples, the speaker uses language to take a snapshot: a picture of predators reclining alongside their former prey, a vision of total darkness, a scene of parched streams and groaning bears. In each case, as the saying goes, one picture is worth a thousand words. Amos does not specify what will happen on the day of the LORD; instead, the image of darkness communicates the general impression that this will be a dreadful time. Similarly, Isaiah paints a series of mental pictures from which his audience can extrapolate that a glorious future will bring peace and harmony among all creatures. In doing so, he taps into a larger motif that signals a return to Eden. With imagery, the poet goes beyond the straightforward language on the page, delivering a more vivid, but less explicit message. Using the listener's various senses, the writer employs a concrete image to convey a more abstract idea.

While a metaphor also evokes an image, what makes it distinct is the presence of an analogy, a comparison between a hypothetical situation and an actual one. For example, in the extended metaphor in Isaiah 5:1–7 (the Song of the Vineyard), the prophet likens the actual situation, God's displeasure about Israel's immoral behavior, to a hypothetical situation: a gardener's disappointment about the way the vineyard he lovingly tended yielded wild grapes.

In a metaphor, the analogy is implicit; in a simile, it is explicit. Examples of similes abound in biblical poetry, as seen in the following passages from the book of Hosea. At several points, Hosea favorably compares God to dew or rain to send the message that God nourishes Israel and will bring about her revival and success. For instance, in Hosea 14:6, God promises:

> I will be to Israel like dew;
> He shall blossom like the lily.

In this simile, the preposition "like" signals the presence of an analogy.

With a metaphor, the speaker crafts the comparison in a variety of ways. The most obvious type of metaphor takes the form of a predicative statement, as in "the LORD is my shepherd" (Ps. 23:1), "All flesh is grass" (Isa. 40:6), and "Israel is a ravaged vine" (Hosea 10:1). Each of these nominal sentences equates one object with another object, thus creating an anomaly. In other instances, the metaphor is introduced by weaving together words connected with the actual situation and vocabulary associated with the hypothetical situation. For example, in the previous citation from Isaiah 1:10, the prophet compares his audience to the archetypal sinners of Sodom and Gomorrah by linking the second person plural imperative verbs and the nouns "leaders" and "people" with the place names "Sodom" and "Gomorrah." The Israelites addressed are not, in fact, residents of Sodom and Gomorrah but are only metaphorically equated with them. In Amos 1:2, the metaphor is more subtle, created by pairing a divine subject with a verb primarily associated with the sound produced by lions:

> The LORD roars from Zion,
> Shouts aloud from Jerusalem.

The combination of "the LORD" and "roars" creates an incongruity that, in part, marks this statement as a metaphor. A metaphor contains both an analogy and an anomaly; in contrast, a simile lacks any sort of anomalous element, for it explicitly compares two entities without equating them.

Interpreting metaphors and similes involves "unpacking" the common features that together make up the analogy. Imagine two overlapping circles (a Venn diagram) with "God" in one circle and "dew" in another. What qualities do the two have in common? What characteristics would fit in the overlapping section of the two circles? In the abstract, we might compile a list of various attributes shared by God and dew. However, when interpreting the simile as it appears in Hosea 14:6, the relevant question is: What specific qualities stand out in this particular verse? In Hosea 14, the larger context allows the interpreter to decipher the qualities that the two words share, and we see that the subsequent verses describe how Israel will flourish like a verdant plant. One can infer from the larger passage that just as dew nourishes trees and flowers, so God will sustain and support Israel so the nation can thrive.

Repetition and Patterning

David's tribute to Saul and Jonathan concludes with two phrases invoked to describe the deceased men:

> How have the mighty fallen,
> The weapons of war perished! (2 Sam. 1:27).

In the first colon, literal language is used to characterize Saul and Jonathan. In the second, David communicates through figurative language, employing the image of abandoned armor to speak of the loss of Israel's military leaders. The phrase "how have the mighty fallen" is repeated two other times in this passage: once at the end of the first verse (2 Sam. 1:19) and again toward the end of the unit (1:25). When a word or phrase recurs at the beginning and end of a composition, it is called an inclusio, or envelope structure. When a word or phrase repeats a number of times, particularly at marked intervals, it is called a refrain.

Repetition stands out as an important way to convey meaning in the Bible. In poetry as well as prose, repetition of key words allows the author to highlight and emphasize central themes. For instance, in Hosea 14:2–9, the root *shuv* (to turn) appears five times. First, the prophet charges his listeners to return to God (14:2,3); then he promises that God will "heal their turning back," for God's anger "has turned away" from them (14:5; also see 14:8). Additional types of repetition can be found in poetic compositions throughout the Bible. In Isaiah 40–66, reduplication, or the side-by-side repetition of the same word, punctuates numerous passages, including the well-known verse: "Comfort, oh comfort My people" (Isa. 40:1). In certain psalms, the same phrase repeats at the beginning of several consecutive lines, such as "how long" in Psalms 13:2–3 or "bless" in Psalms 115:12–13. Even more prominently, in Psalms 150, the phrase "Hallelujah" (Praise Yah) frames the psalm, functioning as an inclusio; in between, the verb "praise" starts each of the subsequent 10 lines. As these examples demonstrate, repetition not only conveys meaning, but also serves as a structuring device and enhances the aesthetic quality of the composition.

In biblical poetry, patterns are created through repetition as well as through other means. In various psalms and in the book of Lamentations, the Hebrew verses are arranged alphabetically, in what is called an acrostic (Lam. 1–4; Ps. 25, 34, 111, 112, 119, 145). A prominent pattern in the Bible is a chiasm, where elements in a verse or over the larger expanse of a text are arranged in reverse order. Genesis 9:6 provides a good example: "Whoever sheds [A] the blood [B] of man [C], by man [C'] shall his blood [B'] be shed [A']" (see the diagram on p. 63).

Another form of repetition and patterning involves the use of sound. Alliteration entails the repetition of the same or similar sound. In the Bible we find many examples of consonance, the more specific category of the repetition of consonants. For instance, listen to the way Amos 5:5 incorporates several recurring sound patterns, which Shalom Paul attempts to capture in his English translation:

> But do not seek Beth–el!
> Nor go to Gilgal!
> Nor cross over to Beer–sheba!
> For Gilgal shall go into galling exile,
> And Beth–el shall become a nullity.

Isaiah 5:7 provides a good example of paranomasia, a play on words using similar-sounding words with different meanings:

> And He hoped for justice,
> But behold, injustice;
> For equity,
> But behold, iniquity!

Other Poetic Devices

Paranomasia is one of a host of literary devices found in biblical poetry. For example, Classical Greek rhetoricians coined much of the terminology that is still used today to label the manifold ways language can be manipulated to produce various rhetorical effects. The few mentioned in this section reflect some of the more prominent of such devices in biblical poetry.

In 2 Samuel 1:27, David speaks of Jonathan and Saul as "weapons of war." He does not compare them to armor, which would constitute a metaphor. Instead, he metonymically speaks of them, using the name of an object with which they are associated. Metonymy involves a connection between two entities related in some sort of a part/whole manner. Amos creates a metonym when he refers to the ruler of Ashkelon as "the one who grasps the scepter" (Amos 1:8), thus linking the king with an action and object associated with him.

The book of Amos contains examples of a number of other poetic effects. Amos employs hyperbole, or emphatic exaggeration, when he expresses the message that God rejects religious rituals if people do not act with justice and morality. The juxtaposition of two verbs in the first half of Amos 5:21 amplifies the tone of the passage:

> I loathe, I spurn your festivals,
> I am not appeased by your solemn assemblies.

Earlier in the book, Amos effectively uses rhetorical questions, constructing a prophecy comprising eight rhetorical questions. He begins by asking: "Can two walk together without having met?" (Amos 3:3). Then, question after question, he draws his audience in so that they eventually recognize his main point: "My Lord GOD has spoken, who can but prophesy?" (Amos 3:8). Deutero-Isaiah cleverly crafts a rhetorical question to respond to the Israelites' feeling of having been abandoned by God:

> Can a woman forget her baby,
> Or disown the child of her womb?
> Though she might forget,
> I never could forget you (Isa. 49:15).

This rhetorical question forms a metaphor that compares God to a mother to reassure the Israelites of God's enduring love and commitment.

Such an example demonstrates the way poetic devices often operate in conjunction with one another. In many cases, we can identify the specific type of poetic device found in a passage. In other cases, a writer's creativity defies easy categorization. None of the stylistic features discussed here is restricted to biblical poetry. They all appear in biblical prose, though not with nearly the same degree of frequency and intensity. Appreciating the artistry of biblical poetry and the depth of its meaning requires being a skillful reader, one who can "unpack" the language, structure, and imagery of a poetic passage and then piece everything back together in a way that gives voice to the ideas conveyed in the elevated discourse of poetry.

Adapted from Andrea Weiss, "Poetry," *Encyclopaedia Judaica*.

THE BOOKS OF THE PROPHETS

Prophets, the second part of the Bible, known in Hebrew as Nevi'im, includes 21 books of the canon, when each of the books are counted. This literature thus composes about one half of the entire Bible and covers about 750 years of biblical history—from the conquest and settlement in the Land of Israel (beginning about 1175 B.C.E.) to approximately a century after the dedication of the Second Temple, in the Persian period (about 425 B.C.E.).

The first part of the prophetic collection is known as the Former Prophets and includes the historical books of Joshua, Judges, 1–2 Samuel, and 1–2 Kings. The second part, the Latter Prophets, is subdivided into the so-called Major and Minor Prophets. The former includes Isaiah, Jeremiah, and Ezekiel; the latter includes all the others—Hosea, Joel, Amos, Obadiah, Jonah, Micah, Nahum, Habakkuk, Zephaniah, Haggai, Zechariah, and Malachi—in a collection of smaller writings known as The Twelve (Prophets).

Prophetic Types

In a literature that spans such a vast period of time and that does so with such different genres, one would expect that the nature, function, and representations of prophets and prophecy would vary greatly—and this in fact the case. Moreover, the terms that designate the prophetic figure are many, and these point to different types of experience's and roles; the modes of expression are also many, and these involve a variety of social spheres and personality types. This said, it should be added that the Hebrew Bible presents all these individuals as legitimate heirs of Moses—the first and greatest of prophets. A charter of proper prophecy is presented in Deuteronomy 18:9–22. According to this document, the foundation of the phenomenon of prophecy in Israel thus coincides with the founding of the nation and the Revelation of the Torah. However, the Torah reports the existence of other prophetic types as well. We are told of the prophetess Miriam, Moses's sister, who sings and dances after the crossing of the sea (Exod. 15:20–21) and of the ecstatic seizure of 70 elders in the desert (as well as two outsiders, Eldad and Medad) when the spirit of God rests on them (Num. 11:25–29). According to yet another tradition, even Abraham is called a prophet in a divine word to Abimelech, the king of Gerar (Gen. 20:7).

The Former Prophets

In the collection of Former Prophets, a number of people are mentioned who have various oracular or ecstatic experiences and are attached to sacred shrines or to specific groups. Such individuals might be called a "seer" (1 Sam. 9:9), a "man of God" (1 Sam. 9:6; 1 Kings 13:1), or a prophet" (2 Sam. 7:2); and they could answer a specific question by an individual or even deliver a message (1 Sam. 9:6–21; 1 Kings 14:5; 2 Kings 22:13)—sometimes at a shrine or during a festival and sometimes also for hire (1 Sam. 9:7–8, 12–13; 1 Kings 14:3; 2 Kings 8:9). The location of the prophet could also be within the royal palace (2 Sam. 7).

In other cases, bands of prophets roam about the countryside. They sometimes fall into ecstatic trances to the accompaniment of music and dance and even influence the state of those who pass nearby (as happens to Saul in 1 Sam. 10:5–6, 10–11) and sometimes do miraculous acts of feeding or healing (as in episodes connected with Elisha and Elijah). Groups of prophets in the employ of kings could also be consulted in times of danger or war, to divine God's will, although this did not mean that all members of these groups were "yes-men," and this divergence among the prophets could result in interesting dynamics (1 Kings 22). Groups of prophets of Baal are also mentioned in these historical sources, and in a famous incident Elijah stems their influence when he successfully intercedes with God to bring an end to a long and deadly drought (1 Kings 18). Very rarely do the prophets mentioned in this literature exceed such acts of divination (speaking or acting for weal or woe, in response to a specific behest or occasion); and even where the prophets mentioned elsewhere appear here, prophetic functions predominate (as when Isaiah pronounces the death of the sick King Hezekiah, then heals him and provides divine signs of God's favor [2 Kings 20:1–11]). But this notwithstanding, several examples exist of rebuke against kings for their egregious crimes. Particularly notable are the bold confrontations of Nathan versus David (2 Sam. 11:1–12:15) and Elijah versus Ahab (1 Kings 20). (Also see "Groupings of the Prophetic Books," on p. 181.)

The Latter Prophets

The Latter Prophets presents a completely different phenomenon. There are, to be sure, similarities within the prophetic types found in the Former Prophets: King Zedekiah consults Jeremiah (Jer. 21:1–2), and elders consult Ezekiel to divine God's will in exile (Ezek. 14:1; 20:1). Moreover, Isaiah is presented as a visionary (Isa. 1:1; 2:1–4); and the visions and trances of Ezekiel dominate his prophetic experience (Ezek. 1; 8–10; 40–28), and he also behaves in bizarre ways (Ezek. 4:4–12). Visions also dominate the prophetic career of Zechariah (Zech. 1–8), and Isaiah was known to engage in strange behavior (Isa. 20:3). But such occurrences hardly offset the abrupt appearance of a new prophetic type in the mid-8th century B.C.E.—perhaps in part a response to the emerging Assyrian empire, poised dangerously on the horizon. From this time on, we find individuals who say that they are compelled by

God and "sent" by Him to the people, for any of numerous reasons. It might be to announce His words of doom or warning, to interpret disasters to come as divine punishment for many sins (immorality most especially), or to condemn foreign nations for assorted crimes and interpret their attacks against Israel and Judah as the rod of God's punishment. It could also be to offer the nation hope in the present if they repent of their sins (though this is not always a possibility, or one long extended) and a future consolation after the divine dooms befall the nation, the Land, and the Temple.

The most characteristic term used by the classical prophets is *navi*, which conveys the sense of a person who speaks on behalf of God and is sent by God to address Israel and the nations. It thus conveys the force of one who is a "verbal medium" of divine messages (see Deut. 18:18 and Jer. 1:7–9). Another striking term, used by the prophet Ezekiel, is *tzofeh*, which conveys the sense of one who is a forecaster of events and also a warner of impending divine punishment (see Ezek. 3:17).

Amos, the first of these great men of mission, utters words of divine rebuke and dramatically declares his difference from the earlier and other breed of prophet when he vigorously rejects the aspersion that he speaks for hire in a shrine. To the contrary, he says, "I am not a prophet, and I am not a prophet's disciple. I am a cattle breeder and a tender of sycamore figs. But the LORD took me away from following the flock, and the LORD said to me, 'Go prophesy to My people Israel.' And so, hear the word of the LORD" (Amos 7:14–16). The call to prophesy thus marks an involuntary break in the life of this individual, and he speaks to the nation in words that are not his own. Indeed, the commission to hear and proclaim the word of God to the people is the singular mark of this person who is a conduit of divine concern. But not only that. Interspersed among the prophecies of doom that forecast a dark day of the Lord, the prophet Amos also tries to intercede with God on behalf of the people ("Oh, Lord GOD, refrain! How will Jacob survive? He is so small" [Amos 7:5]) and sometimes succeeds. A century and a half later, Jeremiah also appears in this double role: at once a spokesman for God to the people, and a spokesman for the people to their God.

Their Oratorical Skill

Amos's self-presentation aside, the classical prophets were hardly rough or untutored individuals. Even Amos betrays himself through his complex speeches, artful rhetoric, and knowledge of national history. Careful study of the words of the prophets shows that these are much more than brief or blunt cries of woe and warning. Rather, they show all the signs of crafted speech—with rhythmic patterns, nuanced emphases, and fixed patterns of emphasis and argumentation. It may be that in certain instances the cries of the prophets were reworked or reformulated by later disciples, who collected and arranged them in thematic clusters or in sequences based on common words. But this editorial process would hardly account for the whole phenomenon. It would rather seem that these people had access to (or were variously trained in) traditional rhetoric and stylistic forms and that this content took on new and renewed modes of expression under the influence of divine inspiration in specific circumstances. Indeed, one is as much impressed by the commonalities among the prophets as by the differences among them.

The content of the prophets' words also opens a window on features of ancient Israelite religion and culture that would not otherwise be known. Much can be learned from their legal rhetoric. Attention to their words informs us about otherwise unknown or variant traditions about the patriarchs or myths, and through their rhetoric we learn how wisdom sayings, as well as poems and songs, lived in the daily voice of the people. Certainly, in some cases, training or background was a factor. Ezekiel's use of priestly images, terms, and laws—often at variance with what is known in the Torah—makes us aware how diverse were the traditions of ancient Israel.

Morality, Obedience, and Other Common Themes

The struggle with Canaanite idolatry and the practice of illicit acts are regularly condemned in this literature—ranging from the rebuke of sympathies for Baal uttered by such prophets as Hosea (Hosea 2) and Jeremiah (Jer. 2), to critiques of fertility practices and forbidden animal offerings even in the late postexilic period (Isa. 57:3–14; 66:3). But by far the most characteristic feature of classical Israelite prophecy is the strong emphasis put on moral right (even over sacrificial rite). From the first, this is the new clarion call. In the 8th century B.C.E., Amos decries the mistreatment of the poor and calls for justice to flow like a mighty stream (Amos 5:24); Isaiah lambasts the people for coming to the shrine with the stain of ethical sin on their hands, and he adds a manifesto of proper acts (Isa. 1:10–17) (see "Isaiah, Proponent of Social Justice," on p. 189). And Micah proclaims "what the LORD requires of you: Only to do justice and to love goodness, and to walk modestly with your God" (Mic. 6:8). Ritual was misbegotten when it was not founded on covenantal morality, and this could result in divine wrath and punishment. Some scholars have even noted this emphasis in some psalms and have suggested that these reflect a distinct prophetic temper (Ps. 15; 24; 50).

Another dominant and emphatic feature of classical prophecy is that the fate of the nation depends on the covenant obedience of the people (and not just on the behavior of the kings, as we often find in 1–2 Kings; by contrast, the apologia for the fall of Samaria in 2 Kings 17:7–23 reflects the classical prophetic ideology) and that the cycle of sin and punishment may be broken by repentance. Hosea's powerful appeal to the people to return to the Lord marks the beginning of the new prophecy (Hosea 14), and repeated reflections on this dynamic can be found in subsequent prophets—leading to various theological assessments of the effects of sin, the nature of divine mercy, and the power of repentance itself (see especially Jer. 18; Ezek. 18; and the book of Jonah). Nevertheless, the possibility of repentance was not always available to the people—after repeated warnings, the gates of repentance could be closed. A striking and poignant statement of God's refusal to heed the intercession of prophets is found in Jeremiah 15:1.

As those who warn and condemn, the prophets were hardly popular figures, and they repeatedly clashed with the people and royal or cultic authorities. Little wonder that in some of the commission scenes, divine protection and support are pointedly emphasized (note especially Jer. 1). For his efforts, Jeremiah was repeatedly put in stocks and ridiculed, and when he went so far as to utter words of doom against the Temple, he was even put on trial for his life (Jer. 7 and 26). This prophet articulates the pathos of the prophetic vocation and also the compulsions of true prophecy: it is, he says, like a fire in the belly, bursting him from within; like a hammer on a rock, producing sparks of fire (Jer. 20:7–13; 23:9–11, 29). How different is this revelation of prophetic psychology from those false prophets who are condemned for speaking the delusions of their own mind, or who plagiarize the prophetic words of each other (Jer. 23:16, 25–26, 31)!

And yet the prophets are not just speakers of doom. In brief and extended visions, they proclaim a future restoration and utopia—a restoration of the Land, the Temple, and a return of the people to their homeland and the reestablishment of the monarchy; and the beginning of an unprecedented era of peace and well-being, which is imagined as a transformation of nature itself. Fertility will increase without end, sowing and reaping will overlap, and the lamb will even lie near the lion—with no fear. But most of all, a new spirit and knowledge of the Lord will manifest itself in this era. Isaiah foresees a time when the entire earth will be filled with the knowledge of or "devotion to the LORD as water covers the sea" (Isa. 11:9). And in an arresting image, Jeremiah envisions a time when the "Teaching [*torah*]" of the Lord will be put into the "inmost being" of the nation and God will "inscribe it upon their hearts." At that time, "No longer will they need to teach one another and say to one another 'Heed the LORD'; for all of them, from the least of them to the greatest, shall heed Me— declared the LORD" (Jer. 31:33–34). The broken tablets of Sinai will thus be made whole and be inscribed in the mind and heart of the people. Obedience to God will not be learned but be a matter of inner instinct. This is the utopian hope.

Gradually, the prophetic corpus as we have it was compiled and edited to preserve the words of the prophets—keeping alive their tirades against injustice and ritual sin; and the visions of hope and restoration. Disciples would particularly want to collect and memorialize the words of their master. In the process of this act of preservation, the words would come alive and be renewed through reinterpretation. This is particularly noticeable in postexilic works. Repeatedly, the words and images of Isaiah 1–12 recur in expanded and revised form in Isaiah 40–66, which date to exilic and postexilic times. Circles of the pious in Maccabean times looked back to the words of Isaiah, especially to the account of the suffering servant of God in Isaiah 52:13–53:12, and found solace and help in their time of persecution (see especially Dan. 12). Such study and application of these old prophetic biblical books are part of their ongoing acceptance—and their transformation from documents of ancient Israel into spiritual resources for early and later Judaism.

From Michael Fishbane, *The JPS Bible Commentary: Haftarot.*

WISDOM LITERATURE

Wisdom Literature is the broad literary category that offers advice on how to succeed in life, as well as reflections on its meanings and problems. Unlike much of the Bible, which is concerned with those unique events in history in which God is revealed to the People of Israel, Wisdom Literature is grounded in the everyday: finding a good wife, parenting, making a living, and the like. It seeks to teach the reader the wisdom necessary for being productive and choosing the right course of action. Doing so will provide the learner with security and well-being and maintain the just social order, in accordance with God's will.

Three books of the Bible are included in this body of writings: Proverbs, Ecclesiastes (also known as Koheleth), and Job, as well as some psalms that resemble Wisdom texts in language and ideas (Ps. 1; 19:8–15; 34; 37; 111–112; 119). Also included are two postbiblical Jewish Wisdom books of the Apocrypha: Ben Sira (also known as Ecclesiasticus) and the Wisdom of Solomon. Some scholars would also include some texts from the Dead Sea Scrolls and some from *Pirkei Avot (Ethics of the Fathers),* in the Mishnah.

Wisdom Literature was widespread in the ancient Near East, where it was cultivated in literate and sophisticated scribal circles and often directed to young men who would join the high officialdom and even serve in the royal court. Some maxims give advice specific to this setting. Most teachings, however, are of general relevance and include folk proverbs from varied walks of life.

Numerous Wisdom writings can be found in ancient Egyptian and Mesopotamian works written from as early as the early third millennium up to Hellenistic times. There is strong evidence that some of these books, or at least some of their sayings and teachings, were translated and transmitted in ancient Israel and that they influenced the book of Proverbs.

There are two types of Wisdom Literature: didactic and critical. Didactic Wisdom Literature offers instruction in the skills of leading a good and virtuous life. This group includes Proverbs, Ecclesiastes, Ben Sira, and the Wisdom of Solomon. Works in the loosely defined category of critical Wisdom Literature reflect on and criticize doctrines and values found in didactic Wisdom Literature. The foremost biblical example of this is Job. Ecclesiastes belongs both to didactic Wisdom Literature (because much of it teaches how to lead the good life) and to critical Wisdom Literature (because it examines and criticizes the assumptions of conventional wisdom). Psalms 49, 72, and 138 are sometimes associated with critical Wisdom Literature, as well.

Proverbs as Wisdom

The most important source of didactic wisdom is the book of Proverbs. Proverbs defines its own contents as wisdom: its prologue (1:1–7) says that the book is "for learning wisdom and discipline; for understanding words of discernment" (1:3) and "for understanding proverb and epigram, the words of the wise and their riddles" (1:6). It often teaches what is wise and urges the reader to strive for it.

The book of Proverbs is a guide to individuals rather than the nation. It is directed particularly to boys and young men, but most of the advice is applicable to all ages and both sexes. It tells readers how to do what is wise in their everyday lives, and it instructs them in the right and prudent ways of behavior that will bring them well-being and success. It teaches them behavior that will bring them "favor and approbation in the eyes of God and man" (4:4). Unlike so many other books of the Bible, it is silent on the nation of Israel, its history and laws, and the Revelation of divine Torah. The basic teaching of the book as a whole is that the possession of wisdom—which is to say, the human intellect—is a necessary and sufficient condition of being good and doing what is good.

The authors of the book of Proverbs borrowed and reshaped wisdom from earlier texts, most notably from the Egyptian *Amenemope* and the Aramaic book of *Ahiqar*. Proverbs is a slice of a tradition that preceded ancient Israel and continued beyond it. This tradition comprised the creation, reshaping, and transmission of wise sayings and teachings about how to live a righteous, productive, and happy life.

READING THE BOOK OF PROVERBS

The book of Proverbs is best read with attention to the different genres it contains. Chapters 10–29 have four collections of proverbs, each comprising mostly independent sayings. The proverbs in these collections speak about a great many issues: the behavior of the righteous and the wicked, actions and attitudes that please or disgust God, the ways of getting along well with others, laziness and diligence, effective and deleterious speech, and more. (See "Proverbs' Literary Collections," on p. 203)

In this part of Proverbs, one can profitably dip in at random and think about each saying by itself. Here are some examples and some thoughts about them:

> Pride goes before ruin,
> Arrogance, before failure (16:18).

Pride can alienate other people and make one blind to the dangers of one's own plans. Then comes the fall. One can think of smug politicians and cynical CEOs who have found themselves exposed, humiliated, and sometimes jailed.

> He who mocks the poor affronts his Maker;
> He who rejoices over another's misfortune will not go unpunished (17:5).

If you insult the poor, you disparage the work of God's hands.

> One who is slack in his work
> Is a brother to a vandal (18:9).

The lazy man not only does his own job poorly but also ruins what others have achieved. A single slacker working on a project can undermine his co-workers' best efforts.

> The poor man speaks beseechingly;
> The rich man's answer is harsh (18:23).

Proverbs like 18:23 observe life's hard realities without offering specific correctives.

> As a dog returns to his vomit,
> So a dullard repeats his folly (26:11).

This is a deliberately disgusting image of repeated stupidity.

Many proverbs are clustered by theme. Proverbs 26:1–12, for example, is a series of sayings on folly. Their point is not primarily to scold fools (who, in the book's view, are a hopeless lot), but rather to condemn certain actions as stupid. Proverbs 16:1–9 is a cluster of proverbs on God's omnipotence and omniscience.

Readers of Proverbs soon realize the variation in content and quality of the sayings. Some are dutiful and predictable expressions of religious feelings and principles, others are penetrating and even surprising observations on human nature, and many offer good practical advice on living a constructive and successful life. Not all sayings will speak to every reader, but everyone can find some that pack insight and good sense into two brief lines.

The book also contains some longer poems. Proverbs 24:30–34 reports an anecdote about laziness, and Proverbs 23:29–35 is a humorous warning against drunkenness, describing the horrid feeling the next morning. In 30:1–9, an otherwise unknown Agur teaches that the most important source of knowledge is the word of God. Proverbs 31:1–10 is noteworthy for being ascribed to a woman, the mother of the otherwise unknown king Lemuel. She warns him that royalty must beware of strong drink and loose women and must instead devote themselves to ensuring justice and the care of the poor. Proverbs 31:11–31 is a song, commonly called "Woman of Valor," in praise of the excellent wife. It describes her energetic investment in the household's well-being and her religious and moral virtues. (See "Woman of Valor," on p. 204)

Part	Verses	Heading (in quotes) or Contents
I	1:1–9:18	"The proverbs of Solomon the son of David, king of Israel"
II	10:1–22:16	"Proverbs of Solomon"
III	22:17–24:22	"Words of the wise" (emended, based on the Greek)
IV	24:23–34	"These too are of the wise"
V	25:1–29:27	"These too are proverbs of Solomon, which the men of Hezekiah king of Judah transcribed"
VI	30:1–31:31	Four Appendices
VIa	30:1–9	The Words of Agur
VIb	30:10–33	Epigrams and Aphorisms
VIc	31:1–9	The Teaching of Lemuel's Mother
VId	31:10–31	Woman of Valor

Major Units of Proverbs

Ecclesiastes (or Koheleth)

As mentioned earlier, Ecclesiastes belongs to both didactic Wisdom Literature and critical Wisdom Literature. The author is reusing, reshaping, and recombining old forms to present new insights into the nature of the world and the powers of wisdom. Koheleth was traditionally identified with King Solomon, but scholars today agree that the book was written in a much later period. Thus it is significant that the speaker is not called Solomon by name. Koheleth speaks as king only once; elsewhere he speaks as a nonroyal sage, one who blames the government for injustices, and the epilogue never indicates that Koheleth is a royal figure. Koheleth is, instead, a literary figure who is given the Solomon-like blessings of power and wealth as well as the wisdom to examine the true value of those assets. (See "Who Is Koheleth?" on p. 209)

Within the book, a number of traditional literary forms can be identified, including the following.

Maxims and proverbs. Much of the book is a collection of (short) proverbs and (longer) maxims praising wisdom, giving advice, and offering observations on the ways of the world. Ecclesiastes 4:17–5:6; 7:1–12,16–21; 8:1b–8; 9:17–10:20; and 11:1–6 contain series of proverbs.

Reflective poems. The book contains three poems contemplating the nature of the world and human life: 1:3–11, on the repetitiveness of natural phenomena; 3:1–9, on the existence of a "time" for every deed and event; and 12:1–9, on the inevitable movement of human life to death and darkness.

> **The Structure of Ecclesiastes**
> Though the book is not organized into a tight structure, its major components can be identified:
>
> Title and statement of principle (1:3)
> The repetitiveness of nature and human history (1:4–11)
> Introduction of Koheleth and his task (1:12–18)
> Reflections and meditations (2:1–4:16)
> Counsels and teachings (4:17–11:6)
> The light of life (11:7–10)
> The darkness of death (12:1–8)
> Epilogue (12:9–14)

READING ECCLESIASTES

Koheleth mentally wanders through life, "turning about" in his heart, as he puts it, to examine human nature, God's treatment of the world, government, and more. The reader is invited to follow him on his journey, which turns out to be a grand circuit, beginning and ending in the lament, "Vanity of vanities! Vanity of vanities!... All is vanity" (1:3 and 12:8).

While Koheleth is observing life, he is also observing himself—reporting what he planned, did, experienced, and thought. Not only should readers consider Koheleth's statements, they should also think of him as a person treading toward understanding and acceptance of life's frustrations and uncertainties. This means that the author is telling us something about the powers and limitations of the human mind. It also implies that some of the feelings and ideas that Koheleth reports may be temporary and transitional, left behind at a more mature stage in his development, as when he says that he had come to loathe life (2:17–18; 4:3) but later declares that it is sweet (11:7).

KOHELETH'S THOUGHT

The book of Ecclesiastes is a reflection on life together with advice on making one's way through it. Koheleth introduces himself as a wise king who sought to examine all that happens on earth (1:12–18), including toil, wisdom, and pleasure. His goal is to determine "what is good for man to do under the heavens during the few days of his life" (2:3). He amassed wealth and belongings, and this accomplishment seems to have given him pleasure, but ultimately he found it senseless (2:4–2:26).

As Koheleth proceeds on his investigation of reality, he judges much of what he sees as *hevel,* a key word that literally means "vapor" but can be translated in several ways, including "vanity," "transient," "futile," "absurd," and "senseless." But alongside this pessimism, Koheleth suggests various ways of adjusting to this reality and maneuvering through life—above all, by enjoying the good things that come to hand (2:24; 3:12,22; 5:17; 8:15; 9:7–9; 11:7–11). Still, he begins and concludes with the judgment that recurs throughout the book, "All is vanity" (1:3; 12:8).

Koheleth stands apart from other ancient Near Eastern sages in his determination to discover truth using his own individual reason and experience alone. This is the approach of philosophy (though very different in method from the Greek philosophers), and its appearance in Ecclesiastes probably reflects a Jewish awareness of this type of thinking among foreign intellectuals.

MAIN INTERPRETATIONS OF ECCLESIASTES

The central message of the book has been understood in various ways, including the following:

1. *Advocacy of Torah study and good deeds.* The traditional approach understands Koheleth as confirming that Koheleth judges matters of this world, all that is *"under* the sun," to be trivial. All that is truly valuable are study of Torah and good deeds.

2. *Advocacy of the enjoyment of life.* Several times Koheleth insists that people should "eat and drink and take pleasure in all their toil" (3:14, for example). Some consider the message of the book to be the importance of enjoying life to the full.

3. *Polemic against traditional wisdom.* Koheleth directs a radical, unrelenting attack on the traditional beliefs of the sages and denies the reality of a moral order. The world is full of injustice. God is an unpredictable and distant ruler. Human wisdom, lavishly praised in the book of Proverbs, disintegrates before life's puzzles. All that is left is the pleasure of the moment, which alone may soothe the troubled spirit.

4. *Living life in the face of life's absurdity.* The underlying issue is the question of whether there is meaning to life, whether life somehow makes sense. The book is full of contradictions, because this is what Koheleth sees; and in his eyes, the contradictions indicate a breakdown of meaning. He perceives,

without resolution, the contradictions of a just God allowing injustices, the righteous suffering the fate that only the wicked deserve, and the wise suffering the fate that only a fool deserves. Still, he does consider some things to be worthwhile, such as moderate work, love and friendship, gaining and using whatever wisdom is within our capacity, being reasonably righteous, fearing God, and, most emphatically, finding temperate enjoyment of the pleasures that come to hand. These good things do not solve the problems Koheleth sees, but they do allow him to conclude that life itself is good and should be enjoyed before death blots out everything (11:7–10).

The author refuses to accept a simple and clear solution. He sees no stable meaning in life and denies the readers a stable resting point where they might find *the* meaning of the book. The book should be read with an openness to the discomfort it expresses and a willingness to pursue the author's meaning while recognizing that the goal cannot be finally and securely achieved.

The epilogue (12:9–14) speaks about Koheleth as a sage of the past whose words are to be appreciated but treated warily. In the end, what is important is fear of God and keeping his commandments. The epilogue is usually regarded as a pietistic warning added by a later scribe. It may, however, be the author's own conclusion. Until now, he has let Koheleth—his literary character—describe his explorations and findings. Now the author speaks in his own voice to remind the reader that philosophical investigations such as Koheleth's are acceptable as long as we do not abandon the essential religious demands, wherever our search might lead us.

Job

The book of Job has a clear and meaningful design, except for two digressions that stand outside this structure and are summarized at the end.

Prologue (chapters 1–2). The book opens, in prose, with a story about the righteous man Job. At the urging of the Adversary (usually called Satan), God decides to test Job by inflicting on him horrendous suffering to see if he will remain faithful. Job bears his pain while maintaining faith in God's justice. Three friends, Eliphaz, Bildad, and Zophar, come from afar to comfort him, and they sit with him for seven days. It is important to note three assumptions inherent in the prologue: Job is innocent, his pain is in no way punishment, and God is basically just, though his infliction of Job is, as God says, "without cause" (2:3); the purpose of the affliction is to test the purity of his piety.

Dialogue (chapters 3–38, excluding 28). Job suddenly bursts out with bitter complaints—first at life itself, then at God's injustice. Job repeatedly insists on his own innocence and demands that God appear to argue his case or at least to specify Job's putative wrongdoings. The friends first comfort Job and then, with increasing vehemence, condemn him. Each speech by Job is followed by the reply of a different friend. There are three such cycles in the extended dialogue, in chapters 3–27. (The third speech of Zophar seems to be lacking. Most likely, however, the speech is still there, after 27:13, but the heading introducing the Zophar's words was accidentally omitted by an ancient copyist, so that the entire chapter now seems to belong to Job.)

In his final speech (chapters 29–31), Job recalls his former good days, when he was in fellowship with God and honored by men, then he bewails his current degradation, and finally he declares his innocence by oath.

God's speeches (chapters 38–42:6). God appears in a whirlwind to Job and challenges him to debate. God speaks about the mysteries and wonders of creation, before which Job can only stand in humility and awe. At the end, Job humbles himself and repents.

Epilogue (chapter 42:7–17). At God's direction, Job's friends ask his forgiveness and are in turn forgiven. God then restores Job's fortunes, making them even greater than before, and he lives out a prosperous and long life.

Two digressions. The poem on wisdom and Elihu's speech do not fit into the book's otherwise clear and logical structure. They might be later additions (note how well God's speeches, starting in chapter 38, would immediately follow Job's final declaration of innocence in chapters 29–31). Alternatively, the digressions might be intended by the author as a way of slowing the pace and putting off the denouement that will come with God's speeches.

The poem on wisdom (chapter 28). This poem asks, rhetorically, "Where can wisdom be found?" The answer is that it cannot be found, even in the farthest reaches of creation. God alone knows where it is. God created it and said to humans that the fear of God and the avoidance of evil alone constitute wisdom. This is the only real wisdom that humans can have.

Elihu (chapters 32–37). After Job and his three friends stop speaking (in frustration at what they see as each other's obtuseness), a new participant, Elihu, speaks up. He says that he held his silence because he is younger than the others, but he can no longer hold back his thoughts. He is angered by what he sees as Job's self-righteousness and irritated at the friends' failure to respond adequately.

Elihu first speaks of the possibility that misery, such as in sickness, can have an educational function, warning people away from further sin. If the sufferer repents, an angel might speak on his behalf and convince God to spare the sufferer. Elihu accuses Job of wickedness and arrogance and declares God's justice, power, and goodness. Much of Elihu's speech, it should be said, is in very obscure Hebrew.

THE CHALLENGE TO THE READER

The interpretations of Job are many and varied. Prominent among the proposals for the central message of the book are the following:

1. *God is mysterious.* Innocent suffering can occur, contrary to the friends' declarations, but humans have to recognize that God's ways are hidden from their comprehension. They may complain of their suffering (as many psalmists do) and insist on their innocence, but in the end they must accept the limitations of human knowledge and humble themselves before God's wisdom and power.

2. *God is gracious.* In the end, God's appearance shows Job that his suffering is not punishment (for God never blames it on Job's sin), and the fellowship that God's appearance offers comforts Job. Fellowship with God is the comfort that sufferers can hope for.

3. *God is unfair.* God did indeed inflict unwarranted suffering on Job, and (in the author's view) Job's railings were justified. When Job humbles himself before God, he does so tongue-in-cheek. After God's speeches, Job says, in 42:6: "Therefore, I recant and relent, being but dust and ashes" (literally, "... on dust and ashes"). Others would translate, " ... and feel sorry for dust and ashes," that is to say, for wretched humans, who are but dust and ashes. Job is cowed by God's power, but he really feels revulsion before the divine dictator and pity for lowly mankind. This is the author's extraordinarily rebellious but carefully hidden message.

It is important to keep in mind that there are three levels of communication in the book of Job. (1) On the human plane, Job and the other characters speak in their inevitable ignorance and try to make sense of what they see. Into this plane God intrudes at the end and speaks with Job, but he brings no new revelation, nothing that Job could not have known otherwise. (2) On the heavenly plane, God communicates with the divine beings (literally, "sons of God," the members of the celestial court). God makes decisions about human fate, of which humans will never know. (3) On the literary plane, above the heads of all the characters, the author communicates with his readers, observing the characters—including God (and possibly judging God). The author tells the readers things that humans could never know: what motivates God, what God cares about, the fact that suffering can occur without guilt, and the importance that God places on individual humans and their genuine righteousness and piety.

Reading a book, especially a challenging one like Job, involves two phases. The first phase is to understand the book on its own terms. This means looking for the message the book is trying to communicate and what it wishes the reader to believe. The second phase is to step back and evaluate this message according to one's own values. Two readers can understand a book's message in the same way, yet one can agree with it and the other reject it. They may agree that God's declaration of God's power and mystery are intended to respond to Job's questions, but while one may find this personally satisfactory, the other may believe that God's response fails to engage Job's real crisis: suffering horrible tragedies for no good reason. God does not offer a response to this crisis, and in any case, Job has all along acknowledged God's power and mystery. It is no argument against a particular interpretation to say that it produces an unsatisfactory answer to the problem the book addresses. Perhaps, after all, there is no satisfactory answer to the problem of unjust suffering. And perhaps, in the end, God implicitly acknowledges this when God ignores Job's suffering to speak about Himself.

Adapted from Michael V. Fox, *The JPS Bible Commentary: Ecclesiastes.*

METHODS OF BIBLE STUDY

What we think the Bible is helps determine the way in which we read it. Traditional Jewish commentators believe that the words of the Bible were revealed by God to Moses. Therefore, when there seem to be contradictions or errors, the commentators set about to harmonize apparent inconsistencies into one true and consistent Bible text. They also try to explain any discrepancies between biblical concepts and the ideas and beliefs of their own time. Interpretation is thus a necessity for every generation.

Modern critical scholarship reads the Bible as a document of religious faith expressed within a specific culture, tied to a specific time, limited by the meaning of the authors. Every text of the Bible, in this view, is time bound. In contrast to this, traditional commentators in every age seek the timeless, eternal voice of God in the words of the Bible; their reading of the Bible is informed by a deep theological commitment to an eternal God whose very word is understood as being imbedded in the text.

Traditional Methods

Over the centuries, traditional commentators have used several different approaches to discover the layers of meaning in the Bible. A convenient way to think about these approaches or levels is through a Hebrew acronym that was created for this purpose: *PaRDeS*. The "Pa" is for *peshat*, "R" for *remez*, "De" for *derash*, and "S" for *sod*.

These ways of reading the Bible for Jews are meant to be complementary, not mutually exclusive. Jewish reading of scripture is not overly concerned with establishing one "correct" reading, and many of the greatest scholars of the tradition have been content to entertain several seemingly opposed interpretations of a single passage.

To illustrate what *PaRDeS* means, let us briefly examine two verses that tell of the journey of Abraham (then known as Abram) from Egypt to Canaan:

> And he proceeded by stages from the Negev as far as Bethel, to the place where his tent had been formerly, between Bethel and Ai, the site of the altar that he had built there at first; and there Abram invoked the Lord by name (Gen. 13:3–4).

Four Approaches to Reading the Bible

Judaism has traditionally fostered a "multiple-lens" approach to reading the Bible. Jews of any background may draw on any or all of these ways of understanding the Bible at any given time:

○ *Peshat* is the **plain sense** reading. It looks to the surface meaning of the text, drawing on knowledge of word meanings, grammar, syntax, context, cognate Semitic languages, archaeology, and history.

○ *Remez* is the **allegorical,** or symbolic, reading. It looks for parallels between the scriptural text and more abstract concepts. This kind of reading sees biblical characters, events, and literary compositions as standing for other truths.

○ *Derash* is the **inquiring** or interpretive reading. It looks for further layers of meaning. Midrash, the Jewish tradition of interpreting the scripture through creative storytelling, derives from this way of reading.

○ Sod is the **mystical** reading. It looks at the biblical text as a symbolic code, which with piety and effort will yield hidden wisdom and personal connection with the Divine. The Jewish mystical tradition known as Kabbalah relies on complex symbolic interpretation of each individual letter of the biblical text.

Adapted from Cullen Schippe and Chuck Stetson, *The Bible and Its Influence.*

The commentators interpret the text using the following approaches:

○ *Peshat:* The plain, literal sense of the verse in its context. Abraham returns to Canaan from Egypt "by stages"; he moves from one oasis to another.

○ *Remez:* The allegorical or symbolic meaning of the verse. The word "Abram" is understood to be the soul; his travels trace his spiritual journey.

○ *Derash:* The homiletic (or interpretive) meaning of the verse as viewed outside of its original context. Specific ideas and values are derived from the text, whether the text, in its literal meaning, could mean this or not. This approach reveals Abram's true intention: to visit many places where he could teach the word of God.

○ *Sod:* The secret, mystical interpretation of the verse. This approach teaches that the Land of Israel draws Abram from a purely nonphysical state of being to one of concrete physical reality.

PaRDeS has become a well-recognized framework for understanding traditional methods of Bible study. No single method of interpretation is considered to be the best, because the Bible is layered with meaning; it is multifaceted. Although each verse means something in its specific context, it can mean many other things as well. This is demonstrated in editions of *miqra'ot gedolot,* a traditional edition of the Bible in which each page contains the biblical text in Hebrew, ancient Aramaic translation of the text, and a number of medieval commentaries in Hebrew. (See *"Miqra'ot Gedolot,"* on p. 133) Different interpretations are placed on the same page, making clear that there is no one definitive interpretation of any verse.

PESHAT AND DERASH

The most important traditional methods of study are *peshat* and *derash. Peshat* is literal; it is exegesis, or "reading out" from the text to understand its original meaning. *Derash* is nonliteral; it is eisegesis, or "reading into" the text. Although it may seem that *peshat* preceded *derash,* the historical fact is that *derash* was the primary Jewish method of study until the 11th and 12th centuries C.E.—the time of Rashi, Ibn Ezra, and Rashbam.

Derash implicitly states that what these words may have meant originally in their context is not necessarily all that they mean. We of a later generation can understand these same words in a different manner.

To illustrate how *peshat* and *derash* produce quite different interpretations, let us focus on Genesis 49:10, a verse that many call the most controversial in all of Genesis. Jacob, the third of the patriarchs after Abraham and Isaac, gives his last will and testament to his 12 sons, including these words to his son Judah.

The JPS translation is:

> The scepter shall not depart from Judah,
> Nor the ruler's staff from between his feet;
> So that tribute shall come to him*
> And the homage of peoples be his.
>
> *Literally, "Until he comes to Shiloh."

Many explanations have been given for the word "Shiloh." Rashbam, a great *peshat* commentator and the grandson of Rashi, states that this verse is a prediction of events that will happen centuries in the future. After the successful reigns of two kings from the tribe of Judah, David and Solomon, Solomon's son Rehoboam will be unable to hold the kingdom together. Rehoboam will come to the northern city of Shechem and antagonize the 10 northern tribes, who will then secede from the United Kingdom. Rashbam explains that the scepter will not depart from Judah until Rehoboam comes to Shechem (which is next to Shiloh), because that is where the kingdoms will be divided. In this interpretation of Genesis 49:10, Jacob predicts that Judah's privilege of sovereignty over his 11 brothers will last only until he (Judah's descendant) comes to (the city of) Shiloh.

This *peshat* interpretation places the verse in a historical context. The verse is a reference to a one-time event that will be fulfilled. If this interpretation is correct, it makes the verse "Until he comes to Shiloh" into a prediction of an event of historical interest.

Derash moves the discussion to a different level. In Rabbinic interpretation, this verse becomes the primary source in the Torah for belief in the Messiah. Thus, in this verse Jacob is blessing and prophesying about his son Judah, the ancestor of King David; Jacob's last words to Judah seem to be a logical place for a reference to the Messiah, who will be descended from Judah and that great king. The ancient Aramaic translation of this same verse is "until the Messiah, to whom the kingdom [Shiloh as *shelo,* or "his"] comes." Unlike Rashbam's comment that the scepter will remain with Judah for only a limited time, this interpretation states that "the scepter will never depart from Judah"—because the Messiah, a descendant of the tribe of Judah, will reign forever.

The literal, *peshat,* meaning of the verse, in its historical context has nothing to do with events 1,000 years after the time of King David. But the *derash* reading takes this verse from a specific historical reference to a verse of the greatest magnitude for Judaism and the future of humankind.

REMEZ

The third element of *PaRDeS* is *remez,* the allegorical, or symbolic, reading. While the great period of this type of interpretation encompassed the 14th through 16th centuries, when such luminaries as Levi Ben Gershom, Isaac Ben Moses Arama, Obadiah Ben Jacob Sforno, and Judah Abrabanel wrote their commentaries, one of the most famous Jewish allegorists is a thinker from the Rabbinic period, Philo of Alexandria.

The *peshat,* or contextual, reading of the passage is that Cain the farmer, murdered Abel, a shepherd, because Cain resented the fact that God preferred Abel over him. Philo's *remez,* or symbolic, interpretation is that Cain and Abel are two aspects of the soul; Cain is every human's capacity to do evil and Abel is every human's ability to do good; and every person's soul is in conflict. The Hebrew root on which the name "Cain" is based means "to acquire, to possess," and Cain's mistake is that he owns the land and its produce. He does not understand that everything comes from God (Philo, *Sacrificiis Abelis et Caini* 2). Cain is possessive and self-centered. God first created Cain, the human soul, but then added Abel, whose ability to be concerned about others is symbolized by his profession of caring for and tending animals. Cain and Abel, then, are no longer characters in a story but the character traits of every human being. The principle of self-love, symbolized by Cain, is modified by God-love, symbolized by Abel. And the law of the Torah commands humans to reach out of themselves and truly fulfill themselves as moral beings.

A human being must not forget the true purpose of life—the fulfillment of the soul. Cain should not have murdered Abel; he should have protected and nurtured him. Humans are capable of both good and evil; our actions affect our souls. The law of the Torah is wise and understands our psychic conflicts; it is the solution to the Cain within us.

In *remez*, a traditional commentary finds broader meaning in the biblical text. A literal interpretation limited in scope is replaced with a symbolic explanation that is more edifying.

SOD

We turn now to mystical interpretation. One of Rashi's most important accomplishments was transmitting the important Rabbinic midrashim (creative interpretations) on the biblical text. Later commentators, however, would often have difficulties with Rashi's presentation of these midrashim at face value. Mystical commentators gave these same midrashim deeper, secret meanings (*sod*).

The following example may more fully illustrate the mystical development of midrashim. In both the story of the Burning Bush (Exod. 3–4) and the Call of Moses in Egypt (Exod. 6–7), we have the same elements:

- God tells Moses of God's plan to save Israel and commands Moses to tell the people of the plan.
- Moses learns God's sacred name, which had not been known before.
- God commands Moses to go to Pharaoh.
- Moses objects that he is of clumsy speech, and Aaron is therefore appointed as a spokesman.
- Moses and Aaron confront Pharaoh and are rejected.

Why does God call Moses a second time—and why are all of these elements, especially the appointment of Aaron, repeated?

Here are two ways of answering these questions. The first is from the sage Yosef ben Akiva (*Midrash Rabbah* 5:22). He said that Moses argued:

> "I know that You will deliver the Israelites one day, but what about those who have been buried alive in the building?" Then did the divine attribute of justice seek to strike Moses, but after God saw that Moses argued in this way only because of Israel's suffering, He retracted and did not allow the attribute of justice to strike him, instead dealing with him according to the divine attribute of mercy.

Moses's question is very much like the question many modern Jews have asked: "It's wonderful and comforting that the State of Israel now exists, but where was

God during the Holocaust while 6 million were being killed?" Here Moses says, "It's wonderful that You're going to save the Israelites from slavery, but what about all of the Israelites who have been killed during their enslavement to these evil Egyptians?" The sages saw God as having two attributes: the attribute of justice, which is represented by the divine name *Elohim,* and the attribute of mercy, which is represented by the divine name *Adonai.* The attribute of justice (*Elohim*) wants to kill Moses for his challenging question, but the attribute of mercy (*Adonai*) wants to save him, because it knows that Moses is asking only out of his anguish for those who have been killed.

God's second call to Moses is, in this reading, part of a dramatic situation that needs a solution, an interesting challenge to God that needs an answer. Moses and God, at odds with each other, must be reconciled. To bring about this reconciliation, God needs to send forth a renewed call, full of reassurance for Moses, who needs to hear everything all over again. And that is why, according to this midrash, God calls a second time, so similar to the call at the Burning Bush.

The second way of answering the two questions comes from the Zohar (the central book of Kabbalah, Jewish mysticism), and it explains that different aspects of God, represented by the *sefirot,* are part of the dramatic dialogue between God and Moses. This *sod* interpretation then goes on to explain that two methods of communication—voice and utterance—are represented by the figures of Moses and Aaron (see next paragraph). The Zohar then wonders how Moses can bring up the problem of speaking again, because it had already been dealt with at the Burning Bush. The apparent redundancy points to an inner meaning. Moses has voice but lacks utterance. Pharaoh can hear God's demands only if voice and utterance are one. God gives Aaron (utterance) to be at the side of Moses (voice). But it was only at Mount Sinai that voice was actually united with utterance. It was only then that Moses was healed of his impediment, when voice and utterance were united in him as their organ.

In modern literary terms, we can speak of the content of God's message, represented by Moses (voice), and the form, symbolized by Aaron (utterance). Traditional interpretation strives to unite the words of the Bible with the revelations of God. If the Bible is the word of God, then its words, its utterance, express the content of God's revelations. Every utterance, every word, must be filled with meaning; it is the task of the commentator to discover the levels of meaning. Moses needs Aaron, content needs utterance, and the Bible needs commentary.

For the reader who believes that the Bible is the word of God, discovering the levels of meaning in the biblical text is a fundamental part of life. But what of the reader who does not believe that the Bible is the revelation of God, who thinks that traditional commentaries are inventing all meaning above the level of *peshat*? For this reader, traditional Jewish commentary can be understood as a fascinating process, a dialogue between the sacred text and the generations of Jews who have kept it at the center of their lives. Commentary is not simply an attempt to know what the Bible is saying, it is also the intellectual foundation for the process by which Judaism has grown, adapting to new environments and cultural situations. The openness to new interpretation assumes the belief, or concept, that God's revelations are still unfolding.

Modern Methods

Unlike traditional interpretive approaches to the Bible, modern biblical criticism is based on two assumptions: (1) Because the Bible is a collection of documents written in human language by human authors, it is subject to the same methods of historical and literary investigation as all other books and documents. Modern critical study ignores the idea of divine authorship, that all levels of meaning emanate from God. (2) The biblical texts must be understood in their original, historical, and cultural contexts. Modern biblical criticism employs many methods of interpretation, the most important of which are textual criticism, source criticism, literary criticism, structuralism, and deconstructionism.

TEXTUAL CRITICISM

Textual criticism attempts to understand the words written by the Bible's human authors. The oldest complete forms of the books of the Bible extant today are in manuscript (handwritten) copies, none of which is earlier than the 10th century C.E. There is, therefore, a gap of as much as 2,000 years between the original writing of the document and the earliest complete copy to which we have access.

Of the several thousand manuscript copies and fragments of the various parts of the Bible that exist today, it is very likely that no two are identical. This is to be expected. How could any literary work that was handed down for many generations be free from error? And yet, the evidence of the Dead Sea Scrolls from Qumran, dating from 2,000 years ago (and thus 1,000 years earlier than the complete copies), confirms the general reliability of the basic textual tradition that has been transmitted.

Modern study of the Bible has benefited greatly from the diligent research of textual critics. This type of criticism is the basis for the translation of the Bible from its original Hebrew and Aramaic into the languages of the modern reader. In that every translation is an interpretation, the basis for translation must be studied carefully.

Many of us naively assume that the Bible we use today is an exact copy of one original text, but there are many versions of the text of the Bible. Most of the English translations of the Bible under Jewish auspices are based on what is called the masoretic text, a text that has been passed down to us by a group of scholars and scribes called the Masoretes, who lived around 1,000 years ago. (See "The Masoretes—Preservers and Protectors of the Hebrew Bible" on p. 20.) This text is the Bible as we know it. We have a Greek translation of the Hebrew Bible that is well over 1,000 years older than the masoretic text. Of the manuscripts that we actually have, the Greek version, the Septuagint, is much closer in time to the original Bible. If there is a difference between the Septuagint text and the Hebrew masoretic text, the Greek is not necessarily more valid simply because it is older. However, when there are significant differences, the Greek version is given serious consideration.

In the masoretic text, we read about Moses's parents in Exodus 6:20: "Amram took to wife his father's sister Jochebed, and she bore him Aaron and Moses." The Greek version of this verse reads: "Amram took to wife the daughter of his father's brother." Why would anyone present a different version of that verse? Probably because the Septuagint translators could not accept the idea that, by the standards of other parts of the Bible, Moses was born out of an incestuous union. Thus, for example, we read in Leviticus 18:12: "Do not uncover the nakedness of your father's sister; she is your father's flesh." The Greek version has Amram marrying his cousin, but the masoretic text states that Amram married his aunt.

Historically speaking, Amram could not have known the prohibitions expressed in Leviticus. But it is difficult to think of Moses as the product of a union that he himself will later call an abomination, especially for a religious person. So the Greek version subtly makes a dogmatic correction in its translation of the verse. This example shows how the slightest divergence in a reading can change a point or avoid difficulties in a text. Because of variant readings, it is a useful method of study to examine all early versions of the biblical text in our search for every possible meaning.

SOURCE CRITICISM

The Torah may seem to present a unified account of Israelite history and law during the Patriarchal and Mosaic periods. Detailed study of the text, however, has led modern critical scholarship to conclude that the Torah is a compilation from several sources, different streams of literary traditions, that were composed and collected over the course of the biblical period (ca. 1200–400 B.C.E.). Because the Torah, in this perspective, is an amalgam of the works of different authors or schools, it contains an abundance of factual inconsistencies; contradictory regulations; and differences in style, vocabulary, and even theology.

The first period of Israelite history is that of the patriarchs, described in Genesis. Beginning with Exodus, the Torah describes events of the Mosaic period.

How did the religion of the patriarchs differ from that of Moses? The Torah makes it abundantly clear that most of the commandments and laws revealed to

Moses are new. What about the faith of Moses as opposed to that of the patriarchs? The Torah presents the idea that Moses had a more intimate relationship with God than the patriarchs did: "God spoke to Moses and said to him, 'I am the LORD [*YHWH*]. I appeared to Abraham, Isaac, and Jacob as El Shaddai, but I did not make Myself known to them by My name *YHWH*'" (יהוה in Hebrew and *"Adonai"* or "the Lord" is often substituted for it) (Exod. 6:2–3). The patriarchs knew God as El Shaddai, but Moses will know God by God's more sacred, more intimate name, *YHWH*.

The revelation of God's name is literally an epoch-making event. When Moses and the Israelites are informed of God's name, they become a special people with the destiny of having a sacred covenant with God. This new revelation of God's name raises two striking questions. First, this name of God was already used in Genesis. In Genesis 4:25–26 we read: "Adam knew his wife again, and she bore a son and named him Seth.... And to Seth ... a son was born, and he named him Enosh. It was then that men began to invoke the LORD [*YHWH*] by name." Thus we learn that long before Moses, even long before Abraham, people used the name *YHWH*. How, then, can Exodus 6 tell us that the patriarchs used the name *El Shaddai* only? There are texts in Genesis that use the name *El Shaddai*, but there are even more texts that use the name *YHWH*. Moses's mother, Jochebed, bears a name compounded with *YHWH*. So how can the name *YHWH* be considered new to Moses?

Second, God had already revealed the name *YHWH* to Moses at the Burning Bush. "Moses said to God, 'When I come to the Israelites and say to them, "The God of your fathers has sent me to you," and they ask me, "What is His name?" what shall I say to them?' And God said to Moses, 'Ehyeh-Asher-Ehyeh'" (Exod. 3:13–14). *Ehyeh-Asher-Ehyeh* means "I will be what I will be," and *YHWH* means "He will be." God explains: "This shall be My name forever, / This My appellation for all eternity" (3:15). If the name *YHWH* had already been revealed to Moses in Exodus 3, why is it given as if for the first time in Exodus 6?

To review, although the distinctively Israelite name of God is *YHWH*, various sources disagree as to when this name was first used. Two sources tell us that *YHWH* was a name not revealed to the Israelites until God revealed it to Moses at the Burning Bush (Exod. 3:13–15) and in Egypt (6:2–3). Both of these sources, however, disagree with the third source, which declares that the name *YHWH* was known from the beginning of history, from the time of the immediate descendants of Adam and Eve (Gen. 4:26). These facts suggest the existence of different theological perspectives concerning the time of the great turning point in Israelite religion, when it becomes a faith very different from that of the surrounding peoples.

The names that are used for God have served as important clues in the separation and discovery of the sources that make up the Torah. The different names of God have led source-critical scholarship to find independent traditions, each of which uses the divine name in a different way. These traditions are independent of and contradict each other. How does scholarship explain all of these variations? Different theories have emerged to explain the divergences along theological, geographic, and chronological lines. Thus there may be a northern and a southern version of the same story, which would account for inconsistencies. The stories were written over the course of centuries and reflect an evolutionary process that incorporated interpretations and additions as the text developed.

There is great agreement among scholars that the Torah in its final form is a work composed and edited from four literary complexes. The oldest of these is the Yahwistic source, designated by the letter J because it consistently uses the name *YHWH* (spelled "Jahweh" in German) and because of its special interest in places located in the Southern Kingdom of Judah. This tradition seems to have been written in the 10th century B.C.E.

The Elohistic source, designated E, is so named because of its use of the divine name *Elohim* and its interest in the northern tribes, of which Ephraim was the most important. It probably was written between 900 and 800 B.C.E., presenting material parallel and supplementary to that found in J.

The Priestly source, designated P, uses the divine name *Elohim* (until Exod. 6) and contains a great many ritual texts. Scholars greatly disagree concerning the date when this source was written. Some place it as early as J and E, but others posit a date as late as the Babylonian exile (6th century B.C.E.). As an extension of this debate, some scholars refer to H, a fifth literary source for the Bible. H is identified with the Holiness Code (Lev. 17–26), which, while considered Priestly literature, is often considered too different from the rest of Leviticus and other Priestly sections of the Bible to have been written at the same time. Those differences have led some scholars to separate out the Holiness Code from other Torah sources.

The Deuteronomic source, designated D, is considered to have been written later (8th to 7th century B.C.E.). It reviews certain stories and presents legislation that sometimes differ from the first four books. It is important to note that contradictions exist not only within narrative material but also within the laws of the Torah. For instance, Exodus 21:2–11 states that a male slave should be released after six years of servitude. This law, however, does not apply to female slaves (21:7). In Deuteronomy 15:12, the same requirement of release is extended to both male and female slaves.

Most scholars believe that the Torah was compiled and edited by Priestly redactors in Babylonia between 600 and 400 B.C.E. (See "The Torah's Four Sources," on p. 10.)

LITERARY CRITICISM

Though source criticism has contributed a great deal to our understanding of the growth of biblical traditions, by definition it ignores the literary unity of the final form of a text. In reaction, literary criticism developed, to examine the literary characteristics (including narrative technique, tone, theme, structure, imagery, repetition, reticence, and character) of the texts. In simple terms, source criticism is interested in cutting up the texts to find the different layers of tradition; literary criticism considers the text as it stands now, as a whole, not as it once may have been. Literary criticism is both like and unlike traditional Jewish commentary. It looks at the Bible as a unified whole but has no theological commitment and sees it as the creation of human authors. Source criticism is interested in the process that wove the different texts, by different authors, together. In contrast, literary criticism sees texts as coherent wholes that create meaning through the integration of their elements, irrespective of the authors and their intentions.

As earlier noted, Exodus 6 repeats a great many of the elements present in Exodus 3. The sages of the Midrash and the mystics of the Zohar created stories to explain this repetition. Similarly, literary criticism does not see the two texts of Exodus 3 and Exodus 6 as contradictory but as different parts of an ongoing narrative. Moses receives a renewed call to action in Exodus 6 because he has become so disenchanted by his early failure to convince Pharaoh to let the people go. This new revelation completes the revelation at the Burning Bush. God tells Moses that the mission for which he was called on at the Burning Bush will occur in due time; Moses should not be dismayed by his initial failures in Pharaoh's court and with his fellow Israelites. He reminds Moses that Abraham, Isaac, and Jacob received revelations and promises, and yet it was not in their times that the promise to possess the land was fulfilled. As the genealogy indicates, the Israelites have gone from being a family to being a people, and so the divine promise will be carried out, the liberation from Egypt will occur, and the Israelites will return to their land.

117

Literary criticism finds unity and purposeful repetition where other approaches find disharmony and contradiction.

STRUCTURALISM AND DECONSTRUCTIONISM

In the past, it was thought that texts communicate meaning straightforwardly and simply. Language was supposed to give an exact picture of the world. In modern thinking, however, it is understood that all words have complex relationships with other words and that it is the patterns of language that give words meaning. All language is figurative; there is a great distance between language about the world and the world itself. Language and literature are cultural phenomena, and structuralism looks at texts and analyzes the basic mental patterns that underlie these social and cultural phenomena.

It was once assumed that the author of a text intended a meaning and that the reader could understand that intention. In modern thinking, however, it is understood that ambiguities in language and context increase the chances of misunderstanding. Even when a writer and a reader live at the same time and in the same place, a reader could still offer different plausible interpretations of a writer's text. When centuries and geography separate writer and reader, misunderstanding is almost certain.

We assume that any text we read has a clear meaning that it is trying to convey. A method called deconstruction claims that a text itself undermines that meaning by presenting evidence against its own case. A text often makes its case by choosing one alternative over another. In the process, however, the other alternative is brought into the picture, enabling the reader to consider it. The writer's preferred alternative is not necessarily rejected as a result, but it now is seen as only one possible option. The authority of the text breaks down, the text folds in on itself (usually at some weak point), and its center no longer holds.

Let us look at Exodus 6 again, this time to demonstrate how a text deconstructs. As we saw from the perspective of source criticism, Exodus 6 seems to be about the name of God. The Patriarchs knew God as *El Shaddai*, but now Moses and the Israelites will know God by God's true name, *YHWH*.

118

But what does it mean to "know the name of God"? When Moses, at the Burning Bush (Exod. 3–4), asks for the name of the god who has sent him to the Israelites on the mission of liberation, God answers, "I will be what I will be [Ehyeh-Asher-Ehyeh]" (3:14). Moses goes to Pharaoh in *YHWH*'s name: "Thus says the LORD, the God of Israel: Let My people go." Pharaoh replies: "Who is the LORD that I should heed Him and let Israel go? I do not know the LORD, nor will I let Israel go" (5:1–2). Moses thinks that he has met with failure: "O LORD, why did You bring harm upon this people? Why did You send me? Ever since I came to Pharaoh to speak in Your name, he has dealt worse with this people; and still You have not delivered Your people" (5:22–23).

What is the "name" of God? It certainly is neither a description nor a definition of God. God's name seems to be God's power. Once both the Egyptians and the Israelites experience the power of God through the plagues, the name of God will be known throughout the world. But God's power is not in God's name.

Indeed, the name *YHWH* is a "non-name" name, a way of undermining the whole idea that God can have a name at all. Moses asks God for God's name, and God replies, "I will be what I will be." Thus this text, which seems to be about the revelation of God's name, contains within it the concept that God cannot have a name at all. Admittedly, the midrash, the Zohar, and the source critics all seek to use the different names of God illustrated in the book of Exodus as a code by which to crack the meaning of the Bible. But there really is only one name of God—*YHWH*—which is not a name at all but an expression of the namelessness of God.

This reading of the texts from Exodus is only one interpretation, and these texts, as the other types of criticism indicate, may be about the revelation of God's name, and the different names of God may each have its own significance.

When a text is deconstructed, however, we are no longer sure what it is trying to say. In the case of the Bible, traditional commentary would agree that no one should claim to have the definitive interpretation of a passage, for every word of the Bible has an infinite range of meanings. Deconstruction tries to be without biases, in contrast to traditional exegesis—which is based on the strongest possible theological basis. Nevertheless it is fascinating that a modern method joins Jewish commentary in striving to keep the biblical text open for our interpretations and for those who will read the Bible in the centuries to come. There is something about the Bible that prevents all commentators, whether traditional or modern, from finding definitive solutions; the problems usually remain problems. The Bible remains open; no one can close it.

From Benjamin Edidin Scolnic, *Etz Hayim: Torah and Commentary.*

COMMENTARIES ON THE BIBLE

The TANAKH, the Hebrew Bible, is the foundational sacred text of the Jewish religion. Of its three divisions, Torah, Prophets (Nevi'im), and Writings (Kethuvim), the Torah is the most hallowed. Even before its final redaction and especially since, the entire TANAKH, but especially the Torah, has been subject to interpretation and reinterpretation to meet the needs of succeeding generations who sought to understand its words and find meaning and instruction in them.

As was explained in the previous chapter, the Bible has traditionally been interpreted according to several methods, which are often referred to by the acronym *PaRDeS;* these stand for *peshat, remez, derash,* and *sod. Peshat* is the plain or contextual meaning of the text; *remez,* the allegorical or philosophical; *derash,* the homiletical; and *sod,* the mystical. (See "Four Approaches to Reading the Bible," on p. 108.)

This chapter focus on *peshat* Bible commentary, beginning with the early Karaites and Saadiah Ga'on. In actual fact, the earliest systematic Jewish biblical commentary to have reached us is the commentary on the Minor Prophets by Daniel ben Moses al-Qumisi, who moved from his home in Persia to Jerusalem in the 9th decade of the 9th century. He was followed a generation later by Saadiah Ga'on, a great scholar and communal leader, and then by Japheth ben Eli, the greatest Karaite commentator of all time.

Peshat interpretation involves determining the grammatical state and fundamental meaning of each word in a verse, the syntactic relationships among those words, and the immediate and broader contexts of each verse to see how the words and the sentences fit together as a meaningful whole.

Why the Need for Commentary?

According to tradition, the Torah contains the literal word of God as dictated to Moses at Mount Sinai, who wrote it down for future generations. Its text was held to be sacred, inviolable, and, on its deepest level, beyond human understanding. The rest of the TANAKH is thought to have been divinely inspired and has also been treated with great reverence. Yet, it was generally accepted that the "Torah was written in human language" and therefore should have meaning on a human level even if ultimately its deepest meaning is unfathomable. Thus each generation of readers has felt compelled to plumb its depths to derive additional meaning from its passages.

Commentary represents the search for meaning. There are two types of meaning that readers can seek in the text, two questions that they can ask of it. First, "What does this text mean?"—that is, what was the writer trying to say when writing this text? Or in other words, "How might the author have expressed him- or herself in plain language if he or she were writing today?" The quest for answers to this question is the foundation of *peshat* commentary. Occasionally, a definitive answer can be given for a particular word, verse, or passage, but quite often we do not have enough information to give such an answer.

The second question is, "What does this text mean for me?" This is a more personal question, one that each commentator, and each reader for that matter, needs to answer for himself or herself. The search for meaning in a sacred text like the Bible is an ongoing enterprise, which engages countless individuals over the course of many generations.

To paraphrase Ecclesiastes 12:12, "Of the making of commentaries there is no limit." Each generation produces its scholars, who provide new insights into the meaning of the text in the first sense, the original intent of the author. And each generation of Bible readers needs its commentators to help individuals read the Bible, understand its meaning, and derive from it new meanings that are relevant to their lives.

The Bible's Challenges to Comprehension

The Bible, a relatively small collection of works of various genres written over a period of at least 500 to 600 years (approximately 7th–2nd centuries B.C.E.), presents many challenges to readers. Many of its words are ambiguous or simply unknown, appearing only once or twice, defying definition. Their meaning must be conjectured, based on context and parallels in other ancient Semitic languages. A frequent footnote in biblical translations to this very day reads: "Meaning of Hebrew uncertain."

The consonantal text of the TANAKH was probably fixed in the tannaitic period (2nd–3rd centuries C.E.), but until the time of the Masoretes the text was transmitted without punctuation or vowels, leaving room for ambiguity and misunderstanding. Even the work of the Masoretes did not eliminate all uncertainties from the biblical text. Sometimes there are extra words; sometimes words may be missing. In a number of cases two alternative readings are given for the same word. The narrative often leaves gaps that need to be filled; occasionally, there are seemingly unnecessary repetitions or needless details; there are problems with chronology, with events apparently related out of sequence; the order of passages often does not make sense or the connections between passages are not readily obvious. Sometimes the biblical text seems to contradict itself.

For the reader who believes that the Bible is the word of God, there are also challenges of a philosophical or theological nature. How do we explain contradictions between our experience and events described in the Bible? What about contradictions between contemporary science and the biblical text, such as in the case of the Creation story in Genesis, or Joshua's battle at Jericho, where we are told that the sun stood still?

All of these issues are troubling and demand resolution. This is where commentary comes into play.

The Commentator's Tools

IN THE MIDDLE AGES

As already mentioned, contextual *peshat* commentary proper began in the early Middle Ages, with the first Karaites and Saadiah Ga'on in the 9th and 10th centuries, who initiated the systematic study of Hebrew grammar and lexicography and the application of these disciplines to the biblical text. Hebrew linguistics developed steadily through the following centuries and was a powerful tool for the biblical commentator. Grammar texts and biblical lexicons or "books of roots" contain a great deal of basic interpretive material. They enabled the comparison of all the instances of the appearance of words of the same root throughout the Bible and the application of these results to verses where the meaning was unclear.

Another important tool for the medievals was comparative lexicography—the mining of other Semitic languages for cognates, words that could possibly have the same or similar meanings as puzzling biblical words. Especially important for this purpose were Rabbinic Hebrew, Aramaic, and Arabic.

Some commentators focused on realia to the extent that they were able, trying to identify species of plants and animals, place names, and geographic features. Their awareness of these disciplines depended on their own education and on contacts they had with other scholars, both Jewish and non-Jewish, and with travelers to the Middle East. In general, this information was spotty.

IN THE MODERN PERIOD

In the Middle Ages and early modern period, knowledge of the archaeology of Palestine and the ancient Near East was nonexistent, as was knowledge of the ancient civilizations that inhabited these areas. All this has changed in the modern period, especially in the last 200 years, which has witnessed a veritable explosion of discovery, producing a wealth of new information about the material and literary cultures, languages, and history of the ancient Near East.

These scientific developments have opened up new vistas for Bible scholars and commentators. Entire languages and their literatures have been discovered and deciphered, creating many opportunities for determining the meaning of puzzling passages. Especially important have been the discoveries of the Ugaritic and Mesopotamian (Sumerian and Akkadian) literatures, but Egyptian literature and Moabite and Phoenician inscriptions have made contributions as well.

The field of archaeology has also shed much light on the biblical period, revealing a great deal about ancient material culture and necessitating the revision of biblical history, calling into question many views that had been long accepted. The debates over issues of dating, chronology, and historicity still rage on, with no resolution in sight.

The discovery of the Dead Sea Scrolls has had a huge impact as well, making accessible for the first time manuscripts that are 1,000 years older than those available in the Middle Ages. (See "The Dead Sea Scrolls," on p. 15.) Important use has also been made of the ancient versions of the Bible, especially the Septuagint and other Greek versions, but also the Aramaic, Syriac, Latin, and Samaritan. All can provide important information for contemporary commentators, enabling them to attain a more accurate picture of the original text.

To all this one may add general advances in all the sciences, which have given us a deeper understanding of how the world works. This vast storehouse of knowledge can be brought to bear on deciphering the ancient biblical texts.

With such new knowledge at their disposal, modern commentators have real advantages over their medieval predecessors. So why bother reading the classical commentaries at all? Because, while they may have been scientifically, linguistically, and archaeologically "challenged," they made up for these deficiencies with their intimate knowledge of the text and a sensitivity to its nuance that few moderns have. Their ability to make associations based on memory, before the age of concordances, CD-ROMS, and other mechanical aids, often yielded startling insights into the biblical text that have not lost their value and significance. And they were intimately familiar with Rabbinic literature, the repository of the Oral Law and lore, which also can be used to elucidate the text. The Rabbis, after all, were also very careful readers, and the word and narrative associations they make are often illuminating and instructive. Many of their comments and insights have the weight and authority of ancient tradition. So, though not every word of every early commentator may appeal to us, a commentator who was an original and insightful thinker is still well worth consulting.

Traditional commentators, with some exceptions (discussed later), generally accept the Mosaic authorship of the Torah (that the Torah was dictated in its entirety by God to Moses at Mount Sinai) and the general inviolability of the masoretic text—the biblical text as established by the Soferim (scribes) of the Talmudic period and the Tiberian scholars called Masoretes, who were active from the early 6th to the early 10th centuries. (See "The Masoretes—Preservers and Protectors of the Hebrew Bible," on p. 20). Modern non-Orthodox commentators accept to a greater or lesser extent the conclusions of modern biblical scholarship: that the TANAKH was the product of a long process of development that culminated sometime in the Second Temple period and involved, especially in the case of the Torah, combining sources from different schools of thought into one more or less cohesive unit. They recognize that the masoretic text, while generally stable and free of error, can on occasion be inaccurate. In general, the text of the Torah is less likely to require correction than that of the other biblical books, but it too is not completely immune.

Many modern, nontraditional commentators adopt a literary approach, which views the text we have as a complete unit whose reputed sources do not concern them. This approach shares much with the approach of the traditional commentators, who were sensitive to nuance and detail and the unusual turn of phrase and who never considered that the text was anything but a unified whole.

Biblical Commentary through the Ages

This section provides a chronological overview of the major biblical commentators, their works, and their methodologies. The availability of English translations is noted.

CLASSICAL COMMENTARIES

Saadiah ben Joseph (Saadiah Ga'on; 882–942). Born in Egypt, Saadiah moved to Iraq, where he rose to prominence, eventually becoming *ga'on* of Sura, the head of the most influential academy of its day. Besides being a communal leader, Saadiah was a prominent scholar who did pioneering work in a number of disciplines, including philosophy, Hebrew grammar, and biblical commentary. He was the first Rabbanite commentator. He translated the entire Bible and commented on many books, including the Torah, Isaiah, Psalms, Proverbs, Job, and the Five Scrolls. All his works were written in Arabic, and very few were translated into Hebrew, so they were not well known in western Europe in the Middle Ages. His commentaries are systematically organized with introductions dealing with grammatical, interpretive, and philosophical issues. He also set out principles for writing commentary, and this guided his work, much of which was directed toward refuting the claims of the Karaites and defending the Oral Law.

Saadiah in English: *Rabbi Saadiah Gaon's Commentary on the Book of Creation*, trans. Michael Linetsky (Northvale, NJ: Jason Aronson, 2002) (on Gen. 1:1–28:9); *The Messiah in Isaiah 53*, trans. Joseph Alobaidi (Bern and New York: Peter Lang, 1998) (on Isa. 52:13–53:12); *The Book of Theodicy: Translation and Commentary on the Book of Job*, trans. Lenn Evan Goodman (New Haven, CT: Yale University Press, 1988); *The Book of Daniel: The Commentary of R. Saadia Gaon*, trans. Joseph Alobaidi (Bern: Peter Lang, 2006).

Japheth ben Eli (10th century). A leader of the Jerusalem school of Karaite scholars, Japheth was the greatest Karaite commentator of all time, perhaps the only one to have translated and commented on the entire Bible. His commentaries became his life's calling and were intended to provide his community with an adequate treatment of scripture that could stand up against the Rabbanites, led by Saadiah Ga'on and his followers. Japheth developed a literary-contextual approach, which was profoundly influential and set the tone for succeeding generations of commentators, both Karaite and Rabbanite. Many of his comments gained currency through the mediation of Abraham ibn Ezra, who quoted him often, sometimes without acknowledgment, sometimes to refute his views. Only a small number of his many commentaries have been published in modern editions. Even fewer have been translated from the original Arabic.

Japheth in English: *The Messiah in Isaiah 53,* trans. Joseph Alobaidi (Bern and New York: Peter Lang, 1998) (on Isa. 52:13–53:12); *Jewish Exegesis of the Book of Ruth,* trans. D. R. G. Beattie (Sheffield, UK: Deptartment of Biblical Studies, University of Sheffield, 1977) (erroneously attributed to Salmon ben Jeroham); *A Commentary on the Book of Daniel,* trans. D. S. Margoliouth (Oxford, UK: Clarendon Press, 1889).

Rashi (Solomon ben Isaac; 1040–1105). Solomon ben Isaac, commonly known as Rashi, the most popular Jewish Bible commentator of all time, was born in Troyes, in northern France, where he lived most of his life, except for a few years spent studying in the talmudic academies of Mainz and Worms. He was one of the leading rabbinical figures of his day, a spiritual and communal leader, renowned for his wisdom, scholarship, modesty, and devotion to the truth.

Rashi wrote commentaries on almost the entire Bible as well as an indispensable and arguably more important commentary on the Talmud. In his commentaries, which are steeped in the Rabbinic tradition, we see a newly discovered awareness of grammar and sensitivity to context, which led to selectivity in the inclusion of midrashic material. The genius of Rashi's commentaries lies in their clarity of language, the felicity of expression, and the skillful selection and editing of his sources. While Rashi's commentaries usually include only what is necessary to explicate the text, occasional reference is made to contemporary social or economic conditions. The impact of the Crusades is especially felt in his commentary on Psalms, written after 1096, in which numerous references to the nation Edom (a symbol of Rome in Rabbinic literature) are applied to the Christian Crusaders. Rashi was a brilliant stylist, and his blend of contextual (*peshat*) commentary and ethical homiletics have helped give his commentary pride of place in the canon of classic Jewish texts that are still studied widely today.

Rashi in English: *Pentateuch with Targum Onkelos, Haphtoroth and Rashi's Commentary,* trans. M. Rosenbaum and A. M. Silbermann (London: Shapiro, 1929–1934; New York: Hebrew Publishing Co., 1934); *The Pentateuch and Rashi's Commentary: A Linear Translation into English,* trans. Abraham Ben Isaiah and Benjamin Sharfman (Brooklyn: S.S. & R., 1949–1950); *The Metsudah Chumash/Rashi,* text trans. Avrohom Davis; Rashi trans. Avrohom Kleinkaufman (vols. 1–2) and Avrohom Davis (vols. 3–5) (Hoboken, NJ: Distributed by Ktav, 1991–1996); *The Torah with Rashi's Commentary,* trans. Yisrael Isser Zvi Herczeg (Brooklyn: Mesorah Publications, 1995–1998). Rashi's entire commentary on Prophets and Writings is also available in the English translation of A. J. Rosenberg; *Miqra'ot Gedolot: A New English Translation* (New York: Judaica Press, 1969–1997). Metsudah is also publishing a linear translation of the TANAKH with Rashi: The Metsudah

Tanach Series (Brookline, MA: Distributed by Israel Book Shop, 1997–2002 to date); so far Joshua (trans. Avrohom Davis), Judges (trans. Yosef Rabinowitz), 1 Samuel (trans. Yaakov Y. H. Pupko), 2 Samuel (trans. Avrohom Davis), 1 and 2 Kings (trans. Yaakov Y. H. Pupko), and the Five Scrolls (trans. Avrohom Davis and Yaakov Y. H. Pupko) have appeared. Mention should also be made of the important scholarly edition and translation of Rashi on Psalms by Mayer Gruber, *Rashi's Commentary on Psalms* (Leiden: Brill, 2004; paperback reprint, Philadelphia: Jewish Publication Society, 2007).

Rashbam (Samuel ben Meir; ca. 1080–ca. 1160). The grandson of Rashi, Rashbam is the foremost figure in the northern French school of *peshat* commentary. He is best known for his Torah commentary (he also probably commented on most of the Five Scrolls and possibly Job), in which he shows himself to be a radical adherent to *peshat* interpretation, even to the point of favoring it over Rabbinic tradition when the two clashed. His stated goal was to gain an understanding of the text as it was written. He distinguished between halakhic commentary, used to establish Jewish practice, and *peshat* commentary, used to determine the meaning of the text, and he saw a legitimate role for both. He was himself a halakhic scholar who wrote commentaries on certain talmudic tractates. He showed considerable interest in matters of grammar and style. For instance, he was the first medieval commentator to notice the biblical literary technique of foreshadowing, providing information in anticipation of a later need for it.

Rashbam in English: *Rabbi Samuel ben Meir's Commentary on Genesis* (Lewiston, NY: Mellen, 1989); *Rashbam's Commentary on Exodus,* trans. and ed. Martin I. Lockshin (Atlanta: Scholars Press, 1997); *Rashbam's Commentary on Leviticus and Numbers,* trans. and ed. Martin I. Lockshin (Providence, RI: Brown Judaic Studies, 2001); *Rashbam's Commentary on Deuteronomy,* trans. and ed. Martin I. Lockshin (Providence, RI: Brown Judaic Studies, 2004); *The Commentary of R. Samuel ben Meir Rashbam on Qoheleth,* trans. Sara Japhet and Robert B. Salters (Jerusalem: Magnes Press, 1985).

Ibn Ezra, Abraham (1089–1164). Ibn Ezra was a prominent Spanish grammarian, biblical commentator, philosopher, and poet who left his homeland in 1140 and wandered through much of western Europe, eventually ending up in London, where he remained for the rest of his life. He produced commentaries on a good number of biblical books, some even in two successive versions. His commentaries are based on a thorough knowledge of Hebrew grammar and lexicography and an appeal to reason and logic. They represent a distillation of the finest achievements of the Spanish school of commentary, which emphasized the importance of grammar and philology. He believed that scripture uses human language and must conform to the rules of grammar, syntax, and rhetoric. In line with other Spanish commentators, he ignored changes in spelling or wording if the meaning of the passage was not affected. Thus textual variants, unusual spellings, and stylistic variation, as are found in parallel halves of many verses of biblical poetry, were not relevant for him.

Ibn Ezra was a steadfast opponent of the Karaites and often criticized them in his commentaries. He was a loyal defender of the Oral Law and never accepted as *peshat* an interpretation that contradicted Jewish law. He incorporated into his commentaries his philosophical views, especially about creation and God's relationship with the Land and People of Israel. While he had a conservative view of the biblical text and rejected all attempts at emendation, he did raise questions about the Mosaic authorship of certain verses in the Torah (for example, Gen. 12:6, 22:14; Deut. 3:11), which he claimed were later additions, and especially of the last 12 verses of Deuteronomy ("the secret of the twelve"), which eulogize Moses and tell of his final hours, and which Ibn Ezra claims were written by Joshua.

Ibn Ezra in English: *Ibn Ezra's Commentary on the Pentateuch*, trans. H. Norman Strickman and Arthur M. Silver, 5 vols. (New York: Menorah, 1988–2004); *The Commentary of Ibn Ezra on Isaiah*, trans. Michael Friedlander, 4 vols. (London : N. Trübner, 1873–1877; reprint, New York: Feldheim, 1964); *The Commentary of Rabbi Abraham Ibn Ezra on Hosea*, trans. Abe Lipshitz (New York: Sepher Hermon Press, 1988).

Kimchi, David ben Joseph (Radak; ca. 1160–1235). Radak was a grammarian and Bible commentator, the most famous member of the illustrious Kimchi family of Narbonne, Provence. He wrote commentaries on the Torah, Prophets, Psalms, Proverbs, Job, and Chronicles. His grammatical works, *Shorashim* and *Mikhlol*, especially the former, also contain considerable material of exegetical value. His commentaries, which often relied on his predecessors, represent the best of the Spanish *peshat* tradition but also are sensitive to the midrashic tradition as exemplified in the commentaries of Rashi.

Radak was a philosophically trained follower of Maimonides who did not shy away from introducing philosophical ideas into his commentaries. He also did not hesitate to apply certain biblical prophecies and psalm verses to the state of the Jews in his own day, and prayers and hopes for the coming of the Messiah and the ultimate redemption are frequently found in his writings. The fact that his commentaries, which were extremely popular, were peppered with anti-Christian polemical statements secured his reputation as a defender of the Jewish faith.

Radak in English: *Hachut hameshulash*, trans. Eliyahu Munk (New York: Lambda, 2003) (on Genesis); *The Longer Commentary of R. David Kimhi on the First Book of Psalms: I–X, XV–XVII, XIX, XXII, XXIV*, trans. G. H. Box (London: SPCK, 1919); *The Commentary of Rabbi David Kimhi on Psalms CXX–CL*, trans. Joshua Baker and E. W. Nicholson (Cambridge, UK: Cambridge University Press, 1973).

Nachmanides (Moses ben Nachman; Ramban; 1194–1270). Bible commentator, talmudist, kabbalist, and communal leader in Gerona, Spain, Ramban is best known for his commentary on the Torah, which marked a new stage in the history of biblical interpretation, being the first that was influenced by both the Andalusian and Ashkenazic traditions. Though a product of Christian Spain, he undoubtedly felt himself to be part of the Andalusian commentary tradition and indeed enriched it with many insightful comments. At the same time, he had absorbed the work of Rashi and the northern French school and held it in high regard. Furthermore, he was wont to draw on the vast resources of Rabbinic literature—Talmud and midrash as well as gaonic and mystical works.

Though certainly trained in grammar and philology, he found the grammatical approach of the Spanish school as exemplified by Abraham ibn Ezra too narrow and limiting. He was therefore sympathetic to Rashi and his selective use of midrashic material, seeking to strike a balance between the two approaches and to adopt a more holistic approach to the text. His commentaries encompass issues of theology, ethics, history, and character analysis, thus weaving a particularly colorful and variegated tapestry that operates on several levels. He is famous for his psychological insights and deep understanding of human nature.

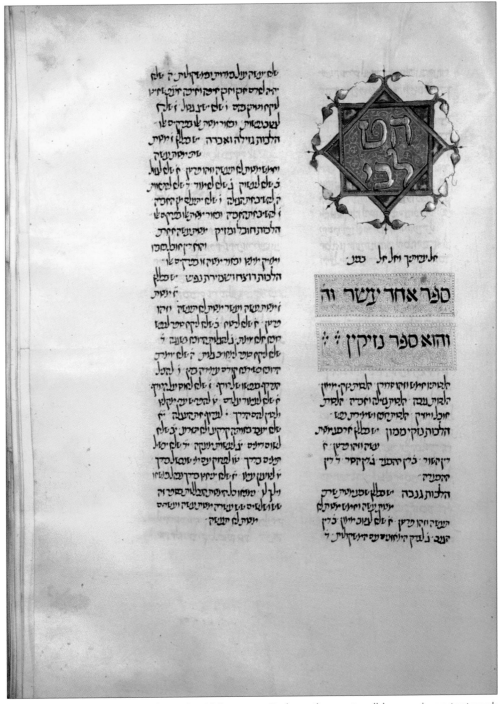

A page from the Mishneh Torah, Spain, 15th century. Perhaps the most well-known, important work of medieval Jewish philosopher Moses Maimonides, the Mishneh Torah is a comprehensive code of Jewish law. It incorporates the positions of the Ge'onim, medieval Jewish scholars, into a code of law that derived from the Talmud. The scope and precision of this work made it a vital contribution to Judaism's Written Tradition. (Courtesy of The Library of the Jewish Theological Seminary.)

Ramban was also a kabbalist, steeped in the mystical traditions of the Provençal school of Kabbalah, and he made numerous allusions to esoteric meanings of various biblical texts. He was also one of the few medieval commentators who made use of typology, seeing the deeds of the Patriarchs as foreshadowing what would happen to their descendants, a theological notion articulated in the expression *ma'aseh avot siman le-vanim* ("the deed of the ancestors is a sign for the offspring").

Ramban in English: Ramban's entire Torah commentary was translated by Charles B. Chavel: Ramban (Nachmanides), *Commentary on the Torah*, 5 vols. (New York: Shilo, 1971–1976). A new translation by Yaakov Blinder and Yoseph Kamenetsky has begun to appear: *The Torah: with Ramban's Commentary*, 3 vols. to date: (Brooklyn: Mesorah, 2004–) (For Genesis and Shmemot-Yitro).

Levi ben Gershom (Ralbag, Gersonides; 1288–1344). A Provençal philosopher and biblical commentator, Ralbag may well have been the most original Jewish thinker of the late Middle Ages. He commented on the Torah, the Early Prophets, the Five Scrolls, and Job. While his commentaries are laced with philosophical insights, they contain much straightforward *peshat* interpretation as well. His commentaries are divided into three sections: (1) an explanation of the difficult words in the passage; (2) an expanded paraphrase of the text; and (3) a list of lessons, both moral and philosophical, that can be derived from the passage. The last may have been inspired by the practice of contemporary Christian commentators.

Ralbag in English: *The Commentary of Levi ben Gerson (Gersonides) on the Book of Job*, trans. Abraham L. Lassen (New York: Bloch, 1946); *Commentary on Song of Songs*, trans. Menachem Kellner (New Haven, CT: Yale University Press, 1998).

Abarbanel, Isaac (1437–1508). Abarbanel (also spelled Abrabanel and, Abravanel), statesman, philosopher, and student of Isaac Arama, was the greatest Spanish biblical interpreter of the 15th century. He produced voluminous commentaries on the Torah, Prophets, and Daniel, which are thoughtful and thought-provoking. The commentaries are arranged in problem/solution fashion. His primary focus was *peshat*, but he also incorporated midrashim that he found acceptable. In his theology, he rejected the rationalist position in favor of one based on faith, which he felt was more in line with that of the sages. As a product of the Renaissance, he was open to new ideas and introduced much contemporary thought into his writing. His commentaries on Samuel and Kings are full of his ideas on the monarchy, which, based on his personal experience, he did not hold in high esteem.

Sforno, Obadiah (1475–1550). The most famous Italian biblical commentator of the 16th century, Sforno wrote commentaries on the Torah and the book of Psalms in the *peshat* tradition. Sforno was a rabbi, a trained physician, and a cultured individual, a true product of Renaissance humanism, whose values infuse his works.

Sforno in English: *Commentary on the Torah*, trans. Raphael Pelcovitz, 2 vols. (Brooklyn: Mesorah, 1987–1989).

Ephraim Solomon ben Aaron of Luntshits (1550–1619). A rabbi, preacher, and communal leader in Prague, Luntshits was the author of *Keli Yeqar* (Precious Vessel; not *Keli Yaqar*, as is

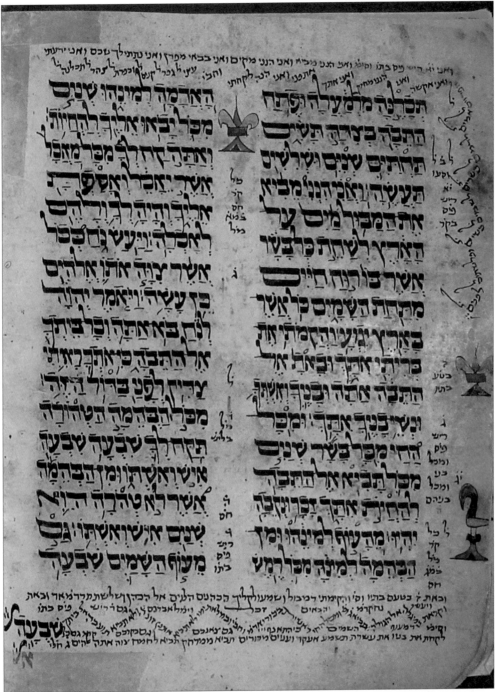

131

A page from a Bible, Yemen, 15th century. Yemenites were prodigious in producing Bible commentaries, especially in the 15th century. Therefore, Bibles such as this one usually contained a short masoretic introduction, and often also contained Arabic commentaries. The pictures and patterned text that decorate the borders of the biblical text itself represent the Yemenite custom of illuminating text and writing commentary notes in the margins. (Courtesy of The Library of the Jewish Theological Seminary.)

commonly assumed; cf. Prov. 20:15), a very popular homiletic commentary on the Torah, reprinted in many editions of *miqra'ot gedolot* down to this day.

Keli Yeqar in English: *Kli Yakar*, trans. Elihu Levine (Southfield, MI: Targum Press; Nanuet, NY: Feldheim, 5762–/2002–) (2 vols. on Exodus); *Kli Yakar: The Commentary of Rabbi Shlomo Ephraim Luntshits, the "Kli Yakar,"* trans. Albert M. Kanter (Skokie, IL: HTC Press, 2003) (on Deuteronomy only).

Ibn Attar, Chayyim ben Moses (1696–1743). Ibn Attar, born in Morocco, was the author of the compendious Torah commentary *Or ha-Chayyim.* This commentary, besides containing elements of *peshat* interpretation based on responses to the writings of his predecessors, includes psychological analyses of the biblical characters and their motives, interpretations of Rabbinic statements, moral instruction and admonition, mystical lore, halakhic discussions, and historical and personal reflections.

The commentary has appeared in many editions, both separately and in *miqra'ot gedolot* editions, and has been published in English translation by Eliyahu Munk; *Or Hachayim: Commentary on the Torah,* 5 vols. (Jerusalem and Brooklyn: Hemed Books, 1995).

Mendelssohn, Moses (1729–1786). Mendelssohn was a German philosopher and man of letters. He was the editor of a new edition of the Bible intended for the educated German-speaking Jewish laity, which featured a carefully edited Hebrew text, a German translation in Hebrew characters, and a commentary in Hebrew called the *Bi'ur* (Commentary), culled for the most part from the best medieval *peshat* commentators (Rashi, Ibn Ezra, Rashbam, Ramban) but also including new linguistic and literary insights. Mendelssohn was assisted in this enterprise by other scholars, including Naphtali Herz Wessely (1725–1805) and Solomon Dubno (1738–1813). The authors of the commentary went out of their way to include both halakhic and aggadic Rabbinic interpretations, trying to demonstrate their beauty and value to an audience that may have had little exposure to Rabbinic literature and probably held it in disdain. The *Bi'ur* went through many editions in the 19th century, making it one of the most popular commentaries of its time.

Meklenburg, Jacob Zvi (1785–1865). A rabbi in Koenigsberg, Meklenburg was the author of *Ha-Ketav veha-Qabbalah* (The Text and the Tradition) (1839; 2nd ed., 1852; 3rd ed., 1880), a commentary on the Torah. While his stated purpose was to demonstrate through linguistic and other means that the Rabbinic interpretations of scripture were reasonable and totally justified, in actuality his commentary is for the most part devoted to *peshat* interpretation, drawing on his contemporaries and predecessors in the German Jewish community. It thus represents a summation of the interpretive work of the late 18th and early 19th centuries.

Ha-Ketav veha-Qabbalah in English translation by Eliyahu Munk, *Haketav vehakabbalah: Torah Commentary,* 7 vols. (Jerusalem: Lambda, 2001).

Luzzatto, Samuel David (Shadal; 1800–1865). Italian rabbi, scholar, and theologian, Shadal has been called the first of the modern Jewish Bible commentators. He lectured on the Bible and biblical criticism at the Rabbinical Seminary in Padua and wrote "Introduction to the Criticism and Interpretation of the Torah" (1829), in which he deals systematically with issues of redaction, textual criticism, and ancient versions and their reliability. He is the author of commentaries on the Torah, Isaiah, Jeremiah, Ezekiel, Psalms 49 and 51, and Ecclesiastes.

> ### *Miqra'ot Gedolot*
> Special editions of the Bible, called *miqra'ot gedolot,* are characterized by their layout: pages have only a few lines of Hebrew text and Aramaic translation to allow room for the notes of an array of commentators. The Hebrew term *miqra'ot gedolot* actually means large-format edition of the Bible, but in practice the size of editions vary from small to oversize.

Shadal's commentary in English: *The Book of Genesis: A Commentary,* trans. Daniel A. Klein (Northvale, NJ: Jason Aronson, 1998).

Hirsch, Samson Raphael (1808–1888). Hirsch, a prominent German rabbi and ideologue of Neo-Orthodox Judaism, produced an extensive commentary on the Torah in German (later translated into English and Hebrew) as well as a commentary on Psalms, which had a unique approach based on his understanding of the symbolic nature of the Hebrew language. Apologetic in tone, the commentaries have as a principal goal the demonstration of the essential moral and ethical superiority of the Jewish faith.

An English translation, *The Pentateuch,* was prepared by Isaac Levy (London: I. Levy, 1958–1962; 2nd ed., 1962–1967).

Malbim, Meir Leibush ben Yehiel Michal (1809–1879). Malbim was a prolific eastern European scholar who strove to demonstrate the unity of the Oral and Written Laws, in response to the perceived attacks by 19th-century reformers. He commented on all of the books of the Bible. His commentary on Leviticus is based on the Rabbinic halakhic midrash *Sifra.* He reproduces the midrashic text and comments on it and the accompanying biblical text in his commentary titled *Ha-Torah veha-Mitzvah* (The Teaching and the Commandment). He produced similar commentaries for Exodus, based on the *Mekhilta de-Rabbi Yishmael,* and on Numbers and Deuteronomy, based on *Sifrei.* For Genesis and other biblical books without halakhic midrashim, he modeled his commentary after that of Isaac Abarbanel, prefacing each section with a series of questions, which he then answered in sequence. Malbim's commentary has been reprinted often and is still highly regarded in traditional circles today.

Malbim in English: *Malbim: Rabbenu Meir Leibush ben Yechiel Michel; Commentary on the Torah,* trans. Zvi Faier, 5 vols. to date (Jerusalem: Hillel Press, 1978–) (on Genesis and the first 12 chapters of Exodus); *Malbim on Mishley: The Commentary of Meir Leibush Malbim on the Book of Proverbs,* trans. Charles Wengrov, abridged and adapted (Jerusalem: Feldheim, 1982); *Malbim's Job: The Book of Job,* trans. Jeremy I. Pfeffer (Jersey City, NJ: Ktav, 2003); *Malbim on the Book of Ruth: The Commentary of Rabbi Meir Leibush Malbim,* trans. Shmuel Kurtz (Jerusalem and New York: Feldheim, 1999) .

Berlin, Naphtali Tzevi Judah (Netziv; 1817–1893). Berlin, head of the prestigious Volozhin yeshivah, published his Torah commentary *Ha'mek Davar* (Delving Deeply into the Matter) in 1879–1880. In this commentary he tried to demonstrate the inseparable link between the words of the Torah and those of the sages and to show that the former must be understood in light of the latter. He stressed over and over again that the Torah is divine and that every word and sentence in it was put there for a reason. He believed that the correct study of the Bible would lead a person to upright behavior. He set as a goal for his students not only intimacy with the biblical text but the ability to derive moral lessons and teachings that would make them better people and bring them closer to God.

Netziv in English: *The Commentary of Rav Naftali Tzvi Yehuda Berlin to Shir Hashirim,* trans. and annotated by Dovid Landesman (Kefar Hasidim: Jewish Educational Workshop, 1993).

MODERN COMMENTARIES—THE ISRAELI SCENE

Sifre ha-Miqra, commentary by E. S. Hartom, ed. Moses David Cassuto et al., 15 vols. (Tel Aviv: Yavneh, 1956–1961); many subsequent printings.

This popular commentary was conceived by Cassuto, a Hebrew University Bible professor, who apparently managed to edit only the first volume before his demise. Hartom completed the work (except for Chronicles, which was completed by others following his method). This is a straightforward *peshat* commentary, intended for a lay audience. It includes no references to other commentaries or scholarly works by other authors and avoids source criticism. It has been very popular in Israel for several generations, especially among high school students preparing for their matriculation exams. It includes some maps but no other illustrations.

Da'at Miqra (Knowledge of Scripture) (Jerusalem: Mosad Harav Kook, 1970–2001).

Produced under the auspices of the prestigious publishing house of the Religious Zionist establishment, this set of commentaries by Orthodox Israeli Bible scholars attempts to remain faithful to the tradition and yet still take into account the findings of modern scholarship and archaeology. Special attention is paid to realia: flora, fauna, and artifacts that would be of special interest to the well-informed Israeli audience. Many of the commentaries focus on the literary aspects of the text. It includes many black-and-white illustrations. So far only the commentary on Psalms by Amos Hakham has been rendered into English: *The Bible: Psalms with the Jerusalem Commentary,* trans. Israel V. Berman, 3 vols. (Jerusalem: Mosad Harav Kook, 2003).

Olam ha-Tanakh (The Biblical World), ed. Menahem Haran, 25 vols. (Tel Aviv: Davidzon-Iti, 1993–1994). (The first edition began to appear in 1983 under the title *Entsiqlopedyah Olam ha-Tanakh* but was never completed.)

A popular scientific commentary, it is intended for an educated lay audience. Copiously illustrated in color with special attention given to archaeology, flora, and fauna, the commentaries are written by a team of Israeli and American Bible scholars, with many comments individually signed.

Miqra le-Yisra'el (A Bible Commentary for Israel), ed. Moshe Greenberg and Shmuel Ahituv (Tel Aviv: Am Oved; Jerusalem: Magnes Press, 1990–).

This scholarly commentary by both Israeli and non-Israeli Jewish Bible scholars is intended for scholars, students, and an educated lay audience. Its stated goals are to provide a modern professional commentary on the Bible based on all aspects of Jewish culture. The entire range of biblical, linguistic, and archaeological scholarship is taken

134

into account, as well as various modern critical methodologies—historical, literary, rhetorical, and redaction criticism—and comparative Semitics and lexicography. The role of each book in the history of Jewish thought and biblical interpretation is also discussed. The following volumes have been published to date: Isaiah 40–66 (Shalom M. Paul), Joshua (Shmuel Ahituv), Judges (Yaira Amit), 1 and 2 Samuel (Shimon Bar Efrat), Joel–Amos (Mordechai Cogan, Shalom M. Paul), Jeremiah (Yair Hoffman), Ezekiel (Rimon Kasher), Obadiah–Jonah (Mordechai Cogan, Uriel Simon), Song of Songs (Yair Zakovitch), Ruth (Yair Zakovitch), and Esther (Adele Berlin).

Leibowitz, Nechama (1906–1997). The quintessential teacher, Leibowitz made a major contribution to the revival of Bible study in modern Israel. She taught thousands of students to appreciate the beauty of the biblical text and the variety of approaches found in the traditional and modern commentaries. In her studies of the weekly Torah portions (*Studies in Bereshit, Studies in Shemot,* and so on, trans. Aryeh Newman [Jerusalem: WZO, 1972–1982]), she cited a dazzling array of sources, from the Talmud and midrash all the way to modern interpreters such as Martin Buber, Franz Rosenzweig, and Benno Jacob as well the occasional Christian commentator, following the long-standing tradition of using the best of the world's knowledge to glorify and exalt the Torah.

Her studies, which grew out of the weekly parashah sheets that she used to circulate among her devoted students, are models of pedagogical technique, presenting various views on a topic in the weekly Torah portion, sometimes indicating her preference, other times leaving the question open for further discussion or reflection.

Leibowitz's approach has been followed by many Bible translators and commentators even if they did not share her theological views. Her influence on Jewish biblical studies, especially in modern religious circles but beyond them as well, has been enormous.

MODERN COMMENTARIES ON THE TANAKH FOR ENGLISH READERS
Soncino Books of the Bible, ed. Abraham Cohen, 14 vols. (Hindhead, UK: Soncino Press, 1945–1952), several subsequent editions.

This series includes the Hebrew text, the Old Jewish Publication Society (OJPS) translation (1917), and a commentary "designed for the ordinary reader of the Bible rather than the student." Textual emendation is scrupulously avoided, and the commentary draws on Rabbinic literature, classical Jewish commentaries, and Christian expositors. The commentaries were prepared by a team of Anglo-Jewish scholars. The commentaries on the books of the Torah differ from the others in that they contain an anthology of classical medieval commentators: Rashi, Ibn Ezra, Ramban, Radak, Rashbam, Ralbag, and Sforno. Authors of commentaries on the other books are as follows: Eli Cashdan (Haggai, Zechariah, Malachi); A. Cohen (Psalms, Ecclesiastes); S. Fisch (Ezekiel); Harry Freedman (Joshua, Jeremiah); S. Goldman (Samuel, Obadiah, Jonah, Micah, Lamentations, Esther); S. M. Lehrman (Hosea, Joel, Amos, Nahum, Habakkuk, Zephaniah, Song of Songs); Victor E. Reichert (Job, Ecclesiastes); Israel W. Slotki (Kings, Isaiah, Chronicles); Judah J. Slotki (Judges, Ruth, Daniel, Ezra, Nehemiah).

Miqra'ot Gedolot: A New English Translation, trans. A. J. Rosenberg (New York: Judaica Press, 1969–1997): *Torah* (B'reishit and Shemot, 5 vols. only); *Prophets and Writings,* 24 vols. (complete).

135

This is a modern edition of the *miqra'ot gedolot* for the English-speaking community. Each volume features the complete Hebrew text of the biblical book in question with the traditional commentaries as well as a concise, modern English translation of the text with extensive commentary. In addition, Rashi's commentary is translated in its entirety, as are selections from Talmud and midrash, Ramban, Sforno, Rashbam, Ibn Ezra, and other commentaries never before translated.

ArtScroll Tanach Series, ed. Nosson Scherman (Brooklyn: Mesorah Publications, 1976–1998).

Included here are individual volumes with Hebrew text and commentary in English anthologized from talmudic, midrashic, and later Rabbinic sources. The following have been published to date: Genesis (6 vols.; Meir Zlotowitz), Leviticus (2 vols.; Nosson Scherman, Hersh Goldwurm), Joshua (Reuven Drucker), Ezekiel (Moshe Eisemann), Minor Prophets (Matis Roberts), Jonah (Zlotowitz), Psalms (5 vols.; Chaim Feuer), Proverbs (Eliezer Ginsburg), Job (Moshe Eisemann), Five Scrolls (Meir Zlotowitz), Daniel (Hersh Goldwurm), Ezra (Yosef Rabinowitz), Nehemiah (Yosef Rabinowitz), 1 and 2 Chronicles (Moshe Eisemann).

This project was never completed and seems to have been suspended in favor of the following one.

The Early Prophets: With a Commentary Anthologized from the Rabbinic Writings, ed. Nosson Scherman (Brooklyn: Mesorah Publications, 2000–), 3 vols. to date (Joshua–Judges, Samuel, Kings).

This new edition by ArtScroll includes the Hebrew text of Rashi, Radak, and the Altschulers (Metzudat David and Metzudat Tziyyon [18th century]). The accompanying commentaries are much shorter than those of the earlier edition.

The JPS Torah Commentary (Philadelphia: Jewish Publication Society, 1989–1996).

The series offers detailed scholarly commentaries on the Five Books of Moses by leading American Jewish Bible scholars (Genesis and Exodus: Nahum Sarna; Leviticus: Baruch Levine; Numbers: Jacob Milgrom; Deuteronomy: Jeffrey Tigay). It is characterized by both scholarly rigor and sensitivity to Jewish tradition.

The JPS Bible Commentary (Philadelphia: Jewish Publication Society, 1999–).

This series follows the same path as the JPS Torah Commentary series. To date the following volumes have been published: *Haftarot* (Michael A. Fishbane, 2002), *Jonah* (Uriel Simon, 1999), *Ecclesiastes* (Michael V. Fox, 2004), and *Esther* (Adele Berlin, 2001).

The Living Nach: A New Translation Based on Traditional Jewish Sources, ed. Yaakov Elman (New York and Jerusalem: Moznaim Publishing, 1994–1999), 3 vols. (*Early Prophets, Later Prophets, Sacred Writings*).

A sequel to Aryeh Kaplan's *The Living Torah* (see below), this publication offers "a clear and modern English translation based on traditional Jewish sources," along with extensive notes citing traditional commentators, as well as maps, bibliography, and index.

Tanach: The Torah, Prophets, Writings, Stone Edition, ed. Nosson Scherman (Brooklyn: Mesorah, 1996).

This volume is a companion to the popular Stone *Chumash* published by ArtScroll/Mesorah (see below).

The Jewish Study Bible, ed. Adele Berlin and Marc Brettler (New York: Oxford University Press, 2003).

This is a one-volume edition of the Bible, modeled after the *New Oxford Annotated Bible,* with commentaries by Jewish scholars and an extensive essay section divided into three parts: (1) "Jewish Interpretation of the Bible," tracing the history of interpretation from the Bible itself (inner biblical interpretation) to modern times; (2) "The Bible in Jewish Life and Thought," which outlines the role of the Bible in Judaism and the Jewish community; and (3) "Backgrounds for Reading the Bible," which deals with various issues in modern biblical and ancient Near Eastern scholarship. The English translation used as the basis for the commentary is the New Jewish Publication Society (NJPS) translation (1985). It is published without the Hebrew text.

The Commentators' Bible: The JPS Miqra'ot Gedolot—Exodus, ed., trans., and annotated by Michael Carasik (Philadelphia: Jewish Publication Society, 2005).

This volume includes the Hebrew text, the OJPS and NJPS translations, fresh translations of Rashi, Rashbam, Ibn Ezra, and Ramban, and selections from other commentators— Joseph Bekhor Shor, Hizkuni, Radak, Abarbanel, and Sforno—all arranged in a similar fashion to the standard editions of the classic *miqra'ot gedolot* text. The nature of the translation is somewhat controversial, as the translator has the medieval exegetes often commenting on the text of the modern English translations. In the author's own words: "A basic assumption of this translation is that commentators are rewriting their original comments today, in contemporary English, for readers who do not know Hebrew."

SYNAGOGUE TORAH COMMENTARIES, OR *HUMASHIM*
The three major modern movements have each produced editions of the Torah with commentary, for use in the synagogue.

Orthodox
Pentateuch and Haftarot, ed. Joseph H. Hertz, 5 vols. (Oxford: Oxford University Press, 1929–1936); 1 vol. (London: Soncino, 1938); 2nd ed., with holiday *haftarot* (London: Soncino, 1979).

This commentary, written by a team of Anglo-Jewish scholars and edited by Hertz, a former chief rabbi of Great Britain and the Commonwealth, draws on a wide range of sources, including ancient versions, classical Jewish commentaries, and many non-Jewish scholars and theologians. The tone is often highly apologetic, as the editor vigorously defends the Mosaic authorship of the Torah and rejects the higher biblical criticism of Julius Wellhausen and his school. This was the *Humash* of choice in many Orthodox and most Conservative congregations for over half a century, until the publication of the Stone (ArtScroll, Orthodox) and *Etz Hayim* (Conservative) *Humashim.*

The Soncino Chumash, ed. A. Cohen, Soncino Books of the Bible (Hindhead, UK: Soncino Press, 1947).

Unlike the rest of the commentaries in the *Soncino Books of the Bible* series (see above), this Torah commentary is anthologized from the classical medieval Jewish commentaries.

The Living Torah: The Five Books of Moses and the Haftarot, a new translation based on traditional Jewish sources, with notes, introduction, maps, tables, charts, bibliography, and index by Aryeh Kaplan (New York: Maznaim, 1981).

The translation is rooted in Jewish sources and follows the traditions of interpretation found in Rabbinic literature. This is especially important in the description of the construction of the Tabernacle and the legal sections in Leviticus. It also avoids archaic or obsolete language to convey the message that the Torah is a living document. Idiomatic language is translated idiomatically. The notes, which are substantial enough to constitute a brief commentary, cite many traditional commentaries and other sources.

The Chumash: The Torah, Haftaros, and Five Megillos, Stone Edition, ed. Nosson Scherman (Brooklyn: Mesorah Publications, 1993).

This edition, published by ArtScroll, has largely replaced the Hertz and the Soncino in Orthodox synagogues in North America. The commentary anthologizes comments from Rabbinic literature, the classical commentaries, and recent generations of *haredi* (piously Orthodox) Torah scholars.

The Gutnick Edition Chumash with Rashi's Commentary, Targum Onkelos, Haftaros and Commentary Anthologized from Classic Rabbinic Texts and the Works of the Lubavitcher Rebbe, comp. Chaim Miller (Brooklyn: Kol Menachem, 2006).

This new edition of the *Humash* for synagogue use, published by the Lubavitch Hasidic movement, includes a new translation based on Rashi's commentary and an anthologized commentary with a distinct Hasidic flavor, featuring the *sichos* (instructional talks) of the Lubavitcher Rebbe. An interesting feature is the column "Classic question," which highlights a problem in the text and offers a number of interpretations from Rabbinic literature and classical commentaries.

Conservative

Etz Hayim: Torah and Commentary, ed. David L. Lieber (New York: Rabbinical Assembly and United Synagogue of Conservative Judaism, 2001).

This volume includes commentary that is based on the JPS Torah and Bible Commentary series, as well as homiletical insights and halakhic instructions, supplemented by 166 pages of essays on biblical topics written by Conservative Bible scholars, a glossary, maps, and a few illustrations.

Reform

The Torah: A Modern Commentary, ed. W. Gunther Plaut (New York: UAHC, 1983).

This very popular one-volume edition of the Torah uses the NJPS translation, with supplementary material, incorporating the findings of biblical scholarship and archaeology into the late 1970s. The original volume, whose text reads from left to right, was intended for adult education classes; a later edition (blue binding), has the text arranged from right to left, for easier use during synagogue services.

The Torah: A Modern Commentary, rev. ed., ed. David E. S. Stein (New York: URJ Press, 2005).

This revision was begun by Gunther Plaut and Chaim Stern in the late 1990s and completed by Stein. It features a new translation by Stern of Genesis and the *haftarot* and a gender-sensitive adaptation of the JPS translation for the rest of the Torah that more accurately reflects the role of women in biblical society, as well as an updated commentary that incorporates recent scholarship and is cognizant of changing social perspectives regarding homosexuality, intermarriage, and divorce.

OTHER TORAH TRANSLATIONS AND COMMENTARIES

The Five Books of Moses: Genesis, Exodus, Leviticus, Numbers, Deuteronomy; A New Translation with Introductions, Commentary, and Notes, trans. Everett Fox (New York: Schocken, 1995).

A translation based on the methods of Martin Buber and Franz Rosenzweig, which attempts to reflect the original as closely as possible and be sensitive to the sounds of the Hebrew text. The translation pays particular attention to instances of wordplay, puns, word repetition, alliteration, and other literary devices of sound and tries to reproduce them in English. The commentary focuses on the "wholeness" of the biblical texts and strives to point out unities, connections, and thematic development. This work does not include the Hebrew text.

The Five Books of Miriam: A Woman's Commentary on the Torah, by Ellen Frankel (New York: Putnam, 1996).

Something of a cross between midrash, meditation, and performance, this book presents a series of conversations on the weekly Torah readings between a variety of characters, mostly biblical women, but also "our daughters," "our mothers," "our bubbes," "the rabbis," "the sages in our own time," "Lilith the rebel," and "Beruriah the scholar." Unlike conventional commentaries, this one does not follow the text verse by verse, but focuses on several topics in each parashah, always from a woman's perspective. This volume does not contain the biblical text, either in the original Hebrew or in translation.

Commentary on the Torah, by Richard Elliott Friedman (New York: HarperCollins, 2003).

Friedman, a well-known Bible scholar (University of Georgia, Athens), has written a commentary in the classical style, presenting an integrated understanding of the biblical text, seeking to elucidate problems that have never been solved and pointing out new problems that have never before been addressed. Friedman wishes to continue the work of the classical commentaries, while adding to them the insights of recent biblical scholarship: archaeology, Semitic philology, ancient Near Eastern history and culture, textual criticism, and ancient versions. Furthermore, like the classical commentators, he tries to show the essential unity of the Torah and to demonstrate its relevance to life. He deals with the usual textual, literary, and historical matters but also with moral issues raised by the text. The book includes the Hebrew text as well as a new English translation, which tries to remain as faithful as possible to the Hebrew text.

The Five Books of Moses, trans. Robert Alter (New York: Norton, 2004).

This is a new translation and commentary by a prominent Berkeley professor of comparative literature and scholar of the Bible as literature. Its fine translation and insightful commentary are based on modern biblical scholarship and the author's deep familiarity with the style and language of the biblical text. Though not ideologically opposed to the idea of multiple authorship of the Torah, Alter is more interested in the Torah as a finished, unified literary product. This work does not include the Hebrew text.

The Contemporary Torah: A Gender-Sensitive Adaptation of the JPS Translation, ed. David E. S. Stein; consulting eds. Adele Berlin, Ellen Frankel, and Carol L. Meyers (Philadelphia: Jewish Publication Society, 2006).

This translation by the editor of the new Reform Torah commentary differs somewhat from the latter, but is based on the same principles. It attempts to assess how ancient Israelites would have understood the gendered language of the biblical texts.

The Torah: A Women's Commentary, ed. Tamara Cohn Eskenazi and Andrea Weiss (New York: URJ Press, 2007).

This volume, published by the Reform movement and written entirely by Jewish women—Bible scholars, rabbis, historians, philosophers, and archaeologists—eighty contributors in all—includes the Hebrew text, an English translation, and an innovative, eclectic commentary. Each Torah portion, or parashah, is preceded by an overview, followed by the Hebrew text and a linear translation, along with a central commentary by a biblical scholar, which draws on modern biblical scholarship and other scholarly disciplines, while highlighting issues pertaining to women. The central commentary on each section is followed by a short counter-commentary offering a different viewpoint. A third contributor offers a post-biblical interpretation, focusing on how Rabbinic literature and traditional Torah commentaries addressed issues pertaining to women. "Contemporary reflections" introduce philosophical, theological, and other approaches relevant to the Bible and Jewish life today; and "creative voices" offer imaginative responses to the text in the form of poems, modern midrash, and other artistic expressions.

Case Studies: Comparing Commentators

Let us now look at a few examples of difficult biblical texts and see how commentators through the ages have dealt with them. Some of these verses have been called cruxes—verses that defy interpretation and have never been satisfactorily explained—others invite a variety of interpretations, none definitive.

GARDEN OF EDEN—A REAL EYE-OPENER

One of the high points of the Garden of Eden story is reached when the serpent succeeds in convincing the woman to partake of the fruit of the tree of knowledge of good and evil.

> When the woman saw that the tree was good for eating and a delight to the eyes, and that the tree was desirable as a source of wisdom, she took of its fruit and ate. She also gave some to her husband, and he ate (Gen. 3:6).

The problematic phrase here is "the tree was desirable as a source of wisdom" (*nechmad ha-etz le-haskil*). The phrase "as a source of wisdom" is *le-haskil* in Hebrew. This word is ambiguous and could have any of several meanings.

Saadiah derives the word from *sekhel* and *haskalah*, meaning "knowledge" and "learning," which basically agrees with the translation cited here.

Rashi comments: "As he [the serpent] had said to her, '(and you will be like divine beings) *knowing* good and evil,'" thus connecting this phrase to the previous verse. Eve was completely taken in by the serpent and believed his words, that eating of the fruit would lead to *knowledge* of good and evil.

Ramban comments: "For with it, one will know [*yaskil*] how to desire [*lachamod*]; lust was ascribed to the eyes and desire to the mind." Ramban thus connects the two parts of the verse "delight to the eyes" and "desirable as a source of wisdom," marking the moment of the awakening of passion and desire in the human psyche.

Robert Alter translates the phrase as "the tree was lovely to look at," pointing to the *Targums* (Aramaic translations of the Bible), which translate *le-haskil* as "to look at." The attraction of this interpretation is that it creates a parallel between *ta'avah*, "lust," and *nechmad* (from the root *chamad*, "to desire") and *la-einayim*, "for the eyes," and *le-haskil*, "to look at."

Another possibility, not mentioned by other commentators is that *le-haskil* means "to achieve success," as it does in several other verses (for example, 1 Sam. 18:14). Thus, the phrase could mean "that the tree was desirable as a means for attaining success." For this verse, there are many possibilities of interpretation, none of which is clearly the correct one.

In the next verse, after Adam and Eve have partaken of the forbidden fruit, we read in the NJPS translation:

> Then the eyes of both of them were opened and they perceived that they were naked; and they sewed together fig leaves and made themselves loincloths (Gen. 3:7).

Here the question is, What happened to Adam and Eve after they ate the fruit? What transformation is described by the phrase "the eyes of both of them were opened"?

Rashi comments: "Scripture speaks about wisdom rather than actual sight. The end of the verse proves this point: 'and they *knew* that they were naked.' Even the blind man knows that he is naked. But what does it mean by 'they knew that they were naked'? They had one commandment to fulfill—not to eat the fruit of the tree—and they were stripped of it."

Rashi, who here, as is often the case, has taken his material from the midrash (*Bereshit Rabbah* 19:6), wishes to teach a moral lesson: The couple attained a certain knowledge and understanding from eating the fruit. The knowledge of their nakedness is not of their physical nakedness but of their lack of commandments to fulfill, since they had violated the only one they had. They were thus spiritually and morally naked and impoverished. For Rashi, the opening of the eyes leads to the attainment of knowledge, which instills in them a sense of guilt.

Radak has a different take: "'Then the eyes of both of them were opened.' The eyes of their heart. That is why it says 'and they knew' and not 'and they saw,' for what they saw now was what they saw then. Rather, after they ate from the fruit of the tree, the lust for sexual intercourse was born within them and the sex organ became hard out of lust. This was an embarrassment to them, that they had lost control of a bodily organ. This is a case of tit for tat since they had abandoned the authority and command of God."

The point here is the meting out of divine punishment for their action in a way that is appropriate to the act. Just as they had violated God's command and defied divine authority, so that God was not in control of them, so would they lose control of a bodily organ, which would take on a life of its own under certain circumstances and cause them embarrassment. For Radak, the opening of the eyes signifies the awakening of sexual desire.

S. R. Hirsch points to the shame that the couple now felt at their nakedness: "As long as Man stands completely in the service of his God, he has not to be ashamed of any part of his body. Even the bodily lures and attractions are pure and godly as long as they submit themselves as means for God's holy purposes.

But when this condition is not entirely there we certainly should be ashamed of displaying them" (*The Pentateuch*, trans. Levy, p. 77). Thus the knowledge that the couple gained is associated with the shame they felt for their nakedness, as a result of their rebellion, a feeling they had not experienced before.

These are only three of an array of interpretations given to this verse. They all have merit and bear witness to the richness and suggestiveness of the text.

THE *AKEDAH* STORY—THE RAM THAT DIDN'T GET AWAY

> And Abraham raised his eyes and saw, and look, a ram was caught in the thicket by its horns (Alter, Gen. 22:13).

At issue here is the phrase "a ram." The masoretic text reads *ayil achar*, literally "a ram, after." Alter's translation reflects the reading in many ancient versions, which read *echad* (one, or the indefinite article "a") for *achar*, replacing the *resh* of *achar* with a *dalet*, which resembles it very closely. But one could challenge this reading by pointing out that *echad* is really superfluous and the verse would read just as well without it. One could also argue that the more difficult reading could be the authentic one, since the natural tendency would be to correct a difficult word to one that is more understandable. Yet there is no question that for those commentators who wish to preserve the reading in the masoretic text, this verse is challenging.

143

Rashi attempts to resolve the problem: "*Achar*. After the angel said to him: 'Do not reach out your hand against the lad,'" he saw it as it was caught, as it says in the *Targum*: 'And Abraham raised his eyes after these things.'" According to Rashi's reading, which is influenced by the midrash, *achar* refers to events that had just happened. The problem with this is the location of *achar*. If this interpretation were correct, *achar* should really begin the verse, which preferably should read, *achar ha-devarim ha-eleh* (after these things) or, even better, *acharei khen* (afterward) (cf. Gen. 25:26).

Ibn Ezra reads the phrase as follows: "after it was caught in the thicket by its horns." According to this reading, the verse should be read with the Hebrew particle *asher* understood before *ne'echaz* (caught). Abraham saw the ram only after it had been caught in the thicket by its horns (*ve-hinneh ayil achar asher ne'echaz ba-sevakh be-karnav*). (Ibn Ezra uses the prefix *she-*, for *asher*, but *she-* appears only in late biblical Hebrew.)

Rashbam has a slightly different take: "*And saw, and look! a ram passed in front of him, after which it got caught by its horns in the thicket.* In other words, afterward [*achar*], he saw the ram while it was passing by get caught in the thicket of the forest. He thought to himself: Certainly this angel must have come to fulfill

God's mission and God prepared this ram for me instead of my son; therefore it got caught in the thicket so that I could take it." He then gives some biblical verses to prove his point that *achar* means "afterward." Netziv (N. Berlin) in *Ha'mek Davar* elaborates on Rashbam. He says that if the ram were already caught in the thicket, Abraham might have thought it belonged to someone who had left it there. If it were running wild, he would have had difficulty catching it. But, in this case, when he watched it first running loose, then getting caught, he sensed that there was providence at work here and that this ram was meant for him.

The reading by Rashbam and Netziv is a valiant attempt to make sense of this difficult passage. It dramatizes the action and tries to explain why Abraham was convinced to sacrifice the ram instead of Isaac. Still this interpretation is not without its own linguistic and grammatical issues. This verse remains a difficult crux.

THE JOSEPH STORY—HOW DEEP IS MY VALLEY?

> He sent him [Jacob sent Joseph] from the valley of Hebron (to find his brothers) [*me-emek Hevron*] (Gen. 37:14).

Many commentators have remarked on the peculiarity of this verse, since it is well known that Hebron is in the mountains. Robert Alter comments simply, "The validity of this designation can be defended only through ingenious explanation because Hebron stands on a height." Nahum Sarna suggests that the text may be referring to the location of the Cave of the Machpelah in a field outside the city. But this hardly sounds like a valley.

Rashi, following the Talmud and midrash, states:

> But Hebron is on a mountain, as it is stated (Num. 13:22): "and they went up into the south and reached Hebron." However, (the valley of Hebron alludes to) the profound counsel [*etzah amuqah*] of that righteous one (Abraham) who is buried in Hebron, to fulfill that which was told to Abraham at the covenant between the pieces "for your seed will be a sojourner in a land not theirs" (Gen. 15:13).

Nechama Leibowitz comments on Rashi's statement:

> Since Hebron was in the mountain and not the valley, the apparently superfluous insertion *emek* is taken, figuratively, to imply "deep," in the sense of "mysterious." Hebron is taken as a figurative expression for the patriarch Abraham who was buried there. Thus we have an allusion to the "mysterious advice" imparted to Abraham regarding the future of his descendants, that they would sojourn in a land not their own. It was this prophecy that Jacob and Joseph were fulfilling unwittingly; the father—in sending, and the son—in going to seek his brothers.

Rashi does not simply see here a geographic designation, the place of Joseph's departure on his way, but a causal designation. The One, who is the cause of all causes and the leader of all travelers, takes Joseph out of his house according to that "profound counsel"—according to that profound plan which he planned and imparted to Abraham and whose meaning is unfathomable (*Studies in Bereshit*, p. 395; second paragraph translation revised by author).

This is a case of a verse for which there is probably no satisfactory *peshat* explanation. In such cases, traditional commentators look for deeper meanings that bring us into other realms, be they theological or mystical in nature.

JACOB'S BLESSING—WHOSE *SHECHEM* IS IT ANYWAY?

As Jacob is approaching death in Egypt, he calls Joseph to his side to give him his final blessing.

> Then Israel said to Joseph, "I am about to die; but God will be with you and bring you back to the land of your fathers. And now I assign to you one portion [*Shechem achad*] more than to your brothers [*al achekha*], which I wrested from the Amorites with my sword and bow" (NJPS Gen. 48:21–22).

This passage raises several questions that have never been satisfactorily explained:

> What is the meaning of *shechem achad*?
> What is the meaning of *al achekha*?
> What exactly did Jacob do to the Amorites? When did he fight them with sword and bow?

The following are some attempts to explain this difficult verse. (It should be noted that there are no capital letters in Hebrew, so proper names cannot be visually distinguished from regular nouns.)

Rashi and many other traditional commentators understand the word *shechem* mentioned here as the actual city of Shechem (near present-day Nablus, in the West Bank), which ended up in the territory of Ephraim, son of Joseph, after the conquest.

In Rashi's words:

> *And now I assign to you.* Since you are going to the trouble of attending to my burial, I have also assigned a place for your burial. Which is it? Shechem, as it is written: "And the bones of Joseph which they had

brought up from Egypt they buried in Shechem (Josh. 24:32). "One portion" (*shechem achad*) "more than to your brothers" (*al achekha*). Shechem itself shall be for you an additional portion over that of your brothers. *With my sword and bow.* When Simeon and Levi killed the inhabitants of Shechem, all the surrounding neighbors gathered together to oppose them and Jacob took up weapons against them.

Rashi's comments serve to edify, in that they praise the virtue of attending to the burial of the deceased. The connection with the city of Shechem resonates because of the later association of that city with the tribe of Ephraim.

But there are problems with this interpretation. The phrase *shechem achad* can hardly refer to the city Shechem. Why modify it with the adjective *achad*, "one Shechem"? This makes little sense. Also the feminine form *achat* rather than the masculine form of the adjective is called for since cities are grammatically feminine in Hebrew. Furthermore, there is no evidence in the biblical story itself that Jacob took up arms.

Rashi himself must have felt discomfort with this line of interpretation, since he offers an alternative:

> Another interpretation: *shechem achad.* This is the birthright, that his sons will get two portions. And *shechem* has the connotation of "portion," and this has many parallels in the biblical text [Rashi cites Ps. 21:13, Ps. 60:8, Hosea 6:9, and Zeph. 3:9; in none of these verses does *shechem* clearly mean "portion"]. *Which I wrested from the Amorites.* From the hand of Esau who committed an Amorite-like deed. Another possibility: He used to stalk his father with the utterances of his mouth [*imrei fiv*, a play on words, *imrei* being reminiscent of Emori]. *With my sword and bow.* This is his wisdom and his prayer.

This line of interpretation follows the midrash fairly closely. The meaning "portion" for *shechem* seems to be derived from the context. None of the supporting verses Rashi brings clearly supports this derivation. Esau was the progenitor of the Edomites. The association of Esau with the Amorites is midrashic and has no textual support. Least of all is there support for the accusation of Esau stalking Isaac with words, which is purely homiletic and intentionally polemical. Finally, the association of Jacob's sword and bow with wisdom and prayer is possibly a reflection of Rabbinic pacifism and an acknowledgment that there is no evidence that Jacob fought anyone with sword and bow. This second interpretation of Rashi is also quite weak.

Ramban associates *shechem achad* with the birthright, explaining that Jacob was prophesying that Joseph's children would inherit two portions of territory; in other words, Joseph inherited the family birthright. The reference to the Amorites is related to the conquest of the land after the Egyptian exile, which began with the Amorites on the east side of the Jordan. This land fell to the tribe of Manasseh. Ephraim also captured land that belonged to the Amorites (Judg. 1:35). "With my sword and my bow" refers to the necessity to capture the land by force. The ability to capture was due to the merit of the forefathers, including Jacob. Ramban also suggests that Jacob alluded to the eventual capture of the land from the Amorites by performing some symbolic act with his weapons, although this is not mentioned in the text. Ramban's interpretation has the advantage that it avoids the awkwardness of referring to the city Shechem with the masculine adjective. It also transfers the events to the future and makes Jacob's words into a prophetic statement applying to the time of the conquest of the land. Nonetheless, it still does not adequately explain the term *shechem achad.*

Robert Alter offers a new reading of this verse. He translates *shechem achad* as "with single intent" and the verse: "As for me, I have given you with single intent over your brothers what I took from the hand of the Emorite (*sic*) with my sword and with my bow." Alter explains:

> The phrase represented here by "with single intent" is a notorious crux, but previous interpreters may have been misled by assuming that it must be the object of the verb "have given." ... But the very phrase used here, *shechem 'ehad,* occurs at one other place in the Bible, Zephaniah 3:9, where it is used *adverbially* in an idiomatic sense made clear by the immediate context: "for all of them to invoke the name of the LORD, / to serve Him *shechem 'ehad* (King James Version, with one consent; Revised English Bible and New Jewish Publication Society Bible, with one accord)." This, then, is an expression that indicates concerted, unswerving intention and execution, and as such is perfectly appropriate to the legal pronouncement of legacy by Jacob in which it appears. Once the phrase is seen as adverbial, the relative clause, "what I took ..." falls into place with grammatical preciseness as the object of the verb "have given," and in this reading, no particular city or region need be specified (*The Five Books of Moses,* trans. Robert Alter, p. 281).

Alter's solution to the *shechem achad* crux has merit, but his translation of the verse still leaves unanswered the question of what it was that Jacob took with sword and bow. The translation "over your brothers" may be overly literal. I would therefore suggest that: *al achekha* could mean "along with" or "in addition to your brothers" (*al* has this connotation in biblical Hebrew; compare with Gen. 28:9, *al nashav,* "in addition to his wives"). This would then signify Jacob's inclusion of Joseph and his sons in the family inheritance, thus formally welcoming him back into the fold. Furthermore, if we follow Ramban's view that this is a prophetic statement and that Jacob is referring here to future conquests, he is then promising Joseph and his sons a fair share in the family inheritance when they return to the land of Canaan and do battle with the Amorites.

The verse might then be translated: "As for me, I promise with single intent to give you, along with your brothers, that which I shall take from the hand of the Amorite with my sword and with my bow."

This example illustrates how interpreters can build on the insights of their predecessors to gain new insights into difficult texts.

"DO NOT GO NEAR A WOMAN"—A FOCUS FOR FEMINISTS

One final example illustrates how certain verses can become controversial due to changing social and cultural circumstances. When the Israelite nation is standing at the foot of Mount Sinai in anticipation of hearing God's words in an awe-inspiring revelatory moment, Moses instructs the people as follows:

> And he [Moses] said to the people, "Be ready for the third day: do not go near a woman" (Exod. 19:15).

At first blush this would seem to be an exclusionary statement, the word "people" apparently including only the men. Does this mean that the women were not meant to be included in the Revelation, or is the intent less sinister?

This verse received very little attention from the classical commentators. Only Rashi addresses the issue, stating on the basis of the Mishnah that this restriction was intended to ensure that the women would be in a state of purity to receive the Torah. Thus the Mishnah, followed by Rashi, offers a way of reading the verse that is inclusive of women in the Revelation event. Nevertheless, the language is exclusionary, and this point is addressed by two of our modern commentaries.

Richard Elliott Friedman states:

> If he is speaking to "the people," which includes both men and women, why does he say, "Don't come close to a woman"? Like many passages, this may have two opposite interpretations. It may be a case of male chauvinism in language, in which an address to the people means the men. Or it may reflect a perception that a command to abstain from sex for three days needs to be particularly directed to men because men are more likely than women to violate the instruction (*Commentary on the Torah*, Friedman, p. 233).

The new Reform commentary adjusts the translation to read: "(the men among) you should not go near a woman" (*The Torah: A Modern Commentary*, p. 475). Further clarification is given in the comment on 20:14, the last commandment of the Decalogue, which again is addressed to men: "The Decalogue is inclusive of women except when the subject is sexuality. In the ancient Near East, sexual mores for men and women were not symmetric" (*The Torah: A Modern Commentary*, p. 480).

Feminist Responses to Moses's Warning

"There can be no verse in the Torah more disturbing to the feminist than Moses's warning to his people in Exodus 19:15," says Judith Plaskow in her book *Standing at Sinai: Judaism from a Feminist Perspective.* "For here," she explains, "at the very moment that the Jewish people stands at Sinai, ready to receive the covenant … Moses addresses the community only of men." Indeed, her book takes its title from this verse, and it has become the *locus classicus* for Jewish feminism; there are essays, poems, and passages in feminist literature that quote this verse as an example of the exclusion of women from tradition.

Feminist scholar Ellen Frankel comments on this passage in her *Five Books of Miriam,* in which she envisions how Jewish women and their biblical foremothers might have responded:

> Before unveiling the Ten Commandments at Mount Sinai, God instructs Moses to tell the people to prepare themselves by entering into a state of purity for three days. But when Moses relays God's instructions to the people, he embellishes them, adding his own warning: "Do not go near a woman." What's he up to—and why does God let him get away with it?

> Huldah the Preacher answers: Throughout the four books of the Bible in which Moses is the main character—Exodus through Deuteronomy— God constantly instructs him to convey messages to the people. And as with any game of telephone, sometimes something gets lost or garbled in the translation.

> Wily Rebecca disagrees: No, in conveying God's message to the people, Moses deliberately changes the audience addressed. God's original instructions—"Be ready for the third day"—include all the people; Moses, however, addresses himself only to men: "Do not go near a woman." In commanding the people to purify themselves for three days, God is asking them to mark a distinction between the profane realm of the everyday and the sacred realm of Revelation. Moses, however, redivides the two realms differently: for him, the profane realm includes all the people; the sacred only men. To enter the latter realm, as Moses sees it, requires isolation from women.

> Lilith the Rebel concurs: In giving Moses these instructions, God entrusts him with a sacred task: to safeguard the people from death, which threatens them if they come too close to holiness or approach it improperly prepared. But Moses violates this trust by adding his own interpretation: "Do not go near a woman." And it's not the only time he does this. in fact, this habit of literary license ultimately costs him his passport to the Promised Land.

Friedman's first comment is probably closer to the mark. In ancient societies, the language often tended to be male-centered and exclusionary. His second comment is more apologetic in tone. The new Reform commentary reminds us that the biblical text needs to be understood in its broader social-historical context.

Each Commentary Offers New Insights

The commentaries discussed earlier in this chapter, which for the most part (except for the Israeli publications and a few of the classical commentaries, such as those of Ralbag, Abarbanel, and Berlin), are available in English translation, and can be grouped into four major categories: (1) the classical medievals, (2) the scientific modernists, (3) the traditional modernists, and (4) the modern traditionalists.

The classical medievals come from different backgrounds and have varying approaches to the text. All are firmly grounded in the rabbinic tradition, but many refer to it only on occasion, preferring to adhere to the *peshat* reading. They resort to external sources to varying degrees. All have gained acceptance in the canon of Jewish biblical interpretation.

> **Women's Contributions to Biblical Scholarship**
> The proliferation of Jewish women's writing on the Bible, in its very diversity, is a force for liberation and transformation. It exemplifies women's access to education and to the institutions of higher education and publication, and it allows women's views to stand alongside those of male scholars in shaping the field of biblical studies. Whether they do or do not view the Bible as a positive force in women's lives, they themselves, as women writers on the Bible, model the possibilities for Jewish women to become engaged and make strong contributions in the form of works that will be read and have influence on other scholars and in the broader community.
>
> From Adele Reinhartz, "Jewish Women's Scholarly Writings on the Bible," *The Jewish Study Bible.*

The scientific modernists are comfortable in the world of contemporary biblical scholarship and are active participants in its discourse, but they tend to avoid its nihilistic excesses, such as recent trends questioning the historical veracity of the Davidic monarchy or dating the entire biblical corpus to the Hellenistic period. Many are faculty members at Israeli or North American universities.

The traditional modernists are open to and use the findings of modern biblical scholarship and archaeology as long as these don't challenge the integrity of the biblical text and traditional attributions of authorship. Source criticism is, for the most part, rejected, but literary analysis is warmly embraced. Proponents of this approach include Shadal (S. D. Luzzatto), Nechama Leibowitz, the authors of the *Da'at Miqra* series, and many faculty members of Bar-Ilan and Yeshiva Universities.

The modern traditionalists are exemplified by the commentators of the ArtScroll *Chumash* and *Tanach* series. These commentators, for the most part, ignore modern biblical scholarship and base their commentaries on a restricted number of approved sources with impeccable religious credentials, such as the classical commentators and luminaries of the yeshivah world.

Awareness of these trends can help one make an informed decision about which commentaries to purchase or consult. The classical medieval and modern traditional commentaries can teach us how to read the text more closely, raise our sensitivity to every detail and nuance in the text, and heighten our awareness of the relationship between small details and the big picture. Modern commentaries such as Friedman's, Alter's, and the more scholarly ones such as *Miqra le-Yisra'el* and the JPS Commentary series are needed to incorporate "the new interpretations being revealed every day," based on new discoveries in archaeology and Semitic philology and the literary, theological, and personal insights of a new generation of scholars and readers.

The Bible is a text that is endlessly open to interpretation. Each comment in every commentary is a link in the great chain of interpretation that joins the generations and ultimately leads back to biblical times. Each of us brings to the Bible his or her own knowledge, understanding, and sensibilities and can provide new insights not seen by previous readers. The process of interpretation is ongoing and unending, keeping the Bible fresh, alive, and full of meaning, commentator after commentator, reader after reader, generation after generation.

Barry Dov Walfish.

MIDRASH

In the book of Genesis, when the twins Jacob and Esau are fighting in her womb, Rebekah goes to ask God for some answers. The verb used for her quest is *lidrosh*, meaning "to seek, to inquire, to search out." This same verb becomes the basis for the word "midrash." Midrash is a unique process of Jewish interpretation that includes both explanation of the Torah and creative legends or ideas that give new meaning to the Torah. Midrash tells what biblical texts say, notices what the texts do not say, and then adds to them. Through midrash, each word in the Bible can become a jumping-off point for a new story. Midrash allows Jewish tradition to keep on growing.

Midrash has been going on for thousands of years. The process of midrash developed, in part, because the Bible often uses few words to tell a story or explain a law. What did the serpent in the Garden of Eden look like? What was the name of Noah's wife? What was Abraham like as a child? How did Jacob feel when he wrestled the angel? Why were the Israelites commanded not to light a fire on the Sabbath? How are we to honor our parents? The Torah does not answer these questions, yet people who take the Torah seriously want answers. So we need a way of reading sacred text that allows them to provide answers where there are none.

How does midrash work? Imagine a page with words written on it in black ink. The words are fixed and holy; they cannot change. Yet around the words are white spaces. In these white spaces, you can write your own thoughts and explanations. The words you scribble are inspired by the original words written in ink. Yet the words you write also reflect your own beliefs and feelings. They even may turn into creative stories based on what you have already read. Your "additions" are interpretations, yet they are also completely new. They do not change the holy text, but if someone reads the text with your ideas next to it, the text will take on new meaning.

This "white margin" way of interpreting the Torah and the Bible began in the Bible itself, but the Rabbis of the Talmud perfected the process we call midrash. The sages commented on every aspect of the Torah, assuming that every single word had secrets and stories in it. They believed each new generation of readers could find more of those secrets and stories. The Rabbis of the Talmud wanted to understand the words of the Bible as well as possible, but their interpretations changed as they themselves grew and changed. The Rabbis created midrash, interpretation, by asking questions of the biblical text, and then answering the questions they asked through parables and stories. By creating midrash, the sages and others produced the laws, ethics, and legends of the Jewish people. Later generations studied these midrashim and added their own ideas.

We know many of the midrashim that ancient Jews wrote or told because they appear in the Talmud and in other written collections from the time of the Talmud and later (300–1000 C.E.). Midrash from this period is called "classical midrash." Yet the process of midrash is so compelling to Jews that they have gone on making midrash in every generation, right up to today. In *Pirkei Avot,* a collection of wise sayings of the sages, it is written: "Turn the Torah and turn it again, for everything is in it." This means that when someone reads the Torah and has a new question, he or she can find an answer, or invent one, through midrash.

How Midrash Works

Let's look at three examples of the way classical midrash asks questions and then offers creative answers.

Example 1

The first example is a comment on Genesis 22:19, a verse at the very end of the story in which Abraham nearly offers his son Isaac as a sacrifice to God, but an angel intervenes at the last moment. The verse reads:

> Abraham then returned to his servants, and they departed together for Beer-sheba; and Abraham stayed in Beer-sheba.

Bereshit Rabbah, a collection of the sages' midrash from the time of the Talmud, comments on this text by saying:

> Where did Isaac go? He went to Shem to study Torah from him.

This midrash asks the question, what happened to Isaac? Isaac was at the mountain and was nearly sacrificed, yet the Torah speaks about how Abraham and the servants go home, but does not mention Isaac. The midrash now must fill in the answer to that question. This midrash imagines that Isaac goes to one of his relatives, Shem, to study Torah.

What's interesting about this answer is that, of course, in the days of Abraham and Isaac there is no Torah to study; the giving of the Torah isn't going to happen for hundreds of years. Why did the Rabbis of the Talmud offer such a strange answer?

First, they themselves were Torah scholars and saw the study of Torah as fundamental to being Jewish, so naturally they imagined Abraham and Isaac, the first Jews, as Torah scholars. They used their midrash to personally identify with the characters in the Bible.

Second, they wanted other Jews who read this midrash to care about Torah study, so they used Abraham and Isaac as role models for learning. They used their midrash to teach a moral lesson.

And third, the Rabbis of the Talmud imagined Torah not just as a document, but as a process. For them, it didn't matter that the written Torah was not given yet in the time of Isaac, just as it didn't matter to them that they themselves were living long after the Torah was given. The Rabbis used their midrash to show that the process of study and interpretation can happen in any generation. That process itself is Torah, no matter when it happens.

(Note that there can be more than one answer to a midrashic question. A different sage answers this same question about where Isaac is by saying that he went to visit his brother, Ishmael!)

Example 2

In the Babylonian Talmud (*Megillah* 10b), the Rabbis are interpreting chapter 15 of the book of Exodus, known as the Song at the Sea. In this passage, the Israelites have just passed through the Sea of Reeds and escaped from Egypt, and they sing a song to celebrate. Meanwhile, the Egyptian warriors who chased them are drowning in the sea.

Exodus 15 begins:

> Then Moses and the Israelites sang this song to the Lord.

The Talmud comments:

> The angels of the heavenly court wanted to sing, but the Holy One said:
> My creatures are drowning in the sea and you want to sing songs?

In midrash, each word in the Torah is important. This midrash is an interpretation of the words "Moses and the Israelites sang." Moses and the Israelites sing, this midrash suggests, but the angels do not sing, because God commands them not to sing. God is sad about the death of the Egyptians, even though they enslaved the Israelites, and so God asks the angels to keep quiet.

This example shows another function of midrash: to express discomfort with the biblical text when it seems not to fit with contemporary values. In the biblical text, the Israelites are cheering while their enemies drown. The sages of the Talmud were uncomfortable with this rejoicing in the face of death. They used this midrash to imagine that God too was uncomfortable with the idea of singing as someone else drowns in the sea.

Example 3

Midrash is used to create traditions, customs, and laws. The Jews of the talmudic period also used midrash to create or clarify Jewish law on a particular subject. For example, the laws of the Sabbath are not spelled out in the Torah. Only a few general verses tell us about biblical Sabbath practices. Later Jewish scholars had to find a way to figure out what activities should be allowed, or forbidden, on the Sabbath. They used midrash to create their vision of the Sabbath.

For example, Leviticus 19:30 reads:

> You shall keep My sabbaths and venerate My sanctuary: I am the Lord.

The Babylonian Talmud (*Yevamot* 6a) asks:

> Is it possible that the building of the sanctuary should be done on Shabbat?… Rather, the Torah says: "You shall keep my Sabbaths and venerate my sanctuary; I am the Lord."

Talmudic Rabbis imagined that because keeping the Sabbath was mentioned in the same verse with honoring the sanctuary, all activities done to build the sanctuary (weaving, dyeing, cutting wood, and so on) were forbidden on the Sabbath. This midrash helped them develop clear ideas about how the Sabbath should be celebrated. Many long passages in the Talmud are based on this one midrash.

In each of these examples, a question is asked of the sacred text, usually a question to which the answer is not obvious from the text itself. Then an answer, or more than one answer, is offered. Midrash combines careful inspection of the words of the Bible with reason and imagination to create a fuller, richer understanding of Torah.

Some Basic Midrashic Rules

The sages were well aware that the sentences of Torah had a literal meaning. The Rabbis called this *peshat*, or the plain meaning of the text. They recognized and honored this literal meaning, saying: "The plain meaning of a scriptural verse should never be ignored." At the same time, they added a more interpretive, fanciful, symbolic meaning, which they called *derash*. It was at this second level of interpretation that midrash happened.

The sages had great autonomy in making midrash, often proposing astonishing solutions to textual problems. For example, Genesis has two Creation stories, one (chapter 1) in which man and woman are created at the same time, and another (chapter 2) in which Adam is created first and Eve is created later. Rabbi Samuel bar Nachman explains this in the following way:

When the Holy One of Blessing created the first human being, it had two faces, and then God split it in two [so that it became a male creature and a female creature] (*Bereshit Rabbah* 8:1).

This midrash, by asking questions about the difference between the two stories, comes up with a solution we would not have expected: first there was one androgynous creature, and then two creatures, male and female. (This story is based on a Greek story by Plato. The Rabbis did sometimes borrow legends from other cultures.)

No creative idea was off-limits in making midrash. However, the sages did use some rules to help them interpret biblical stories. These rules allowed them to find answers to their questions even when the Bible did not offer any obvious clues.

RULE 1: LOOK AT WHAT IS NEARBY

One rule the Rabbis used is called *semikhut parshiyot*, or "the closeness of one section of Torah to another." If one tale in the Torah is unclear, another tale that appears before or after it is used to explain the first. For example, in Genesis 23, Sarah dies, but we are not told why or how she dies. How can the sages answer this question of how Sarah dies, with no information to go on?

Immediately before the story of Sarah's death, we are told of the binding and near-sacrifice of Isaac. One midrash from *Va-yikra Rabbah* concludes that Sarah dies because she hears about what nearly happened to Isaac. The shock is too much for her. This kind of midrash uses the rule of *semikhut parshiyot* to suggest that the Torah hints at why Sarah dies by putting the story of her death close to the story of her son's trauma.

RULE 2: JUST DESSERTS

Another rule the sages used is called *middah keneged middah*, or "measure for measure," and sometimes defined as "poetic justice." The Talmud assumes that events in the Torah about a person's life (good or bad) happen because that person has done something to deserve them.

For example, the Patriarch Jacob serves his uncle Laban for seven years in order to marry Laban's daughter Rachel. On his wedding night, Laban tricks Jacob and gives him Rachel's elder sister Leah as a bride. In the morning, as light dawns, Jacob realizes that he has been with Leah all night. Yet the Torah does not tell us what Jacob and Leah say to one another. *Bereshit Rabbah* imagines that Jacob says, "Deceiver and daughter of a deceiver! All night I called you Rachel and you answered me!" Leah responds, "Is there a teacher without students? Didn't your father call you Esau, and you answered him?" Leah is invoking the principle of *middah keneged middah*.

Another example is in Exodus 7:20, where Moses and Aaron tell Pharaoh that a plague of blood will come upon Egypt because Pharaoh has enslaved the Israelites. Yet only one person strikes the river: "he lifted up his rod and struck the water." Who does the striking? Is it Moses or Aaron?

A midrash in *Shemot Rabbah* says that it must have been Aaron who struck the Nile River to turn it into blood. Why? Because the Nile once saved Moses's life, when he was a baby floating in a basket. It is fitting (*middah keneged middah*) for Moses not to strike the Nile at the time of the Exodus, for the Nile did not strike Moses when he was an infant. And so this is an explanation for why Moses steps aside when the plague of blood begins.

RULE 3: SIGNS FOR THE FUTURE

Another idea the sages used often when making midrash is known as *ma'aseh avot siman le-vanim,* "the actions of the ancestors are a sign for the children." This means that actions that happen in the Bible can be a sign of events that will happen later in history. For example, take the beautiful scene in which a dove brings an olive branch to Noah to let him know that dry land has appeared and the Flood is over. *Midrash Tanhuma,* a 12th- to 14th-century commentary, says the following:

> The Holy One of Blessing said: Just as the dove brought light to the world, so you, who are compared to a dove in Scripture, brought olive oil and lighted a lamp before me.

The dove's taking of an olive branch signifies that the Jews will one day light a lamp filled with olive oil, a menorah, in the Temple.

The sages also used this principle when discussing the quarrel between Esau and Jacob. These two brothers, sons of Isaac and Rebekah, fight over their inheritance. Jacob has to run away from his home because of the conflict, but eventually wins the inheritance. Many midrashim see this conflict as a sign of later conflicts to come between Romans and Jews, and between Christians and Jews, and tell stories of Jacob's spiritual superiority to Esau, even though Esau is stronger.

Midrash can have a contemporary political meaning. In this kind of midrash, a story told about the Bible reflects how someone feels about a situation that is happening to them at the moment. The sages, oppressed by Roman or Christian authorities, used stories about Jacob and Esau to express their conviction that one day they would come out on top.

RULE 4: NAMES TELL THE STORY

When interpreting the Bible, the Rabbis also liked to use the meaning of people's names to add to the story. This principle is sometimes called *k'shmo kein hu,* "a person is like his name." For example, at the beginning of the book of

Exodus, two midwives named Shifrah and Puah save Israelite children from Pharaoh, they refuse to kill the children at Pharaoh's command. In a collection called *Shemot Rabbah*, the sages say that Shifrah is Yocheved, Moses's mother, and Puah is Miriam, Moses's sister:

> Yocheved is called Shifrah because she cleans up [*meshaperet*] the child when it is born... and Miriam is called Puah because she blows [*po'ah*] into the child's mouth when others say it has been born dead [and brings it to life again].

Here, we learn more about Yocheved and Miriam. They are not just members of an illustrious family, but expert and caring midwives. Midrashim like this one help give personality characteristics to biblical characters by using the meaning of names.

RULE 5: NO BEFORE OR AFTER IN THE TORAH

A basic rule of the midrash is that time does not matter in the Torah: *ain mukdam u'meuchar ba-Torah*, "there is no early or late in the Torah." For example, Genesis tells us that Abraham dies before Jacob and Esau are born. However, a midrash looks at the relative ages of Abraham, Jacob, and Esau and insists that Abraham lived many years while Jacob and Esau were alive. In fact, this midrash tells us that the meal of lentils that Jacob serves to Esau is actually a mourning meal for their grandfather Abraham. The midrash lends power to Jacob and Esau's confrontation by putting their conversation about lentil stew in an intense emotional context: their grandfather has just died.

In midrash, any two events in Torah can be related. The stone Jacob uses as a pillow can become the cornerstone of the Temple, and Jacob's wily uncle Laban can be the same person as the wily prophet Balaam, who appears hundreds of years later. The text of the Bible becomes fluid, able to move through time.

RULE 6: CONNECTING THE VERSES

The classical midrash is often written in a style where two verses in the Bible are linked to one another even if they appear to have nothing to do with one another. The rest of the midrash then tries to prove how those verses are linked. Leaps of logic, intuition, and imagination help connect the verses to one another. Here, too, every part of Torah can link to every other part.

For example, the collection known as *Midrash Tanhuma* begins by interpreting the very first verse in Torah: "In the beginning, God created the heavens and the earth." *Midrash Tanhuma* connects this verse to a different verse from the book of Proverbs: "God has founded the earth with wisdom." After linking these two verses, the midrash goes on to say that the "beginning" at the start of Genesis is really a code word for "wisdom," or Torah, and that the Holy One used Torah to create the world:

> The Holy One consulted with Torah and created the world.
> How was this Torah written? In black fire on white fire.

This extraordinary midrash imagines Torah, not as words in a book, but as a vast force of wisdom, present at the dawn of Creation. Torah helps build the world. The midrashist, by telling new legends about the Torah, is revealing new secrets of Creation.

Chain Midrash

Sometimes one midrash becomes so popular that it is repeated over and over again, from ancient through medieval, mystical, modern, and contemporary times. As this midrash becomes famous, more stories are told using that midrash. A single story becomes many linked stories, all using the same midrashic idea. This is sometimes called a chain midrash.

One chain midrash is the story of Serach, daughter of Asher. Serach, granddaughter of Jacob, is mentioned in only a few genealogies. There are no biblical stories about her. However, *Midrash ha-Gadol,* a 13th-century collection from Yemen, imagines a story about her. When Joseph's brothers come home from Egypt, they have discovered that their brother Joseph, whom they sold into slavery, is alive. They are afraid this news will shock their father, Jacob, who has grieved for Joseph for many years. So they ask young Serach to tell him. She waits until her grandfather is praying and sings the news to him. Jacob is so grateful to hear the news that he gives Serach a blessing that she will never die.

Because of this extraordinary blessing, Serach lives through the slavery in Egypt and is there when the children of Jacob promise to bring Joseph's bones with them from Egypt when they are freed. Hundreds of years later, it comes time for the Hebrews to leave, and Serach is the only one who knows where Joseph's bones are. *Midrash Tanhuma,* a 12th-century collection, says the following:

> How did Moses know where Joseph's grave was to be found? They say that only Serach daughter of Asher had survived from that generation, and that she revealed to Moses where Joseph's grave was located. The Egyptians had made a metal coffin for him and then sunk it into the Nile. Moses went to the bank of the Nile... and called out, "Joseph, Joseph, the time has come for the Holy One of Blessing to redeem his children. The Shekhinah and Israel and the clouds of glory await you. If you will reveal yourself, good, but if not, we shall be free of your vow." Whereupon Joseph's coffin floated to the surface.

Notice that Serach has now been used to answer two midrashic questions: how Jacob was told that Joseph was alive, and how Moses knew where to find the bones of Joseph. Midrashists often find it elegant to use the same solution for two or more problems in the Torah. Following this rule, interpreters were able to explain why, before the Exodus, the enslaved Hebrews believed that Moses had come to save them. Serach, the oldest member of the community, was able to identify Moses as a true redeemer, because she remembered that her father had told her what the redeemer would say when he arrived.

The existence of chain midrash shows how Jews read and told midrashic stories and then added to them. In fact, much of the midrashic tradition is not only commentary on the Torah but also commentary on other commentary. It is hard to trace the origin of any particular midrash because each legend or idea has been passed on through so many people and so many generations.

Medieval and Mystical Midrash

In a sense, Jewish history is one tremendous chain midrash. The role of midrash in interpreting Torah and in creating Judaism is so powerful that Jews have gone on doing midrash in every era of Jewish history. The time of classical midrash eventually ended, but the medieval years were also a very fruitful time for midrash. Great commentators arose to retell midrashim and invent new ones. New approaches to creating midrash arose, and old midrashim were also gathered and retold.

For example, Rashi (a scholar of 11th-century France) is considered one of the greatest interpreters of the Bible. Rashi was skilled at identifying the *peshat* (literal meaning) of a verse by using grammar and common sense, yet he was also skilled at quoting midrashic stories of the sages in short, clear sentences. Rashi retold many complex midrashic tales in ways that are easy to understand. For example, Rashi wrote about the first commandment given on Mount Sinai, the first of the Ten Commandments:

> I the Lord am your God who brought you out of the land of Egypt, the house of bondage.

Rashi said:

> At the shore of the Sea, God was revealed as a strong warrior, and here [on Sinai] God is revealed as an old man full of mercy.... Even though I change appearance, do not say that there are two powers in heaven, for I am the one who brought you out of Egypt.

In very few words, Rashi explained that God appears in different forms throughout the Bible, yet is still the same Deity. Rashi also invited us to imagine the confusion of the Israelites, who saw God making war on Egypt and are now asked to believe that God is kind and merciful. They may ask, "Why does God appear differently at different times if God is One?" By retelling a midrash, Rashi encapsulated a major dilemma of faith in a single comment.

Each interpreter in the Middle Ages has a special way of looking at text. Maimonides (12th-century Spain) quoted midrashim that emphasize ethics and law, rather than miraculous events. Nachmanides (13th-century Spain), on the other hand, often used mystical teachings in his comments. Ibn Ezra (12th-century Spain) often contradicted earlier midrash if he found it too fanciful. For example, a midrash from the time of the Talmud claims that Abraham's third wife, Keturah, is the same person as his first wife, Hagar, but she has two different names. Ibn Ezra flatly said that according to the text, this is not true. His dislike of certain kinds of midrash was honest, if unusual in Jewish history.

Medieval midrash sometimes take the form of a kind of novel. *Sefer ha-Yashar*, a 12th-century novel-like retelling of the tale of Joseph, contains many midrashim put together in story form. And collections like the *Yalkut Shimoni* from 13th-century Germany put together midrashim from many sources and embellish them into larger stories.

The rise of mysticism among Jews started a whole new variety of midrash. The Zohar, a 12th-century mystical work from Spain, expresses the idea that every verse of the Torah holds a secret meaning in which the different biblical characters represent different aspects of God. For example, consider the following biblical text about the Garden of Eden:

> The Lord God planted a garden in Eden, in the east, and placed there the man whom He had formed.

The Zohar (25b) does not see this verse as being about a real garden. To the Zohar, the "garden" where the human will live is the *Shekhinah*, the feminine indwelling presence of God. No matter where they go, humans will be connected to this indwelling presence. This kind of mystical midrash continued to be popular through the 17th-century in Sefad, a city in the Land of Israel where Kabbalah thrived.

In the early modern period, a kind of midrash arose that represented a different way of thinking. These midrashim were written by rabbis of the Hasidic movement, European Jews who believed in a spiritual, joyful approach to life. Commentaries like the *Sefat Emet* (Rabbi Yehudah Leib Alter, 19th-century Poland) and the *Mei ha-Shiloach* (Rabbi Mordechai Yosef of Isbitza, 19th-century Poland) look at events in the Torah as stories about one's inner life. For example, they might look at the conflict between the Israelite people and the tribe of Amalek (an enemy tribe who fought the Israelites) and see it as a story about the conflict between the inclination to do right and the inclination to do wrong. Or, the story of Jacob's ladder might be seen as a symbol of a soul's connection to heaven and earth. This midrashic style, which focuses on how Torah can teach about a person's inner self, helped create what we know today as modern midrash.

Modern Midrash

As Jews entered the modern period, yet another kind of midrash evolved. While the sages and medieval rabbis were full of imagination, they saw their midrash as part of a process of Torah interpretation. They would never have thought of themselves as "making something up." While some modern Jews continue retelling and reinventing older midrash, others create midrash that is meant to be creative; it is separate from the Bible and even questions or criticizes the Bible. This individualism is what makes modern midrash unique.

The poet Yehuda Amichai, one of the foremost poets of Israel, is a wise and irreverent midrashist who uses biblical characters and stories in his poems in unexpected ways. In one of his many poems on the Binding of Isaac, published in the book *Open Closed Open*, Amichai writes in a verse from the "The Bible and You, and Other Midrashim" section:

> Abraham had three sons, not just two:
> Yishmael, Yitzchak, and Yivkeh....
> Yishmael was saved by his mother Hagar,
> an angel saved Yitzchak,
> but Yivkeh was not saved by anyone.

In this midrash, Amichai imagines that Abraham had three sons and that the youngest son (the one not mentioned in the Bible) was offered up on Mount Moriah in place of Isaac. In Amichai's version of the Bible, there was no ram; an actual child was killed. This bold move allows Amichai to express his anger at the wars and religious battles that sacrifice children and his rage at those who want to cover up this reality with stories of divine rescue. Amichai uses this midrashic method to express a critique of his tradition and his modern reality.

Malka Heifetz Tussman, a Yiddish poet, writes a midrash on the creation of Eve called "Water without Sound," (from Howard Schwartz, *Voices within the Ark: The Modern Jewish Poets*). She looks out her window at a canal shaped like a rib and imagines the sea has torn a rib from its side and commanded it to acknowledge the sea's superiority. Tussman expresses sadness at the fate of this silent canal and thus critiques the assumption that Eve is an inferior being. Dan Pagis, a Holocaust survivor, also imagines Eve. In his brief and stunning poem, "Scrawled in Pencil on a Sealed Railway Car" (an English version can be found in David Curzon, ed., *Modern Poems on the Bible*), Eve is in a cattle car with her son Abel. She is looking for her son Cain, who has apparently joined the oppressors. Like Tussman, through the vehicle of midrash Pagis expresses his anger about how humans hurt one another.

Modern midrash has a great deal in common with ancient midrash in that it builds on other midrash as well as biblical text. In her poem "The Songs of

163

Miriam" (in Rebecca Schwartz, ed. *All the Women Followed Her*), Alicia Ostriker, an American poet and critic, writes of Miriam the prophet: "You who remember my music, you will feel me under your footsoles like cool ground water under porous stone—follow me, follow my drum." Ostriker is alluding to an ancient midrash in which a well of water follows the prophet Miriam through the desert. This well quenches the thirst of the Israelites, who are walking through the desert on their way to the Land of Israel. Ostriker uses this old midrash connecting Miriam to water, and she imagines the voice of Miriam and the sound of her drum as "underground," since Miriam's voice is not often present in the biblical text. Yet the flowing watery songs of Miriam lead the people toward freedom.

Jewish writers in all languages have written midrash, and non-Jewish writers have also created midrash. Modern midrash can come in a variety of forms: novels, poetry, dance, painting, sculpture, drama. Visual artists can depict biblical texts in ways that offer new meaning, from the dreamscapes of Chagall to the work of contemporary abstract painters, sculptors, or mask-makers. All of these techniques continue to add to the rich treasury of midrash.

What Type of Midrash Is It?

"Midrash" is a Hebrew word deriving from the root word *d-r-sh*, meaning "to explain." It refers to a method of interpreting a biblical text. The term "midrash" also can refer to a compilation of midrashic teachings on the Bible.

There are two types of midrash: *halakhah* and *aggadah*. When a midrash is about Jewish law or practice, it is called *midrash halakhah*. When it tells a story or a parable, or interprets a narrative in the Bible in some fashion—in prose, poetry, song, art, drama, or another artistic expression—it is called *midrash aggadah*. *Aggadah* means "telling" in Hebrew, and any midrash that is not *halakhah* is considered *aggadah*.

Both kinds were at first preserved only orally; but they began to be written down in the 2nd century, and the practice continues to this day.

Conclusion: A Story without an End

How close does a midrash have to remain to the text to be considered a midrash? It is difficult to answer that question. Some would say novels like Anita Diamant's *The Red Tent* are in the tradition of midrash, while others believe only classical midrashim by the sages really "count." How a person defines midrash will help to define what kind of Jew he or she chooses to be. Yet all Jewish sects and traditions honor midrash in some way.

Midrash is like the nervous system of the Jewish people. It allows people to respond to Torah in real time, out of the events and emotions of their own lives. Midrash does not force us to read sacred text one way; it opens us to read sacred text in many ways. This is why the sages say, "There are seventy faces of Torah." Through midrash, readers of the Bible in every generation can add their thoughts and ideas to the text and experience moments of new understanding.

Jill Hammer

Sampling of Important Works of Midrash

Interpretations of Jewish law and practice and legends and stories from the Bible, creative interpretation of sacred text, can be found in a variety of works spanning more than 2,000 years.

Some interpretive works, like those from the apocryphal books Jubilees and Judith, were written after the Bible but before the time of the Talmud. *Bereshit Rabbah* and others were written around the time of the Talmud, and there are those from medieval times, like *Yalkut Shimoni* and *Midrash Tanhuma*. The kabbalists of Spain wrote midrash, too, as did the Hasidim in the 18th and 19th centuries. There are many modern works as well, created by poets, prose writers, artists, and scholars of our own age.

All in all, there are thousands of works of midrash; here is a sampling of some of the most noteworthy of them.

ANCIENT WORKS
Mekhilta de-Rabbi Ishmael. A collection of halakhic (legal) midrashim that interprets the legal sections of the book of Exodus (chapters 12–23, 31, 35). *Mekhilta de-Rabbi Ishmael: A Critical Edition,* trans. by Jacob Z. Lauterbach (Philadelphia: Jewish Publication Society, 2004).

LATE ANTIQUITY/EARLY MEDIEVAL WORKS
Midrash ha-Gadol. According to many, the crowning glory of the legendary works of Yemenite Jewry. It is the most extensive midrash on the entire Torah; it was probably compiled during the 13th and 14th centuries by R. David ben Amram. It is not available in English; the only complete version is *Midrash ha-Gadol* (Hebrew), by Rabbi David ben Amram Adani, 10 vols. (Mossad HaRav Kook, 2004). However, *Praise Her Works: Conversations with Biblical Women,* ed. by Penina Adelman (Philadelphia: Jewish Publication Society, 2005) is a collection of midrash based loosely on this early work.

Midrash Rabbah. A collection of Rabbinic interpretive commentaries on the Torah and the Five Scrolls (Song of Songs, Ruth, Lamentations, Ecclesiastes, and Esther), dating from 400 to 1000 C.E. *Midrash Rabbah: Genesis I, II, & III,* ed. by Rabbi Dr. H. Freedman and Maurice Simon, trans. by S. M. Lehrman (Brooklyn: Soncino Press, 1951);

Midrash Rabbah: Exodus, ed. by Rabbi Dr. H. Freedman and Maurice Simon, trans. S. M. Lehrman (Brooklyn, Soncino Press, 1951). *Midrash Devarim Rabah,* Oxford MS. no. 147 (Yahorimin, 1964). *Golden Bells and Pomegranates: Studies in Midrash Leviticus Rabbah,* by Burton L. Visotzky (Tubingen, Germany: Paul Mohr Verlag, 2003). *Midrash Rabbah: Esther,* ed. Rabbi Dr. H. Freedman and Maurice Simon, trans. S. M. Lehrman (Brooklyn: Soncino Press, 1951).

Pesikta de-Rav Kahana. A central and classic text of midrashic literature, commenting on the Torah readings of all the major festivals and special Sabbaths of the Jewish year. Because this collection of midrashim relates to the destruction and redemption of Jerusalem, it can be said that *Pesikta* is one of the most "Israel-focused" midrashic works. Before 1832, no manuscript or text of the *Pesikta* was known. *Pesikta de-Rab Kahana,* trans. William G. Braude and Israel Kapstein (Philadelphia: Jewish Publication Society, 2002).

Sefer ha-Yashar. A 12th-century Jewish commentary from Muslim Spain. Known also as *Toledot Adam* and *Dibre ha-Yamim be-Aruk,* it concerns itself with the history of the Jews from the time of Adam to the Judges. *Sefer HaYashar: The Book of the Righteous,* trans. Seymour J. Cohen (Jersey City, NJ: Ktav Publishing House, 1973). *Sefer Ha-Yashar or The Book of Jasher,* trans. J. H. Parry (Providence, RI: Providence University, 2007). *Sefer Ha-Yashar or The Book of Jasher,* trans. M. M. Noah (Whitefish, MT: Kessinger Publishing, 2007).

Yalkut Shimoni. An anthology of midrashim to the entire Bible, compiled from more than 50 works. The first part (963 sections) deals with the Torah; the second part (1,085 sections) covers the Prophets and the Writings. The author is thought to be Shimon ha-Darshan, who lived in Frankfurt in the 13th century. *L'kutei Bosar L'kutei: An Anthology of Interpretations and Interpreting Comments on Midrash Rabba, Midrash Tanchuma Yalkut Shimoni,* trans. Rabbi Shmuel Alte (Nanuet, NY: Philipp Feldheim, 1971).

LATE MEDIEVAL AND EARLY MODERN WORKS

Mei ha-Shiloach (Rabbi Mordechai Yosef of Isbitza). Commentary written by a 19th-century Hasidic rabbi of Poland, known for his creative, compassionate, and mystical commentary. *The Living Waters: The Mei HaShiloach,* 2 vols. trans. Betalel Philip Edwards (Northdale, NJ: Jason Aronson, 2000).

Sefat Emet (Rabbi Yehudah Leib Alter). A 19th-century Hasidic master from Poland, known for a mystical and psychologically aware approach to Torah. *The Language of Truth: The Torah Commentary of Sefat Emet,* by Arthur Green (Philadelphia: Jewish Publication Society, 1998).

Shulchan Aruch. A 16th-century law code of Joseph Caro, a Jewish legal scholar of Spain, accompanied by commentary by the Ashkenazic authority Moses Isserles. *Code of Jewish Law (Kitzur Shulhan Aruh): A Compilation of Jewish Laws and Customs,* by Solomon Ganzfried, trans. Hyman E. Goldin (New York: Hebrew Publishing Co., 1963).

MODERN WORKS

The Book of Legends. A translation of *Sefer ha-Aggadah,* a 1991 anthology of Rabbinic tales and parables collected by Hayim Nahman Bialik and Yehoshua Hana Ravinsky. *The Book of Legends,* trans. William G. Braude (New York: Schocken, 1992).

Legends of the Jews. The classic collection of midrashim about the major characters and events of the Bible, gathered by Ginzberg from around the world and retold by him. Originally published in seven volumes from 1909 through 1938, it was republished in 2003 in two volumes with a new, extensive index. *Legends of the Jews,* by Louis Ginzberg (Philadelphia: Jewish Publication Society, 1909–1938; 2003).

The Nakedness of the Fathers. Ostriker employs a mix of poetry, essays, and literary criticism to formulate midrash from the perspective of the contemporary Jewish woman. *The Nakedness of the Fathers: Biblical Visions and Revisions,* by Alicia Suskin Ostriker (New Brunswick, NJ: Rutgers University Press, 1994).

Sisters at Sinai. Hammer has created a collection of midrashim by rewriting biblical stories from the perspective of their female protagonists. In her commentary at the back, Hammer explains how she came to write each story and explains its connection to biblical and rabbinic sources. *Sisters at Sinai: New Tales of Biblical Women,* by Jill Hammer (Philadelphia: Jewish Publication Society, 2001).

Summaries of the Books of the Bible

Genesis

TITLE: "Genesis" is a Greek word signifying "origin" or "beginning." In Hebrew the book is called "Bereshit" (in the beginning). As the first book of the Bible, it sets the precedent of taking its title from the first significant word in the text itself, *bereshit*.

CONTENTS: Genesis is a book about beginnings. It outlines the origins of the universe and of humankind, and it wrestles with the nature of the relationship between God's creation and God. The book begins with an account of the creation, the exile of Adam and Eve from the Garden of Eden, and the early history of humankind. This first part of Genesis contains these stories: the initial covenant with humankind; the intrusion of sin through the account of the first murder (of Abel by his brother Cain); the Flood, with which God threatens to eradicate the "mistake" of creating humans, because they have proved themselves capable of great evil; a second covenant (with Noah), wherein God vows to never again flood the world; the repeopling of the earth from Noah's lineage; and the confusion of tongues at the Tower of Babel, concluding with the genealogy of Shem down to Terah and Abraham.

The next segment of Genesis contains the special history of the patriarchs, the ancestors of the Jewish people. Here Abraham is the prominent figure, and the history of his call from God is recorded, along with detailed accounts from the Patriarchal era: tales of Abram and Sarai in Egypt (before their names are changed by God to Abraham and Sarah); the covenant between God and Abram; internal family conflict between Sarai and her handmaid, Hagar, who flees from maltreatment at home and returns at God's request to "father" Ishmael; the surprising conception, birth, and circumcision of Isaac; God's decision to destroy Sodom and Gomorrah, despite Abraham's resistance; and Abraham's offering of Isaac on an altar to God (the *Akedah*, the Binding of Isaac), which is interrupted and halted by an angel of God at the last moment.

These are then followed by stories of Isaac, Rebekah, and their children Jacob and Esau. One of the most well known of these stories is that of Jacob, Leah, and

Rachel: Rebekah sends her son Jacob to live with his uncle Laban, who later tricks him into marrying his daughter Leah instead of Rachel, the daughter he desires. Jacob strikes a deal with Laban to work for seven additional years to earn Rachel's hand in marriage. And so Jacob marries Leah and Rachel and also fathers twelve sons, who become the Twelve Tribes of Israel. (See "The Twelve Tribes of Israel," on p. 182) The dramas that unfold in the lives of Jacob's children—of Joseph and his brothers, and of Dinah—ultimately lead to the emigration of Jacob and his family to Egypt. Later chapters tell the history of Jacob and Joseph, to the death of Joseph in Egypt.

Genesis tells the story of the creation of the world, and then it follows one family across the generations, weaving the narrative through space and time until the family's descendants dwell in Egypt, thereby setting the stage for the narrative to come, in the successive biblical books.

Setting the Foundation for the Religion of Israel

The theme of Creation, important as it is, serves merely as an introduction to Genesis's central motif: God's role in history. The opening chapters are a prologue to the historical drama that begins in chapter 12. They serve to set forth the worldviews and values of the civilization of the Bible, the pillars on which the religion of Israel rests. They provide us with the fountainhead of ideas and concepts from which all future developments spring: the divinely ordained history and destiny of Israel, the nature of God, the nature of humankind as created by God, and the relationships between the two.

We learn in these early chapters that the God of Genesis is the wholly self-sufficient One, absolutely independent of nature, the supreme Sovereign of the world, who is providentially involved in human affairs—Lord of history. And the human being in Genesis—the pinnacle of Creation—is a creature of infinite preciousness who enjoys a unique relationship with God. Humankind is endowed with free will and, consequently, is also charged with moral responsibility and inescapable accountability. Moreover, the human race constitutes a single family whose ultimate destiny is determined by God. This universal opening serves as the background for the rest of the book of Genesis and, indeed, for the remainder of the Bible.

Adapted from Nahum M. Sarna, *JPS Torah Commentary: Genesis.*

OF SPECIAL SIGNIFICANCE: Unlike many other early Creation stories, the biblical story of Creation in Genesis is strikingly monotheistic. The Bible opens with an impressive presentation of the fundamental religious truth: that all of creation owes its existence to the One God. This is undoubtedly the most significant

Beginning of the book of Genesis (Bereshit), Pentateuch, Berlin, 1933. The Soncino Gesellschaft der Freunde des jüdischen Buches was a society of Jewish bibliophiles in Germany dedicated to producing Jewish and Hebrew books that met the highest typographical standards. This Pentateuch was part of the society's attempt to publish a new Hebrew Bible featuring a new Hebrew font. Type designer Markus Behmer based the font on Gershom Cohen's 1526 Prague haggadah. However, the society never had the chance to publish the Bible in full, as this Pentateuch was one of the last legally printed Hebrew books under the Third Reich before the Nuremburg Laws went into effect. In 1937, the Gesellschaft was liquidated by the Nazis, and the unique type in its Pentateuch was never used again. (Courtesy of The Library of the Jewish Theological Seminary.)

revolution recorded in the biblical narrative. Abraham is chosen as the Patriarch and his family lineage is traced in these stories because later Rabbinic tradition says he is the world's first monotheist.

Genesis, in its breadth and depth, embraces the world and the entire human race, while showing the ways in which God is revealed to the first ancestors of the Jewish nation. By outlining the specific stories of the individuals of Abraham's family and the dynamics of their lives, it is possible to attain deep insight into universal psychological and sociological human truths. Herein lies the beauty of Genesis: in the very particularity of this family and their struggles is the universality of every family's story.

This opening book of the Bible presents us with God, who is supreme, above all else. And it presents us with human beings, who have a special relationship with God; they are endowed with free will, but also with moral responsibility and accountability to God.

Exodus

TITLE: "Exodus" is derived from the Greek word signifying "departure" or "going out," referring to the descendants of Abraham "going out" from bondage in Egypt to the Promised Land. The Hebrew title, "*Sefer ve'elah shemot,*" which means "the book of 'And these are the names,'" is based on the opening words of the book. This is often shortened to *Shemot,* or "Names."

CONTENTS: Exodus gives an account of the early history of Israel as a nation, one that was enslaved, redeemed, set apart, and then dedicated to following God's commandments. The four major themes—liberation, law, covenant, and the presence of God—provide a structure that is meant to maintain an ongoing relationship between God and Israel.

The events in Exodus extend from the birth of Moses to the construction of the Tabernacle. The first chapters give an account of the oppression of the Israelites in Egypt, the early life of Moses and his call to be the deliverer of Israel, the Ten Plagues, the liberation from slavery, the passage through the Sea of Reeds, the journey to Mount Sinai, the arrival at Sinai, the construction of the Golden Calf in Moses's long absence on the mountain, and finally, the preparations for receiving the Law (the Decalogue, or Ten Commandments).

Exodus then turns to matters of law: the promulgation of the Law; and the ratification of the covenant between the Israelites and God, with commandments and guidelines to dictate values and behavior sanctioned by God. These commandments include the Mosaic Covenant—both absolute commands such as the Ten Commandments, which are given without explanation or justification, and more conditional laws, with the rationale for them.

The Decalogue, or Ten Commandments

The Decalogue, in Exodus 20:2–14 is the only collection of laws that, according to biblical tradition, God revealed to Israel without an intermediary, and this helps account for its significance within biblical and later religious traditions.

The usual name for these laws, "the Ten Commandments," is not found in the Bible and is inaccurate. The first statement in the Decalogue reads: "I the Lord am your God who brought you out of the land of Egypt, the house of bondage" (20:2); this is not a commandment but an utterance or statement. The term "Decalogue," from the Greek *deca* (10) *logos* (words), is more appropriate.

Both of the commonly used terms, "Decalogue" and "Ten Commandments," follow the tradition of Exodus and Deuteronomy in that this text is divided into 10 sections. This most likely reflects a notion of 10 as a number expressing perfection. Yet the Decalogue comprises as many as 13 separate statements:

1. (v. 2) I the Lord am your God who brought you out of the land of Egypt …
2. (v. 3) You shall have no other gods besides Me.
3. (v. 4) You shall not make for yourself a sculptured image….
4. (v. 5) You shall not bow down to them or serve them.
5. (v. 7) You shall not swear falsely by the name of the LORD your God …
6. (v. 8) Remember the sabbath day and keep it holy
7. (v. 12) Honor your father and your mother …
8. (v. 13) You shall not murder.
9. (v. 13) You shall not commit adultery.
10. (v. 13) You shall not steal.
11. (v. 13) You shall not bear false witness against your neighbor.
12. (v. 14) You shall not covet your neighbor's house:
13. (v. 14) You shall not covet your neighbor's wife …

The Decalogue, or Ten Commandments (continued)

The version in Deuteronomy 5 differs from that in Exodus 20 in both small and large ways. For example, a totally different reason is given in Deuteronomy for why the Sabbath should be observed, and that text introduces the Sabbath injunction using a different verb, as may be seen from the following juxtaposition:

Exodus 20:8–11

Remember the sabbath day and keep it holy. Six days you shall labor and do all your work, but the seventh day is a sabbath of the LORD your God: you shall not do any work—you, your son or daughter, your male or female slave, or your cattle, or the stranger who is within your settlements. For in six days the LORD made heaven and earth and sea, and all that is in them, and He rested on the seventh day; therefore the LORD blessed the sabbath day and hallowed it.

Deuteronomy 5:12–15

Observe the sabbath day and keep it holy, as the LORD your God has commanded you. Six days you shall labor and do all your work, but the seventh day is a sabbath of the LORD your God; you shall not do any work—you, your son or your daughter, your male or female slave, your ox or your ass, or any of your cattle, or the stranger in your settlements, so that your male and female slave may rest as you do. Remember that you were a slave in the land of Egypt and the LORD your God freed you from there with a mighty hand and an outstretched arm; therefore the LORD your God has commanded you to observe the sabbath day.

Adapted from Marc Zvi Brettler, *How to Read the Bible*.

The latter part of Exodus gives the orders for making the Tabernacle, for the consecration of the family of Aaron to the Priesthood, and for making their vestments. It also records the sin and punishment of the Israelites for making the Golden Calf.

The Tabernacle

After Moses received the Ten Commandments at Mount Sinai, the Israelites built a portable shrine for their worship, the Tabernacle, or Tent of Meeting, with Aaron and his family as priests. The shrine was a tent, its construction and appearance given to Moses in a vision on Mount Sinai (Exod. 25–40). Constructed with great care from precious materials, it held a sacrificial altar and many ritually important objects. Within the Tabernacle was a smaller, curtained enclosure, the Holy of Holies. This enclosure, which was entered only on Yom Kippur by the High Priest, housed the Ark of the Covenant and the tablets of the Ten Commandments.

The term "tabernacle" is a translation of the Hebrew word *mishkan*, "dwelling place." It was thought to be a literal dwelling place of God. During the Israelites' 40 years of wandering, a cloud signaling the presence of God formed over the Tabernacle, disappearing when it was time to move to the next encampment. Then the Israelites dismantled the Tabernacle and reconstructed it in the center of the next camp, under the relocated divine cloud. When the Israelites reached Canaan, they gave the Tabernacle a more permanent residence in Shiloh.

175

OF SPECIAL SIGNIFICANCE: "Let My people go!" is a well-known and oft-quoted verse from Exodus. The second half of this same verse is, "that they may worship Me" (7:26, 8:16, 10:3:1), thereby providing a reason for the slaves' liberation from bondage. The Israelites' liberation from Egypt is followed by the introduction of covenantal law, which is meant to create a context for an abiding presence of God. The explicitly stated purpose of liberation is for the people to live in covenantal relationship with God. This special relationship and centuries of celebrating the Passover holiday provide a way to see alternative possibilities in the world—for oppressed peoples to imagine their own potential for freedom and the possibility that God hears their cries for liberation. Therefore, the covenantal relationship is, in fact, revolutionary in that it creates a world in which divine authority supersedes all other systems of authority.

Other themes and values elucidated in the narratives of Exodus are the management of anger (epitomized in Moses's punishment by God); defeating Amalek, the archenemy of the Israelite people; Jethro's advice to Moses to delegate leadership to decentralize the power and responsibility and to make leadership more manageable for Moses; the Revelation at Mount Sinai, including the giving of the Ten Commandments; the rebellion against God in the Israelites' construction of the Golden Calf at the foot of the mountain; and finally, instructions for constructing the Tabernacle.

In this series of events lies a deep spiritual appreciation for loyalty, forgiveness, and rebuilding a relationship after a violation of trust. God's giving the instructions for building a Tabernacle immediately following the people's abhorrent building of an idol provides an example of the way in which God understands the psychology of the people and their need for a physical representation of the Divine, so that they might worship God in a sanctified and acceptable manner within the bounds of the holy relationship.

Leviticus

TITLE: Like many of the biblical books, the name "Leviticus" is taken from the Greek, literally meaning "things pertaining to the Levites," because much of the book is concerned with the priests themselves (who formed part of the tribe of Levi) and priestly matters. In Hebrew, the term "Priestly Law" is often used to describe the book, as it consists mainly of laws for the priests.

CONTENTS: Leviticus contains many laws: those concerning the different kinds of sacrifices; the consecration of Aaron and his sons; the punishment of two of them, Nadab and Abihu, for offering "alien fire" (10:1); laws concerning clean and unclean foods, personal purity, and leprosy; the ordinance for the Day of Atonement; and the laws of holiness. Emphasis is placed on holiness as a quality distinguishing Israel, demanded of Israel by God, and regulating the Israelite's life. Of particular concern are the slaughter of animals; unlawful marriages and lusts; the priests; sacred times, seasons, and festivals; the lights of the sanctuary; the episode concerning a blasphemer and his punishment; the sabbatical year and the jubilee. It concludes with promises and warnings (also called "blessings and curses"), involving vows, tithes, and offerings to God.

OF SPECIAL SIGNIFICANCE: Leviticus is distinctive in that it completely excludes historical narrative, with the exception of the sections relating to the consecration of the priests, the death of Nadab and Abihu, and the stoning of the blasphemer. It relates the history of only one month (the first month of the second year of the Exodus), and all the events in the whole book take place at Sinai. The book also outlines the sacrificial system, explaining the burnt offering, meal/grain offering, well-being offering, and the purification offering. Leviticus establishes this sacrificial system as the sanctified manner in which the community can access God: to communicate repentance or thanksgiving, to purify oneself after a transgression, and to maintain the purity of the community as a whole. The book also explains the way in which the priest is consecrated through anointment as a rite of passage, as well as the rules regarding the dietary laws, rituals after childbirth and purification after contracting the "scale disease." The Holiness Code, which lists punishments and spells out requirements for the Israelites to remain "holy," is found here.

Numbers

TITLE: The name "Numbers" is likely derived from the Greek translation, the Septuagint, which named the book after the census taking in the first chapters of Numbers and again at the end of the wanderings of the Israelites. The book covers a period of 38 years and 3 months, from the completion of the giving of the Law until the 5th month of the 40th year.

The Hebrew name is "Be-midbar," or "in the desert," taken from the fifth Hebrew word in the first chapter of the book. It refers to the setting of the book, as the Israelites leave behind the slavery of Egypt and journey through the desert wilderness toward the Promised Land, Canaan.

CONTENTS: Numbers begins by describing the last days at Sinai: the first census; the arrangement of the army; the service of the Priestly Levites; various additional laws; and a description of the cloudy pillar, a symbol of God's ever presence. The book then proceeds to describe the Israelites' travels from Sinai to the borders of Canaan, including the appeal of Moses to Hobab; the burning at Taberah; the giving of the quails; the murmuring of Aaron and Miriam against their brother, Moses; Miriam's subsequent skin disease (often identified as leprosy); the sending of the spies, their report, and the murmuring of the people; and, finally, the rash attack on the Canaanites and their response.

The third section of Numbers outlines the 38 years of wandering: various laws are given; the rebellion of Korah, Dathan, and Abiram and their punishment are described; and the dues payable to the Levites are proscribed, followed by an explanation of the way defilement by the dead is to be handled. The book ends with the description of the last year of the Israelites' journey: the death of Miriam; the sin of Moses and Aaron; the circuit around Edom; the death of Aaron; the conquest of the Amorites; the episode of Balaam; the sin of Baal-peor and its consequences; the second census; laws of inheritance, offerings, and vows; the war against the Midianites; settlement of Gad, Reuben, and Manasseh; a summary of the places that the Israelites stopped during their 40 years of wandering through the desert; levitical cities and cities of refuge (where individuals convicted of crimes and expelled from the community are sent) are all outlined.

OF SPECIAL SIGNIFICANCE: Numbers is unique in that it is the record of the formation of a holy community dedicated to the service of God with a covenant initiated at Sinai.

The celebration of Passover is recorded in the book, as is the subsequent preparation for the walk through the wilderness. Much of this first generation's time in the wilderness is marked by conflict, dissent against the leadership, and death. The threats are real, and they come from both internal and external sources.

Also of note in Numbers is the stark candor of the reporter. The writer freely exposes the faults not only of the people but also of Aaron and Miriam. The author extols the generosity of Moses, his meekness, and his self-effacement, but also records his tendency to despondency and the weaknesses that prevented him from entering the Promised Land.

Deuteronomy

TITLE: "Deuteronomy" comes from the Greek and signifies "repetition of the Law." The first giving, most notably the Decalogue, is in Exodus (see "The Decalogue, or Ten Commandments," on p. 173). In Hebrew, Deuteronomy is known as "Devarim," which means "these are the words," the opening phrase of the book.

CONTENTS: Deuteronomy consists mainly of three addresses given by Moses in the 40th year of the Exodus and the last year of his life. Of the three addresses, the first is introductory, reminding the people of their deliverance from bondage, of God's guidance and protection in their wanderings, and their frequent ingratitude. It closes with a warning from the past and an exhortation to follow God's teachings, to secure the inheritance of the Land, which is now within reach.

The second address, starting with the Decalogue, consists of a speech from Moses, introducing the importance of the Ten Commandments and the sacred covenant with God, seemingly retroactively, reminding them of the promises they already made at Horeb to follow God's teachings. This address is followed by the laws in three main groups: those concerning religion, the administration of justice, and private and social rights. It concludes with teachings commonly known as "the blessings and the curses," which are said to be consequences of behaviors either sanctioned or prohibited by God.

At the close of these addresses there is an account of the delivery of the Law to the Levites, a song sung by Moses, the final benediction of the Twelve Tribes of Israel, and the closing scenes of Moses's life.

To some extent, Deuteronomy is a restatement of previously given written law, with an important difference: the law here requires all sacrifices to be offered, not at many places, as previously assumed, but at one place only—in the Promised Land that the Israelites are about to inherit.

OF SPECIAL SIGNIFICANCE: Though a book of law, Deuteronomy is penetrated throughout by a religious and ethical spirit dominated by the fundamental belief in the unity of God and the conviction of the consequent necessity of the Israelites' wholehearted devotion to the Divine. In Deuteronomy, it is stated for the first time that no other god exists, and that only the Lord has performed divine deeds. This is epitomized by the central prayer in Judaism, the *Shema*, in chapter 6, and demonstrated by Moses when he recounts the Exodus and the events at Mount Sinai.

This is the book from which stems the belief that God made a covenant with Israel at Sinai, with the Torah embodying the terms of that covenant. Thus the people's continuity is staked not on worship, but on obedience to covenantal law. In fact, half of the laws laid out in Deuteronomy are followed by explanations that are meant to inspire obedience by demonstrating how each law is logical, just, or beneficial. And the Israelites are also told of the harsh consequences for disobedience. When Moses recounts how an entire generation perished wandering in the desert on the journey from Mount Sinai to the Promised Land, he does so to demonstrate the consequences of Israel's faithlessness.

However, worship itself is deemphasized and circumscribed in Deuteronomy. Sacrifices, festivals, and purification rites are limited to the central sanctuary in the religious capital, making it difficult for most Jews, who did not live near the central sanctuary, to engage in these practices. The Temple itself is no longer viewed as the dwelling place of God. While the Promised Land remains important in Deuteronomy, it is the law that allows Judaism to thrive as a living religion, independent of a fixed geographical location.

179

Loyalty to the Lord

The main theme of Deuteronomy is the ardent and exclusive loyalty that Israel owes the Lord, as expressed in 6:4–5: "Hear, O Israel! The Lord is our God, the Lord alone. You shall love the Lord your God with all your heart and with all your soul and with all your might."

Moses constantly exhorts Israel to worship the Lord alone and to shun pagan occult practices. No other book demands such a vehement campaign to prevent Israelites from worshiping other gods: it prescribes execution for Israelites who do so, or even advocate doing so; it requires the destruction of the native Canaanites, to prevent them from influencing Israel to adapt their gods and abhorrent practices, such as ritual murder; and it warns that worshiping other gods will lead to Israel's destruction and exile. In times of war, as a corollary of loyalty, Israel must trust God completely and face the enemy without hesitation.

From Jeffrey H. Tigay, *JPS Torah Commentary: Deuteronomy.*

Moses addresses the people for the last time before his death; they must become acclimated to new leadership, as Moses will not be permitted to travel with them into the Promised Land. Throughout Deuteronomy, military campaigns are waged and laws reiterated so that the people are prepared to enter the Holy Land as a holy people. The Ten Commandments are restated, Moses's final instructions and warnings. The Deuteronomic law code is explained, including laws dealing with the purity and unity of monotheistic worship; the sanctification of time; transitions in public leadership and shifts in authority; and matters of life and death, general conduct, and gratitude. It is here that many of the basic tenets of Jewish observance are given: the yearly festivals, ritual objects—the mezuzah, tefillin (prayer boxes or phylacteries), and tzitzit (prayer shawl fringes)—and the *Shema*. At the end of the book, Moses sings a last song, offers blessings, and then dies.

Joshua

TITLE: The name "Joshua" (Hebrew for "God is salvation") was substituted by Moses for Joshua's earlier name, "Hoshea," on the occasion of sending out the 12 spies (Num. 13:16). Just why this name change was made is unknown, but a midrash explains that the addition of the letter *yud* (rendered in English as "j"), which has a numerical value of 10, is said to foreshadow Joshua standing against 10 of the other spies. Joshua was born in Egypt while the Israelites were slaves there. He first appears as a military captain at Rephidim during the attack of the Amalekites. He is Moses's attendant at the giving of the Law and is later sent to spy out the land of Canaan for the tribe of Ephraim. When Moses dies, Joshua is appointed by God as Moses's successor and leader of the people, settling the Israelites in Canaan.

CONTENTS: The book of Joshua is predominantly concerned with the conquest of Canaan by the Israelites and the partitioning of the land among the tribes. (See "The Twelve Tribes of Israel," on p. 182) Once this is accomplished, Joshua bids farewell to the people and dies. (The general impression in this book is that the Israelites, acting together under Joshua, conquered all of Canaan within a period of a few years. However, there are hints within the text that the conquest and occupation of Canaan by the Israelites were a more gradual process and not altogether due to the actions of a united people.) The narrative tells how Joshua leads the Israelites across the Jordan River into the Promised Land, after wandering for 40 years from Egypt, since the Exodus. Then there are detailed descriptions of how the land is divided up between the tribes, incorporating boundaries and cities. Joshua's final speech to all the tribes assembled at Shechem, followed by a short epilogue, closes the book.

OF SPECIAL SIGNIFICANCE: The conquest of Canaan is in many ways the long-anticipated climax of the previous biblical narratives, the conclusion of the early

> **Groupings of the Prophetic Books**
> The biblical books of the Prophets, or Nevi'im, are sometimes grouped into categories:
>
> **Former Prophets**—The books of Joshua, Judges, Samuel, and Kings are the historical narratives of the early days of the Land of Israel.
>
> **Latter Prophets**—The books of Isaiah, Jeremiah, and Ezekiel are mostly in poetic style and are filled with prophecies about how sinners will be punished and with calls for redemption.
>
> **Major Prophets**—The books of Isaiah, Jeremiah, Lamentations, Ezekiel, and Daniel are so named because of their length, not their importance.
>
> **Minor Prophets**—The books of Hosea, Joel, Amos, Obadiah, Jonah, Micah, Nahum, Habakkuk, Zephaniah, Haggai, Zechariah, and Malachi are called minor because they are shorter in length than the Major Prophets.

Israelite experience. After a full generation of Israelites have died (those who were once enslaved in Egypt), God delivers on the ancient promise to their ancestors Abraham, Isaac, and Jacob for a land of their own. This book provides a triumphant end to the liberation of the Israelites from slavery, delivering them to their promised destination under the divine guidance of God, through Joshua.

The book also serves to illustrate the transition of leadership from Moses to Joshua, thereby signifying that God remains the true leader, regardless of the specific identity of the human being enacting God's will. Joshua shows the people that life after Moses is possible and that their redemption from Egypt led them to this place and time.

Judges

TITLE: Judges receives its title from those who were raised up to be the deliverers of the Israelites from their enemies, after the death of Joshua. The Hebrew word for these deliverers is *shofet;* its plural is *shofetim,* which has come to mean "judges."

CONTENTS: Judges opens with an account of the conquest of territories in the land of Caanan by the different Israelite tribes. Each of them was given a portion of the Promised Land, which was their inheritance and responsibility to cultivate. Next it tells the stories of Ehud, Deborah, Barak, Shamgar, Gideon and his son

The Twelve Tribes of Israel

Jacob's 12 sons come to Egypt to escape famine. When their descendants leave Egypt and wander the desert for 40 years, they separate into their own communities, or tribes. Upon reaching Canaan after the Exodus, these tribes divide the land into 12 territories, 1 each for the tribes descended from Reuben, Simeon, Judah, Issachar, Zebulun, Dan, Gad, Naphtali, Asher, and Benjamin, with the remaining two territories taken by the tribes of Joseph's two sons, Ephraim and Manasseh. The descendants of Jacob's remaining son, Levi, form a Priestly tribe with no territory of its own.

The territories unite under Saul but split into two kingdoms, the Southern Kingdom, or Judah, from the territories of Judah, Simeon, and part of Benjamin; and the Northern Kingdom, or Israel, from the other 10 territories—with Levites in both kingdoms. In 722 B.C.E., Assyrians conquer the Northern Kingdom, scattering the 10 tribes living there. Because of this, most modern Jews claim to be descendants of the Southern Kingdom tribes and Levi.

After the Assyrian conquest, the scattered northern tribes become known as the Ten Lost Tribes. They never return to Canaan, giving birth to numerous tales and legends about their history and whereabouts. Some scholars think they survived in Mesopotamia, possibly merging with the later exiles from Judah; some may have come back to Israel later. While most modern scholars consider these legends to be fictional and assume that these tribes intermarried with their new neighbors and lost their separate identity, many groups have been identified with the Ten Lost Tribes. Groups—Jewish and otherwise—in India, the Middle East, and Africa have all claimed to be transported descendants of the lost tribes.

Abimelech, Jephthah, and Samson, with briefer accounts or notices of others, including minor judges. This time period is characterized by successive periods of national sin, punishment, penitence, deliverance, and peace.

The final part of Judges contains a record of two remarkable incidents: that of Micah and the Danites; and the "outrageous act" (20:6) performed at Gibeah and the consequent war that led to the near extermination of the tribe of Benjamin. The latter portion of Judges explains the extent to which some of the Israelite families were demoralized. Phinehas, the grandson of Aaron, and

Jonathan, the son of Gershom and the grandson of Moses, are said to be living during this time period, indicating that only a generation separates Judges chronologically from the events in the first five books of the Bible.

OF SPECIAL SIGNIFICANCE: The book of Judges begins in an era of decline, following the deaths of Moses and Joshua. The judges come to leadership during various times and states of military emergency. The transition from leadership by Moses and Joshua, who were elected by divine authority, now to the rule by kings who are elected by the populace, is a turbulent one.

Judges is often connected to the repetitive cycle in which the people sin, God sends an enemy to oppress them, the people cry out, and God responds by sending a deliverer. The Bible is rife with examples of this cycle: every prophet records a similar pattern of sin, punishment, repentance, and forgiveness.

Jerusalem and Its Temple

In Judges, the city of Jerusalem appears as the stronghold of the Jebusites, resisting all assaults of the Israelites. The citadel of Zion remains unconquered until captured by David. From that time on Jerusalem is the capital and the center of Jewish national life. David transfers the Ark to Zion, making this the great sanctuary of the nation. Solomon builds himself a palace and the Temple on Zion. Part of the wall is broken down by Jehoash, but rebuilt by Uzziah and Jotham. The city and Temple are destroyed by Nebuchadnezzar (586 B.C.E.) and then restored under Ezra and Nehemiah. In 37 B.C.E. Herod rebuilds the Temple with great magnificence, and he encloses the city by restoring a second and outer wall. A third wall is built by Agrippa. In 70 C.E. Jerusalem is finally taken and destroyed by the Romans under Titus.

183

1 Samuel and 2 Samuel

TITLE: The books of Samuel are so called not because Samuel was the author, but because he is the most prominent actor in the opening portion, and the great instrument in the establishment of the Kingdom of Israel, which occurs throughout the remainder of 1 and 2 Samuel. The two books are in reality a single work and are so regarded in the original Hebrew canon.

CONTENTS: The books of Samuel address three biographies, those of Samuel, Saul, and David. The period covered is approximately 1050–970 B.C.E. 1 Samuel is the connecting link by which the judgeship passes on to monarchy. Whereas

Judges reflects a cry for stable leadership, here this cry is translated into a request for a king. It is unclear precisely where the power lies—with the priest, the prophet, the judge, or the king. The fact that these books are named after Samuel (a prophet) rather than Saul or David (who were both kings) exemplifies the tension between the kings' authority as political leaders and their subordination to God, whose will is communicated through prophets. In Deuteronomy 17:14, there is an explicit prohibition against kingship, and here the people are defying this prohibition by crying out for the establishment of a monarchy. They want a king to end the reign of political chaos resulting from the charismatic leadership appointed by God. The books of Samuel are essentially the point in Israelite history where the people demand personal responsibility for their leadership.

1 Samuel starts with Hannah's poem and introduces the monarchy; 2 Samuel begins by highlighting the death of Saul and reminding the reader that the narrative of conquest and struggle for power in 1 Samuel continues here. David's reign as the next king becomes the central focus of 2 Samuel. He eliminates his rivals, principally from the house of Saul, establishes a capital Jerusalem, and subdues external enemies. There is a great deal of bloodshed both preceding and following David's rise to power. Still, David emerges from these battles initially as a strong ruler of a unified nation, centered on a royal city that celebrates the blessings of God.

David's personal life looms large throughout these stories, ever present as a potential threat to his successes. David is one who is willing to go to extremes to achieve his heart's desire: murder, adultery, deception, and betrayal are means to an end for this king and warrior. But as the personal life of David unravels, so too does the monarchy itself. Following sexual transgressions and familial violence and betrayal in the House of David, Jerusalem becomes dangerous, and David is forced into exile. In his son Absalom's rebellion and revolt, David experiences the threat of another charismatic leader, thereby reliving the trauma experienced by Saul at the start of David's career as a king. Unlike the preceding stories of succession and military triumphs, however, the future of the monarchy is not determined by battles won. Rather, survival is the single most important factor in determining the heir to the throne, and it is Solomon, not Absalom, who ultimately survives.

At the conclusion of 2 Samuel, there is some moral resolution: David takes responsibility for the suffering of his people; and the monarchy, after a tumultuous beginning, becomes strong.

OF SPECIAL SIGNIFICANCE: Samuel's personal character, administrative skill, and intellectual ability transform anarchy into a peaceful monarchy with a respect for justice. It is easy to see why Samuel became one of the "heroes of Hebrew history"—why, as the last representative of the judges, the first in the regular succession of prophets, and the inaugurator of the kingdom, he could be associated with Moses and Aaron in Psalms. 1 Samuel opens with a scene in which a barren woman, Hannah, prays to God for a child, promising to dedicate her offspring (Samuel) to God's service. The priest assumes that the weeping woman, whose lips are moving without uttering words aloud, must be drunk, but Hannah proves to be the first person to pray silently to God in her heart, thereby serving as a biblical precedent for silent prayer.

King Saul begins well but ends badly. He is brought down by his fits of melancholy and jealousy, his bitter persecution of David, his moments of remorse, and his final defection, exhibited in his consulting the woman of En-dor just before the disastrous battle of Mount Gilboa. Often called "the witch of En-dor," the woman is a mystic, one who can bring dead spirits to life. Saul has made necromancy (consulting dead spirits) illegal, yet he comes to the woman of En-dor in disguise, begging for her services so that he might receive counsel from the deceased prophet Samuel before proceeding into battle. He believes that Samuel might provide hope or strength to him as he heads toward his certain downfall as the first monarch of Israel. Proud, selfish, reserved, obstinately stiff-necked, and profane, as he appears in parts of Samuel, Saul seeks to govern absolutely, instead of as the servant of God. But he is never sovereign of more than the central part of the country. Rather, he is more the pastoral chief of amalgamated tribes than the monarch of a kingdom.

In David, for the first time we see a true monarch, and he becomes the founder of a dynasty that lasts for four centuries. In his career we note his early life as preparation for his subsequent career, his life at court and as an outlaw, his elevation to the throne after long and varied discipline, his devotion to Jonathan and his magnanimity toward Saul, his valor, his musical and poetic gifts, the depths to which he falls when he gives way to the temptations of passion, the seriousness of his contrition, and the severity of the punishment that follows the great sin of his life. David is a masterful politician and public speaker. He uses his strengths to gain widespread public affection while revealing few of his own motivations or emotions. He is saved again and again by those who love him (most notably Jonathan), though his weakness for women and his willingness to use their love to his own political advantage ultimately serve to expedite his downfall as a ruler and hero.

1 Kings and 2 Kings

TITLE: The books of Kings are so named because they recount 400 years of Israelite history through its kings—from David's final years to the Babylonian exile, from approximately 970 to 586 B.C.E. In the original Hebrew both books

Kings Saul, David, and Solomon

When Israelite tribes find themselves faced with invasion by the Philistines in the 11th century B.C.E., they demand that the judge and prophet Samuel choose a king to unite them. Fearful of tyranny, Samuel is reluctant to do so, but he eventually yields and asks God to choose for him. Samuel anoints Saul, who is successful in pushing back the Philistines and then the Amalekites. Despite victory, Saul's battle with the Amalekites causes him to lose the support of Samuel when Saul spares the Amalekite king, in defiance of Samuel's orders. Saul effectively remains king until his defeat in a second battle against the Philistines. Seeing his army—including his sons—slaughtered, Saul falls on his own sword and dies (1 Sam. 9–2 Sam. 1).

Samuel becomes disenchanted with Saul after his failure to kill the Amalekite's king, and so he anoints a young soldier and musician, David, in his place. David comes to the prophet's attention both for single-handedly defeating the Philistine giant Goliath and for his musical talent; his playing soothes Saul's depression. While Saul continues as king, David gains followers and military victories, even allying himself at times with Saul's enemies. When Saul dies, David takes the throne. His reign is a golden age for the Land of Israel; the Twelve Tribes are united as a powerful nation ruling all Canaan and much of the surrounding territory (2 Sam., 1 Kings 1–2).

David is succeeded by his son Solomon. Anointed by the priest Zadok and the prophet Nathan, Solomon acts as both a civil and religious leader. He builds a palace, fortifies the city, strengthens the army, and maintains political ties with nations from Phoenicia to Arabia. Solomon builds the First Temple and is said to have written the biblical books Proverbs, Ecclesiastes, and Song of Songs (although his authorship is questionable). Despite the peace and prosperity of Solomon's reign, resentment grows over his 700 political marriages and heavy taxation, leading to the division of the kingdom following his death (1 Kings 6–12).

The dynasty of David continues to rule the Southern Kingdom of Judah until the Babylonian invasion in the 6th century B.C.E. In the Northern Kingdom of Israel, members of many families assume the kingship until the kingdom is destroyed in 722 B.C.E.

of Kings were one book, called "The Book of Kings." It was broken into two parts by the Greek translators of the Septuagint, and this division was adopted in all later Christian and Jewish Bibles.

CONTENTS: The narrative falls into three parts: (1) the reign of Solomon and the undivided kingdom at the height of its power; (2) a parallel account of the two divided kingdoms, Judah and Israel, until the Babylonian exile; and (3) the history of the Kingdom of Judah until the Babylonian conquest of Jerusalem by Nebuchadnezzar and the captivity of the people. (For a list of the kings and the dates of their reigns, see "Chronology of the Monarchies," on p. 259).

OF SPECIAL SIGNIFICANCE: Throughout this period, the role of the prophet, as defined by Samuel, assumes special prominence. The prophets become the monarch's closest advisers, counseling him on certain issues, while criticizing him on others. They are also teachers, giving the people instruction from God. It is their function to defend and interpret the moral law, in order to guarantee the keeping of the covenant and to denounce oppression and injustice. The religious behavior of the monarchs is all-important and a determining factor in the fate of their kingdoms. The religious devotion of David and Solomon protects their people, but the impiety of the kings who come after them results in moral corruption and the ultimate fall of their kingdoms.

187

Isaiah

TITLE: The prophet Isaiah's name, meaning "God is salvation," serves as the title of the book. Isaiah son of Amoz is called to prophesy in the year that King Uzziah dies (about 740 B.C.E.) and continues his work at least until 701 B.C.E. Of his personal history we know little. His wife, "the prophetess," and his sons, whose names bear witness to his prophetic announcements, are mentioned. He has access to the kings of his time (Uzziah, Jotham, Ahaz, and Hezekiah).

The era in which he prophesies is critical. The state of the nation is somber, as described by Amos, who lived somewhat earlier, as well as by Isaiah himself and the prophets Hosea and Micah. Luxury, oppression, idolatry, immorality, vain confidence in humankind, and lack of confidence in God, together with zealous attendance to the ceremonials of religious worship, are the characteristics of both the kingdoms of Israel and Judah. Assyria enters into a period of its greatest power and expansion, and Syria and Palestine are exposed to its severity. The Israelites' nearest neighbors also suffer from the Assyrian advance. The destinies of all these kingdoms are touched on by Isaiah, though the Israelites are foremost in Isaiah's thoughts. In every victory and defeat, Isaiah sees divine intention and intervention.

Biblical Politics: The Kingdoms of Israel and Judah

The period of biblical history from the end of the Exodus through the Babylonian conquest in the 6th century B.C.E. centers on the Israelites' settlement in the area between the Jordan River and the Mediterranean Sea, known as the Land of Israel, Palestine, and also Canaan. Initially, this region is divided into 12 largely independent tribal territories, which support each other but lack a central authority. This changes in the 11th century B.C.E., when the Philistines begin to threaten Israel.

In response to the Philistine invasion, the Israelites develop a monarchy. Three kings in turn—Saul, David, and Solomon—rule this territory and rebuff invaders. They, in turn, expand their kingdoms into an empire centered in Israel. Religion as well as politics becomes more developed; the building of the Temple in Solomon's reign brings the Priestly cult and Jerusalem to new heights.

After Solomon's death, his son and heir, Rehoboam, fails to keep his kingdom intact. The 10 northern tribes secede with the bulk of the territory to form the Northern Kingdom, also known as the Kingdom of Israel. It continues as a monarchy, but it lacks a stable dynasty; politics in the Kingdom of Israel are marred by internal strife and civil war. In the first half of the 8th century B.C.E., Jeroboam expands the kingdom, but it collapses after his death. Already weakened by internal discord, the Northern Kingdom falls to the Assyrians in 722 B.C.E., and its people are scattered.

The Southern Kingdom, the Kingdom of Judah, continues from the divide following Solomon's death until 586 B.C.E., more than a century and a half after the demise of the Northern Kingdom. The Southern Kingdom continues the dynastic tradition; with the exception of one queen, all of its rulers are descendants of David. The queen, Athaliah, assumes the throne after the deaths of her husband, Jehoram, and her son, Ahaziah, both descendants of David. Her attempt to consolidate power by eradicating the line of David fails; her grandson Joash survives the purge and successfully rises against her. The Kingdom of Judah grows in population following the destruction of the Kingdom of Israel at the hands of the Assyrians but is reduced to a subject of Assyria.

The final crest in the history of the Southern Kingdom comes in the reign of Josiah, in the late 7th century B.C.E. He expands the kingdom to the west and north, including areas that had been part of the Northern Kingdom. The embattled Assyrians, however, ally themselves with Egypt. Josiah is killed in a final battle against the Egyptian forces, after which the Kingdom of Judah falls under the yoke of first Egypt and then Babylonia. In the end, Babylonian forces, led by Nebuchadnezzar, put down a revolt of Zedekiah, the last king of Judah, and they destroy Jerusalem and the First Temple.

CONTENTS: Isaiah consists of two distinct parts: chapters 1–39 and chapters 40–66. The first closes with the narratives derived from 2 Kings and records the events of the last great period of Isaiah's career. The second part never mentions Isaiah and seems to have nothing to do with him.

Isaiah 1–39 is a combination of various collections of prophecies and prophetic narratives mostly belonging to the age of Isaiah. They do not all purport to have been written by Isaiah, but it is Isaiah himself who records his call to prophecy, as well as certain other experiences of his earlier life. Later parts of this section read like a narrative about the prophet written by someone else. Some of the prophecies in this first half of the book of Isaiah predict the fall of Israel to Assyria. But Isaiah predicts that Israel and the holy city of Jerusalem will be restored and that a just and pious Judean king from the line of David will rule Israel.

Isaiah 40–66 focuses on the salvation of Israel, on the people's release from exile in Babylonia to return to the Land of Israel. It prophesies that there will be peace on earth, with all people under one God, the end of paganism. The author, or more likely authors, of these chapters are not known and are often referred to as Deutero-Isaiah, or Second Isaiah, and Trito-Isaiah, or Third Isaiah.

OF SPECIAL SIGNIFICANCE: As Isaiah is convinced of the coming redemption from the suffering of his people and of God's purposes bound up with it, the prophet sets himself to rouse the Israelites in exile from their unbelief and despondency by telling them of the uniqueness of God, that other gods (those of Babylon, for example) are not real gods. He also insists on the power and might of God and of God's ability to deliver the Israelites into freedom and restore them to their land. Isaiah and the other authors of the book speak of the Israelites' destiny to be a people who might bring their religion to the other nations.

Isaiah, Proponent of Social Justice

Isaiah was well known for his teachings on social justice. Speaking for the voiceless and downtrodden, he rails against land speculators who "add house to house and join field to field" (5:8); against clever dissemblers and manipulators "who call evil good and good evil; who present darkness as light and light as darkness" (5:20); and against distorters of justice and due process, "who vindicate him who is in the wrong in return for a bribe, and withhold from him who is in the right" (5:23). Against this, Isaiah tries to give the people positive instructions in order to redress their crimes. "Devote yourself to justice" he teaches, "aid the wronged; uphold the rights of the orphan; defend the cause of the widow" (1:17).

From Michael Fishbane, *JPS Bible Commentary: Haftarot.*

Isaiah is the most familiar of the prophetic books. Many *haftarot* (readings that accompany the weekly Torah portions read during synagogue services) are taken from Isaiah, and there are some often-quoted passages here. There are roots of both Jewish and Christian beliefs in the Messianic Age and in social justice. Despite this, the book is not easy to read and understand; much of it is in verse, and the poetry is complex and its meaning often ambiguous.

Jeremiah

TITLE: As the title suggests, the main character of this book is the prophet Jeremiah. His name in Hebrew means "God will rise." In Jeremiah's most famous confrontation with authority, he threatens the king: "I will hurl you out of this land to a land that neither you nor your fathers have known…" (16:13), a prophecy that includes a possible pun on another translation of Jeremiah's name, "God shoots or hurls."

Jeremiah is the son of Hilkiah and a priest of the Priestly city of Anathoth, three miles north of Jerusalem. He is called to prophesy when still a youth, in the 13th year of King Josiah (about 626 B.C.E.), and he continues to prophesy in Jerusalem and in other cities of Judah for 40 years, until the final capture of the city (586 B.C.E.). After the capture, he warns the people at Mizpah and their governor Gedaliah against going down to Egypt, but he is nonetheless carried there against his will by his countrymen, where he protests against their idolatry until the end. Some believe he was murdered in Egypt by those angered by his prophecies. There is no reliable record of his death; he may have died at Tahpanes or, according to a tradition, may have gone to Babylon with Nebuchadnezzar's army.

CONTENTS: According to a narrative found within Jeremiah, more than 20 years after his call to prophesy Jeremiah is directed to prepare a book of his prophesy. He does this, but the book is destroyed by King Jehoiakim. Jeremiah writes another book, and it is portions of this book that most likely survive in Jeremiah 1–25. The majority of the poems and narratives in these chapters are told in the first person and have a character of their own, which distinguishes them from the rest of Jeremiah. Chapters 26–45 consist mainly of narratives about the prophet and his life before 604 B.C.E. and are thought by most scholars to be mainly the work of his disciple Baruch. The third part of Jeremiah consists of a collection of prophecies concerning foreign nations.

Although Jeremiah struggles to understand and come to terms with the horror of the destruction of the Temple and banishment from the Land, he looks to a time when the Temple will be rebuilt and his people will return to Jerusalem, praising God, "for the LORD is good, for His kindness is everlasting!" (33:11).

OF SPECIAL SIGNIFICANCE: No prophet reveals more to us about the inmost recesses of his mind than Jeremiah. Naturally shy and timid, subject to despondency and sadness, he is called to a work requiring undaunted resolution and rare courage. Belonging to the orders of both priest and prophet, he is compelled to witness against each when these offices sink into the lowest state of degradation. He is devoted to his duty and maintains his work to the end.

His style reflects the sadness of his mission; his poetry expresses the painful imagery that colors his thoughts. The book varies between prose and poetry and contains history mingled with prophecy. The prophetic utterances are often broken by out-bursts of prayer or complaint, and the bitter opposition of his enemies wrings from him occasionally words of indignation and cries for vengeance.

Ezekiel

TITLE: Ezekiel is a prophet whose name means "God strengthens." He is the son of Buzi and of Priestly descent through the House of Zadok. He is taken away with King Jehoiachin at the time of Nebuchadnezzar's second attack on Jerusalem and settles with a Jewish colony on the banks of the river Chebar in Babylonia, where he sees visions. He continues to prophesy for 22 years, beginning 5 years after he goes into captivity.

CONTENTS: The first part of Ezekiel contains prophecies uttered before the destruction of Jerusalem to caution the people against the false hope of relief from their suffering in Egypt and to exhort them to repent for their unfaithfulness to God. It includes Ezekiel's call to prophecy, the general carrying out of his commission, the rejection of the people because of their idolatry, the sins of the age in detail, the nature of the judgment, and the guilt that caused it.

The second section announces God's judgments on the seven heathen nations—Ammon, Moab, Edom, Philistia, Tyre, Sidon, and Egypt—and is largely written between the beginning of Nebuchadnezzar's siege of Jerusalem and the news of its fall. It also foretells the re-creation of the Land of Israel and of its people and contains a detailed vision of the restored Temple, Jerusalem, and the nation.

OF SPECIAL SIGNIFICANCE: Ezekiel is a prophet who, unlike the other prophets, loves drama. It is not unusual, for instance, for him to hold up a potter's flask and smash it in front of people as he speaks, to symbolize that Jerusalem will be destroyed and the people will be scattered to the winds.

Ezekiel believes it is his prophetic mission to reach people one by one and win them back to God, and he considers himself personally responsible for every individual soul. Ezekiel plants his hope for the future on two things: law and worship. In response, the people become a congregation, political aims and tasks no longer exist, and monarchy and state become subservient to all-powerful God. With no other prophet are vision and ecstasy so prominent. Ezekiel repeatedly refers to symptoms of severe maladies striking his body, such as paralysis of the limbs and of the tongue, and he is relieved of these physical ailments only after he announces the downfall of Jerusalem.

Early Jewish mysticism is based on Ezekiel's vision of the chariot in the first chapter.

Hosea

TITLE: The book is named after the prophet Hosea, whose name means "God has saved." Hosea is of the Northern Kingdom. He begins to prophesy toward the close of the reign of Jeroboam II (before the overthrow of the House of Jehu) and continues to do so during the anarchic period of the kings that follows. In spite of the external prosperity of the reign of Jeroboam II, there are corrupting influences that assert themselves during the anarchy following his death. The kings are recklessly wasteful; the priests fail to teach the knowledge of God, and moral standards plummet; God is forgotten, and the rulers are forced to look to Assyria or to Egypt for help in their misfortunes.

CONTENTS: The opening chapters give us the key to the imagery that colors all of the prophet's language thereafter. The unfaithfulness of Hosea's wife, who has borne him two sons and one daughter, is used as a symbol of the idolatry of the nation in the sight of God. Degraded as she is, so "... the Israelites shall go a long time without king and without officials, without sacrifice and without cult pillars, and without ephod and teraphim. Afterward, the Israelites will turn back and will seek the LORD their God..." (3:4–5).

The second part of Hosea consists, under the most vivid imagery, of accusations against the Israelites for their sins, which the prophet denounces unsparingly: their dishonesty, idolatry, distrust of God, and unwillingness to return to God. But it concludes with a hope for Israel's return to God's favor through repentance.

OF SPECIAL SIGNIFICANCE: What is especially significant about Hosea is his marriage to the prostitute Gomer, at God's command, so that Hosea might understand firsthand how it feels to be betrayed by a beloved. Like Hosea, God has been betrayed by the Israelites, who idolize others' gods, and God severely punishes them and then forgives them.

The relationship between God and the Israelites is expressed in rural and domestic pursuits, such as the snaring of birds, sowing, reaping, threshing, and baking bread, and this gives us insight into the daily life of the time. The women are decked with earrings and jewels, the feasts and Sabbaths are days of mirth, the people sacrifice on mountaintops and burn incense on hills, while the priests, forgetful of their functions, lie in wait "Like the ambuscade of bandits,/ Who murder on the road to Shechem..." (6:9).

Joel

TITLE: The prophet Joel, whose name means "Adonai/Lord God is God," is the son of Pethuel and prophesies at a time not directly stated in the book or elsewhere.

CONTENTS: In the opening chapters, Joel describes an impending visitation of locusts and drought, which may represent the threat of invasions. He exhorts the people of Judah to repent, fast, and pray to avert these calamities. He then promises a blessing in their stead, declaring that while there will be a judgment of the heathen in the Valley of Jehoshaphat and Edom and that Egypt will be wasted, Judah will be blessed.

OF SPECIAL SIGNIFICANCE: The prophet Joel speaks out against the people's worship of Baal and their rejection of God. He criticizes them for their sins and their impiety, making many references to nature: planting and fertility, birth and growth. His prophesy about the threat of locusts, for example, is very vivid and poetic, describing them first in the form of agricultural devastation and then as a marching army. His concern, however, is not limited to such a disaster. He sees them as a symbol of deeper significance: a sign of future judgment, "the day of the LORD." In fact, five of the 19 explicit references to "the day of the LORD" in the Bible are found in this short book.

Hosea, along with Amos and Isaiah, his contemporaries, is one of the earliest prophets of ancient Israel whose prophecies were recorded.

Amos

TITLE: The prophet Amos, whose name is a derivative of the word that means "to bear a burden," is a native of Tekoa in Judah, about 12 miles from Jerusalem, a "cattle breeder and a tender of sycamore figs" (7:14). Like many of the other biblical prophets, Amos was not an official or professional prophet, but someone who suddenly felt called by God. The imagery of his visions is full of country life; he writes about the "lion roar in the forest" (3:4); the shepherd rescuing "from the lion's jaws, / Two shank bones or the tip of an ear..." (3:12); the "bird drop on the ground—in a trap—/With no snare there" (3:5); "blight and mildew" (4:9); the "fish baskets" (4:2); "the rain from you, /Three months before harvesttime" (4:7); dangers from "a lion" and "a bear" (5:19); "the king's reaping" (7:1) and "the late-sown crops" (7:1); "shakes [sand] in a sieve" (9:9); "the plowman shall meet the reaper, /And the treader of grapes" (9:13); "a wagon is slowed, /When it is full of cut grain" (2:13). The prophet also shows knowledge of the great historical movements not only of his own nation, but of other nations as well.

CONTENTS: In the reign of Jeroboam II, king of the Israelites, and Uzziah, king of Judah, Amos is sent to Bethel to prophesy against the Israelites. His prophecies include an announcement of the coming of a day, when, captured by the Assyrian invaders, the priest's wife will be reduced to earning her living by infamy; that the priest's sons and daughters will be slain by the sword; that the Israelites will be enslaved; and that the priest himself will die in a polluted land. After delivering his message at Bethel in rebuke of the people's vices (extreme luxury, revelry, and debauchery, combined with cruelty and oppression of the poor), however, he delivers a final message of comfort and hope to the Israelites.

OF SPECIAL SIGNIFICANCE: Amos is most known today for being the prophet who cries out for social justice in a wealthy, corrupt society. In its essence, the book is a long prophetic poem with refrains in which the prophet denounces the sins, especially the inhumanity, of the nations bordering on Israel and Judah—Syria, Philistia, Tyre, Edom, Ammon, and Moab—and, at greater length, the sins of Israel itself. He speaks of the iniquities of the Israelites, the elect people of God, and the punishment that is to come to them—in five striking visions. The book concludes with words of hope and promise, depicting the raising up of the Temple and the final restoration of God's people.

Obadiah

TITLE: The name of Obadiah the prophet means "worshiper of God." We know nothing of his personal history

CONTENTS: A considerable part of this brief book reappears in Jeremiah, and it is not clear which was written first, which of the two prophets repeats the denunciations of the other. The prophecy contains two parts: the first is the denunciation of Edom, sketching its punishment and the sins of the people that led to that punishment; the second predicts the future restoration of the Israelites, who, after their return, should possess the land of Edom and Philistia and rejoice in the establishment of the kingdom of God.

OF SPECIAL SIGNIFICANCE: Obadiah is the shortest book in the Bible, only one chapter long, describing the animosity between Edom and the Israelites. The hatred between the Edomites and the Israelites is one of the oldest examples of deep conflict in human and familial relationships. It began even before their ancestors, Esau and Jacob, were born, jostling each other in the womb of their mother Rebekah. Later, the Edomites refused to let the Israelites pass through their land on the way to the Promised Land. The animosity continued for centuries, and Obadiah prophesies a message of inevitable doom for the Edomites because they are the Israelites' enemy, despite their familial connection.

Jonah

TITLE: The prophet Jonah's name means "dove." Jonah is the son of Amittai, who was born at Gath-hepher, a village in Zebulun.

CONTENTS: This book, unlike those with which it is grouped, is not a book of prophecies, but rather a story about a prophet. Jonah is commissioned to proceed to Nineveh, the capital of Assyria, which is a city of sinners. Being an unwilling prophet (and believing the people of Nineveh to be beyond salvation), Jonah refuses and hastens to Joppa, where he boards a ship set for Tarshish. A furious storm arises, and at his own request, the mariners fling him into the sea. Here a great fish swallows him, and he remains in its belly 3 days and three nights. He prays earnestly, and the fish casts him out onto the land. Bidden a second time to go to Nineveh, he dares not disobey, and once there he proclaims his message: that in 40 days Nineveh shall be overthrown. Hearing this, the king and people of Nineveh repent, their penitence is accepted, and they are saved from impending doom. Disappointed and angry, the prophet sits in a booth of woven boughs outside the city, waiting in vain for the judgment he had denounced. The book closes with an exhibition of Jonah's petulance and God's tender mercy even toward the sinners of Nineveh.

OF SPECIAL SIGNIFICANCE: Unlike the other prophetic books, Jonah is a narrative. One of the most well-known stories in the Bible, it is the story of the enforcement of profound religious truths about the nature of divine command, reprimand, repentance, compassion, and forgiveness. It describes one man's journey toward understanding that God is merciful and forgiving.

Jonah is read on Yom Kippur because of the connection of the book's theme of repentance to the holiday.

Micah

TITLE: The prophet Micah, whose name means "who is like (unto God?)," was a native of Moresheth-gath, in Judah. He prophesied during the reigns of Jotham, Ahaz, and Hezekiah, during the late 8th and early 7th centuries B.C.E. He is contemporary with Isaiah, and in much the same style as Isaiah, Micah rebukes those who are corrupt, including wealthy landowners and the "chiefs of the House of Israel" (3:1).

CONTENTS: The prophecies in Micah fall into three sections, each opening with a call to listen to God's message. In the first three chapters, a threatening tone dominates. Micah proclaims that the immoral and the false prophets are heading for disaster and ruin and that Jerusalem will be destroyed. In the next section, the tone and contents shift abruptly: restoration of Zion and of its Temple and its people are promised. In the final section, the sins of the past are recounted, followed by instructions for reform. Micah promises God's forgiveness and the restoration of the nation of God.

OF SPECIAL SIGNIFICANCE: Like many of the other prophets, Micah speaks out against the oppression of the people by both spiritual and secular leaders. According to Micah, injustice shows itself in coveting what belongs to others, in perverting justice, and in hypocritical religiosity. From his words, it is possible to clearly see his self-confidence and his mission. He says, "But I, / I am filled with strength by the spirit of the LORD, / And with judgment and courage, / To declare to Jacob his transgressions / And to Israel his sin" (3:8). This confidence distinguishes Micah from the other prophets.

Nahum

TITLE: The prophet Nahum, whose name means "consoler," was a native of Elkosh. It is not known when he lived, and scholars are not certain when in the 7th century B.C.E. the book was written. Nahum may have been the son of an Israelite captive. Those who believe so say it is because the prophet could not have described the doom of Nineveh in language so pictorially vivid if he had not drawn the scenes from personal observation, and they point to the interspersion of Assyrian words in his writing as an indication that Assyria was the scene of his prophecies.

CONTENTS: Nahum comes to the people to console them and to foretell the overthrow of Assyria. Unlike many of the other prophets, his prophecy is devoted to a single theme: the coming destruction of Nineveh, the capital of Assyria. Assyria had long been dominant in this region, and for the past century Judah had suffered severely as a result of the harsh Assyrian rule. Nahum hardly speaks directly about Judah; rather, his words simply predict the downfall of its enemy.

Nineveh is notorious for brutal violence, cruelty, and bloodshed as well as blasphemy and hostility against God. Nahum pronounces that its destruction is near and will be swift and complete. There are three very distinct predictions: (1) a general description of God sitting in judgment; (2) the certain fall of Nineveh, with a vivid picture of the siege and sack of the city, aided by the sudden inundation of the Tigris River; and (3) Nineveh's utter destruction and desolation, a desolation so complete that the city vanishes entirely from view, and Alexander can march over it.

OF SPECIAL SIGNIFICANCE: Nahum presents God as a warrior-god who is sovereign over all things, people, nations, and history itself; God is holy and just; God will simply not endure sin forever. Nahum is not so much communicating his own private thoughts about the people of Nineveh (whom God had saved in the time of

Jonah, after their repentance) as he is proclaiming God's frustration with these sins. Though some argue that Nahum conveniently overlooks the sins of his own people, his intention in his prophecy is not to discuss the sins of Judah (who will likely be punished as well for sinning), but to preach specifically against Nineveh.

Habakkuk

TITLE: "Habakkuk" is an ambiguous Hebrew name, which might come from the same root as the modern Hebrew word *hibbuk*, which means "close embrace." We know nothing of the prophet himself, but from the musical directions attached to chapter 3 of Habakkuk, a psalm, "For the leader; with instrumental music" (3:19), some conjecture that he is a Levite.

CONTENTS: Writing after the great reformation in the days of Josiah, Habakkuk has to sustain hope and teach patience under difficult circumstances. Neither sincere repentance, nor earnest turning to God and the removal of the "high places" (referring to practices of idolatry), nor the great national fast removes the threat of invasion of the Kingdom of Judah by the Chaldeans. Thus the suffering of the chosen people of God from cruel, ruthless oppressors, "Fleeter than wolves of the steppe" (1:8), seems like a mysterious trial.

In chapter 1, the prophet appeals to God and asks how long the people will suffer. Habakkuk then describes the fierceness of the Chaldeans, and he stands on his watch and waits for an answer. He is told that "the righteous man is rewarded with life / For his fidelity" (2:4). Habakkuk is also assured that the suffering shall be removed and the oppressor shall perish. Then, a series of "woes" follow, and Habakkuk breaks into a note of prayer, which introduces the great hymn of faith, recounting the miraculous deliverances of old as indication of future redemption from suffering.

OF SPECIAL SIGNIFICANCE: This book focuses on an attempt to grow from a faith of perplexity and doubt to a place of absolute trust in God. Habakkuk is unique among the prophets in that he openly questions the wisdom of God. In the first part of the first chapter, he sees injustice and asks why God does not take action, crying, "How long, O LORD, shall I cry out / And You not listen, / Shall I shout to You, 'Violence!' / And You not save?" (1:2). Then, at the end of the first chapter, Habakkuk expresses shock at God's choice of instrument for judgment and awaits God's response to his challenge. God explains that the Chaldeans will also be judged harshly, whereupon Habakkuk expresses his ultimate faith in God, even if he doesn't fully understand.

Zephaniah

TITLE: The prophet Zephaniah, whose name means "God has hidden," was the son of Cushi and the great-grandson of Hezekiah; he tells us himself that he prophesies "during the reign of King Josiah son of Amon of Judah" (1:1), in the late 7th century B.C.E. The date of his prophecy was at about the time of Jeremiah's call, before Josiah's reformation suppressed worship to the god Baal, which Zephaniah denounces.

CONTENTS: The prophecy of Zephaniah begins with a harsh denunciation of the idolatry of Judah and a description of God's judgment day. It continues with a call to repent and escape the punishment that is to fall on the Philistines, Moab, Ammon, Ethiopia, and Nineveh. It concludes with promises that the day of Zion's restoration will come and the judgment of wicked nations will end.

OF SPECIAL SIGNIFICANCE: The major themes of Zephaniah are prevalent ones in the books of the Minor Prophets: judgment and deliverance. The book explicitly states that God will judge those in Judah who practice pure paganism and who mix the worship of God with the worship of other deities, who choose to identify with the heathen by their dress, who practice violence and deceit, and who have abused their authority and forsaken their stewardship. Zephaniah then states that divine judgment is the means by which God removes sins, which will lead to the ultimate deliverance of these people.

Haggai

TITLE: The prophet Haggai, whose name comes from the Hebrew word meaning "festive," is the first of the prophets after the Babylonian exile. He was a contemporary of Zerubbabel; of Joshua, who led those who returned from Babylon; and of the prophet Zechariah, with whom he is mentioned in Ezra.

CONTENTS: Haggai was inspired by God to rouse the people to support Zerubbabel and Joshua in building the Temple. His prophecies consist of two chapters, and they were all delivered in the second year of Darius Hystaspes, very probably spoken directly to the people at the festivals of the New Moon and of the Feast of Tabernacles, which is the season of the autumn rains. Haggai's prophesies all aim to scold the people for their lethargy and encourage them to complete the Temple.

The book begins by rebuking the apathy of the people for not devoting themselves in earnest to restoring the Temple and for listening to those who tried to persuade them that the time is not opportune for such work. Haggai's words are persuasive, and the people resume the rebuilding of the Temple. Haggai encourages them with the assurance that the glory of the rebuilt Temple will be greater than that of the former. Then he promises them that from the day they begin the restoration in earnest, the harvests will become more plentiful and the years of drought and famine will change into blessings. Finally, Haggai's words contain a special word of encouragement for Zerubbabel.

OF SPECIAL SIGNIFICANCE: The key words of Haggai's prophecies and their repetition are worth noting, for they highlight the importance of his message to the people at a critical time in history: "Be strong... be strong... be strong" (2:4), and "Consider how you have been faring... Consider how you have fared... take thought... Take note" (1:5,7; 2:15,18).

Zechariah

TITLE: The prophet Zechariah, whose name means "God has remembered," is the son of Berechiah and grandson of Iddo, who is the head of one of the Priestly houses. A contemporary of Haggai, he begins to prophesy two months after Haggai's first prophecy and continues for two years.

CONTENTS: Like Haggai, Zechariah's goal is to rouse the people from their lethargy, but his style is very different. In a series of night visions received during the rebuilding of the Temple, he seeks to ignite in the people a national enthusiasm for the great work.

This book, the longest of the Minor Prophets, consists of two distinct parts: the first contains Zechariah's prophecies and visions, and the second contains anonymous prophecies. Zechariah's prophecies and visions include a call to repentance and a series of visions. It concludes with a command to make a crown for "the Branch" (King David's lineage). After the last vision, there is a two-year pause in Zechariah's prophetic activity, but in the fourth year of King Darius, the word of God again comes to him. Certain people ask a question about continuing to fast as they had done in the past, as Chaldeans set fire to Jerusalem. It seems ridiculous to them to continue fasting, as they suffer losses and tragedies even as they repent. They long for a prophet to come who might expound on the nature of a true fast and then convert these fasts into feasts of joy and gladness

The anonymous prophesies at the end of Zechariah present greater difficulties than the rest of the book. Many hold that there are two distinct prophets, while others maintain their connection with the rest of Zechariah. In general, like most prophecy after the exile to Egypt, these chapters are prophecies of promise. Judah, now subject to foreign rulers, is promised its own native king and that it will become supreme, with Jerusalem as the religious center of the world.

OF SPECIAL SIGNIFICANCE: The visions of Zechariah distinguish him from the other prophets. His first vision is of the four horsemen of God. The second is of four horns and four smiths, symbolizing the approaching judgment of the heathen. The third is of a man with a measuring line who is enlarging the boundaries of Jerusalem, symbolizing the inclusion of the nations. The fourth is of the cleansing of the Priesthood and the advent of "the Branch." The fifth vision is of the golden candelabrum, symbolizing the restored community, fed by two olive trees, representing the two heads of the community, Joshua and Zerubbabel. The sixth is of a flying scroll, or vengeance on the ungodly. The seventh is of a woman hidden in an *ephah* (a lidded tub, commonly thought to be a symbol of the hidden or entrenched wickedness of the Israelites) and borne eastward, symbolizing the departure of that guilt from Judah. In Zechariah's vision, the lid is removed from the *ephah*, and the hidden woman is exposed. Finally, the eighth vision is of four chariots issuing from two brazen mountains, symbolizing the course of divine providence. Many of these images are also thought to be symbolic of God's mercy and forgiveness.

Malachi

TITLE: The prophet referred to as Malachi, which means "my messenger," was most likely of the Priestly order or had close relations with the priesthood. Nothing is known of his life including his real name and personal history. Though his book is the last of the prophetic books, he is not the latest prophet whose writings survive. Most scholars agree that Malachi wrote in the period after the Babylonian exile, when Nehemiah is absent for 12 years at the court of Artaxerxes.

CONTENTS: After dwelling on the affection of God for Judah, speaking of God as a loving father and ruler of God's people, Malachi rebukes the priests as the leaders of the spiritual defection that he witnesses. Then he rebukes the mixed marriages and also the divorces, evidenced by the deserted wives weeping at the altar. Finally, he predicts the coming of a faithful messenger who will purify the people of their sinful ways. He pleads with them to remember the Torah and to look forward to the coming of Elijah, who will "reconcile parents with children and children with their parents" (3:24).

OF SPECIAL SIGNIFICANCE: Malachi, unlike the other prophetic books, stresses ceremonial observance, that the priest is God's messenger, and that the laws of Moses must be strictly observed. Malachi talks of the social duties that people owe to one another, explaining that ceremonial observance of laws and statutes is valuable only so long as these practices lead to spiritual service. He scathingly reveals and curses the degeneracy of his time and is especially severe toward those who enter into wedlock with heathen women.

Psalms

TITLE: In Hebrew, Psalms is called "Sefer Tehillim," "the Book of Praises" or simply "Praises." The Greek translated the Hebrew *mizmor*, meaning a song with musical accompaniment, as *psalmos*, "psalms," and titled the entire collection "Psalms."

When we speak of "the psalms of David," it is not to imply that all of them were actually written by King David, but rather that they are written in the style of David. Only about half of them are attributed to him; some were attributed to Asaph, Solomon, the sons of Korah, and to others we do not know.

Categorizing the Psalms

Because they express so many different emotions, and there are often seemingly conflicting emotions in the same psalm, the poems and prayers of the book of Psalms cannot be rigidly categorized by theme, but in a very general sense there are three kinds of psalms: (1) hymns (songs of praise to God), (2) elegies or laments (poetry or personal or communal sorrow), and (3) didactic (teaching) poems. Bible scholars have identified other groupings, useful for comparison. Here are some common ones.

Type	Identifying Features	Example
Praise	Praise of God's power and might, acknowledgment of the universality of God's reign	Psalm 24
Thanksgiving	Personal or national gratitude for God's help in a specific time of distress or war, contrast of God's power with that of other gods	Psalm 115
Nature	Celebration of God's actions in creation or use of natural images to describe God's power	Psalm 104
Trust	Humble surrender to God's care, statement of faith in God's providence, contentment	Psalm 23
Pilgrimage	Longing for the Temple, praise of Jerusalem as the city of David, celebration of liturgical gathering, invocation of peace	Psalm 122
Royal	Praise of Israel's king as a representative of the divine kingship of God, invocation of God's help for the ruler	Psalm 21
National lament	Cry for God's attention, description of the nation's unjustified suffering at the hands of enemies, plea for God's help, promise to return to faithfulness	Psalm 79
Personal lament	Vivid description of the speaker's distress, reminder of the covenant, protestation of innocence, condemnation of evildoers, profession of faith in God's ability to save	Psalm 22
Confession	Admission of personal or national wrongdoing, plea for forgiveness, promise of conversion	Psalm 51
Didactic Poem	Recounting of God's past actions on behalf of Israel, reminder of the wisdom of keeping the covenant, contrast of good and evil or wisdom and foolishness	Psalm 145

From Cullen Schippe and Chuck Stetson, *The Bible and Its Influence.*

CONTENTS: Psalms is the longest book of the Bible, with 150 chapters, or psalms. There is no narrative here, nor connection from one psalm to the next; each psalm stands on its own.

Psalms is a collection of great variety and the full range of human emotions. At times, it is the pure intensity of the language—especially the language of rebuke—that moves us. The energies of the Psalmist can abruptly shift from a seemingly rational consideration of the enemy or the powers of the world to a description of the passion and suffering experienced by the poet at the hand of God. Other psalms move swiftly from rebuke to lament, speak of yearning to be close to God, or ask God for favors. As a collection, they express the entire the range of human emotions and provide a language for those wishing to express longing, loneliness, disgust, exasperation, hope, or love for the Divine.

In Second Temple times, each day had its special psalm. Psalm 24 is for Sunday, Psalm 48 is for Monday, Psalm 82 is for Tuesday, Psalm 94 is for Wednesday, Psalm 81 is for Thursday, Psalm 93 is for Friday, and Psalm 92 is titled "A psalm. A song; for the sabbath day." There are psalms for remembrance (38:1), which may indicate that they were sung at the offering of incense; and psalms "for praise" (100:1). There are 15 psalms that bear the title of "A song of ascents" or "A song for ascents" (120–134). Some believe that they were the songs sung either by the Jewish exiles on their return from Babylon or by the Jewish pilgrims on their journeys up to Jerusalem for the annual feasts. There are psalms that can also be classified according to their subjects: psalms that are instructive, devotional, messianic, and historical.

OF SPECIAL SIGNIFICANCE: The psalms, more than any other text, have captured the heart of the human audience, and they are integral to the prayer books of both synagogues and churches; cycles of psalms mark the liturgical life of both traditions. The language of the psalms has so shaped the very language and ethos of religious life that it is difficult sometimes to remember the source of that influence.

Proverbs

TITLE: Proverbs opens with the words "The proverbs of Solomon son of David, king of Israel" (1:1), from which the abbreviated title in the Hebrew Bible "Mishle" ("the proverbs of") originates. Proverbs consists of teachings for everyday life, which come in numerous literary forms, not just as short proverbs. Wisdom is the highest goal here, and it is viewed as a latent, God-given quality in all people. Thus, divine revelation becomes unnecessary, placing Proverbs in tension with many books in the Torah. The Hebrew word *mashal* means "to rule" or "to govern," suggesting that Proverbs are not just wise sayings but rules spanning a broad range of topics that govern life. Just as Psalms is often called "the psalms of David" because David is considered the author of many of them, Proverbs is thought to be connected to Solomon, even though he was most likely not the actual author.

CONTENTS: Proverbs is a manual of practical rules for daily life, a book of lessons for all ages and for all men and women. Its preface sets forth the general character of the contents, introducing the value of wisdom and the character of wisdom, a central theme of the book as a whole. The purpose of Proverbs is to teach, not to argue or debate, but to provoke thought by vivid pictures and pithy language.

Proverbs' Literary Collections

The book of Proverbs is made up of at least seven different literary collections. They are separated by internal titles, and each of them has a slightly different literary form.

1. The Proverbs of Solomon, Son of David, King of Israel: This collection extends from 1:1 to 9:18 and is made up mostly of long poems, while much of the rest of Proverbs is composed of short sayings. The style of this collection is often like that of a parent admonishing a child.

2. The Proverbs of Solomon: The sayings in this collection, which include 10:1–22:16 and 25:1–29:27, are connected by catchwords like "the wise" and the "foolish." The literary style consists of brief and somewhat disconnected sayings.

3. The Words of the Wise: There is a distinct change in style and content in this collection as well, which extends from 22:17 to 23:11. Many of the sayings are found in the writings of a famous Egyptian sage.

4. The Sayings of the Wise: The style here (23:12–24:34) is that of slightly longer poems with similes and metaphors. The collection also deals with some strong moral issues.

5. The Words of Agur: This collection is found in chapter 30. The literary form here is that of an oracle, a series of riddle-like sayings to force the listener to think along with the speaker.

6. The Words of King Lemuel: The literary style of 31:1–9 is "an oracle that his mother taught him."

7. Praise for the Capable, or Good, Wife: The final collection is 31:10–31, often called "Woman of Valor." It is an acrostic poem in Hebrew, organized alphabetically by the first Hebrew letter of each opening line.

Adapted from Cullen Schippe and Chuck Stetson, *The Bible and Its Influence.*

OF SPECIAL SIGNIFICANCE: Proverbs is part of the Wisdom Literature of the Bible (along with Job and Ecclesiastes) because its main themes focus on the pursuit of knowledge and the centrality of the knowledge of God. (See the chapter "Wisdom Literature.") The implication that reverence and respect for God in all circumstances bring true knowledge is emphasized in Proverbs again and again. God's people are taught that Torah is something that is part of life and it is our duty to obey it. Proverbs calls this kind of obedience "the fear of the LORD" (1:7, 10:27, 15:33). This sacred obligation of creating and maintaining a connection to the Divine through everyday actions is similar to the ancient command to "know God." Therefore, "knowledge of God" (2:5) is synonymous with holy behaviors, involving reverence, gratitude, and commitment to do the will of God in every circumstance.

"Woman of Valor"

The poem "Eishet Chayil" ("Woman of Valor") (Proverbs 31:10–31) is a tribute bestowed on a woman who exemplifies traditional Jewish values, such as running a home, raising children, and doing good deeds (*mitzvot*). But she not only manages the household estate with great competence, she is also a successful businesswoman, independent of her husband. This is a significant development, because Proverbs (and indeed most all Wisdom Literature in the Bible) addresses only the ideal virtues of men and boys.

The poem's first line is often quoted: "A woman of valor, who can find? Her price is far beyond rubies"—or, as in the NJPS translation: "What a rare find is a capable wife! Her worth is far beyond that of rubies." Jewish lore has it that Solomon wrote it for his mother, Bathsheba, but others say it was written by Abraham as a eulogy for Sarah, his wife. The poem is often recited at the graveside of a Jewish woman.

While some feminist scholars have critiqued "Eishet Chayil" as perpetuating sexist notions of a woman's place in society, others have argued that in valorizing wives and mothers, the poem compliments and supports women. In ancient Israel, everything that married mothers did was seen as essential to the financial and spiritual sustenance of the family. Hence, ascribing the virtues described in "Woman of Valor" to a wife was not considered confining or degrading, but empowering. It is a traditional Sabbath ritual for men to pay homage to their wives by reading "Eishet Chayil" to them. Today, however, some prefer to substitute their own, more modern interpretation of this tribute.

Job

TITLE: The title comes from the name of its main character, Job, a righteous man, whose life illustrates the theological question of why "bad things happen to good people." It is uncertain when Job was written, but features of its language point to a dating after the Babylonian exile in the 6th century B.C.E. In any case, the issues Job raises are timeless and not dependent on a particular time.

CONTENTS: Job is a wealthy, God-fearing man living in patriarchal style in the land of Uz. Without warning, he is struck by a succession of calamities and is stripped of his property, his children, and his health—all because God enters into a wager with Satan: Will Job continue to be a faithful servant even if his loved ones and his comforts in life are taken away? The book begins with a prose narrative about the cause and extent of Job's sufferings; it affirms that Job is righteous and that sin is not the cause of his calamities (though this assertion is not known to Job or his mortal friends, only to the omniscient narrator and the reader).

Then prose turns to poetry in the conversations between Job and his friends—musings about the cause of Job's (and more generally, of human) suffering. His friends affirm that the cause is sin, and they exhort Job to repent. Job denies their accusations and claims that he is righteous. Moreover, he asserts that other righteous men such as he suffer, while some wicked men prosper. This conversation consists of a series of speeches: Job's complaint, followed by assertions of Eliphaz, Bildad, and Zophar, each being successively answered by Job; another series of speeches by the three friends, and Job's responses; and then a speech by Eliphaz and Bildad, and Job's replies. Finally, another friend, Elihu, argues that sufferings are remedial and for the good of the one afflicted, and Job asserts that he is righteous despite his suffering, and then Elihu replies by again defending God's justice with a magnificent description of God's wonderful works in the world of nature.

205

Then God, speaking from out of a whirlwind, puts a series of questions to Job, intended to compare the unfathomable wisdom and power of God with the littleness of humankind. The book continues with what some consider a confession by Job that he had spoken beyond his limited knowledge. Its conclusion, in prose, reaffirms Job's righteousness, condemns the friends for their ungrounded accusations, and tells of the peace and prosperity that Job enjoys for the rest of his life.

OF SPECIAL SIGNIFICANCE: One of the most striking things about Job is that in all its 42 chapters there is not a single reference to Israelite history. Job appears to be "everyman."

There is irony in the fact that while most scholars concur that Job is best described as one of the books of Wisdom Literature, it takes an "anti–Wisdom Literature" stance. God rejects the theories of Job's friends (God says at the end of the book that the friends "have not spoken the truth about Me" [42:7, 42:8]," as did Job), even though their beliefs reflect many generally held tenets articulated within Wisdom Literature (and throughout the Bible), such as the assumption that good is rewarded and evil is punished and that God is a judge of supreme justice. These beliefs include the assumption that Job is certainly being punished for some unknown sin, which necessitates his repentance and prayer to God for forgiveness (4:17). God seems to refute these assumptions at the end, thereby making the book truly unique within biblical theology. (See also the chapter "Wisdom Literature.")

Song of Songs

TITLE: The Hebrew title "Shir ha-Shirim," "the Song of Songs," may mean the greatest or sweetest of all songs in the same way that "King of kings" means "Supreme King." The book claims Solomon as its author, which accounts for its being called "Song of Solomon" in most Christian Bibles.

CONTENTS: Song of Songs consists in large part of dialogue, words exchanged between two or more people. The theme of the dialogues is love. Two alternative theories of Song of Songs are that it is a drama involving two or three chief characters and that it is a collection of popular Hebrew songs, of a simple dramatic nature.

OF SPECIAL SIGNIFICANCE: Song of Songs separates itself immediately from the other books in the Bible: the opening words introduce a poetic work whose subject is romantic love and its physical expression. It is one of the most enigmatic books in the Bible because there is no consensus about many of its elements. Are there two main characters or three? How does one divide the speaking parts? What is the structure of the book? Who wrote it? How many people wrote it? For centuries, the common wisdom among Jews concerning Song of Songs was to view it strictly as an allegory—expressing the love between the People of Israel and God. The logic that prompted such a view was that all books in the Bible are about God, and since Song of Songs is in the Bible, it is about God. Still, there is really no internal or external justification for this assumption of allegory; some say its only benefit is to justify why Song of Songs is in the Bible. Its inclusion in the scripture was long debated and quite controversial. This is due in large part to the radically different tone of the book and its sensuality and eroticism, to its passion and seeming disregard for social mores of the time.

Song of Songs is read during Passover because it is a spring holiday and the themes of the blossoming of nature, love, and awakening beauty are all motifs of springtime. Some say it is because the book speaks of Pharaoh's chariots.

Ruth

TITLE: Ruth is named for its heroine and is set in the times of the judges.

CONTENTS: During a period of famine, Elimelech and Naomi leave Bethlehem with their two sons, Mahlon and Chilion, to seek a home in the land of Moab. There Elimelech dies, and then his sons, who have married two of the daughters of Moab, Orpah and Ruth, die also. Naomi prepares to return to her native town, and Ruth, who cannot be dissuaded, accompanies her. Reaching Bethlehem, Ruth goes to glean in the fields of Boaz, a wealthy relative of Elimelech. Struck by Ruth's loyalty to her mother-in-law, Naomi, Boaz permits Ruth to share in the harvest set aside for his servants to glean. Naomi urges Ruth to claim kinship with Boaz, who would then be obliged, under the levirate law, to marry her to maintain the family line. Boaz first offers a closer relative the opportunity to fulfill this duty, but he refuses, and so Boaz marries Ruth. Through Ruth, Boaz becomes the father of Obed, the grandfather of King David.

OF SPECIAL SIGNIFICANCE: This moving narrative is a familiar Bible story, with its poignant themes of loyalty and lovingkindness (*hesed*) and of redemption. Socially, the Israelites were aware of their responsibility to protect the weak and unprotected among themselves. Redemption secures the life of the people as a community, not just as individuals. In this story, Boaz is called the "redeemer" of Ruth (and Naomi) when he fulfills the familial obligation to marry the widow of a deceased relative who never was able to father children, to both continue the family line and protect the otherwise vulnerable single women in the family.

Perhaps the overall theme in Ruth is about the real actor, God. God's actions, not a series of commendable human qualities, are praised in Ruth. God accomplishes more than we could ever hope or imagine, demonstrated through the lovingkindness of ordinary people.

It is possibly this ability to see God in every action that makes this story of loyalty and kindness a favorite among readers of the Bible. Ruth's promise to Naomi is often quoted and repeated by others who wish to invoke an act of supreme loyalty: "Do not urge me to leave you, to turn back and not follow you. For wherever you go, I will go; wherever you lodge, I will lodge; your people shall be my people, and your God my God." (1:16). Even her vow of loyalty involves God and is seen by many as the first story of religious conversion after that of Abraham in Genesis.

Ruth is traditionally read on the Jewish holiday of Shavuot, because it is a harvest festival and Ruth meets Boaz during harvesttime and because (as a convert) she accepts the Torah, which was given at Shavuot.

Lamentations

TITLE: The name "Lamentations" comes from the Hebrew word *kinot*, which is the plural of the term applied to David's funeral song for Saul and Jonathan, considered by many to be the quintessential dirge in biblical literature.

CONTENTS: Lamentations is not a single poem, but five distinct poems. Chapter 1 dwells on the desolation and grief of the city; chapter 2 describes its destruction and acknowledges that it is the result of sin. Chapter 3 complains of the bitter cup that God's people have to drink but traces God's mercy in the infliction of their miseries. Chapter 4 describes the horrors of the siege and capture of the city, and the last chapter repeats many of the painful details, concluding with a prayer for deliverance.

OF SPECIAL SIGNIFICANCE: Lamentations provides a detailed description of Jerusalem under siege and of the destruction of the First Temple, told in an intricate set of dirges. It bewails Jerusalem, once teeming with life and now sitting abandoned and alone like a solitary widow, capturing the horror of the siege: children pleading for water and bread in vain, the cannibalism of hunger-maddened mothers, nobles hanged, women raped, priests defiled.

Lamentations is read on the Jewish occasion of Tisha b'Av, the Ninth of Av, commemorating the anniversary of the destruction of the First and Second Temples.

Ecclesiastes

TITLE: The title of this book in Hebrew is "Koheleth" (the assembler), after the book's narrator. The English title, Ecclesiastes, is the ancient Greek rendering of the Hebrew, which means "a member of the assembly." The intention of the title may be to call together an assembly, a group of people, to address them on the subject of wisdom. Ecclesiastes, along with Job and Proverbs, is part of the Wisdom Literature of the Bible. (See the chapter "Wisdom Literature.") Ecclesiastes is written in the person of Solomon, son of King David, but many facts point to the book being the work of a writer whose name is unknown, living long after the Babylonian exile, when his people were the subjects of a foreign government, either Persian or Greek.

CONTENTS: Ecclesiastes consists in the main of reflections on and illustrations of the complete vanity of life. According to Ecclesiastes, people can get nothing new or satisfying out of all of their toil. The fate of humankind is not determined by their conduct in this life, and there is no life beyond death for humans any more than there is for beasts: The righteous may meet with calamity, the unrighteous with prosperity.

Mingled with such reflections are others that contradict them: the certainty of a judgment that distinguishes the righteous from the unrighteous, and that we

> **Who Is Koheleth?**
> Koheleth was traditionally identified with King Solomon, but scholars today do not regard Solomon as the author of Ecclesiastes. It is significant that the speaker is not called Solomon by name, as he could have been if the author had wished to actually identify him with that king. Koheleth speaks as king only once (Eccles. 1:12–2:26); elsewhere he speaks as a non-royal sage, one who blames the government for injustices (5:8), and the epilogue (12:9–14) makes no mention of Koheleth's royal station. Koheleth is a literary figure, not a historical one, who is given the Solomon-like blessings of power, wealth, and wisdom to qualify him to examine the true value of those assets.
>
> Michael V. Fox

should fear God. This combination of opposing viewpoints in the same book has been be explained by some as the work of a single writer presenting the conflict between a higher and a lower self, and by others as the work of one writer whose words were added to by another.

In addition, there is no single genre in Ecclesiastes: the work is a mixture of poetry and prose. The whole of Ecclesiastes seems to imply a diversity of opinions and rhetorical styles on each topic it addresses.

OF SPECIAL SIGNIFICANCE: Ecclesiastes consists of personal or autobiographic teachings, largely articulated in pithy statements and maxims interspersed with reflections on the meaning of life and the best way to live one's life. The work emphatically proclaims all the actions of humans to be inherently "meaningless," as the lives of both wise and foolish people end in death. Ultimately the author concludes that this search for meaning in life points to the fact that humankind's paramount duty is to fear God and keep God's commandments, while enjoying simple pleasures whenever possible.

Ecclesiastes is read in most Ashkenazic and some Sephardic synagogues on the Sabbath during Sukkot, possibly because it speaks about the transience of life, like the temporary booth, the sukkah.

Esther

TITLE: The title of the book comes from the name of the main heroine, Esther. It is either from the Persian word for "star" or the name of the Babylonian goddess Ishtar, even though we are told that Esther's Hebrew name is Hadassah, meaning "myrtle." She is selected, in place of Queen Vashti, to become the favorite wife of the Persian king.

209

Why Is Esther in the Bible?

The events in Esther are implausible as history and, as many scholars now agree. The book is better viewed as imaginative storytelling, not unlike others that circulated in the Persian and Hellenistic periods among Jews of the Land of Israel and of the Diaspora. This story seems to have been known in several different versions, or to have gone through a number of different stages in its development before it was linked with Purim and incorporated into the Bible.

As a diaspora story—a story about, and presumably for, Jews in the Diaspora during the Persian period—it provides an optimistic picture of Jewish survival and success in a foreign land. In this it resembles other diaspora stories such as the biblical book of Daniel (chapters 1–6) and the apocryphal books of Judith and Tobit. But unlike those books, Esther lacks overtly pious characters and does not model a religious lifestyle.

Esther is the most "secular" of the biblical books, making no reference to God's name, to the Temple, to prayer, or to distinctive Jewish practices such as dietary laws. Yet Esther, of all the biblical books outside of the Torah, is the only one that addresses the origin of a new festival. For this reason, if for no other, Esther should be considered a "religious" book. Its main concern, the very reason for its existence, is to establish Purim as a Jewish holiday for all generations. In fact, the book of Esther, more than anything else, is responsible for the continued celebration of Purim. It also opened the way for the establishment of later holidays that, like Purim, could be instituted without divine command if they commemorated an important event or served an important function in the life of the Jewish people.

From Adele Berlin, *JPS Bible Commentary: Esther.*

CONTENTS: Esther's cousin, the Jew Mordecai, who "sat in the palace gate" (2:19), discovers that the eunuchs are planning to assassinate the king. He divulges this information, thereby saving the king's life, and the record of his services is entered in the royal chronicles. But he has a rival for the royal favor: Haman, an Agagite, a descendant of the ancient Amalekite kings. Haman, jealous of Mordecai, forms a plot for the wholesale destruction of the Jewish exiles, especially when he learns that Mordecai refuses to bow down to him.

Mordecai discovers Haman's plans to destroy the Jews and informs Esther. She puts her life at risk, interceding with the king on behalf of the Jews, and Haman is hanged on the very gallows he had designed for Mordecai, while Mordecai is advanced to high honor in the Persian court.

The Jews, saved from peril themselves, slaughter their enemies, and thereafter celebrate their victory on the holiday of Purim.

OF SPECIAL SIGNIFICANCE: The feast of Purim, meaning "lots," is a holiday still celebrated among Jews to commemorate the ironic destruction of their great enemy Haman and in memory of their miraculous survival in the face of a plot that sought to destroy them. It is likely that because the festival Purim has its origins in the book of Esther (or, as it is commonly called, Megillat Esther, "Scroll of Esther"), this biblical book became part of the Jewish canon.

It is doubtful that the events told in this humorous, at times even hilarious, book of the Bible are historically accurate; rather, they are a parable of the seemingly miraculous survival of the Jewish people throughout history. It is interesting that there is no mention of God in the unfolding of the events of the Purim story; this is the *only* biblical story that does not explicitly attribute its successful outcome to divine intervention.

Daniel

TITLE: Daniel was a Jew in exile in Babylon in the 5th century B.C.E. He was recognized by the rulers there as "intelligent and proficient in all writings and wisdom without blemish, handsome, proficient in all wisdom, knowledgeable and intelligent, and capable of serving in the royal palace" (1:17) and also for his ability to interpret dreams and decipher messages in strange writings. Because of these abilities he was appointed one of the three highest officials in the land. Daniel is at the center of the stories in the first half of the book and is the visionary in the second half.

CONTENTS: The first part of Daniel, chapters 1–6, is in many ways linked to the second, chapters 7–12: The first section contains in the interpretation of Nebuchadnezzar's dream an apocalyptic element, while the second contains Daniel's visions of disastrous events, of apocalypse. Both parts are written partly in Aramaic, partly in Hebrew. That is, Daniel 1:1–2:4a is in Hebrew, then 2:4b–7:28 is in Aramaic. Chapters 8–12 switch back to Hebrew.

The most well known of the stories is of Daniel in the lions' den. Officials in the court of the Persian ruler Darius, jealous of Daniel, arrange for Darius to forbid the worship of any gods. Daniel, faithful to God, ignores the ordinance and continues to pray, and for this he is arrested and thrown into a den of lions. But he is not killed by the lions, for God protects him. When Darius sees this, he is in awe of God and reverses his order; now all must worship Daniel's god.

OF SPECIAL SIGNIFICANCE: The date of the book of Daniel is likely shortly before the death of Antiochus Epiphanes in 164 B.C.E., after the defilement of the Temple, the cessation of the Jewish daily service, and the erection of an altar to Zeus Olympus in the Temple. Written under such circumstances, the author's intent was to inspire and build up the morale of the Jews. He did this in two ways: first, by telling stories of those who, like Daniel, stood firm to their religion under severe trials, and then, by contrasting the power of God with the impotence of the most exalted and proud earthly monarchs.

Daniel's visions were later interpreted by Christians as predictions of Christ's resurrection. The Rabbis thus deemed Daniel a seer, but not a prophet. Therefore, in Jewish Scripture the book of Daniel is placed with Kethuvim (Writings), while in the Christian Old Testament Daniel is placed with the major prophets Isaiah, Jeremiah, and Ezekiel.

Ezra

TITLE: Ezra, whose name means "help," is the son of Seraiah and was probably born in Babylon. He is a scribe who went to Jerusalem with a later group of returning Jewish exiles.

CONTENTS: Ezra consists of two sections, with a considerable interval of time between the writing of the two. The first is an account of the return of the Jews from Babylon at the beginning of the reign of Cyrus, 538 B.C.E. and of the rebuilding of the Temple. The second, which takes place more than half a century later, tells of the second return of exiles in the 7th year of Artaxerxes (457 B.C.E), led by Ezra. The entire period covered by the book extends over 79 years.

The Temple

In the 10th century B.C.E., King Solomon built the Temple in Jerusalem, larger than the Tabernacle but of similar design. Surrounded by a great courtyard, it consisted of a main hall with the sacrificial altar and an inner chamber, the Holy of Holies, for the Ark of the Covenant (2 Sam. 7; 1 Kings 6).

This First Temple was destroyed in the 6th century B.C.E. by Nebuchadnezzar, who drove the Israelites into exile in Babylon (2 Kings 25). After the Israelites' return half a century later, the high priest, Joshua, oversaw the rebuilding of the Temple, following the plan of the First Temple. It was sacked in the 2nd century B.C.E. by Antiochus and restored three years later by the Maccabees (1 Maccabees).

Sometime between 37 B.C.E. and 5 C.E., Herod expanded the Temple, doubling its size and adding a room in which the judicial court met. The Second Temple was finally destroyed in 70 C.E. by the Roman warrior Titus, although the Western Wall still stands and remains a holy site.

Some scholars contend that Ezra may have originally been part of a larger work, along with Nehemiah and Chronicles, but Ezra appears to contain within it practically unaltered extracts from memoirs written by Ezra himself, plus other sections from his memoirs modified by the editor.

OF SPECIAL SIGNIFICANCE: Ezra begins where 2 Chronicles ends (even though Chronicles comes later in the Bible). Ezra, along with Nehemiah, records the fulfillment of God's promise to restore God's people to their land after 70 years of Babylonian enslavement. Ezra stresses the theme of God's covenant with God's people, reflected especially in God's special presence in the Temple and Israel's special access through God-appointed sacrifice. Religious reform must be accompanied by spiritual and ethical reform, and so marriages to foreign women are outlawed to renew religious purity. The overall focus in Ezra is on the return of God's people to the worship of the God and to the keeping of the covenant, to the land God promised them, and to religious and ethical purity. Thus the rebuilding of the altar and the Temple and the offering of sacrifices receive considerable attention in this book.

Nehemiah

TITLE: Nehemiah means "God comforts." The son of Hacaliah of Judah, he is among the Jews exiled to Babylon. After the Babylonian empire falls to the Persians, Nehemiah becomes the royal cup-bearer in the palace of the Persian king Artaxerxes, and upon the Jews' return from exile, he is made the civil governor of Jerusalem, where Ezra is High Priest.

The books of Nehemiah and Ezra are very closely linked, and although recent scholarship questions it, some scholars speculate that they were once one unified work, written by Ezra. These two books are the only ones in the Bible that contain memoirs.

CONTENTS: Nehemiah and Ezra have a common goal: to renew their community with a rebuilt Temple and rededication to the laws of God. When Nehemiah hears of the deplorable condition of Jerusalem and of the residents in Judah, he is filled with sorrow and prays to God. God opens the heart of Artaxerxes to give Nehemiah a commission to rebuild the walls of his ancestral city. (Zerubbabel had previously rebuilt the Temple, but not the city walls.) Many oppose Nehemiah's work, but he prevails, calling on everyone in the city, of every rank and order, to work with him night and day, and in 52 days the wall is complete.

After holding the position of governor of Jerusalem, Nehemiah returns to the court of Artaxerxes. During this absence, the residents of Jerusalem stray from the Law, and when he is informed of this, Nehemiah once more leaves the Persian court for Jerusalem, so that he can put down abuses, restore the holiness of the Sabbath, denounce mixed marriages, and lead a second reformation.

Large parts of Nehemiah are told in the first person and may be extracts from memoirs written by Nehemiah himself or perhaps based on his memoirs. In other sections, both Ezra and Nehemiah are referred to in the third person, though the narrative may be based on the memoirs of Ezra.

OF SPECIAL SIGNIFICANCE: Whereas both Ezra and Nehemiah focus on the rebuilding of the Temple and the renewal and restoration of the purity of the people, their leadership style is very different. Ezra's is one of collaboration, while Nehemiah's is that of an outspoken and charismatic leader. They exemplify how two people living at the same time and in the same place approach leadership differently.

1 Chronicles and 2 Chronicles

TITLE: 1 and 2 Chronicles are one work in the Hebrew, "The Acts [or Annals] of the Days," from which comes the title "Chronicles." As mentioned earlier, until recently, 1 and 2 Chronicles, Ezra, and Nehemiah were all thought to have originally been one book; today modern scholars believe that they were separate books but that the writer of Chronicles, referred to as "the Chronicler," had read Ezra and Nehemiah and was influenced by them.

CONTENTS: 1 and 2 Chronicles, the last books of the Bible, tell the history of the Temple and its Priesthood, emphasizing its centrality to religious continuity. They also describe the House of David and the tribe of Judah, guardians of the Temple, and state the case for their importance in Jewish history.

The books are naturally divided into four parts. The first consists of genealogies from Adam: the line from Adam to Abraham; from Judah to Elishama; the kingly line of David through Zerubbabel; priests to the Babylonian exile; and the three leading families of singers, one of which is the line of Samuel. The second part tells the history of David and is remarkable both for its omissions of the narrative that is found in 1 and 2 Kings and for many new facts not given in those biblical books. The third part contains the reign of Solomon, and the fourth recounts the history of the kings of Judah up to the exile.

OF SPECIAL SIGNIFICANCE: Chronicles shows us the methods used by a redactor of a historical work. By comparing Chronicles with Samuel and Kings, we can see how the Chronicles' redactor sometimes incorporated the earlier material practically unaltered, sometimes abbreviated it, sometimes expanded it, and corrected its theology, as when he wrote that it is Satan, not God, who compels David to take a census of the people (1 Chron. 21:1; 2 Sam. 24:1). Accordingly, the value of Chronicles is that it reveals the interests, ideas, and temperament of certain Jewish circles about 300 B.C.E. Along with Ezra and Nehemiah, it is a key source of knowledge about this period.

214

Compared with the parallel histories of Samuel and Kings, the redactor of Chronicles has a great tendency to dwell on the details of Temple worship, on the arrangement of the Priestly vestments, and on the Levites as well. He has a marked bias for genealogical tables and for assigning names to persons engaged in any of the events narrated. Finally, when it comes to discussing Solomon's reign, the building of the Temple, and the ensuing history of Judah, not only is Judah and its subsequent kings treated sympathetically, but all references to the Northern Kingdom of Israel are omitted.

Chronicles was evidently not intended to supersede Samuel and Kings, for knowledge of the history contained in those books is in several places presupposed, while many sections in Chronicles agree almost verbatim with those of Samuel and Kings. Others are found only in Chronicles. The most important of these are certain songs at the bringing up of the Ark by David, the account of the organization of Temple ritual, various incidents in the history of the kings and the "calls" to prophecy by several of the prophets, and the account of the great Passover feasts kept by Hezekiah and Josiah.

What makes Chronicles unique is its overriding belief in God's compassion and forgiveness. While on the surface it recounts the history of Israel, there is a strong message of hope here: that people who repent for their sins will be forgiven, and those who do good deeds will be rewarded.

215

GLOSSARY
OF WORDS AND TERMS, AND MOST IMPORTANT PEOPLE AND PLACES IN THE BIBLE

Note: Words in boldface are defined in their own entries. For books of the Bible, see "Summaries of the Books of the Bible."

Aaron—The older brother of **Moses**. Aaron is a leading figure in the Passover story and the **Exodus** from Egypt. He was the first High Priest of the ancient Hebrews.

Abel—The younger brother of **Cain** and the second son of **Adam** and **Eve**. He was a shepherd, while Cain was a farmer. When the brothers came to present their offerings to God, the sacrifice of Abel (the firstlings of his flock) was preferred to that of Cain, who gave of the fruits of the earth. God's acceptance of Abel's offering aroused the jealousy of Cain, who, in spite of the warnings of God, wreaked his vengeance on Abel by killing him.

Abihu—Abihu and his brother, with **Moses** and **Aaron,** are the leaders of the elders of **Israel** who ascended **Mount Sinai** to eat the **covenant** meal. Abihu was the second son of Aaron and Elisheba, and with his father and brothers was consecrated to the Priesthood. He and **Nadab** were put to death for offering "alien fire" to God.

Abiram—A member of the tribe of **Reuben**, son of Eliab. With **Dathan**, he made an effort to incite the people against their leader.

Abraham—The first of the three **Patriarchs** of the Jewish people. God commands Abraham, "Go forth from your native land and from your father's house to the land that I will show you. I will make of you a great nation" (Gen. 12:1–2). Abraham and his wife, **Sarah,** had a son, **Isaac.** Later, God tested Abraham's loyalty by telling him to sacrifice his beloved son. (See *Akedah*.) Abraham and his wife's servant, **Hagar**, had a son, **Ishmael**, who is considered by Muslims to be the ancestor of the Arab people.

Adam—The first human being. "God formed man from the dust of the earth. He blew into his nostrils the breath of life" (Gen. 2:7). Adam and the first woman, **Eve**, lived in the **Garden of Eden,** and God provided for all their needs until they ate the forbidden fruit of the **Tree of Knowledge** of Good and Evil. God punished them and banished them from Eden, telling Adam that he must make his way in the world by the sweat of his brow. Adam was the father of **Cain** and **Abel**. See also **Garden of Eden**.

Adonai—A title for God, and the one used most often in prayers, and to represent the attribute of merci in the Divine. Because God's name is so sacred, it is not spoken as it is written; the **Hebrew** letters (*yud, heh, vav,* and *heh*) that spell the name are read only as *Adonai*. See also **Tetragrammaton** and *Elohim*.

aggadah (aggadic, adj.)—The nonlegal (non-halakhic) aspects of the **Talmud**: legends, teachings, sayings, prayers, and historical information.

Ahasuerus—The ruler of ancient **Persia** (486–465 B.C.E.) during the time of the Purim story. According to the Purim **megillah**, Ahasuerus was a foolish king who allowed his adviser, **Haman**, devise a plot against the Jews. First married to Queen **Vashti**, Ahasuerus later took a young Jewish woman, **Esther**, as his bride.

Akedah—The incident in Genesis when God told **Abraham** to bind his son **Isaac** and prepare to sacrifice the boy. At the last moment, God stopped Abraham from going through with the deed, providing instead a ram for the sacrifice. Some interpret the *Akedah* as God's test of Abraham's obedience or proof that God never would allow human sacrifice.

Aleppo Codex—The earliest-known **Hebrew** manuscript of the **Bible.** Although only about two thirds of it is extant, it is considered the most authoritative and most accurate document for the biblical text. Sometimes referred to as the Crown of Aleppo.

aliyah—Literally, "going up." 1. The honor of reciting the blessings before and after the reading of the **Torah.** 2. An individual section of the liturgical reading of the Torah over which blessings are recited.

altar—In biblical times, a structure, usually of stones or of a single stone, on which certain animals or parts of animals were burnt and their blood sprinkled. The first mentioned was that built by **Noah.** God commanded the **Hebrew** altars to be made of earth or of unhewn stones, and without steps. In the **First Temple** and **Second Temple** of **Jerusalem**, the brazen altar of burnt sacrifice was in the court, in front of the **Holy of Holies.** The golden altar of incense stood inside.

Am ha-Aretz—Literally, "people of the land." A term that originated during the time of the **Second Temple,** referring to the common people who were neither learned in **Torah** nor religiously pious. In the **Bible** it also refers to landowners.

Amalek/Amalekites—Amalek stands as a symbol of the timeless enemy of the Jews. Amalekites were ancient nomadic people who lived in the **Sinai** desert and southern portions of **Canaan.** They attacked the **Israelites**, who were on their way from Egypt to **Mount Sinai**, at **Rephidim**, but they were eventually fought off. After this incident, God commanded that the Amalekites be annihilated. **Saul's** failure to fulfill this obligation led to the revocation of his descendants' rights to succeed to the throne of **Israel.** However, **David** went on to defeat the Amalekites, and they were finally wiped out during the reign of King Hezekiah of **Judah.**

Antiochus IV—A Syrian king who ruled Judea from 175 to 163 B.C.E. Antiochus forbade many Jewish practices, including circumcision and Sabbath observance. He desecrated the **Second Temple** in **Jerusalem** with animal sacrifices and statues of Greek gods. The **Maccabees'** rebellion against Antiochus and rededication of the Temple is the story of Hanukkah.

Apocrypha—A group of 14 Jewish books written in the **Second Temple** period; they are in the Catholic and some Protestant and Orthodox Bibles but not in the Jewish Bible.

Aramaic—An ancient Near Eastern language closely related to **Hebrew** that was regionally dominant during the **Second Temple** period up until the Islamic conquests. Along with Hebrew and Greek, it was the language used most by Jews for more than 1,000 years. Parts of the TANAKH (for example, Daniel), the **Talmud**, and the Zohar were written in Aramaic.

ark—1. The boat **Noah** built in Genesis, before the Great Flood. 2. The Ark of the Covenant, the ancient chest built by **Moses** at God's command to house the stone tablets inscribed with the **Ten Commandments.** It was carried in front of the people on their march by the **Levites**. After King **Solomon** built the **First Temple** in **Jerusalem,** the Ark of the Covenant was kept in the **Holy of Holies.** It was lost, probably during the **First Temple** period.

Asher—The eighth son of **Jacob** and the second son of Zilpah, who was Jacob's concubine and **Leah**'s handmaiden. Asher is also the name of one of the **Twelve Tribes of Israel**, whose members were said to be descended from him. The tribe occupied the northwestern part of **Canaan.**

Ashkenazim—Jews originally from, or descendants of, Jews from Germany and France. The term derives from *Ashkenaz*, which is the **Hebrew** name for Germany, though these Jews spread across eastern Europe as well. Yiddish was the primary language of Ashkenazic Jews in Europe, where they greatly outnumbered Sephardic Jews. Today, the majority of Jews are of Ashkenazic descent.

Assyria—Northern **Mesopotamia**, whose ancient empire conquered much of the Near East, including the Kingdom of **Israel** in 722 B.C.E.

atzei hayim—Literally, "trees of life." The poles to which a **Torah** scroll is attached. The ends of the poles, which are generally made of wood or ivory, protrude to serve as handles for lifting and carrying the Torah and rolling it to the next section of text.

Babylon—The capital of **Babylonia**, built by Nimrod; the location of the tower of Babel.

Babylonia—Modern-day central Iraq. This ancient empire conquered much of the Near East, including the Kingdom of **Judah** in 586 B.C.E. The Jews were exiled there at that time.

Balaam—**Balak**, king of **Moab**, requested the soothsayer Balaam to come and pronounce a curse against **Israel**, with whom the Moabites were at war. Along his journey, an angel of God with a drawn sword in his hand showed himself three times to Balaam's donkey, which was then given the power of addressing its rider in human speech. The angel then became visible to Balaam and permitted him to go on with the Moabites, enjoining him to say "nothing except what I tell you" (Num. 22:35). Instead of cursing Israel as was Balak's command, Balaam found that he could only bless them with the words of God.

Balak—The king of **Moab** in the days of **Moses**, who requested that the soothsayer **Balaam** pronounce a curse against **Israel**, with whom the Moabites were at war. He was afraid that Israel, who had just defeated the Amorites, would attack Moab, and because of their great numbers would likely defeat the Moabites as well.

Barak—He helped the prophetess **Deborah** defeat the Canaanite army led by King Jabin by taking 10,000 men from the tribes of **Naphtali** and **Zebulun** to Mount Tabor to fight.

Beer-sheba—**Abraham** built an altar here, on the border of the Southern Desert, and planted a sacred grove around it, which became the first fixed sanctuary in **Palestine**. Here Abraham also received orders to take **Isaac** and sacrifice him, and here all the chief events of Isaac's life were enacted: his birth, and that of **Esau** and **Jacob**; the purchase by Jacob of Esau's birthright; and Jacob's reception of Isaac's blessing. Here **Samuel**'s sons sat as judges, and **Elijah** left his servant here when fleeing to **Mount Sinai.** It became the center of local government for the southern tribe of **Judah.**

Benjamin—The 12th and youngest son of **Jacob** and 2nd son of **Rachel**, who died during his birth. Benjamin is also the name of one of the **Twelve Tribes of Israel**, whose members were said to be descended from him. When the Israelite kingdom divided after the death of King **Solomon** in 930 B.C.E., the two southern tribes, **Judah** and Benjamin, remained loyal to King **David** and his descendants.

Beth-el—**Jacob**, fleeing from **Esau**, had a vision of angels, and gave to the spot its name, "house of God"; returning after 20 years to perform his vow there, he rebuilt the altar, set up a pillar, and received from God his new name (**Israel**). In the days of the Judges it was chosen as the resting place of the **Ark** for a time, and here an altar was set up. **Jeroboam** I made a sanctuary, setting up a calf and an altar, which **Josiah** long afterward destroyed. But in **Elijah**'s last visit to the place before he was taken up to God, a school of the prophets existed there. Under Jeroboam II it was a royal residence, with a royal chapel and chaplains, and it was then that the prophet **Amos** was sent there to warn Israel.

Bethlehem—About five miles south of **Jerusalem**, it is also called Ephrath (and Ephrathah) to distinguish it from the northern city of the same name. On the road to it was the scene of **Rachel**'s death and burial; it was the residence of **Boaz** and **Ruth,** and the birthplace of **David.** It was once captured by the **Philistines,** and it was the last rallying point of the remnant of **Judah** after the invasion of **Nebuchadnezzar.**

Bible—The word "Bible" derives from the Greek *biblia,* meaning "books." By its very name "the Bible" refers to "*the* collection of books"—that is, the one that is deemed to be authoritative, or canonical.

Biblia Hebraica Stuttgartensia—A scholarly edition of the **Leningrad Codex**, the oldest dated manuscript of the complete **Hebrew Bible**.

Bilhah—**Jacob**'s concubine and **Rachel**'s maidservant. Rachel, who could not conceive, told Jacob to take Bilhah as a concubine so that, according to the custom of the time, any children born from the maid would be considered Rachel's. She bore two sons, **Dan** and **Naphtali**, whose descendants would go on to become two of the **Twelve Ttribes of Israel.**

bimah—The raised platform from which the cantor, rabbi, or other leader conducts services and reads from the **Torah**. In Ashkenazic synagogues it is located at the front of the sanctuary, while in Sephardic synagogues it is in the center.

Birkat ha-Kohanim—The Priestly Benediction. In ancient times, the *Kohanim* (the Temple priests) would bless the people each day from a platform in front of the Holy **Ark.** In this ceremony, the *Kohen* stood with his hands and arms outstretched and his fingers forming a V while he recited a blessing from the book of Numbers.

Boaz—Husband of **Ruth**, with whom he fathered Obed, King **David**'s grandfather. He and Ruth were brought together by Ruth's mother-in-law **Naomi.**

Burning Bush—Bush that marked the presence of God for Moses. Living in **Midian** after having fled Egypt, **Moses** was tending the flock of his father-in-law, **Jethro,** near **Mount Sinai**. There he saw an angel appear in a burning bush, yet the bush was not consumed. God appeared to Moses with the name Ehyeh-Asher-Ehyeh ("I will be what I will be") and told him to go to **Pharaoh** with God's blessing to free the **Israelites** from slavery.

Caesarea—**Herod** the Great built this city and harbor in the 1st century B.C.E. and made it the seat of Roman government and troops.

Cain—Firstborn of **Adam** and **Eve.** He became a farmer and made an offering of its fruits, which God did not accept, though God had accepted the offering of **Abel.** Cain was angered and slew Abel, and therefore was cursed by God so that the soil should yield no return from his labor, and he should be driven out to wander over the earth. At Cain's appeal, God "put a mark on Cain, lest anyone who met him should kill him" (Gen. 4:15). Cain went forth to the land of Nod, east of Eden; his wife bore him a son, **Enoch,** after whom he named a city that he had built.

Canaan—The ancient region between the **Jordan River,** the **Dead Sea,** and the Mediterranean Sea, also called **Palestine** from Roman times. It was the land that God promised to **Abraham** in the book of Genesis. After the **Exodus** from Egypt, **Moses** appointed a delegation to go ahead and see what the land of Canaan and the people who lived there were like. The scouts returned, reporting on a bountiful, beautiful land "flowing with milk and honey" (Exod. 3:8)—a phrase still used today to describe **Israel.** Canaan is often referred to as "the **Promised Land.**"

canon—The authoritative collection of books recognized as Holy Scripture.

canonization—Process by which certain literary works of ancient **Israel** were determined to be divinely inspired and ultimately entered into the **Hebrew Bible;** the process is generally thought to have been concluded by the 2nd century C.E.

cantillation—The chanting in public recital of biblical texts, in which the system of accents depends on the rhythm and sequence of the syllables in which they are chanted.

Chosen People—The belief that as descendants of **Abraham,** the Jewish people have been chosen by God. This idea comes from a phrase in Deuteronomy (7:7) that reads, in part, "It is not because you are the most numerous of peoples that the LORD set His heart on you and chose you."

221

codex (codices, pl.)— The precursor of a book as we know it: handwritten manuscript pages bound together, particularly for Bibles and other holy works. Codices began to replace scrolls around the 2nd century C.E. (though only for Christians at that time).

commandments—According to the Talmud, the 613 specific obligations, or mitzvot, required for leading a good Jewish life. Many of these, which are detailed in the **Bible,** could be classified as "good deeds," like visiting a sick friend or giving to charity. Others have to do with leading a Jewish life, such as keeping kosher or reciting prayers, and some are ethical and moral obligations, such as the prohibition against incest.

concordance—An index to a text, such as the Bible, listing each occurrence of a given word, along with its context, so users can see how that word is used.

covenant—The agreements made between God and the Jewish people. The **Torah** tells of the covenant God made with **Abraham**, promising him that he would be the **patriarch** of great nations. In return, Abraham agreed that every male would be circumcised, as a sign of this covenant. God also made a covenant with **Moses** as he prepared to receive the **Ten Commandments**. God told Moses: "Now then, if you will obey Me faithfully and keep My covenant, you shall be My treasured possession among all the peoples" (Exod. 19:5). God also made a covenant with **Noah**, a non-Jew, after the Great Flood, giving him the **Noahide Laws** and promising never again to destroy the world; God created a rainbow in the clouds as a sign of this covenant.

Cyrus—The Persian king who conquered **Babylon** in 539 B.C.E. He then authorized the exiled Jews to return to their land and rebuild the **First Temple.** He also returned the utensils of the Temple, which **Nebuchadnezzar** had brought to Babylon, to Sheshbazzar, leader of the returning captives.

Damascus—The city north and east of **Palestine** where **Abraham**'s ancestors had settled and from where the wives of **Isaac** and **Jacob** came; roughly the region of modern northern **Syria** and northwestern Iraq.

Dan—1. The fifth son of **Jacob,** and the first of **Bilhah** (who was Jacob's concubine and **Rachel**'s maidservant). Dan is also the name of one of the **Twelve Tribes of Israel**, whose members were said to be descended from him. 2. A city in northern **Israel**.

Daniel—One of the prisoners carried by **Nebuchadnezzar** to **Babylon** after the capture of **Jerusalem,** in the third year of the reign of Jehoiakim. Inspired by God, he interpreted King Nebuchadnezzar's dream, and the king in return made him ruler over the whole province of Babylon and chief over all the wise men of Babylon. Daniel was cast into the lion's den for refusing to follow a decree forbidding anyone to ask anything of God, or of any man except the king, after he continued to pray three times a day. He was rescued by God and honored anew by the king. He retained his influence until the third year of **Cyrus**'s reign over **Babylon** (to 536 B.C.E.) and prophesied the future of God's kingdom.

Dathan—Son of Eliab, of the tribe of **Reuben.** He conspired with his brother **Abiram** against **Moses** and **Aaron**.

David—The second king of **Israel**, who reigned from approximately 1010 to 970 B.C.E. As a young man, David, armed with only a slingshot and faith in God, gained fame for defeating the Philistine giant **Goliath.** As king, David united the warring tribes into the nation of Israel, with **Jerusalem** as its capital. Today, part of Jerusalem is still called the City of David, and it remains the physical and spiritual capital of Israel.

Dead Sea—The mineral-rich, landlocked lake in the valley southeast of **Jerusalem,** between **Israel** and Jordan. A super-salty body of water, the Dead Sea is also the lowest place on earth—1,348 feet below sea level.

Dead Sea Scrolls—Leather and papyrus scrolls containing partial texts of the **Bible** and other ancient documents. In 1947, a Bedouin shepherd wandered into a rocky cave on a cliff at **Qumran**, an area northwest of the **Dead Sea**, and discovered pottery urns containing fragments of biblical books and other documents dating from the late **Second Temple** period (200 B.C.E.–68 C.E.). The Dead Sea Scrolls are written primarily in **Hebrew**, some in **Aramaic**, and a few in Greek. Most scholars believe that the scrolls were written by the **Essenes**, a monastic, separatist sect of Judaism that took refuge at Qumran in reaction to Maccabean policies.

Deborah—A prophetess described in the book of Judges, she wrote the Song of Deborah, which tells of her victory over King Jabin of **Canaan**'s army, with the help of **Barak.**

Decalogue—See **Ten Commandments**.

Delilah—The Philistine woman who seduced **Samson** into telling her the source of his power. Once he revealed that it was his hair, she had him shaved.

derash—The interpretative meaning of a Jewish text, in which the presence of certain words or phrases gives added meaning to a passage.

devar Torah—A short commentary on an issue related to the weekly **Torah** portion. It is considered an honor to deliver a *devar Torah.*

Diaspora—Outside the Land of **Israel**.

Dinah—the daughter of **Jacob** and **Leah.** Dinah was raped by **Shechem,** the son of Hamor the Hivite, the ruler of the city of **Shechem** during the days of Jacob.

dukhan—The platform in front of the **Ark** of the Covenant from which priests would bless the people each day in ancient times. See *Birkat ha-Kohanim.*

Elijah—A prophet of the 9th century B.C.E. who, according to the Bible, ascended to heaven in a chariot. According to tradition, he will reappear one day to announce the arrival of the **Messiah.** An angry prophet, Elijah often thought God had forsaken him and that he was the last righteous man.

Elisha—The son of Shaphat, a wealthy landowner in Abelmeholah, Elisha was summoned from the plow by the prophet **Elijah,** whose disciple and successor he became. Elisha predicted Hazael's impending succession to the throne. By his direction one of the sons of the prophets anointed Jehu as king, with the purpose of dethroning Joram and destroying Ahab's dynasty. His last act was his prediction to King Joash, who visited him on his deathbed, that he would be victorious over the Syrians.

Elohim—One of the many terms used to refer to God. Often used to represent the attribute of justice in the Divine. Also the general term used for any deity. See also *Adonai* and **Tetragrammaton.**

Enoch—1. Son of **Cain,** who named the city he founded after him. 2. Son of **Midian,** a grandson of **Abraham** and Keturah, whom Abraham married after Sarah's death. He was an ancestor of the Midianites.

Ephraim—Second son of **Joseph** and his wife Asenath, an Egyptian. Ephraim is also the name of one of the **Twelve Tribes of Israel**, whose members were said to be descended from him. Joseph was given a double portion of land, which he later gave to his two sons, **Manasseh** and Ephraim. The tribe of Ephraim occupied the central region of **Canaan.**

Esau—Twin brother of **Jacob**, son of **Isaac** and **Rebekah.** Esau was a skillful hunter and Isaac's favorite. As the older twin, he sold his birthright to Jacob for a bowl of stew. Later, when Isaac was near death and nearly blind, Esau's blessing was given to Jacob who, aided by Rebekah, disguised himself as his brother and served his father food. Esau did end up getting a blessing, too.

Essenes—A sect of Jews distinguished by their members' withdrawal from the mainstream of society, their piety, and its ascetic ideals. Because Essenes lived in ancient **Israel** in **Qumran** near the **Dead Sea** during the time of the **Second Temple** (538 B.C.E.–70 C.E.), many scholars identify this group as responsible for the **Dead Sea Scrolls.**

Esther—The Jewish woman who became queen of ancient **Persia**, the second wife of King **Ahasuerus**, during the 5th century B.C.E. Her story is retold in the biblical book of Esther, also referred to as the Megillat Esther.

Ethics of the Fathers—The English name for Pirkei Avot, one of the sections of the **Mishnah.** It contains many ethical teachings and Rabbinic sayings from the ancient Jewish **sages,** including Hillel, Akiva, Ben Zoma, and others.

Eve—The first woman. Eve and the first man, **Adam,** lived in the **Garden of Eden,** and God provided for all their needs. The serpent tempted Eve with the forbidden fruit of the **Tree of Knowledge** of Good and Evil. She ate the fruit and gave some to Adam. When God found out what they had done, God punished them and banished them from Eden. Eve was the mother of **Cain** and **Abel.**

exegesis—An interpretation of a text in its historical and literary contexts. The word comes from a Greek verb meaning "to lead out of."

Exodus—1. The term used to describe the **Israelites'** flight to freedom from slavery in Egypt. 2. Also, the second book of the **Bible.**

First Temple—The central holy place of worship and sacrifice in ancient **Jerusalem.** Erected by **Solomon** circa 960 B.C.E., it was destroyed by the Babylonians under **Nebuchadnezzar** in 586 B.C.E. See also **Second Temple.**

Five Books of Moses—Another name for the **Torah**, the first five books of the **Hebrew Bible**, which include Genesis, Exodus, Leviticus, Numbers, and Deuteronomy. Also called the **Pentateuch** and the *Humash.*

folio—A sheet in a manuscript or in a **codex.**

Former Prophets—The biblical books of Joshua, Judges, Samuel and Kings, which are primarily historical in nature.

Gad—The seventh son of **Jacob** and first son of Zilpah, who was Jacob's concubine and **Leah's** handmaiden. Gad is also the name of one of the **Twelve Tribes of Israel**, whose members were said to be descended from him. His tribe occupied the mountainous region northeast of the **Dead Sea.**

Garden of Eden—The place where **Adam** and **Eve** resided.

ga'on—Head of a rabbinic academy; the term originated as the title for the heads of Babylonian academies in Sura and Pumbedita, starting in the 6th century. The gaonic period lasted from approximately the mid-6th to the mid-11th centuries. The title *ga'on* is an abbreviation of *rosh yeshivat ga'on Yaakov* (head of the academy that is the pride of **Jacob**), *ga'on* literally means "pride" in biblical **Hebrew**. *Ge'onim* authored responsa, which were answers to queries about talmudic and halakhic matters that became semi-canonical in many areas during the gaonic period.

Gemara—Literally, "learning." A compilation of 300 years of **rabbis'** legal and ethical commentaries on the **Mishnah**, edited in the 5th century C.E. Together, the Gemara and the Mishnah make up the **Talmud.**

genizah—A repository for obsolete documents and worn-out books, usually sacred **Hebrew** texts. Jewish law says that objects containing the word of God should be properly interred when they are no longer able to be used. This tradition has existed since ancient times. The most notable *genizah* is the Cairo Genizah in Egypt.

Gibeon—Situated on an isolated hill about five miles north of **Jerusalem**, it was the chief city of the Hivites, and consequently of great strength. Falling into the hands of **Joshua**, it was allotted to **Benjamin** and assigned to the priests. It was the site of the **Tabernacle** under **David** and **Solomon**, and it contained the altar of sacrifice, but not the **Ark**, which was in Jerusalem.

Gilgal—The first camping place of the **Israelites** after crossing the Jordan, it is two miles southeast of **Jericho**. It was the residence of **Elisha** and site of a school of prophets.

Golden Calf—An idol that the **Israelites** worshiped during their wanderings through the desert. This disobedient act of worship caused God to smash the **Ten Commandments**.

Goliath—the nine-foot-tall leader of the **Philistines** against **Saul**'s army. **David** defeated the giant when he knocked Goliath down with a rock fired from his slingshot, then he cut off Goliath's head with a sword. When this happened, the Philistines desisted, running back to their cities.

Gomorrah—One of the five "Cities of the Plain" (**Sodom**, Gomorrah, Admah, Zeboiim, and Zoar), four of which were destroyed by fire and brimstone. These cities stood in the Jordan Valley, immediately north of the **Dead Sea.**

Goshen—A fertile district in Egypt, immediately to the east of the ancient delta of the Nile, and west of the south section of the Suez Canal. It was here that **Jacob** and his descendants settled until the **Exodus.**

haftarah (haftarot, pl.)— A reading from the biblical books of **Nevi'im** (**Prophets**) that is recited in synagogue immediately following the reading of the **Torah**. The passage, which consists of a chapter or two, is usually relevant to that week's Torah portion. Unlike the Torah, the haftarah is usually read from a bound book that contains **Hebrew** vowels.

Hagar—The mother of **Ishmael**, who is considered by Muslims to be the ancestor of the Arab people. Egyptian handmaiden to **Sarah**, Hagar conceived Ishmael with **Abraham.**

Hagiographa—Another name for the third of the three sections that compose the TANAKH, along with **Torah** and **Nevi'im**. It is known in English as **Writings** and in **Hebrew** as **Kethuvim.**

halakhah (halakhic, adj.)— Jewish law; pertaining to the legal aspects of Judaism.

Haman—An adviser to King **Ahasuerus** of ancient **Persia**. According to the book of **Esther**, Haman hatched a plot to kill the Jews of Persia. But his plot was found out and stopped by Queen Esther**.**

Hannah—The mother of **Samuel** and, along with Peninnah, one of the wives of Elkanah. Constantly tormented by fertile Peninnah, Hannah was barren until she made a pilgrimage to the shrine at **Shiloh**, where she vowed that if she gave birth, she would make her son a Nazirite, completely devoted to the worship of God. She subsequently gave birth to Samuel and kept her vow. She later also gave birth to three more sons and two daughters.

ha-Shem—See **Tetragrammaton**.

Hasmonean—Dynasty of the **Maccabees**, Jewish rulers of Judea from the Maccabean uprising to the Roman conquest (142–63 B.C.E.).

Hebrew—1. The scholarly and holy language of the Jews, used in prayer. It is the language in which most of the TANAKH was originally written. A Semitic language, Hebrew was the language of the ancient **Israelites** until the 2nd century B.C.E., when **Aramaic** took its place as the everyday language. 2. A term sometimes used for Israelites and Judeans before the Babylonian exile in 586 B.C.E.

Hebron—This city is situated on a cluster of heights about 19 miles southwest of **Jerusalem. Sarah** died here and was buried in the Cave of **Machpelah**, which was also the burying place of **Abraham**, **Isaac**, **Rebekah**, **Leah**, and **Jacob.**

hermeneutics—The technical term for the process of interpreting the meaning of texts.

Herod—Declared king of the Jews by the Senate in Rome in 40 B.C.E., he then captured and reigned over **Jerusalem,** where he refurbished and enlarged the **Second Temple**. He rebuilt the cities of **Samaria** and **Caesaria**.

historical-critical method—Reading biblical text within the context of the place and time in which it was written.

Holy of Holies—The inner sanctum in the ancient **First Temple** and **Second Temple,** where the **Ark** of the Covenant (the chest containing the **Ten Commandments**) was kept. The Holy of Holies was entered only once a year, by the High Priest on Yom Kippur.

Holiness Code—Part of the book of Leviticus, and so called because it lists punishments and spells out requirements for the **Israelites** to remain holy. The Holiness Code requires the Israelites not to take part in the contemporary religious practices of their neighbors, the Canaanites. The Israelites were to remain separate—to be like their God and not like other people. They were to be "holy," set apart, different.

homiletic—Of or related to oratory such as sermons, explications of **Bible** verses, and lectures on moral themes.

hoshen—The breastplate, usually made of silver, that beautifies the **Torah**. Modern breastplates are reminiscent of the one worn by the High Priest in biblical times, which had 12 precious stones engraved with the names of the **Twelve Tribes of Israel**. The *hoshen* is attached to a chain and draped over the *atzei hayim*, the poles, after the scrolls have been "dressed." Usually a small box is soldered to the plate; it contains silver nameplates for each holiday and special Sabbath**.**

Humash—A bound book containing the **Five Books of Moses** that is used in synagogue or for study. A *Humash* contains the weekly **Torah** portions in **Hebrew** and English, and some editions also contain commentaries and explanations along with the weekly **haftarah** portions. In synagogue, congregants use it to follow the Torah readings. See **Pentateuch**.

Isaac—The second of the three **patriarchs** of the Jewish people; son of **Abraham** and **Sarah**; half-brother of **Ishmael**. Isaac was born when his mother was 90. When he was a young man, his father was ready to sacrifice him to show his obedience to God, but God sent an angel to intervene, and Isaac was saved. Isaac married **Rebekah** and fathered twin sons, **Esau** and **Jacob**. See *Akedah.*

Ishmael—Son of **Abraham** and **Hagar;** the ancestor of the Arab people.

Israel—1. Jewish ties to the Land of **Israel** go back 4,000 years, when tradition holds that God told **Abraham** to go there and promised him and his descendants that land. The creation of the modern State of Israel was the culmination of the Zionist dream for a Jewish homeland. 2. In ancient times, the Northern Kingdom of the Jews, home to 10 of the **Twelve Tribes of Israel**. It was part of the kingdom united by **David** and held by **Solomon**. Israel broke off from **Judah**, which was home to the remaining 2 tribes. 3. The new name given to **Jacob** after he wrestled the angel (in the book of Genesis).

Israelites—The ancient term for the Jewish people, who were descended from the **Twelve Tribes of Israel**. In ancient times, these descendants of **Jacob** inhabited the land then known as **Canaan**, which is present-day **Israel**.

Issachar—The ninth son of **Jacob** and the fifth son of **Leah**. Issachar is also the name of one of the **Twelve Tribes of Israel**, whose members were said to be descended from him. The tribe occupied the west bank of the **Jordan River**. During the time of King **David**, the tribe was known for its wise men, and its descendants were considered men of learning.

Jacob—The third of the three **patriarchs** of the Jewish people; the second son of **Isaac** and **Rebekah**. Jacob tricked his twin brother, **Esau,** into handing over Esau's birthright; later, with the help of his mother, he intercepted his father's blessing for Esau. Jacob worked for **Laban** for seven years in order to marry **Rachel**, Laban's younger daughter, but on the wedding night, Laban tricked Jacob into marrying **Leah**, his older daughter. Jacob married Rachel one week later and worked for Laban for seven more years as a condition of his father-in-law's approval of the marriage. Jacob had 12 sons with Leah, Rachel, **Bilhah**, and Zilpah, and these sons became the leaders of the **Twelve Tribes of Israel**, **Israel** being the spiritual name God gives to Jacob when appearing to him a second time.

Jericho—About 15 miles northeast of **Jerusalem**, in the valley of the **Jordan River**, it was the first conquest of **Joshua**, miraculously delivered into his hands, and burned by him at God's command.

Jeroboam—Once the northern tribes seceded, splitting the United Kingdom, they chose Jeroboam as king of **Israel**. He expelled the **Levites,** who were loyal to the kingdom of **Judah,** and recruited priests from the common people, whom he personally appointed and ordained. There was constant war between the kingdoms of Israel and Judah during his reign.

Jerusalem—Since biblical times it has been regarded as a holy city by Jews and later by Christians and then Muslims. King **David** made Jerusalem his capital (hence its name, the City of David), and the ancient Jewish First and Second Temples were built here.

Jethro—Priest of **Midian** and father-in-law of **Moses**. Happening one day to be at the well where Jethro's daughters were drawing water for their flocks, Moses had occasion to defend them against some shepherds who attempted to drive them away. Jethro, out of gratitude, gave him his daughter **Zipporah**. After Moses and the **Israelites** had crossed the **Sea of Reeds**, Jethro went to Moses with the latter's wife and two sons. When Moses told Jethro of all the miracles done for the Israelites by God, Jethro, rejoicing, exclaimed, "Now I know that the LORD is greater than all gods" (Exod. 18:11) and offered burnt offerings and sacrifices. After this, Jethro returned to his own country.

Jochebed—The daughter of **Levi**, **Jacob**'s son, and the mother of **Moses**, **Aaron**, and **Miriam**. After Moses was born, Jochebed placed him in a basket and sent the basket down the Nile River, hoping to save him from **Pharaoh**'s decree to kill all newborn Jewish boys. After one of Pharaoh's daughters rescued Moses, Jochebed was brought to Pharaoh's palace to nurse him. According to the **Rabbis,** Jochebed was also one of the chief Jewish midwives at the time, responsible for delivering the Jewish children in Egypt.

Joppa—The seaport of Judea. The timber from Lebanon for building the **First Temple** came through this port. Jonah embarked from here when he fled to Tarshish.

Jordan River—Along with the **Dead Sea** and the Mediterranean Sea, one of the borders of the **Promised Land**. The **Israelites** crossed the Jordan River as the beginning of their conquest of **Canaan**. The major cities of Judea and **Samaria** lay on the river's west bank.

Joseph—The 11th son of **Jacob** and the firstborn son of **Rachel**. Joseph was his father's favorite. He was sold into slavery in Egypt by his jealous brothers and eventually, because of his ability to interpret dreams, became a confidant of **Pharaoh** and later became the viceroy of Egypt. When **Joshua** divided the land of **Canaan** among the **Twelve Tribes of Israel**, he gave Joseph a double portion of land, which Joseph passed on to his two sons, **Manasseh** and **Ephraim**.

Joshua—The son of Nun; servant and successor of **Moses.** Joshua led the Israelite troops to victory over the **Amalekites**. He was one of the spies sent to explore **Canaan**. Returning from this mission, it was he who with Caleb allayed the apprehension of the excited people, bravely taking the risk of being stoned to death. For this fidelity, he and Caleb, alone of all the **Israelites** 20 years old and upward at the time of this episode, were to enter the **Promised Land**. Moses appointed Joshua as his successor, and upon his death, Joshua began his conquest of **Israel** with the miraculous victory at **Jericho.** Joshua continued to capture the rest of the country and then divided it among the **Twelve Tribes of Israel.**

Josiah—King of **Judah** from 639 to 608 B.C.E., Josiah began his reign at the age of eight. He was the son and successor of Amon and grandson of **Manasseh.** In the 18th year of his rule, Josiah began a great religious reformation, beginning with the repair of the Temple. He then set about the task of cleansing the land from idolatry. The most important of the results that followed this reformation were the centralization of religious worship at the Temple in **Jerusalem** and the acceptance of a sacred book of spiritual and ethical teaching as canonical and authoritative.

JPS—See **NJPS** and **OJPS**.

jubilee year—A special year of rest and forgiveness observed every 50th year by the ancient **Israelites**, when slaves were set free, property given back to its original owner, and the fields left unplanted.

Judah—1. Fourth son of **Jacob** and **Leah.** Judah was one of the **Twelve Tribes of Israel**, whose members were said to be descended from him. The tribe inhabited **Jerusalem** during the reign of kings **David** and **Solomon**. 2. The southern part of the Israelite kingdom. The land was divided in two after the death of King Solomon in 930 B.C.E.

Kabbalah—Jewish mystical theology, which appeared in the 12th and 13th centuries in Provence and northern Spain, that believed that there were secrets in the **Torah** that, if uncovered, would provide a direct connection to God. This connection could be established through a system of 10 *sefirot,* or emanations from the *Ein Sof,* or Godhead. By meditating on the *sefirot* and seeking to unite them, people can experience the Divine. The classic text of this mystical tradition is the Zohar, compiled by Moses de Leon around 1290. Kabbalah became a major influence in the development of Hasidism.

Karaites—Members of a Jewish sect that originated in **Babylonia** in the 8th century C.E. that rejected the **Oral Law** of the **Rabbis** and relied on the **Bible** for religious faith and practice.

Kethuvim—The third of the sections of the Tanankh, along with **Torah** and **Nevi'im.** Kethuvim, known by the English name **Writings,** includes a variety of texts, including Psalms, Proverbs, the book of Job, and the historical books of Ezra, Nehemiah, and Chronicles. Kethuvim also includes five books recited on Jewish holidays—Esther, Ruth, The Song of Songs, Ecclesiastes, and Lamentations—that are known as *megillot.* It is also called **Hagiographa.**

230

klaf—The parchment from the skin of a kosher animal (one that is acceptable according to the Jewish dietary laws), on which the **Torah** is written by a *sofer.*

Kohen (*Kohanim,* pl.)—A member of the tribe of **Levi** authorized to perform the **Temple** service and other sacred, priestly duties.

Korah—During the journey of the **Israelites** in the wilderness, Korah, with **Dathan**, **Abiram**, and 250 other men, rebelled against the leadership of **Moses** and **Aaron**. God punished them by causing the earth to swallow them with their families and all their possessions.

Laban—Employed **Jacob** for seven years, then tricked him into marrying **Leah,** Laban's oldest daughter, when he really wanted to marry **Rachel**, Laban's youngest daughter. Laban approved Jacob's marriage to Rachel on the condition that Jacob work for him for another seven years.

Latter Prophets—The biblical books of Isaiah, Jeremiah, and Ezekiel, and the 12 **Minor Prophets**, which are made up primarily of the speeches of the prophets whose names they bear.

Leah—One of the four **matriarchs** of the Jewish people; the first wife of **Jacob**, one of the three **patriarchs**. Leah was wed when her father, **Laban,** tricked Jacob into marrying her instead of his true love, her younger sister, **Rachel**. Leah had seven children: **Reuben, Simeon, Levi, Judah, Issachar, Zebulun,** and **Dinah**.

Leningrad Codex—The oldest complete manuscript of the **Hebrew Bible**, which was copied in 1009 C.E. from a manuscript written by the Masorete Aaron ben Moses ben Asher.

Levi—Third son of **Jacob** and **Leah**. Levi's daughter, **Jochebed**, was the mother of **Moses** and **Aaron**. Levi is also the name of one of the **Twelve Tribes of Israel**, whose members were said to be descended from him. His descendants are known as Levites.

levirate law—The obligation of the surviving brother of a childless, deceased man to marry the widowed sister-in-law, in order to maintain the family line.

Levite—A member of the tribe of **Levi**. Levites carried the **Tabernacle** and later assisted at the Temple by serving as gatekeepers, teachers, musicians, and assistants to the priests (*Kohanim*). The Levites were chosen for service to God because, in Exodus, they refused to worship the **Golden Calf.** The Levites had no tribal land of their own but were spread among the other tribes.

levitical cities—The six cities of refuge assigned by **Moses** for those individuals convicted of crimes and expelled from the community, as prescribed in the book of Numbers. Three others were also assigned by him as refuge cities in Transjordan.

Lost Tribes of Israel—The 10 tribes of **Israel** that disappeared from biblical accounts after the Northern Kingdom of Israel was conquered by the Assyrians in 722/1 B.C.E. The tribes lost their separate identity during their exile and captivity and are thought by some to have intermarried with the Assyrians. Throughout history, various groups around the world have claimed that they are descendants of the lost tribes, pointing to their ancient Hebraic customs and beliefs as proof. Perhaps the best known of these are the Falashas of Ethiopia and the **Samaritans** of Nablus.

Maccabee, Judah—The third son of Mattathias, Judah led the rebellion against King **Antiochus** of **Syria** in the 2nd century B.C.E. after his father died. Nicknamed "Maccabeus"—the hammerer—because of his strong fighting style, Judah led the revolt against the Syrians that eventually returned control of **Jerusalem** and the **Second Temple** to the Jews.

Maccabees—The band of Jewish revolutionaries, led by Judah **Maccabee**, who fought from 167 to 165 B.C.E. for religious freedom and the right to reclaim **Jerusalem** from King **Antiochus** and Syrian control. Also see **Hasmonean.**

Machpelah—**Abraham** needed a burying place for **Sarah** and bought the field of Machpelah near **Hebron**, at the end of which was a cave. He paid 400 silver shekels for it. The cave became the family burying place, Sarah being the first to be buried there; later, **Abraham, Isaac, Rebekah, Leah,** and **Jacob** were placed there.

maftir—The final three or four verses of the weekly **Torah** reading (parashah).

Major Prophets—The biblical books of Isaiah, Jeremiah, and Ezekiel.

Manasseh—First son of **Joseph** and his wife, Asenath, an Egyptian. Manasseh is also the name of one of the **Twelve Tribes of Israel**, whose members were said to be descended from him. Joseph was given a double portion of land, which he later gave to his two sons, Manasseh and **Ephraim.** The tribe of Manasseh occupied the mountainous region northeast of the **Dead Sea**.

manna—Food that was miraculously supplied to the **Israelites** in the wilderness during the **Exodus** from Egypt. When the Israelites questioned **Moses** about his decision to flee slavery in Egypt to an uncertain future, he and **Aaron** told the people that God would provide. The next morning, God rained "bread from heaven"—manna—to sustain the Israelites. Manna was described as white in color and delicious to eat.

mappah—1. The cloth placed over a table on which the **Torah** is read so that the Torah does not touch bare wood. 2. The decorative, embroidered cloth mantle used to protect and beautify the Torah. It has two openings at the top to accommodate the *atzei hayim,* the poles. The mantle is placed on the Torah before the breastplate, *hoshen,* and crown are put on, in a process known as dressing the Torah.

Masoretes—Literally, those who preserve the *masorah,* the tradition; a group of Jewish **sages**, living between the 7th and 9th centuries c.e., who preserved the text of the **Hebrew Bible** with great accuracy.

masoretic text—The traditional authoritative **Hebrew** text of the **Bible,** with its consonants, vowels, and **cantillation** marks, as preserved by the **Masoretes**.

Matriarchs—The "founding mothers" of the Jewish people: **Sarah, Rebekah, Rachel,** and **Leah;** the wives of the three **Patriarchs**.

Mattan Torah—The term used to describe God's giving the **Torah** to **Moses** and the **Israelites** at **Mount Sinai**.

megillah (*megillot,* pl.)— Literally, "scroll." This term is often used to refer to five books of the **Bible** (The Song of Songs, Ruth, Lamentations, Ecclesiastes, and Esther) that are part of **Kethuvim** and read on Jewish holidays. In ancient days the *megillot* were written on scrolls of parchment, like the **Torah**. When the word "megillah" is used without specifying which one, it is most often capitalized and usually refers to the Scroll of Esther, Megillat Esther, the best known of the *megillot.*

Mesopotamia—Modern-day Iraq; the land of the early **Sumerian** civilization as well as the later Assyrian and Babylonian civilizations.

Midian/Midianites—Midian was the son of **Abraham** and Keturah. His five sons, Ephah, Epher, Enoch, Abidah, and Eldaah, were the progenitors of the Midianites.

midrash (midrashim, pl.)— A creative interpretation that elaborates on the biblical text, be it a story, law, custom, or ritual of Jewish life. Ancient collections of midrashim date back thousands of years and are attributed to famous **sages** and **Rabbis.** In these discussions, the Rabbis dissect the **Torah** verse by verse, looking for explanations and meaning in each word. Midrashim in all art forms—including stories, poetry, paintings, and song—are still being created today.

Minor Prophets—The biblical books of Hosea, Joel, Amos, Obadiah, Jonah, Micah, Nahum, Habakkuk, Zephaniah, Haggai, Zechariah, and Malachi. They are called minor because of their length, not their importance.

Miriam—The sister of **Moses** and **Aaron**. Miriam watched her brother, the baby Moses, float down the Nile until he was safely rescued by **Pharaoh**'s daughter; she then brought their mother to the palace to serve as Moses's nurse. During the **Exodus** from Egypt, after the **Israelites** safely crossed the parted **Sea of Reeds,** Miriam led the women in joyful song and "dance with timbrels."

mishkan—see **Tabernacle.**

Mishnah—Text in which the **Oral Law** was written and codified in the 2nd century C.E.. The **Talmud** is a compilation of two books: the Mishnah, and the **Gemara**, which consists of commentaries on the Mishnah. Much of the Talmud follows a format in which a law from the Mishnah is cited, followed by Rabbinic discussions and rulings on its meaning.

Mishneh Torah—A comprehensive book of Jewish law completed in the 12th century C.E. by the Rabbinic scholar and philosopher Moses Maimonides. The *Mishneh Torah* is a lengthy discussion of the **Torah**'s 613 **commandments**. It covers subjects such as Jewish rituals, customs, and holiday celebrations as well as business ethics and civil dealings.

mitzvah (mitzvot, pl.)— 1. Commandment, often translated as good deed. 2. One of the 613 specific obligations, or **commandments**, required for leading a good Jewish life.

Moab—Land overlooking **Canaan**, east of the **Jordan River** and southeast of the **Dead Sea**. It is where **Moses** died at the age of 120 after he led the **Israelites** through the **Exodus** and their 40 years of wandering the desert. Though **Israel** and Moab were often at war, Moabites weren't always portrayed negatively in the **Bible; Ruth** was from Moab.

Mordecai—A cousin of Queen **Esther**, Mordecai served as a palace official during the reign of the Persian King **Ahasuerus**. Mordecai was responsible for Esther's upbringing, and when he refused to bow down to **Haman,** he incurred Haman's wrath upon the Jews.

Moses—Biblical prophet, lawgiver, and leader of the ancient Jewish people. Son of Amram and **Jochebed**, brother of **Miriam** and **Aaron.** The story of his life is told in the books of Exodus, Leviticus, Numbers, and Deuteronomy. After growing up in the Egyptian court, Moses was appointed by God to lead the **Israelites** out of slavery in Egypt. Moses received the **Ten Commandments**, the basis of Jewish law, from God on **Mount Sinai** and served as God's messenger to the people. Moses also led the Israelites in the wilderness for 40 years, preparing them to enter the land of **Canaan.** He died at the age of 120 in the land of **Moab**, overlooking Canaan. There are several explanations as to why God punished Moses by not allowing him to enter the **Promised Land**, including that he argued with God, he smashed the Ten Commandments when he saw the Israelites worshiping the **Golden Calf**, and he disobeyed God in the desert.

Mount Sinai—According to the **Torah**, the mountain on which God gave **Moses** the stone tablets containing the **Ten Commandments**. The location of the mountain is not specified in the Torah. See *Torah mi-Sinai.*

Nadab—Eldest son of **Aaron** and Elisheba; one of the leaders of the children of **Israel** who went with **Moses** to **Sinai** and saw the God of Israel. Nadab was consecrated to the Priesthood with his three younger brothers, but he and his brother **Abihu** perished for having offered "alien fire."

Naomi—Wife of Elimelech and mother-in-law of **Ruth.** Naomi accompanied her husband and two sons into the land of **Moab;** but after the death of her husband and sons she returned to **Bethlehem** with her daughter-in-law Ruth, whom she endeavored in vain to dissuade from following her. Naomi contributed to bring about the marriage of **Boaz** and Ruth and became the nurse of their child.

Naphtali—The sixth son of **Jacob** and the second son of **Bilhah**, who was Jacob's concubine and **Rachel**'s handmaiden. Naphtali is also the name of one of the **Twelve Tribes of Israel**, whose members were said to be descended from him. The tribe settled northwest of the Sea of Galilee.

Nebuchadnezzar—Babylonian emperor who captured and destroyed **Jerusalem** and the Temple in 586 B.C.E., ending the **First Temple** period.

Nevi'im—Also known as **Prophets**, the second of the three sections of the TANAKH, along with **Torah** and **Kethuvim (Writings)**. Nevi'im includes historical narratives (Joshua, Judges, 1 and 2 Samuel, and 1 and 2 Kings); writings of the three **Major Prophets** (Isaiah, Jeremiah, and Ezekiel); and writings of the 12 **Minor Prophets** (Hosea, Joel, Amos, Obadiah, Jonah, Micah, Nahum, Habakkuk, Zephaniah, Haggai, Zechariah, and Malachi). These 21 sections trace Jewish history from the time of **Moses**'s death until the destruction of the **First Temple** in **Jerusalem** and the exile of the Jews to **Babylonia**. They contain detailed history and commentary on ancient Jewish civilizations. The weekly *haftarah* readings in Jewish liturgy are taken from the various books in Nevi'im.

Nineveh—The capital of **Assyria**. Built on the Tigris River by Nimrod. Visited by the prophet Jonah, when the population was so great that the number of children alone was computed to be 120,000.

NJPS—The new Jewish Publication Society **Bible** translation, first published in its entirety in 1985. See **OJPS**.

Noah—When he was about 600 years old, Noah was commanded by God to make a great **ark**, in which he and his family were to find safety from the waters of a great flood. This deluge was to destroy all living things except those brought into the ark. For 40 days the rain fell, but finally, after 150 days, the vessel rested on the "mountains of Ararat" and a rainbow appeared in the sky as a sign of the **covenant** made with Noah that "the waters shall never again become a flood to destroy all flesh" (Gen. 9:15).

Noahide Laws—The seven ancient laws that Judaism considers relevant to all people. These laws were initially given to **Noah** in Genesis 9. The first six prohibit idolatry, blasphemy, murder, adultery, robbery, and the eating of flesh cut from a living animal. The seventh commandment is an injunction to establish courts of justice. While Jews are expected to keep all the laws of the **Torah**, non-Jews are expected to keep only these seven laws. A non-Jew who keeps these laws is considered one of the righteous of the nations of the world and therefore guaranteed a place in the world to come.

OJPS—Old (first) Jewish Publication Society **Bible** translation, published in 1917. See also **NJPS.**

omer—A biblical unit of measure used for grains and dry goods. (The omer was equal to 0.1 ephah, which is believed to equal approximately 43 ounces). The word *"omer"* is sometimes translated as "sheaf," meaning an amount of grain large enough to require bundling. An omer of barley was a traditional offering on the second day of Passover during the period of Temple sacrifice. Also, when God sent **manna** to the **Israelites** wandering in the desert, they were instructed to collect "an *omer* to a person for as many of you as there are; each of you shall fetch for those in his tent" (Exod. 16:16).

Omri—King of **Israel** who built **Samaria** and made it the capital of the kingdom in the 9th century B.C.E. He made peace with **Judah,** ending the war between the two kingdoms that had been going on since the death of **Solomon.** He made an alliance with the Phoenician kingdoms of **Tyre** and **Sidon**, and he recovered the lost territory east of the **Jordan River**, including the kingdom of **Moab.**

Oral Law—In addition to the **Torah**, called the **Written Law,** Judaism has a long tradition of Oral Law. The body of commentaries, expositions, and Rabbinic explanations of points of Torah that were passed down from generation to generation in ancient times, starting with **Moses**, according to tradition. For example, the Torah does not specify what is necessary for a Jewish marriage ceremony; these specifics are part of the Oral Law. Around 200 C.E., the Oral Law was written down and codified in a text called the **Mishnah.** The Mishnah and the **Gemara** together make up the **Talmud.**

Palestine—The Romans' name for the ancient land on the east coast of the Mediterranean Sea, known in ancient times as **Canaan.** Palestine has been inhabited and conquered by many nations since biblical times. The **Philistines**, **Israelites**, Babylonians, Romans, Crusaders, Muslims, and British all conquered ancient Palestine and laid claim to the region.

parashah (*parashot,* pl.)—The **Torah** is divided into 54 sections (one for each week of the **Hebrew** lunar calendar), and a specific portion, or parashah, is read each week during synagogue services. Each portion has a Hebrew name. Also known as *sidrah* (*sidrot,* pl.).

PaRDeS—An acronym for the four types of understanding possible when studying the **Torah**. These are *peshat,* the literal, obvious meaning of the text; *remez,* the allegorical meaning; *derash,* the symbolic, interpretive meaning of the text; and *sod,* the secret, hidden, or mystical meaning of the passage.

parochet—The curtain that covers the **Torah** scrolls inside the **ark** in a synagogue. The ark has a solid door made of wood or another material. When that door is open, the *parochet* further shields the Torah scrolls. It is considered an honor to be asked to open the curtain during a service, an act called ***petichah.***

235

Passover (Pesach)—The holiday when a meal called a seder is held, and a text called a haggadah is read, to recall the plight of the **Israelites** in ancient Egypt. Though they were slaves, **Moses** demanded that the **Pharaoh** let them go, but when he refused, God brought down the Ten Plagues on the people of Egypt. However, when the final plague came and God killed the firstborn son of every Egyptian, God had the Jews mark the doors of their houses so the Angel of Death would pass over them. The Pharaoh let the Israelites go, but then changed his mind. As the Egyptian army chased them, God parted the **Sea of Reeds**, so that the Israelites could cross, then closed it, and the Egyptians drowned. After the **Exodus** from Egypt, the Israelites would go on to receive the **Ten Commandments** at **Mount Sinai.**

Patriarchs—The "founding fathers" of Judaism: **Abraham, Isaac,** and **Jacob;** the husbands of the four **Matriarchs.**

Pentateuch—From the Greek words for "five books." Another name for the **Torah.** This is also the name given to the actual book used in synagogue that contains the Torah and commentaries on it. See *Humash.*

Persia—Indo-European empire bordered by India, Rome, and the Tigras-Euphrates. **Esther** became queen of Persia when she married King **Ahasuerus** in the 5th century B.C.E. Esther and her cousin **Mordecai** thwarted **Haman**'s plans to have the Jews of Persia killed, according to the book of Esther.

peshat—The straightforward or "plain" meaning scholars give to a Jewish text. It can also refer to the simple interpretation of any issue or question.

petichah—The act of opening the doors or curtain (*parochet*) on the Holy **Ark** just before the **Torah** is taken out of the ark to be read.

Pharaoh—The title of the kings of ancient Egypt. The word in Egyptian literally means "great house," referring to the king's palace. In the books of Genesis and Exodus, the pharaohs mentioned were referred to only by that title, while in the later historical works of Kings and Jeremiah the individual pharaoh's names were recorded.

Pharisees—A group of Jews in **Second Temple** times (536 B.C.E.–70 C.E.) who constituted the spiritual forebears of the talmudic **Rabbis.** Led by lay teachers of the **Torah,** they emphasized the tradition of the **Oral Law.** This tradition of ongoing interpretation of, rather than strict adherence to, the **Written Law** would become the basis for the **Talmud.** The Pharisees believed in the coming of a Messianic Age and an afterlife in which God would punish the wicked and reward the good. They became the dominant sect, and because the **Sadducees** and **Essenes** died out, the Pharisees are considered the ancestors of all modern Jews.

Philistines—A group who invaded, and then settled in, **Canaan** in the 12th century B.C.E. after having been defeated in an attempt to invade Egypt. They originated in the Aegean and had a Semitic deity, Dagon, as their god. The arrival of the Philistines on the Canaanite coast coincided with the arrival and settlement of the **Israelites** in Canaan's central hill country. As both groups sought to expand their territories, they came into conflict and fought numerous battles. When the Philistines captured the **Ark,**

the Israelites pressed for the establishment of a monarchy, leading to the appointment of **Saul** as the first king. Around 1000 B.C.E., King **David** finally defeated the Philistines, and they never appeared in the **Bible** again as a threat to the Israelites.

Phinehas—Son of Eleazar and grandson of **Aaron**. Through his zeal he stayed the plague that had broken out among the **Israelites** as a punishment for their sin; for this act he was approved by God and rewarded with the divine promise that the Priesthood would remain in his family forever. After this event Phinehas accompanied, as priest, the Israelite expedition that destroyed the **Midianites.**

Phoenicia—Canaanite land north of **Israel**, whose capital was **Sidon** and commercial center was **Tyre**. The Phoenicians were well known for trading and colonizing over the entire Mediterranean basin and for developing a linear alphabet, which was then used by the **Israelites** and many others in the ancient Near East. The prophet **Elijah** sought to preserve the Israelite religion when the influence of a form of Phoenician worship, the cult of Baal, spread.

Promised Land—The land promised to the patriarch **Abraham** as an everlasting inheritance. The Promised Land, also known as **Canaan**, is the portion of ancient **Palestine** between the **Jordan River** and the Mediterranean Sea, plus some of Transjordan.

prooftext—Text from the **Bible** used to support a particular point.

Prophets—See **Nevi'im, Major Prophets,** and **Minor Prophets.**

pseudepigrapha—Religious texts and writings composed under a pseudonym from the time of the **Second Temple.** Pseudepigrapha are distinct from **A**pocrypha, but both are often referred to as extraneous or extra-canonical books. While they are ascribed to prophetic and patriarchal figures of antiquity like **Moses** and **Solomon,** they were mostly written by Hellenistic Jews.

Qumran—The site of the caves on the western shore of the **Dead Sea** where the **Dead Sea Scrolls** were found, beginning in 1947.

Rabbinic period—The period from the destruction of the **Second Temple** and exile from **Jerusalem** in 70 C.E. to the completion of the Babylonian **Talmud** around 600 C.E. During this time, as Rabbinic academies flourished, the Talmud was compiled and **rabbis** ascended to a new position of prominence in Jewish society and religious tradition.

rabbis—1. Rabbis can serve as spiritual leaders of Jewish congregations but also as teachers, scholars, or counselors. Literally meaning "teacher," the name "rabbi," is often what students call their teachers as a sign of respect. 2. When capitalized, the word refers to the members of a specific movement within ancient Judaism; the Rabbis compiled the **Talmud.**

Rachel—One of the four **Matriarchs** of the Jewish people; the second wife of **Jacob,** one of the three **Patriarchs.** Rachel was the woman whom Jacob truly loved and whom he married after his father-in-law tricked him into first marrying her older sister, **Leah.** After struggling to conceive, Rachel gave birth to **Joseph** and **Benjamin**, but died giving birth to the latter.

realia—Objects from real life, both naturally occurring (such as animals and plants) and human made (such as coins, tools, and artifacts).

Rebekah—One of the four **Matriarchs** of the Jewish people; wife of **Isaac,** one of the three **Patriarchs**. Rebekah, known for her beauty and kindness, was the mother of the twins **Esau** and **Jacob,** who struggled with each other even in the womb. While Esau was Isaac's favorite, Rebekah favored Jacob and helped him trick Isaac and get a blessing that had been meant for Esau.

Red Sea—See **Sea of Reeds**.

redactor—Editor; as related to the **Bible**, one of those who selected and arranged the text that became the Bible.

Rehoboam—Succeeded his father **Solomon** as the king of **Israel**, but the northern tribes seceded and chose **Jeroboam** as their king. The southern tribes, including **Judah**, **Simeon**, and **Benjamin**, became the kingdom of Judah, and maintained Rehoboam as their king. He waged constant war against Israel, but held on to the hope that the old kingdom would reunite.

remez—An allegorical reading that looks for parallels between the scriptural text and more abstract concepts.

Rephidim—Located on the edge of the desert of Sin, the Children of **Israel** encamped here after crossing that desert. At Rephidim, **Amalek** attacked Israel from behind. The people suffered here from lack of water; they complained, and **Moses** smote water from the rock.

Reuben—The firstborn son of **Jacob** and **Leah.** Reuben is also the name of one of the **Twelve Tribes of Israel**, whose members were said to be descended from him. His tribe settled on the east side of the **Jordan River** after the conquest of **Canaan**, but it was small and soon disappeared.

rimonim—Literally, "pomegranates." 1. The name for the two small, decorative silver crowns placed on the *atzei hayim*, the poles to which the **Torah** scrolls are attached. 2. The Sephardic term for the finials, or ornamental end pieces, on these poles. Originally the finials were carved like pomegranates.

Ruth—A Moabite woman who married one of **Naomi**'s sons and thereby, according to Rabbinic interpretation, converted to Judaism. After the death of her husband, Ruth pledged her loyalty to her widowed mother-in-law, Naomi, declaring, "For wherever you go, I will go; wherever you lodge, I will lodge; your people shall be my people, and your God my God. Where you die, I will die, and there will I be buried. Thus and more may the Lord do to me if anything but death parts me from you" (Ruth 1:16–17). Later Ruth married **Boaz**, and they had a son, Obed. Obed was the father of Jesse, who was the father of **David.** Ruth, a convert, was therefore the great-grandmother of King David.

Sadducees—A sect of Jews from the **Second Temple** period (536 B.C.E.–70 C.E.), connected primarily with the priestly aristocracy, who rejected the nonbiblical practices followed by the **Pharisees**.

Samaria—Ancient name of the land on the west bank of the **Jordan River**. The city was built by **Omri**, king of **Israel**, who made it his capital in place of **Tirzah**. After the kingdom was conquered by the Assyrians in 722/1 B.C.E., the Northern Kingdom was known as Samaria. It was rebuilt by **Herod** the Great in the 1st century B.C.E., who named it Sebaste. Today, it is known as Sebastiyeh.

Samaritans—According to the **Bible**, they were foreigners brought in by the Assyrians after the Assyrians conquered Israel. When Jews returned from the Babylonian exile, they rejected the Samaritans on religious grounds and would not let them worship at the **Second Temple** in **Jerusalem.**

Samson—The twelfth and last of the judges, his birth was predicted by an angel to his barren mother. Though he had massive strength, which was fueled by his uncut hair, he was seduced into revealing that source of power by the Philistine **Delilah**, who then had him shaved.

Samuel—The prophet and judge Samuel was called on by God to annoint the first king of **Israel**. Samuel chose **Saul**, but Saul proved to be an unsatisfactory ruler, and God removed him from the throne. God sent Samuel to **Bethlehem** to visit Jesse and choose one of his sons to be king. After observing all of Jesse's sons at a feast, Samuel sent for **David**, the youngest, who was in the fields tending the flocks. Upon meeting him, Samuel was commanded by God to anoint him as king.

Sanhedrin—The Supreme Court of the Jews who lived in ancient **Israel.** Composed of 71 wise elders who dispensed legislation and judgment, it was the chief judicial and legislative body during the time of the **Second Temple** and for several hundred years after its destruction. It disbanded in 425 C.E.

Sarah—One of the four **Matriarchs** of the Jewish people; wife of **Abraham**, one of the three **Patriarchs**. Because Sarah could not bear children, Abraham had a child, **Ishmael**, with **Hagar**, Sarah's handmaiden. When Sarah was 90 years old, God told her that she would have a child, and she laughed. Then, **Isaac,** whose name refers to his mother's "laughter," was born.

Saul—Chosen to be **Israel**'s first king in the 11th century B.C.E., Saul successfully fought the **Philistines**, Moabites, and **Amalekites**. Ultimately, he lost favor with the prophet **Samuel,** who chose young **David** to be the next king. In his last battle, when all was lost, Saul fell on his sword and killed himself.

Sea of Reeds—The **Hebrew** term for the **Red Sea**, *Yam-Suf,* literally translates as "Sea of Reeds." This name has led to some controversy over whether the **Israelites** actually crossed the Red Sea during the **Exodus,** or if they crossed a more shallow, marshy body of water instead.

Second Temple—The most holy place of worship and sacrifice in **Jerusalem** in ancient **Israel.** The Second Temple was built on the site of the **First Temple** 70 years after its destruction. Construction began in 520 B.C.E. and was finally completed in 515 B.C.E.; the process is described in the **Bible** in the book of Ezra. The Temple was refurbished and enlarged by King **Herod** during the 1st century B.C.E. and remained in use until it was destroyed by General Titus and the conquering Roman Empire in 70 C.E. See also **Holy of Holies**.

sefer Torah—A continuous parchment scroll on which a *sofer* has written the **Hebrew** words of the **Five Books of Moses**. A portion, or *parashah*, of **Torah** is read from a *sefer Torah* in synagogue every Monday and Thursday, on Shabbat, and on festivals and the High Holy Days.

Sephardim—Jews who lived in Spain, Portugal, the Mediterranean basin, North Africa, and the Middle East, and their descendants. *Sepharad* is the **Hebrew** name for Spain, where most of these Jews lived before their expulsion in 1492. Hebrew or Ladino was their language of prayer, while Judeo-Spanish (Judezmo) was their everyday language in Europe. Sephardic Jews have been, and continue to be, a notably smaller group than Ashkenazic Jews.

Septuagint—Jewish translation into Greek of the **Hebrew Bible**, beginning in the 3rd century B.C.E., to meet the needs of the Jewish community of Alexandria; this translation later became authoritative scripture for the church. Its meaning, "seventy," derives from the legend that it was composed by 72 Jewish scholars. It is often abbreviated as LXX, the Roman numeral 70.

Shechem—The first spot on which **Abraham** built an altar. **Jacob** rescued this altar from the Amorites and rebuilt it on the parcel of land he bought from the children of Hamor. It was the scene of the rape of **Dinah** and the subsequent slaughter of the Shechemites by **Simeon** and **Levi**. At Shechem **Joshua** assembled the **Israelites** to offer sacrifice and to read out the blessings and curses of the Law, immediately on entering the **Promised Land**; and here again he assembled them to renew the **covenant** before he died, when he set up a pillar as a witness. At this pillar, Abimelech was made king, and **Rehoboam** met the heads of tribes who sought redress. Here the 10 tribes revolted and made **Jeroboam** their king.

shemitah—The seventh, or sabbatical, year. According to Leviticus, all the land in the Land of **Israel** was to lie fallow every seventh year; plowing, planting, watering, and harvesting were forbidden. In addition, all debts were to be forgiven.

Shiloh—Here **Joshua** had set up the **Tabernacle**, made the allotment of **Canaan** to the tribes, and dismissed them to their possessions with his benediction. A temple stood there from early days, in which the **Ark** of the **Covenant** was kept. Here Eli lived and died, **Samuel** ministered before God, and an annual festival was held in honor of the Ark. The prophet Ahijah, who announced **Jeroboam**'s rise, came from Shiloh.

shofar—A hollowed-out ram's horn that is blown like a trumpet. The shofar is an ancient musical instrument used for communication and celebration. Tradition says the shofar was sounded at **Mount Sinai** when the Jewish people promised to honor and obey God's **commandments**.

Sidon—The mother city of **Phoenicia**, which was already famous in **Joshua**'s time. Its architects were the best in **Syria**. It was captured by Shalmaneser in 720 B.C.E. and again by the Persians in 350 B.C.E.

240

sidrah (*sidrot*, pl.)—The **Hebrew** word for *parashah*, the weekly portion of the **Torah** read in synagogue.

Simeon—The second son of **Jacob** and **Leah.** Simeon is also the name of one of the **Twelve Tribes of Israel,** whose members were said to be descended from him. The tribe lived in the southernmost part of **Canaan.**

Sinai—The arid, mountainous peninsula bounded by the Mediterranean Sea on the north, **Israel** on the northeast, the Gulf of Aqaba on the southeast, the **Red Sea** on the south, the Gulf of Suez on the west, and Egypt on the northwest. The mountain where **Moses** saw the **Burning Bush** and received the **Ten Commandments** from God is somewhere in the Sinai Desert.

sod—A mystical reading of the **Bible** that interprets the text as a symbolic code, which can reveal hidden wisdom and personal connection with the Divine.

Sodom—God was determined to destroy the "Five Cities of the Plain" (Sodom, **Gomorrah**, Admah, Zeboiim, and Zoar) because of their wickedness, but promised **Abraham** to spare Sodom if as few as 10 of its inhabitants should be found righteous. Abraham, however, failed to find even 10 righteous in Sodom, and God rained fire and brimstone upon all five cities and overthrew them.

sofer—Scribe; a specially trained scholar who carefully inscribes the **Hebrew** words on **Torah** scrolls and on the parchment of other holy documents. There are many laws governing the work of the *sofer.* The writing must be done by an observant Jew, using black ink and a quill from a goose or other fowl in accordance with Jewish dietary laws. The writing must be perfect, with no errors.

Solomon—The son of King **David,** Solomon became king of **Israel** in the 10th century B.C.E. Regarded as a wise and great king, he was known for his brilliant and just decisions. Solomon was the last king to rule over the united Kingdom of **Judah** and Israel. He was responsible for building the **First Temple** in **Jerusalem.** Jewish tradition says he was the author of three biblical books: Song of Songs, Proverbs, and Ecclesiastes.

source criticism—An analysis that divides the text of a work into earlier written documents that have been combined by editors, or **redactors**. When applied to the **Torah** as a whole, it suggests that the Torah is composed of four main sources—four originally separate, (more or less) complete documents, labeled J, E, P, and D.

stichography—The convention of visually distinguishing poetic passages.

Sumer—An ancient urban civilization of Southeast **Mesopotamia**.

Syria—The region around Damascus. From the middle of the second millennium B.C.E. it was chiefly populated by Aramean peoples.

ta'amim—See **trope**.

Tabernacle—The tent structure used to house the portable wilderness sanctuary that served as the center of ancient **Israelite** worship until the construction of the **First Temple** in **Jerusalem** by King **Solomon**. It was set up, taken down, and carried by the **Levites;** when stationary, the Pillar of Cloud rested on it. The inner sanctum of the **Tabernacle,** called the **Holy of Holies**, contained the **Ark** of the **Covenant**; it was surrounded by curtains. The **Hebrew** word for the Tabernacle is *mishkan.*

Talmud—The collection of ancient Rabbinic laws, commentaries, and traditions related to the **Torah.** The Talmud is a compilation of two books: the **Mishnah,** or **Oral Law,** and the **Gemara**, which consists of commentaries on the Mishnah. There are 63 areas of study that make up the Talmud, called tractates. Much of the Talmud follows a format in which a law from the Mishnah is cited, followed by Rabbinic discussions and rulings on its meaning. The Talmud explains and elaborates on every aspect of Jewish life, including daily prayers, mitzvot, and holiday celebrations. There are two versions: the **Jerusalem** (*Yerushalmi*) or Palestinian Talmud, compiled in the late 5th century C.E., and the more extensive and more widely used Babylonian (*Bavli*) Talmud, compiled in the late 6th century C.E.

Tanakh—An acronym for the three collections that make up the Jewish **Bible:** the **Torah, Nevi'im,** and **Kethuvim.** The Torah is the **Five Books of Moses:** Genesis, Exodus, Leviticus, Numbers, and Deuteronomy. Nevi'im contains the books of **Prophets,** from which come the *haftarot.* Kethuvim, or **Writings,** includes Proverbs, Psalms and Job, historical accounts, and the five scrolls, or *megillot.* Also spelled Tanach.

Targum—**Aramaic** translations of the **Hebrew** biblical books, believed to have been written in the **Second Temple** era.

tas—A silver plaque that is inscribed with the name of a particular holiday or Shabbat service. It is placed in a window on a **Torah**'s breastplate (*hoshen*), indicating that the **Torah** has been rolled to the right place for the reading for the upcoming occasion. These nameplates are stored in a small box soldered to the *hoshen.*

Temple—See **First Temple, Second Temple.**

Ten Commandments—According to the Jewish tradition, the Ten Commandments are as follows: (1) I am the Lord your God, (2) you shall have no other gods besides me and shall not create or worship false idols, (3) you shall not swear falsely nor take God's name in vain, (4) remember the Sabbath and keep it holy, (5) honor your father and mother, (6) you shall not murder, (7) you shall not commit adultery, (8) you shall not steal, (9) you shall not bear false witness against your neighbor, and (10) you shall not covet anything that belongs to your neighbor. Jewish tradition says that the stone tablets containing the Ten Commandments were given to **Moses** by God at **Mount Sinai.** The first four commandments describe the relationship of humankind to God; the next six describe the relationship of person to person. Also known as the **Decalogue.**

Tetragrammaton—The four **Hebrew** letters—*yud, heh, vav, heh*—that compose the inexpressible name of God. These letters are usually transliterated as *YHVH.* Today, because Jews believe that God's name is sacred, it is not spoken; instead the letters are usually read as *Adonai* or *ha-Shem.*

Tirzah—The second capital of **Israel**, lying about 11 miles to the northeast of **Shechem** (the first capital). Here Zimri murdered Elah; here also he burned his own palace over his head when the city was taken by **Omri**.

Torah—The first five books of the Bible, also called the **Five Books of Moses** and the **Pentateuch.** The Torah is the most revered and sacred book of Judaism. It begins with Genesis and the creation of the world, and ends with Deuteronomy and the death of **Moses.** The Torah codifies the principles of the **Ten Commandments** and contains much of the ancient history and traditions of the Jewish people. The books of the Torah—the **Written Law**—are Genesis, Exodus, Leviticus, Numbers, and Deuteronomy.

Torah mi-Sinai—Literally, "**Torah** from **Sinai.**" The traditional belief that the Torah and all aspects of Jewish law are the direct word of God, given to **Moses** on **Mount Sinai**.

Tree of Knowledge—The tree in the **Garden of Eden** whose fruit gave knowledge to those who tasted it.

Tree of Life—The tree in the **Garden of Eden** whose fruit gave immortality to those who tasted it.

trope—The special musical notes, designated by a series of lines and dots, that indicate the tune for chanting prayers and readings from the **Torah** and **haftarah.** Trope symbols are not written in the Torah scroll; they are printed in a book called a *tikun* and are also printed in most vocalized editions of the **Bible**. There may be slight variations in trope marks from one edition to another. Trope may also be included in a *Humash.* To chant the Torah portion, the reader must learn the trope along with the **Hebrew** words. Trope symbols were created by scholars known as **Masoretes**, who lived in **Israel** during the 9th and 10th centuries C.E. Also called masoretic accents and *ta'amim.*

Twelve Tribes of Israel—The 12 clans into which the **Israelites** were divided in biblical times. Each tribe was descended from one of **Jacob**'s 12 sons: **Reuben, Simeon, Levi, Judah, Dan, Naphtali, Gad, Asher, Issachar, Zebulun, Joseph,** and **Benjamin.** When **Joshua** led the Israelites into **Canaan,** he gave each tribe, except Levi, a particular territory according to its size.

Tyre—An ancient Phoenician city whose marvelous wealth and commerce are described by Ezekiel, who also foretold of its destruction by **Nebuchadnezzar** after a 13-year siege. It was rebuilt on an island rock, but again stormed by Alexander. **David** and **Solomon** made peace with Hiram, its king.

Ur of the Chaldees—The birthplace of **Abraham**, located in southern **Babylonia**.

Valley of Hinnom—This valley was the scene of the idolatrous worship of a god named Molech by the **Hebrew** text. In the religious reforms of **Josiah**, the worship was abolished, and the valley desecrated forever. Henceforth, the Jews used it as a place into which they cast all manner of refuse and the bodies of animals and criminals. To prevent infection, great fires were kept always burning, and the place became the symbol of the place of future punishment, Gehennom, or Gehenna.

243

Vashti—Queen Vashti was the first wife of King **Ahasuerus** of **Persia**. She displeased the king by refusing to show off her beauty at a banquet and was deposed and replaced by **Esther**.

Vulgate—Latin translation of the **Hebrew Bible** by the church father Jerome (345–420 C.E.). It became the official Latin version of the Bible for the Roman Catholic Church.

Western Wall—The archaeological site in the Old City of **Jerusalem**, which is believed to be the outside retaining wall of the mount of the **Second Temple**. Previously referred to by some as the Wailing Wall.

wimpel—The long band of material, usually two to three inches wide, that encircles and holds together the two rolls of a **Torah** scroll, like a belt. It is placed around the *sefer Torah* before the mantle, breastplate, and crown are put on, in a process known as "dressing the Torah."

Wisdom Literature—The biblical books Proverbs, Job, and Ecclesiastes, which are characterized by praise of God, sayings that give advice about living a virtuous life, and criticisms about the assumptions of conventional wisdom. Parts of Psalms are considered by some to be part of Wisdom Literature, as are the apocryphal books the Wisdom of Solomon and Ben Sira (also called Ecclesiasticus and sometimes spelled Ben Sirach).

Writings—See **Kethuvim**.

244

Written Law—The **Torah, the Five Books of Moses**. The term "Written Law" is used in contrast to **Oral Law**, which includes all the commentaries, expositions, and Rabbinic explanations of points of Torah that were passed down from generation to generation since ancient times. Traditional Jews believe in the concept of *Torah mi-Sinai,* that the Torah and all aspects of Jewish law are the words of God, as given to **Moses** (and written down) at **Mount Sinai**.

yad—Literally, "hand." A small pointer used when reading the **Torah.** Because a *sefer Torah* is fragile, handwritten, and easily damaged by dirt and oil from human hands, the *yad* is used to point to the words so the reader does not touch the scroll. A *yad* also allows the reader to follow the words without obscuring the view of others gathered around the podium for *aliyot*. A *yad* often is shaped like a human hand, with the index finger pointing outward. Usually made of wood or silver, the *yad* is attached to a chain or a string and hung from the Torah.

YHVH—See **Tetragrammaton**.

Zadok—A biblical priest during the reign of **David**, his genealogy traces back to **Aaron**. The High Priesthood remained in the hands of the Zadokites from this time until the rise of the **Maccabees.** The descendants of Zadok increased in rank and influence, so that his son Azariah was one of the officers of **Solomon,** and his son Ahimaaz married a daughter of Solomon.

Zebulun—Tenth son of **Jacob** and sixth son of **Leah.** Zebulun is also the name of one of the **Twelve Tribes of Israel,** whose members were said to be descended from him. The tribe inhabited the northern part of **Canaan.**

Zerubbabel—Took a prominent part in the reorganization of the community upon returning from the exile in **Babylon** and shortly afterward succeeded to the governorship of **Judah.**

Zion—1. One of the biblical names for the ancient city of **Jerusalem.** Zion included the Temple Mount and the walled city. 2. Poetic name for ancient **Israel.**

Zipporah—Daughter of **Jethro** and wife of **Moses.** Moses and Zipporah had two sons, Gershom and Eliezer.

Contributions from Joyce Eisenberg and Ellen Scolnic, *Dictionary of Jewish Words.*

FAMILY TREE OF THE TORAH:

Adam

Cain

Enoch

Irad

Mehujael

Methusael

Zillah (1) · · · · · · · · · · Lamech · · · · · · · · · · Adah (2)

Naamah Tubal-cain   Jubal Jabal

Japheth

Tiras Gomer Magog Madai Tubal Javan Meshech   Elam Asshur

Togarmah Ashkenaz Riphath   Elishah Tarshish Kittim Dodanim

Joktan

Jobab Ophir Uzal Abimael Obal Diklah Sheba

Hazarmaveth Jerah Sheleph Hadoram Almodad Havilah

Haran   Keturah (3) · · · · · · · · Hagar (2) · · · · · · ·

1st Daughter (1) · · · Lot · · · 2nd Daughter (2)

Moa Ben-Ammi

Jokshan Shuah Zimran Midian Ishbak Medan Ishmael

Sheba Dedan   Epher Abida Enoch Eldaah Ephah

Leummim Letushim Asshurim

Kedmah Jetur Massa Dumah Kedar Adbeel Mahalath

Naphish Mishma Hadad Tema Mibsam Nebaioth

Zilpah (4) · · · · · · · Bilhah (3) · · · · · ·

Basemath (3) · · · Esau · · · Oholibamah (2) · · · Adah (1)   Gad Asher   Dan Naphtali

Reuel Jeush Jalam Korah Eliphaz

Timma Teman Omar Zepho Gatam Kenaz Amalek

Nahath Shammah Mizzah Zerah

Gershon

Libni Shimei

Elisheba · · · Aaron

Eleazer Nadab Abihu Ithamar

Phinehas

ADAM THROUGH MOSES'S DESCENDENTS

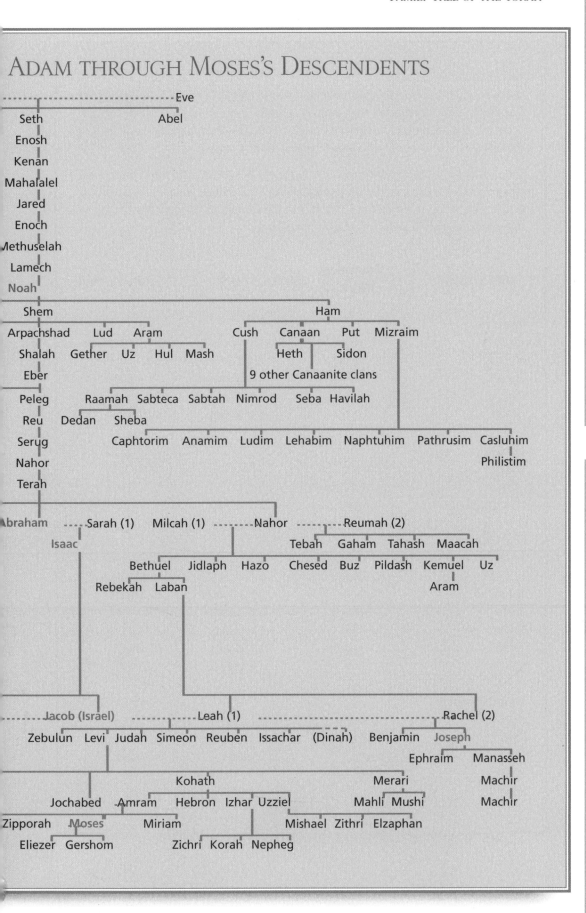

Weights and Measures

Many things in the Bible are given precise measurements: Noah's Ark, the Ark of the Covenant, the Tabernacle, the Temple, priestly vestments, and other objects. Offerings and sacrifices are also measured: the books of Ezekiel and Leviticus give the weights or volume for offerings of grain, oil, and wine.

The shekel, just under ½ ounce, was the basic unit of weight. And the cubit, the distance from the elbow to the fingertips, about 17 ½ inches, was the basic unit of length. The omer, the traditional offering at the Temple of the new barley crop on the second day of Passover, is about ½ dry gallon.

NJPS English	Equivalent Measure	U.S.	Metric
Weights			
Talent	60 minas	75.6 pounds	34.3 kilograms
Mina	50 shekels	20.1 ounces	571.2 grams
Shekel	20 gerahs	176.3 grains	11.4 grams
Pim	0.67 shekel	117.5 grains	5.7 grams
Gerah		8.8 grains	0.57 gram
Length			
Cubit	2 spans	17.5 inches	0.43 meter
Span	3 handbreadths	8.7 inches	0.22 meter
Handbreath	4 fingers	2.9 inches	0.07 meter
Dry Measure			
Homer, kor	2 lethechs	6.5 bushels	229.7 liters
Lethech	5 ephahs	3.6 bushels	114.8 liters
Ephah	3 seahs	20.9 quarts	22.9 liters
Seah	3.3 omers	6.6 quarts	7.7 liters
Omer	1.8 kavs	2.1 quarts	2.3 liters
Tenth of a measure	0.1 ephah	2.1 quarts	2.3 liters
Kav		1.6 quarts	1.3 liters
Liquid Measure			
Kor	10 baths	60.7 gallons	230 liters
Bath	6 hins	6.07 gallons	23 liters
Hin	3 kabs	1 gallon	3.8 liters
Kab	4 logs	1.5 quarts	1.4 liters
Log		0.1 pint	0.3 liter

In Genesis 6–9, God tells Noah to build an ark 300 cubits long, 50 cubits wide, and 30 cubits high. That is about 145 yards long—longer than a football field—and 24 yards wide.

According to Exodus 25 and 26, the Ark of the Covenant measures in at 2½ cubits long, 1½ cubits wide, and 1½ cubits high—about 3½ feet by 2 feet by 2 feet.

The Ark sits in the Holy of Holies, 10 cubits by 10 cubits—15 feet by 15 feet—within the Tabernacle, 10 cubits by 30 cubits—15 feet by 45 feet.

More impressively, the Tabernacle used 29 talents and 730 shekels of gold: almost 2,210 pounds of gold, worth more than 20 million dollars today.

Timeline of Biblical Events

NOTE: The dates below, until the division of the kingdom, are based on the internal biblical chronology (e.g., Exod. 12:40) and, when possible, on scholarly approximations. The number of years that each king reigned, as reported in the Bible, does not always coincide with the internal chronology, due to the fact that in many cases the heir to the throne, before becoming king on his own, was co-regent with his father.

From the Patriarchs to the death of King Solomon

20TH CENTURY B.C.E.

1950   Abraham is born in Ur of the Chaldeans (situated in today's Iraq).

19TH CENTURY B.C.E.

1875   Abraham emigrates with his wife Sarah and his nephew Lot from Haran, (situated in today's Turkey), to Canaan, (today's Israel), at the age of 75.

1850   Isaac is born.

1810   Isaac at the age of 40 marries Rebekah.

18TH CENTURY B.C.E.

1790   Jacob is born.

1750   Hyksos (possibly a Canaanite people) invade Egypt and seize control.

17TH CENTURY B.C.E.

1660   Jacob with his family settles in Egypt.

1643   Death of Jacob in Egypt.

1600   Alphabet writing is developed, probably in Canaan.

16TH CENTURY B.C.E.

1570   Ahmose I expels the Hyksos and restores native Egyptian control to Egypt.

13TH CENTURY B.C.E.

1230   Exodus of the People of Israel from Egypt, after having been 430 years in Egypt (Exod. 12:40), led by Moses.

12TH CENTURY B.C.E.

1190   After wandering 40 years in the desert of Sinai, the Hebrew tribes enter Canaan, under the command of Joshua, and defeat and destroy a number of Canaanite cities.

1150   The Peoples from the Sea invade Egypt but are turned back. Part of them, the Philistines, settle in the southern coast of Canaan, where they set up a network of five cities: Ashdod, Ashkelon, Ekron, Gaza, and Gath.

1120   The northern tribes of Israel, under the leadership of Deborah, defeat Sisera.

1100   Gideon is judge over Israel. After his death, his son Abimelech destroys the city of Shechem.

11TH CENTURY B.C.E.

1075   The city of Geba is destroyed during an intertribal war against the tribe of Benjamin.

1050   The Philistines destroy Shiloh and capture the Ark of God. Samuel becomes judge over Israel.

1020   Saul is anointed by Samuel as the first king of Israel. He unites the tribes, which until then had formed a loose confederation.

1005   Saul is defeated by the Philistines and dies. David is chosen king of Judah in Hebron at the age of 30.

10TH CENTURY B.C.E.

998   After reigning seven years over Judah in Hebron, David becomes king of all the tribes, when the northern Israelite tribes join Judah in recognizing David as king.

990   David conquers Jerusalem from the Jebusites and makes it the capital of his kingdom.

970   Absalom attempts to overthrow his father, David.

965   David dies at the age of 70 after reigning for 40 years, seven over Judah in Hebron and 33 in Jerusalem over the united country. He is succeeded by his son Solomon.

961   Solomon starts the building of the Temple.

954   King Solomon finishes the Temple, a project that took seven years.

928   Rehoboam succeeds Solomon. The northern tribes secede and choose Jeroboam as king of Israel, while Rehoboam remains king of Judah.

From the division of the Kingdom to the fall of Israel

10TH CENTURY B.C.E.

923   The Egyptian pharaoh Sheshonk I (called Shishak in the Bible) invades Judah and takes with him all the treasures that he finds in the Temple and in the palace in Jerusalem. He also destroys several cities in both Judah and Israel.

922   Jeroboam moves his capital from Shechem to Tirzah and establishes two shrines at both ends of his kingdom, Bethel and Dan.

913   Abijah succeeds Rehoboam in Judah and reigns for three years.

908   Asa succeeds Abijah in Judah and reigns for 41 years.

907   Nadab succeeds his father, Jeroboam, in Israel and reigns for one year.

906   Nadab is killed by one of his officers, Baasha, who usurps the throne of Israel, and reigns for 23 years.

9TH CENTURY B.C.E.

886   King Asa asks King Ben Hadad of Damascus for help against Baasha, who is trying to seize the territory just north of Jerusalem.

883   Baasha of Israel is succeeded by his son Elah, who reigns one year.

882   Elah, king of Israel, is killed by Zimri, one of his army commanders, who reigns for only seven days, until Omri, acclaimed king by the people, takes Tirzah, the capital city. Zimri, seeing that he is lost, finds refuge in the palace, burns it, and dies in the flames. Tibni challenges Omri for the Kingdom, but Omri prevails and Tibni dies.

871   Omri of Israel dies, after reigning the first years in the old capital of Tirzah and his final years in Samaria, which he founded and made his capital. His son Ahab succeeds him and reigns for 21 years.

867   Asa, king of Judah, dies and is succeeded by his son Jehoshaphat, who reigns for 21 years.

853   The Assyrian record of Shalmaneser III mentions that king Ahab took part in the battle of Qarqar with 2,000 chariots and 10,000 soldiers. This event is not mentioned in the Bible.

850   Ahab, king of Israel, is mortally wounded in battle. His son Ahaziah succeeds him. During Ahab's reign, his wife Jezebel, a Sidonian princess, introduces in Israel the worship of the Phoenician god Baal, against the protest and resistance of the prophet Elijah.

848   Elisha succeeds Elijah as the leading prophet. Ahaziah, the king of Israel, dies and is succeeded by his brother Jehoram (Joram).

846   Jehoshaphat of Judah dies, and is succeeded by his son Jehoram.

843   Jehoram, king of Judah, dies and is succeeded by his son Ahaziah.

842   King Jehoram of Israel and King Ahaziah of Judah are killed in a revolt by Jehu, who becomes king and kills all the members of the royal house of Israel, together with members of the royal family of Judah. Athaliah, the queen mother, liquidates the surviving members of the royal house of Judah, with the exception of Jehoash, who is hidden by the High Priest.

836   Athaliah is killed in a palace revolt, and Jehoash is proclaimed king in Judah.

814   Jehu, king of Israel, dies and is succeeded by his son Jehoahaz.

800   Jehoahaz, king of Israel, dies and is succeeded by his son Jehoash, during whose reign the prophet Elisha becomes very ill and dies.

8TH CENTURY B.C.E.

798   Jehoash of Judah is killed by palace conspirators. His son, Amaziah, succeeds him.

784   King Jehoash of Israel dies and is succeeded by his son Jeroboam II, during whose rule the prophet Amos is active.

769   King Amaziah of Judah is murdered by conspirators. His son Uzziah succeeds him.

748   King Jeroboam II of Israel dies and is succeeded by his son Zechariah. He rules six months and is murdered by Shallum, who, after being king for only one month, is himself murdered by Menahem, who becomes king.

739   Uzziah of Judah dies and is succeeded by his son Jotham.

737   Menahem of Israel, who had become a tributary of Assyria, dies and is succeeded by his son Pekahiah.

735   King Pekahiah of Israel is killed by Pekah, one of his commanders, who succeeds him as king.

733   Tillegath-pilneser, king of Assyria, invades Israel, captures a number of cities and exiles many inhabitants.

732   Hoshea plots against Pekah, king of Israel, assassinates him, and succeeds him as king, with Israel becoming a vassal kingdom of the Assyrian Empire. Jotham, the king of Judah, dies and is succeeded by his son Ahaz.

725   Hoshea revolts against Assyria. King Shalmaneser of Assyria invades Israel, and besieges Samaria. Micah prophesies the fall of the city.

722/1   Sargon II, king of Assyria, sacks Samaria and exiles a large segment of the population. The kingdom of Israel comes to an end. The deported Israelites—the legendary Ten Lost Tribes—do not survive as a community; they assimilate into their new localities and disappear from history. Esarhaddon, king of Assyria, and after him his son Ashurbanipal, bring foreigners (whose descendants are later known as Samaritans) to settle in the abandoned cities of Israel.

From the fall of Israel to the fall of Judah

8TH CENTURY B.C.E.

727   Jotham of Judah dies and is succeeded by his son Ahaz.

716   King Ahaz of Judah dies and is succeeded by his son Hezekiah, who encourages the immigration of the northerners who escaped exile.

701   The Assyrians, under Sennacherib, lay siege to Jerusalem, but King Hezekiah, with the moral encouragement of the prophet Isaiah, does not surrender, and the Assyrians retire without taking the city.

7TH CENTURY B.C.E.

688   King Hezekiah of Judah dies and is succeeded by his son Manasseh, who becomes an Assyrian vassal and promotes foreign cults in Judah.

642   King Manasseh of Judah dies and is succeeded by his son Amon.

640   Amon is murdered by his officers in the palace. The people of Judah kill the assassins and make his son Josiah king of Judah, during whose kingdom the prophets Zephaniah, Jeremiah, and Nahum are active.

609   Josiah, while trying to stop an expedition force of Pharaoh Neco, is killed in battle and succeeded by his son Jehoahaz, who is dethroned after three months by Pharaoh Neco and succeeded by another of Josiah's sons, Jehoiakim, who becomes an Egyptian vassal.

605   Pharaoh Neco is defeated by Nebuchadnezzar, who makes Jehoiakim a vassal of Babylon.

6TH CENTURY B.C.E.

598   Jehoiakim dies and is succeeded by his son Jehoiachin.

597   Nebuchadnezzar lays siege to Jerusalem; the king surrenders and is taken prisoner to Babylon, together with the treasures in the Temple. Zedekiah, uncle of the deposed king Jehoiachin, is named king by the Babylonians and governs as a puppet, until a few years later when he revolts.

586   After two years of siege the Babylonians breach the walls of Jerusalem. King Zedekiah escapes but is caught, blinded after seeing his sons get killed, put in chains, and taken to Babylon. Nebuzaradan, commander of the Babylonian army, burns down the Temple, the palace, and most of the city and exiles the people to Babylon.

From the fall of Judah to the return to Zion

6TH CENTURY B.C.E.

585   Gedaliah, appointed governor of Judah by Babylon, is murdered by Judean nationalists who consider him a Babylonian collaborator. Other Babylonian supporters flee to Egypt, taking the prophet Jeremiah with them.

561   Upon the death of Nebuchadnezzar, Evilmerodach, the new king of Babylon, releases Jehoiachin from prison and lets him stay in the Babylonian court.

550   Cyrus the Persian gains control of the Median Empire.

539   Cyrus, king of Persia, conquers Babylon.

538   Cyrus authorizes the exiles to return to their land. A number of them do, led by Sheshbazzar, a member of the Judean royal family.

522   Zerubbabel, a descendant of the royal family, is made governor of Judea, which is now a Persian province.

520   The reconstruction of the Temple begins.

515   The Temple is completed.

5TH CENTURY B.C.E.

486   Xerxes I succeeds his late father Darius as king of Persia. Most scholars identify him as King Ahasuerus in the book of Esther.

450   The book of Malachi is written.

445   A Jewish official of the Persian court, Nehemiah, is appointed governor of Judea and is sent to Jerusalem, where he rebuilds the walls of the city.

437   The Jerusalem walls are completed.

433   Nehemiah returns to Babylon. Eliashib, the High Priest, allows Tobiah, governor of the Persian province of Transjordan and bitter enemy of Nehemiah, to stay in the Temple.

431   Nehemiah is reappointed to Jerusalem. Upon his arrival he expels Tobiah and enforces observance of the Sabbath and the ban on intermarriage.

428   The priest-scribe Ezra arrives in Judah, authorized by the Persian government to teach the Jews the laws of Moses. He forces those who had married foreign women to divorce them and to commit themselves to the exact observance of the religious laws.

From the return to Zion to the reign of Herod

The following events are postbiblical.

4TH CENTURY B.C.E.

330   Alexander the Great conquers Persia, and the whole Middle East including the Land of Israel.

323   Alexander the Great dies of malaria in Babylon. His generals divide the empire between them. Ptolemy gets control of Egypt. Seleucus controls Babylonia.

301   Ptolemy I of Egypt conquers the Land of Israel.

3RD CENTURY B.C.E.

250   The Hebrew Bible is translated to Greek in Alexandria.

217   Antiochus III of Syria conquers the Land of Israel, but Ptolemy IV defeats him and recovers it.

2ND CENTURY B.C.E.

198   The Seleucids conquer the Land of Israel.

175   Antiochus IV Epiphanes, descendant of Seleucus, becomes king.

169   Antiochus IV plunders the Temple treasuries.

167   Antiochus bans Jewish religious practices and desecrates the Temple.

166   The Hasmonean family of priests in the Judean town of Modiin leads a rebellion against the Hellenistic priests in Jerusalem and against the regime of Antiochus. The revolt begins when the Hasmonean patriarch slays a Jew making a sacrifice ordained by Antiochus.

164   Judah Maccabee, leader of the rebellion, is victorious over the Syrian armies, captures Jerusalem, and rededicates the Temple.

160   Judah Maccabee dies in battle. His brother Jonathan assumes the leadership.

142   Jonathan is murdered. His brother Simeon assumes the leadership. The independence of Judea is recognized by the Syrians. Judea signs a treaty with Rome.

134   Simeon is assassinated. John Hyrcanus assumes the leadership.

1ST CENTURY B.C.E.

67   Civil war starts between Hyrcanus II and his brother Aristobulus II.

63   Pompey captures Jerusalem, brings Palestine under Roman rule, and appoints Hyrcanus II High Priest.

44   Julius Caesar is assassinated by Brutus, Cassius, and others.

40   The Parthians invade Palestine and help Antigonus, son of Aristobulus II, to seize control. The Senate in Rome proclaims Herod, son of the Idumean Antipater, king of the Jews.

37   Jerusalem is captured by Herod, who starts his reign.

31   Octavius defeats Mark Anthony and becomes master of the Roman world.

27   Octavius is proclaimed emperor under the name Augustus (the Exalted).

22   Herod begins the construction of the Roman port of Caesarea in the Mediterranean.

From the death of Herod to the fall of Masada

1ST CENTURY B.C.E.

4   Death of Herod. The Romans divide his kingdom among his three sons: Judea, Samaria, and Idumea to Archelaus, Galilee to Herod Antipas, and the Lebanon districts to Philip. Birth of Jesus.

1ST CENTURY C.E.

6   Augustus deposes Archelaus and puts Judea under the direct control of a Roman governor.

14   Tiberius succeeds Augustus.

37   Caligula succeeds Tiberius.

41   Claudius succeeds Caligula. Herod Agrippa I is appointed king of Judea.

44   Herod Agrippa dies, and Judea reverts to direct Roman government under a procurator.

53   Nero succeeds Claudius.

66   The Jews revolt against Rome.

70   Titus takes Jerusalem and burns down the Temple.

73   Masada, the last Jewish fortress, falls to the Romans. Hundreds of defenders commit suicide, choosing to die before becoming slaves.

Adapted from David Mandel, *Who's Who in the Jewish Bible*.

Chronology of the Prophets*

Nathan (10th c.) (In the time of David and Solomon)

Ahijah (mid-late 10th c.) (Solomon)

Elijah (mid-9th c.) (Ahab)

Elisha (mid-late 9th c.) (Jehoram, Jehoshaphat, Joram, Ahaziah, Joash, Jehu)

Amos (early-mid 8th c.) (Uzziah and Jeroboam II)

Jonah (early-mid 8th c.) (Jeroboam II)

Hosea (8th c.) (Jeroboam II-Hoshea)

Micah (mid-8th-early 7th c.) (Jotham, Ahaz, Hezekiah)

Isaiah (early 8th-early 7th c.) (King Uzziah's death, Ahaz, Pekah, Hezekiah)

Zephaniah (mid-late 7th c.) (Josiah)

Jeremiah (mid-7th-early 6th c.) (Josiah, Jehoahaz, Jehoiakim, Jehoiachim, Zedekiah)

Nahum (late 7th c.)

Habakkuk (late 7th c.)

Ezekiel (586, in the time of the Babylonian exile)

Haggai (late 6th c.) (Zerubbabel)

Zechariah (late 6th c.) (Zerubbabel)

Obadiah (early 5th c.)

Malachi (mid-5th c.)

Joel (4th or 5th c.)

*Note: all dates are B.C.E.

Chronology of the Monarchies*

Israel and Judah United

1020 – 1005	Saul
998 – 965	David
965 – 928	Solomon

928 Kingdom Divides—Israel (Northern Kingdom)

928 – 907	Jeroboam
907 – 906	Nadab
906 – 883	Baasha
883 – 882	Elah
882 – 882	Zimri
882 – 872	Tibni
882 – 871	Omri
871 – 850	Ahab
850 – 848	Ahaziah
848 – 842	Jehoram
842 – 814	Jehu
814 – 800	Jehoahaz
800 – 784	Jehoash
784 – 748	Jeroboam II
748 – 748	Zechariah
748 – 748	Shallum
748 – 737	Menahem
737 – 735	Pekahiah
735 – 732	Pekah
732 – 725	Hoshea

722 – 721 Fall of Samaria to the Assyrians and fall of Israel

928 Kingdom Divides—Judah (Southern Kingdom)

928 – 913	Rehoboam
913 – 908	Abijam
908 – 867	Asa
867 – 848	Jehoshaphat
846 – 843	Jehoram
843 – 842	Ahaziah
842 – 836	Athaliah
836 – 798	Jehoash
798 – 769	Amaziah
769 – 739	Uzziah
739 – 732	Jotham
732 – 716	Ahaz
716 – 688	Hezekiah
688 – 642	Manasseh
642 – 640	Amon
640 – 609	Josiah
609 – 609	Jehoahaz
609 – 598	Jehoiakim
598 – 597	Jehoiachin
597 – 586	Zedekiah

586 Fall of Jerusalem and fall Judah

259

*Note: all dates are B.C.E.

Familiar Quotations from the Bible

There are many biblical passages that are familiar to modern readers, even those readers not well versed in the Bible. These passages have a special place in our language and in our literature because they are either central to tradition, liturgy, or teaching or are very familiar as English expressions or idioms.

In the beginning God created the heaven and the earth (Gen. 1:1).*

"Let there be light" (Gen. 1:3).

And God said, "Let us make humankind in our image, after our likeness" (Gen. 1:26).**

The Lord said to Cain, "Where is your brother Abel?" And he said, "I do not know. Am I my brother's keeper?" (Gen. 4:9).

Noah was a righteous man; he was blameless in his age; Noah walked with God (Gen. 6:9).

The Lord said to Abram, "Go forth from your native land and from your father's house to the land that I will show you" (Gen. 12:1).

"Take your son, your favored one, Isaac, whom you love, and go to the land of Moriah, and offer him there as a burnt offering" (Gen. 22:2).

"The voice is the voice of Jacob, yet the hands are the hands of Esau" (Gen. 27:22).

A new king arose over Egypt who did not know Joseph (Exod. 1:8).

I have been a stranger in a strange land (Exod. 2:22).*

He gazed, and there was a bush all aflame, yet the bush was not consumed (Exod. 3:2).

"[A] land flowing with milk and honey" (Exod. 3:17, 13:5, and others).

"Let My people go that they may celebrate a festival for Me in the wilderness" (Exod. 5:1).

Love your fellow as yourself (Lev. 19:18).

Proclaim liberty throughout the land unto all the inhabitants thereof (Lev. 25:10).†

The Lord bless you and protect you! The Lord deal kindly and graciously with you! The Lord bestow His favor upon you and grant you peace! (Num.6:24–26).

"Would that all the Lord's people were prophets " (Num. 11:29).

Hear, O Israel! The Lord is our God, the Lord alone. (Deut. 6:4).

[A] human being does not live on bread alone (Deut. 8:3).**

I have put before you life and death, blessing and curse. Choose life—if you and your offspring would live (Deut. 30:19).

How have the mighty fallen (2 Samuel 1:27).

"My son Absalom! O my son, my son Absalom! If only I had died instead of you!" (2 Sam. 19:1).

"O my son Absalom! O Absalom, my son, my son!" (2 Sam. 19:5).

And they shall beat their swords into plowshares
And their spears into pruning hooks:
Nation shall not take up Sword against nation;
They shall never again know war (Isa. 2:4).

No, this is the fast I desire: To unlock the fetters of wickedness, And untie the cords of the yoke, To let the oppressed go free; To break off every yoke. It is to share your bread with the hungry, And to take the wretched poor into your home; When you see the naked, to clothe him, And not to ignore your own kin. (Isa. 58:6–7).

"He has told you, O man, what is good,
And what the Lord requires of you: Only to do justice
And to love goodness, And to walk modestly with your God" (Mic. 6:8).

Out of the mouth of babes and sucklings hast thou ordained strength because of thine enemies, that thou mightest still the enemy and the avenger. (Ps. 8:2).*

Guard me like the apple of Your eye (Ps. 17:8).

Familiar Quotations from the Bible (continued)

The Lord is my shepherd; I shall not want (Ps. 23).*

Teach us to count our days rightly, that we may obtain a wise heart (Ps. 90:12).

I have strayed like a lost sheep (Ps. 119:176).

He who spares the rod hates his son,
But he who loves him disciplines him early (Prov. 13:24).

What a rare find is a capable wife! Her worth is far beyond that of rubies.
(Prov. 31:10).

"Naked came I out of my mother's womb, and naked shall I return there; the Lord
has given, and the Lord has taken away; blessed be the name of the Lord (Job 1:21).

Yea, the price of wisdom is above rubies (Job 28:18).†

Oh, give me of the kisses of your mouth, For your love is more delightful than wine
(Songs 1:2).

My beloved is mine/And I am his (Songs 2:16).

For wherever you go, I will go; wherever you lodge, I will lodge; your people shall
be my people, and your God my God (Ruth 1:16).

[V]anity of vanities; all is vanity (Eccles. 1:2).*

There is nothing new
Beneath the sun! (Eccles. 1:9).

A season is set for everything, a time for every experience under heaven
(Eccles. 3:1).

[T]he race is not to the swift, nor the battle to the strong, neither yet bread to the
wise, nor yet riches to men of understanding, nor yet favor to men of skill; but
time and chance happeneth to them all (Eccles. 9:11).†

Those noted with an asterisk (*) are from the *King James Version*; those with a dagger (†),
from the OJPS TANAKH, and those with a double asterisk (**), from *The Contemporary Torah*.
All others are from the NJPS TANAKH.

Maps of Biblical Lands

263

264

THE NEAR EAST IN THE TIME
OF THE PATRIARCHS

Caspian
Sea

Persian
Gulf

ELAM

BABYLON

Ur

Erech

Babylon

Tuttul

ASSYRIA

Tigris River

Nineveh

MITANNI

HURRIANS

Euphrates River

Mari

ARABIA

Haran

Tadmor

Carchemish

Hamath

Qatna

Damascus

Aleppo

Kadesh

ARAM
(SYRIA)

AMORITES

Ugarit

Byblos

Sidon

Tyre

Hazor

Megiddo

CANAAN

Shechem

Bethel

Jerusalem

MOAB

Gaza

Gerar

Beer-sheba

EDOM

Isaac's route

MIDIAN

CYPRUS

Mediterranean Sea

SINAI

Zoan

Memphis

EGYPT

Nile River

ARZAWA

Empire of Hammurabi,
early 18th cent. BCE

Empire of Thutmose III,
c. 1468 BCE

Abraham's wanderings

0   100   200 Miles
0   100   200 Kilometers

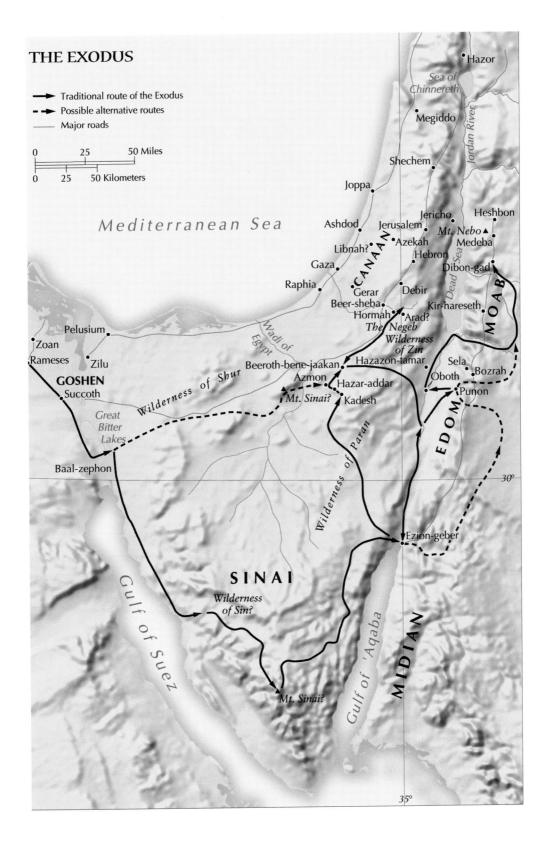

THE EXODUS

→ Traditional route of the Exodus
▸ Possible alternative routes
— Major roads

0   25   50 Miles
0   25   50 Kilometers

Mediterranean Sea

Hazor

Sea of Chinnereth

Megiddo

Shechem

Joppa

Jericho   Heshbon

Ashdod   Jerusalem

Libnah?   Azekah   *Mt. Nebo* ▲   Medeba

Gaza

Beer-sheba

Gerar   Debir

Raphia

Hebron

Dibon-gad

CANAAN

Hormah   Arad?

The Negeb

Wilderness of Zin

Hazazon-tamar

Sela   Bozrah

Oboth

Azmon   Hazar-addar

Beeroth-bene-jaakan

Punon

Mt. Sinai?   Kadesh

Pelusium

Zoan

Rameses   Zilu

GOSHEN

Succoth

Wilderness of Shur

Wadi of Egypt

Great Bitter Lakes

Baal-zephon

MOAB

EDOM

Wilderness of Paran

30°

Ezion-geber

SINAI

Wilderness of Sin?

Gulf of Suez

Gulf of 'Aqaba

MIDIAN

Mt. Sinai?

35°

Jordan River

Dead Sea

Kir-hareseth

265

TWELVE TRIBES OF ISRAEL

Sidon

Mt. Hermon

DAN

Tyre

Dan

Kedesh

ASHER

Hazor

33°

NAPHTALI

MANASSEH

Chinnereth

Sea of
Chinnereth

GESHUR

BASHAN

Achshaph?

ZEBULUN

Hammath

Ashtaroth

Kishon R.

Mt. Tabor

En-dor

Golan

Jokneam

ISSACHAR

Yarmuk River

Edrei

Dor

Megiddo

Jezreel

Kamon?

Taanach

Mt.
Gilboa

Beth-shean

Ramoth-gilead

Jordan River

MANASSEH

Shechem

Zaphon?

Pirathon

GILEAD

Aphek

Jabbok River

Gath-rimmon?

EPHRAIM

Shiloh

GAD

AMMON

Joppa

Bethel

Rabbah

DAN

Gezer

Ai

Gilgal

Gibeon

Gibbethon

Jericho

Heshbon

Ekron

Aijalon

BENJAMIN

Gibeah

Bezer?

Ashdod

Valley of Elah

Beth-shemesh

Jerusalem

Mt. Pisgah

Ashkelon

Gath

Bethlehem

Mt. Nebo

Jarmuth

REUBEN

Gaza

Lachish

JUDAH

Hebron

Aroer

Debir

Ziph

En-gedi

Arnon River

Gerar

Eshtemoa

Arad?

Dead Sea (Salt Sea)

Beer-sheba

MOAB

SIMEON

The Negeb

Zered River

Wilderness
of Zin

EDOM
(SEIR)

Bozrah

Mediterranean Sea

PHILISTINES

266

35°

| 0 | 20 | 40 Miles |
| 0 | 20 | 40 Kilometers |

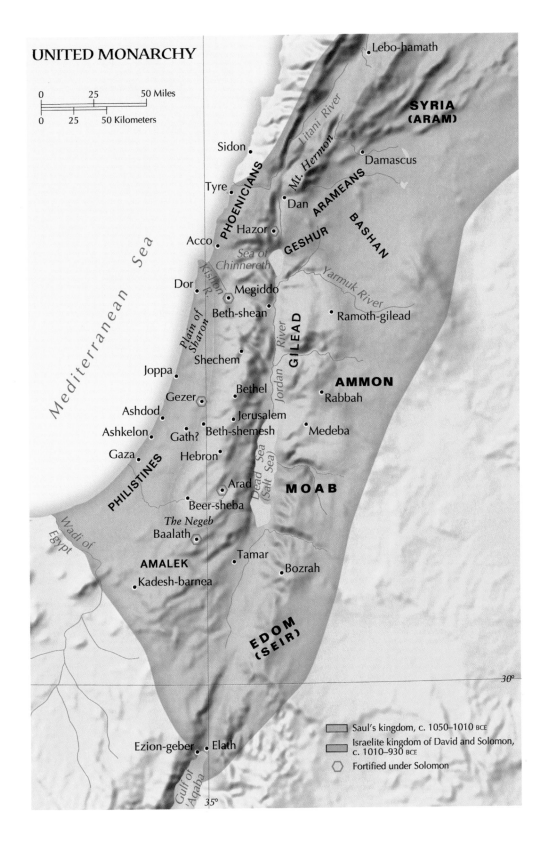

UNITED MONARCHY

0 — 25 — 50 Miles
0 — 25 — 50 Kilometers

Lebo-hamath

**SYRIA
(ARAM)**

Sidon

Litani River

Damascus

Tyre

Dan

Mt. Hermon

PHOENICIANS

ARAMEANS

Hazor

BASHAN

Acco

GESHUR

*Sea of
Chinnereth*

Yarmuk River

Dor

Kishon R.

Megiddo

Beth-shean

Ramoth-gilead

Plain of Sharon

GILEAD

Shechem

Jordan River

Joppa

Bethel

AMMON

Gezer

Rabbah

Ashdod

Jerusalem

Ashkelon

Gath?

Beth-shemesh

Medeba

Gaza

Hebron

PHILISTINES

Mediterranean Sea

Arad

MOAB

Beer-sheba

*Dead Sea
(Salt Sea)*

The Negeb

Baalath

Tamar

AMALEK

Bozrah

Kadesh-barnea

Wadi of Egypt

**EDOM
(SEIR)**

30°

267

Ezion-geber • Elath

Gulf of 'Aqaba

35°

◻ Saul's kingdom, c. 1050–1010 BCE
◻ Israelite kingdom of David and Solomon,
c. 1010–930 BCE
⬡ Fortified under Solomon

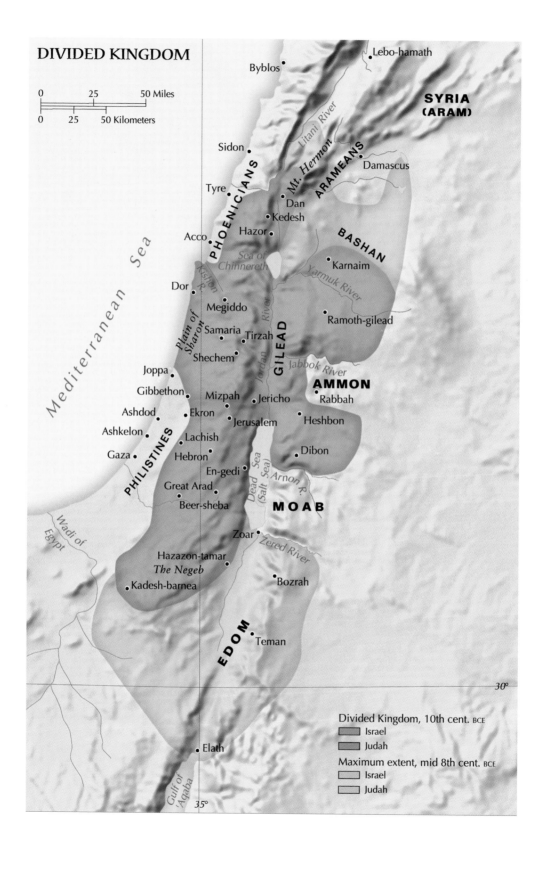

DIVIDED KINGDOM

0   25   50 Miles

0   25   50 Kilometers

Lebo-hamath

Byblos

SYRIA (ARAM)

Litani River

Sidon

Mt. Hermon

ARAMEANS

Damascus

Tyre

PHOENICIANS

Dan

Kedesh

BASHAN

Acco

Hazor

Sea of Chinnereth

Karnaim

Yarmuk River

Dor

Kishon R.

Megiddo

Ramoth-gilead

Plain of Sharon

Samaria

Tirzah

GILEAD

Shechem

Jordan River

Jabbok River

Joppa

AMMON

Gibbethon

Mizpah

Jericho

Rabbah

Ashdod

Ekron

Jerusalem

Heshbon

Ashkelon

Lachish

Gaza

PHILISTINES

Hebron

Dibon

En-gedi

Dead Sea (Salt Sea)

Arnon R.

Great Arad

Beer-sheba

MOAB

Mediterranean Sea

Zoar

Zered River

Wadi of Egypt

Hazazon-tamar

The Negeb

Bozrah

Kadesh-barnea

EDOM

Teman

30°

Elath

Gulf of 'Aqaba

35°

Divided Kingdom, 10th cent. BCE

Israel

Judah

Maximum extent, mid 8th cent. BCE

Israel

Judah

268

Caspian Sea

Persian Gulf

MEDIA

ELAM

MINNI

L. Urmia

PEKOD

Cuthah

BABYLONIA (CHALDEA)

Nippur

Larsa

ARARAT

L. Van

Turushpa

Arbela

Dur-sharrukin

Arrapkha

Sippar

Babylon

Borsippa

Erech

Ur

Tigris River

Nineveh

Calah

Asshur

NAIRI

ASSYRIA

Gozan

BETH-EDEN

Euphrates River

ARABIA

Haran

Rezeph

Tadmor

Tiphsah

QEDAR

Carchemish

Calno

Arpad

Aleppo

HATTINA

Kadesh

SYRIA

Damascus

COMMAGENE (KUMUKHU)

MUSRI

Hamath

TUBAL

Arvad

AMMON

Jerusalem

MOAB

QUE

Gebal (Byblos)

Sidon

Tyre

Acco

ISRAEL

EDOM

Ezion-geber

CILICIA

CYPRUS

Samaria

JUDAH

Gaza

Raphia

SINAI

Mediterranean Sea

Pelusium

Tahpanhes

Heliopolis

Zoan

Sais

Memphis

Nile River

Hermopolis

EGYPT

LYDIA

Sardis

50°

40°

30°

269

THE NEAR EAST IN THE TIME OF THE PROPHETS

☐ Approximate extent of Assyrian domination, latter part of the 8th cent. BCE

0   100   200 Miles

0   100   200 Kilometers

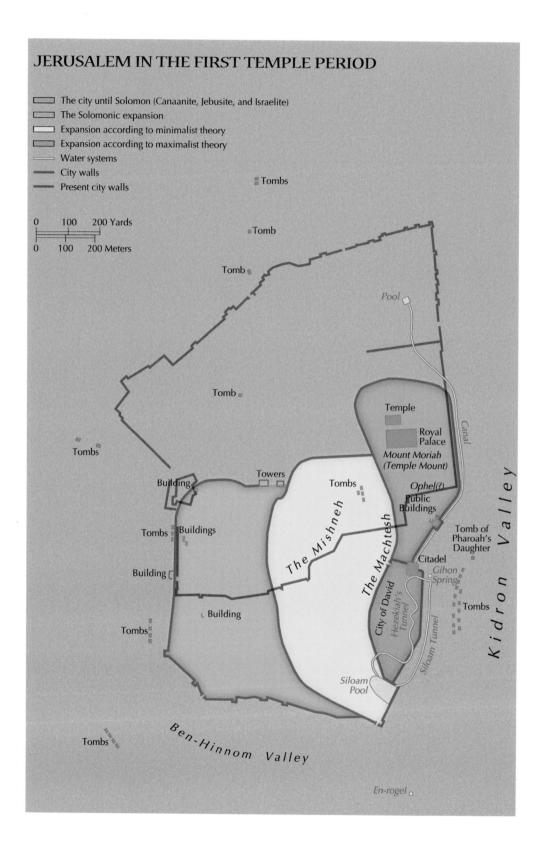

JERUSALEM IN THE FIRST TEMPLE PERIOD

☐ The city until Solomon (Canaanite, Jebusite, and Israelite)
☐ The Solomonic expansion
☐ Expansion according to minimalist theory
☐ Expansion according to maximalist theory
—— Water systems
—— City walls
—— Present city walls

■■ Tombs

0   100   200 Yards
0   100   200 Meters

Tombs

■ Tomb

Tomb ■

Pool ☐

Tomb ■

Tombs

Temple

Royal
Palace

*Mount Moriah
(Temple Mount)*

Towers

Tombs

Ophel(?)
Public
Buildings

Building

The Mishneh

Tombs ■ Buildings

Tomb of
Pharoah's
Daughter

Building ☐

Citadel

The Machtesh

*Gihon
Spring*

City of David

*Hezekiah's
Tunnel*

Tombs

Building

Siloam Tunnel

Canal

Kidron Valley

Tombs

*Siloam
Pool*

Tombs

Ben-Hinnom Valley

En-rogel ○

270

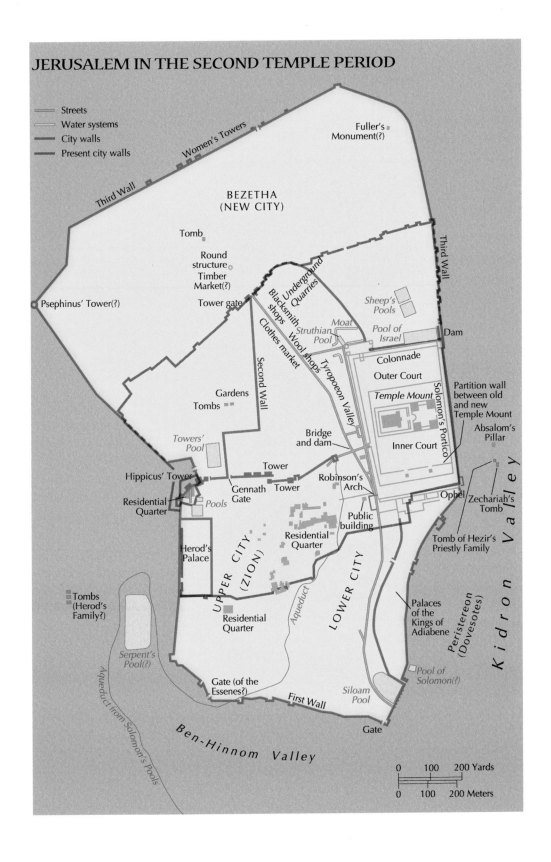

JERUSALEM IN THE SECOND TEMPLE PERIOD

Streets
Water systems
City walls
Present city walls

Women's Towers

Fuller's
Monument(?)

Third Wall

BEZETHA
(NEW CITY)

Tomb

Round
structure
Timber
Market(?)

Third Wall

Psephinus' Tower(?)

Tower gate

Underground
Quarries

Sheep's
Pools

Blacksmith
shops
Wool shops

Struthian
Pool

Moat

Pool of
Israel

Dam

Clothes market

Second Wall

Tyropoeon Valley

Colonnade

Outer Court

Temple Mount

Solomon's Portico

Partition wall
between old
and new
Temple Mount

Gardens

Tombs

Bridge
and dam

Inner Court

Absalom's
Pillar

Towers'
Pool

Tower

Robinson's
Arch

Hippicus' Tower

Gennath
Gate

Tower

Ophel

Zechariah's
Tomb

Residential
Quarter

Pools

Public
building

Tomb of Hezir's
Priestly Family

Residential
Quarter

Herod's
Palace

UPPER CITY
(ZION)

LOWER CITY

Kidron Valley

Tombs
(Herod's
Family?)

Residential
Quarter

Aqueduct

Palaces
of the
Kings of
Adiabene

Peristereon
(Dovesotes)

Serpent's
Pool(?)

Aqueduct from Solomon's Pools

Gate (of the
Essenes?)

First Wall

Siloam
Pool

Pool of
Solomon(?)

Gate

Ben-Hinnom Valley

0   100   200 Yards

0   100   200 Meters

A SHORT LIST OF RECOMMENDED BOOKS AND WEBSITES

Note: See also Bible commentaries listed in "Commentaries on the Bible" and a sampling of midrashic works in "Midrash."

Books

Armstrong, Karen. *The Bible: A Biography*. New York: Atlantic Monthly Press, 2007.

> A short history of the Bible: how, when, and by whom it was written, plus a look at 2,000 years of biblical interpretation by Christians and Jews, scholars and mystics, theologians and critics. Armstrong is author of over 20 books on religion, such as *A History of God* and *The Great Transformation*.

Berlin, Adele, Marc Zvi Brettler, and Michael Fishbane, eds. *The Jewish Study Bible*. New York: Oxford University Press, 2003

> This volume contains the JPS translation with biblical book introductions and extensive sidebar commentary by leading Jewish scholars, plus 24 themed essays, maps, charts, and index. Berlin is professor of Hebrew, University of Maryland. Brettler is professor of biblical studies at Brandeis University. Fishbane is professor of Jewish studies at the University of Chicago Divinity School.

Brettler, Marc Zvi. *How to Read the Bible*. Philadelphia: Jewish Publication Society, 2005. (Also available in paperback, as: *How to Read the Jewish Bible*. New York: Oxford University Press, 2007.)

> Brettler believes that readers can understand the ancient Hebrew Scripture only by knowing more about the culture that produced it. And so, with emphasis on the historical-critical method of interpretation, he takes readers through key sections of the Bible by explaining how they were shaped by the historical conditions, ideological assumptions, and literary conventions prevalent at the time they were written. Brettler is professor of biblical studies at Brandeis University.

Cherry, Shai. *Torah through Time: Understanding Bible Commentary from the Rabbinic Period to Modern Times*. Philadelphia: Jewish Publication Society, 2007.

> Here are six case studies in comparative biblical interpretation, dealing with such issues as the creation of humanity, the rivalry between Cain and Abel, Korah and his gang, and the daughters of Zelophehad. Cherry has a Ph.D. in Jewish thought and theology and has taught at Vanderbilt University, American Jewish University, and UCLA.

Coogan, Michael D. *The Old Testament: A Historical and Literary Introduction to the Hebrew Scriptures*. New York: Oxford University Press, 2005.

Employing the narrative chronology of the Bible itself and the history of the ancient Near East as a framework, Coogan introduces the books of the Hebrew Bible and the Apocrypha with attention to their historical context, literary genre, and distinctive features, with key terms and questions for each chapter, a glossary, time lines, photos, illustrations, and maps. Coogan is professor of religious studies at Stonehill College.

Encyclopaedia Judaica, 2nd ed. Jerusalem: Keter Publishing House; Detroit: Macmillan Reference USA, 2007.

This 22-volume set is a comprehensive reference work about the history and culture of the Jewish people, including entries on the Bible. There are approximately 22,000 entries, over 600 maps, charts, archaeological plans, and chronologies as well as a thematic outline and expansive index.

Freedman, David Noel, ed. *The Anchor Bible Dictionary*. Doubleday, 1992.

This six-volume work is a comprehensive treatment of biblical subjects and scholarship, with nearly 1,000 contributors representing Protestant, Catholic, Jewish, and Muslim traditions, as well as secular interpretation. Freedman is chair of Hebrew biblical studies, University of California, San Diego.

Friedman, Richard E. *Who Wrote the Bible?* San Francisco: HarperCollins, 1997.

Relying on biblical and archaeological evidence, Friedman leads his readers on a fascinating investigation and analysis of the authors of the Torah. He looks at the historical circumstances that led to the writing of the various biblical texts (known as the J, E, P, D, and R sources) and how they were ultimately woven together into the Torah. Friedman is the Ann and Jay Davis Professor of Jewish Studies at the University of Georgia.

273

Ginzberg, Louis. *Legends of the Jews*, 2nd ed. Philadelphia: Jewish Publication Society, 2003.

This is the classic collection of biblical midrash, originally published 1909–1938, and reissued in this two-volume set, with four new indexes and a new introduction by postbiblical and medieval Hebrew literature scholar David Stern, Ruth Meltzer Professor of Classical Hebrew, University of Pennsylvania.

Holtz, Barry W., ed. *Back to the Sources*. New York: Simon & Schuster, 1986.

A classic introduction to classic Jewish texts, including the Bible, Talmud, legal commentaries, midrash, and other texts associated with Kabbalah, Hasidism, and Jewish philosophy. Each chapter, written by an expert in the field, explains what the work is and who wrote it, its literary significance, and how to read the work with greater understanding. Holtz is professor of Jewish education at the Jewish Theological Seminary.

The JPS Bible Commentary series. Philadelphia: Jewish Publication Society, 1999–. Available to date: *Ecclesiastes* (Michael V. Fox), *Esther* (Adele Berlin), *Haftarot* (Michael Fishbane), and *Jonah* (Uriel Simon).

Like The JPS Torah Commentary series, below, each volume in this ongoing collection contains the Hebrew Torah text alongside the JPS English translation, with line-by-line commentary.

The JPS Torah Commentary series. Philadelphia: Jewish Publication Society, 1989–1996. *Genesis* (Naham M. Sarna), *Exodus* (Naham M. Sarna), *Leviticus* (Baruch A. Levine), *Numbers* (Jacob Milgrom), and *Deuteronomy* (Jeffrey H. Tigay).

As in The JPS Bible Commentary series, above, each volume contains the Hebrew Torah text alongside the JPS English translation, with line-by-line commentary below. There are also supplementary essays that elaborate on key words and themes, a glossary of commentators and sources, and notes.

JPS Hebrew-English TANAKH. Philadelphia: Jewish Publication Society, 1999.

The oldest-known complete Hebrew version of the Bible (the masoretic text from the Leningrad Codex), side by side with the NJPS (1985) English translation. The TANAKH is also available in several English-only editions from JPS.

Kugel, James L. *How to Read the Bible: A Guide to Scripture, Then and Now.* New York: Free Press, 2007.

This book includes ancient interpretive approaches as well as an introduction into modern historical-critical approaches to reading the Bible. Kugel styles this work like an introductory course on the Bible, acquainting readers with all its major figures and events, and in the process creates a narrative of the evolution of ancient Israel and of the Hebrew Bible itself. Kugel is professor of Bible and director of the Institute for the History of the Jewish Bible at Bar Ilan University in Israel.

Lieber, David L., ed. *Etz Hayim: Torah and Commentary.* New York: The Rabbinical Assembly and United Synagogue of Conservative Judaism. Produced in Philadelphia by The Jewish Publication Society, 2002.

Etz Hayim includes the 1985 JPS translation of the Torah, broken into weekly *parshiyot*, with accompanying *peshat, derash*, and halakhic commentary, and the *haftarot* readings and commentary. In addition, there are essays on key themes by prominent Conservative rabbis and scholars, maps, a glossary, a brief time line of biblical events, and index. Lieber is president emeritus of the University of Judaism.

Mandel, David. *Who's Who in the Jewish Bible.* Philadelphia: Jewish Publication Society, 2007.

This comprehensive biographical dictionary covers all those named in the Bible— close to 3,000 people. Arranged in A to Z format, each entry includes biographical descriptions, the origin and meaning of their name, the dates he or she lived (if known), and the book, chapter, and verse of the first appearance in the Bible.

Metzger, Bruce, and M. Michael D. Coogan, eds. *The Oxford Companion to the Bible.* New York: Oxford University Press, 1994.

This encyclopedic volume, containing 700 entries from 250-plus Bible scholars, treats the formation, transmission, circulation, socio-historical situations, interpretation, theology, uses, and influence of the Bible. Coogan is professor of religious studies at Stonehill College; Metzger was professor emeritus at Princeton Theological Seminary.

Plaut, G. W. *Torah: A Modern Commentary, Revised Edition.* New York: URJ Press, 2005.

This volume includes a gender-sensitive version of the JPS translation of the TANAKH, with updated commentary and translations. It includes talmudic sources, as well as modern scholarly writings, only adding to what has become the standard *humash* of the Reform movement. Plaut is a leading scholar and rabbi in the Reform movement.

Rabin, Elliott. *Understanding the Hebrew Bible: A Reader's Guide.* Jersey City, NJ: KTAV Publishing House, 2006.

In this introductory overview, Rabin devotes one chapter each to storytelling, law, history, prophecy, wisdom, and poetry in the Bible, plus another to the history of the Bible itself. Rabin is director of education at Makor, a Jewish adult education program in New York City.

Rainey, Anson F., and R. Steven Notley. *Carta's New Century Handbook and Atlas of the Bible.* Jerusalem: Carta, 2007.

A concise overview of biblical history and geography told through an extensive collection of detailed maps and accompanying interpretive texts. Rainey is professor emeritus of the Department of Archaeology and Ancient Near Eastern Studies at Tel Aviv University. Notley is professor of biblical studies at Nyack College–New York City campus.

Scherman, Nosson, ed. *ArtScroll Tanach Series.* Brooklyn: Mesorah Publications, 1976–1998.

The entire Torah, as interpreted by the classic sages of talmudic and rabbinic literature, is included in this volume. Rabbi Scherman collaborated with an international team of Torah scholars to create this comprehensive work.

Stein, David E. S. *The Contemporary Torah.* Philadelphia: Jewish Publication Society, 2006.

A gender-sensitive adaptation of the NJPS translation of the Torah. The preface explains the methodology used for making decisions about God language and gender attributes, and the "Dictionary of Gender in the Torah" in the back of the book provides notes about the translation of key words. Stein is project editor of *Etz Hayim,* and editor of *The Torah: A Modern Commentary,* rev. ed. and the *JPS Hebrew-English TANAKH.*

Helpful Websites

Note: *Online resources often change and move locations. Some of the URLs below, and the links to other sites on these web pages, may have been altered or relocated since this list was created.*

http://orion.mscc.huji.ac.il/index.html

The Orion Center for the Study of the Dead Sea Scrolls and Associated Literature, which provides resources for the study of the Scrolls, a virtual tour of the caves at Qumran, and information about the center's activities and programs.

http://www.aleppocodex.org

Here you can read the Aleppo Codex, the oldest-known manuscript of the complete Hebrew Bible, as well as background on the Codex, the Bible, and the Masoretes.

http://www.bl.uk/treasures/gutenberg/homepage.html

View the British Library's two copies of the Gutenberg Bible, perhaps the first book ever printed by Gutenberg using his printing press in the 1450s. You can also find information on the history of the Bible.

http://www.bookreviews.org

This is the website for the *Review of Biblical Literature*, which was founded by the Society of Biblical Literature. It presents digital and print versions of reviews of books in biblical studies and related fields, thus making the site a great starting point for anyone looking to learn more about these subjects.

http://www.etana.org/abzu

Abzu is a searchable guide to online open access data relevant to the study of the ancient Near East and the ancient Mediterranean world. It is operated by, and linked to, the research archives of the Oriental Institute of the University of Chicago, another resource for information on the ancient Near East.

http://www.ibiblio.org/expo/deadsea.scrolls.exhibit/intro.html

The "Scrolls from the Dead Sea: The Ancient Library of Qumran and Modern Scholarship" exhibit at the Library of Congress, which brings together a selection of Dead Sea Scrolls with a description of their content and of the Qumran community from which they likely originated. The story of their discovery, as well as challenges associated with researching the Scrolls, are also covered.

BIBLIOGRAPHY OF WORKS CITED

Alter, Robert. *The Art of Biblical Narrative.* New York: Basic Books, 1981.

_____. *The Art of Biblical Poetry.* New York: Basic Books, 1985.

_____. *The David Story.* New York: W. W. Norton, 1999.

_____. *The Five Books of Moses, A Translation with Commentary.* New York: W. W. Norton, 2004.

Berlin, Adele. *The JPS Bible Commentary: Esther.* Philadelphia: Jewish Publication Society, 2001.

Amichai, Yehuda. *Open Closed Open.* New York: Hartcourt, 2000.

_____. *The Dynamics of Biblical Parallelism,* rev. ed. Grand Rapids, MI: Eerdmans, 2007.

Brettler, Marc Zvi. *How to Read the Bible.* Philadelphia: Jewish Publication Society, 2005.

Clifford, Richard J. *Proverbs.* Old Testament Library. Louisville, KY: Westminster John Knox, 1999.

Clines, D. J. A. *Job 1–20.* Word Bible Commentary. Waco, TX: Word Books, 1980.

_____. *Job 21–27.* Word Bible Commentary. Waco, TX: Word Books, 2007.

Crenshaw, James L. *Ecclesiastes: A Commentary.* Old Testament Library. Philadelphia: Westminster, 1987.

Curzon, David, ed. *Modern Poems on the Bible.* Philadelphia: Jewish Publication Society, 1994.

Diamant, Anita. *The Red Tent.* New York: St. Martin's Press, 1997.

Eisenberg, Joyce, and Ellen Scolnic. *Dictionary of Jewish Words.* Philadelphia: Jewish Publication Society, 2001.

Encyclopaedia Judaica, 2nd ed. "Poetry." Jerusalem: Keter Publishing House; Detroit: Macmillan Reference USA, 2007.

Fishbane, Michael. *The JPS Bible Commentary: Haftarot.* Philadelphia: Jewish Publication Society, 2002.

Fox, Everett. *The Five Books of Moses. The Schocken Bible,* Vol. 1. New York: Schocken Books, 1995.

Fox, Michael V. *The JPS Bible Commentary: Ecclesiastes.* Philadelphia: Jewish Publication Society, 2004.

_____. *Proverbs 1–9.* Anchor Bible. Garden City, NY: Doubleday, 2000.

_____. *Proverbs 10–31.* Anchor Bible. Garden City, NY: Doubleday, 2008.

Frankel, Ellen. *The Five Books of Miriam.* San Francisco: HarperSanFrancisco, 1998.

Friedman, Richard Elliott. *Commentary on the Torah.* San Francisco: HarperCollins, 2003.

Gordis, Robert. *The Book of Job.* New York: Jewish Theological Seminary, 1978.

Greenberg, Moshe. *Understanding Exodus.* New York: Behrman House, 2006.

Holy Bible: Contemporary English Version. New York: American Bible Society, 1995.

The Holy Bible: King James Version. Peabody, MA: Hendrickson Publishers, 2006.

Holy Bible: New International Version. Colorado Springs, CO: International Bible Society, 1984.

Holtz, Barry W., ed. *Back to the Sources.* New York: Simon and Schuster, 1986.

Kaplan, Aryeh. *The Living Torah: The Five Books of Moses.* New York: Moznaim, 1981.

King James Version Reference Bible. New York: Oxford University Press, 2005.

Knohl, Israel. *The Divine Symphony.* Philadelphia: Jewish Publication Society, 2003.

Kugel, James. *The Idea of Biblical Poetry: Parallelism and Its History.* New Haven, CT: Yale University Press, 1982.

Lieber, David L., ed. *Etz Hayim: Torah and Commentary.* Philadelphia: Jewish Publication Society, 2002.

Milgrom, Jacob. *The JPS Torah Commentary: Numbers.* Philadelphia: Jewish Publication Society, 1990.

Murphy, Roland E. *Ecclesiastes.* Word Bible Commentary. Waco, TX: Word Books, 1992.

_____. *Proverbs.* Word Bible Commentary. Waco, TX: Word Books, 1998.

New American Bible. New York: Oxford University Press, 1990.

The New Revised Standard Version Bible with Apocrypha. New York: Oxford University Press, 1990.

Perdue, Leo G., and W. Clark Gilpin. *The Voice from the Whirlwind.* Nashville, TN: Abingdon, 1992.

Philo. "De Sacrificiis Abelis et Caini." In *Philo,* Vol. 2. Trans. F. H. Colson and G. H. Whitaker. Cambridge, MA: Loeb Classical Library, 1929.

Plaut, W. Gunther, ed. *The Torah: A Modern Commentary.* New York: UAHC, 1983.

Plaut, W. Gunther, and David E. S. Stein, eds. *The Torah: A Modern Commentary,* Rev. ed. New York: URJ Press, 2005.

Pope, Marvin H. *Job.* Anchor Bible. Garden City, NY: Doubleday, 1965.

Reinhartz, Adele. "Jewish Woment's Scholarly Writings on the Bible," in *The Jewish Study Bible*, Adele Berlin and Marc Brettler, eds. New York: Oxford University Press, 2004.

Sandberg, Ruth. *Rabbinic Views of Qohelet*. Lewiston, NY: Mellen, 1999.

Sarna, Nahum M. *The JPS Torah Commentary: Genesis*. Philadelphia: Jewish Publication Society, 1989.

Scherman, Nosson, ed. *ArtScroll Tanach Series*. Brooklyn: Mesorah Publications, 1976–1998.

Schippe, Cullen, and Chuck Stetson, eds. *The Bible and Its Influence*. Fairfax, VA: BLP Publishing, 2006.

Schwartz, Howard. *Voices within the Ark: The Modern Jewish Poets*. New York: Avon Books, 1980.

Schwartz, Rebecca, ed. *All the Women Followed Her: A Collection of Writings on Miriam the Prophet and the Women of Exodus*. Mountain View, CA: Rikudei Miriam Press, 2001.

Seow, Choon-Leong. *Ecclesiastes*. Anchor Bible. Garden City, NY: Doubleday, 1997.

Simon, Uriel. *Reading Prophetic Narratives*. Bloomington, IN: Indiana University Press, 1997.

Stein, David E. S. *The Contemporary Torah*. Philadelphia: Jewish Publication Society, 2006.

Tanach: The Stone Edition. Brooklyn, NY: Mesorah Publications, 1996.

TANAKH: The Holy Scriptures. Philadelphia: Jewish Publication Society, 1917.

TANAKH: The Holy Scriptures—The New JPS Translation According to the Traditional Hebrew Text. Philadelphia: Jewish Publication Society, 1985.

Tigay, Jeffrey H. *The JPS Torah Commentary: Deuteronomy*. Philadelphia: Jewish Publication Society, 1996.

Van Leeuwen, Raymond. *Proverbs*. New Interpreter's Bible. Nashville: Abingdon, 1997.

Visotzky, Burton L. *The Midrash on Proverbs*. New Haven, CT: Yale University Press, 1992.

CONTRIBUTORS

Marc Zvi Brettler, Dora Golding Professor of Biblical Studies, Brandeis University, Waltham, Massachusetts.

Joyce Eisenberg, author and editor of travel books and kosher cookbooks; coauthor of *Dictionary of Jewish Words*.

Michael Fishbane, Nathan Cummings Professor of Jewish Studies, University of Chicago, Chicago, Illinois.

Michael V. Fox, Hills-Bascom Professor of Hebrew, University of Wisconsin, Madison, Wisconsin.

Frederick Greenspahn, Gimelstob Eminent Scholar in Judaica, Coordinator of Jewish Studies, and Director of Religious Studies, Florida Atlantic University, Boca Raton, Florida.

Leonard Greenspoon, Professor of Classical and Near Eastern Languages and of Theology, and Philip M. and Ethel Klutznick Chair in Jewish Civilization, Creighton University, Omaha, Nebraska.

Jill Hammer, Director of Spiritual Education at the Academy of Jewish Religion; Director of Tel Shemesh, a website and community celebrating and creating Jewish traditions related to the earth.

Stuart Kelman, now retired, is the founding rabbi of Congregation Netivot Shalom, Berkeley, California, and is a trained *sofer*.

Adriane Leveen, Assistant Professor of Bible, Hebrew Union College, Los Angeles, California.

David Mandel, Founder of Computronic Corporation, an Israeli software development company that specializes in biblical software.

Lionel Moses, Rabbi of Shaare Zion Congregation in Montreal, Canada; Secretary of the Joint Beth Din of the Conservative Movement.

Shalom Paul, Past Professor of Bible, Jewish Theological Seminary, New York, New York; Professor Emeritus of Bible and Past Chair of Bible, Hebrew University, Jerusalem, Israel.

Adele Reinhartz, Professor of Classics and Religious Studies, University of Ottawa, Ottawa, Ontario, Canada.

Nahum M. Sarna, former Dora Golding Professor Emeritus of Biblical Studies, Brandeis University, Waltham, Massachusetts.

Cullen Schippe, Vice President, Religious Education, Pflaum Publishing Group; former Vice President of Macmillan/McGraw-Hill.

Benjamin Edidin Scolnic, Rabbi of Temple Beth Sholom, Hamden, Connecticut; Biblical Consultant, the North Sinai Archaeological Expedition; Adjunct Professor of Bible, Southern Connecticut State University.

Ellen Scolnic, writer on topics of Jewish interest; coauthor of *Dictionary of Jewish Words.*

David E. S. Stein, revising editor of *The Contemporary Torah: A Gender-Sensitive Adaptation of the JPS Translation*; general editor and revising translator for *The Torah: A Modern Commentary,* rev. ed.; project editor for the *JPS Hebrew-English Tanakh* (1999).

Chuck Steton, Chairman of the Board and Managing Director, Private Equity Investments, Inc., New York, New York.

Jeffrey H. Tigay, A. M. Ellis Professor of Hebrew and Semitic Languages and Literature, University of Pennsylvania, Philadelphia, Pennsylvania.

Barry Dov Walfish, Judaica Specialist at the University of Toronto Libraries, University of Toronto, Toronto, Ontario, Canada.

Andrea Weiss, Assistant Professor of Bible, Hebrew Union College-Jewish Institute of Religion, New York, NY.

Ziony Zevit, Distinguished Professor of Biblical Literature and Northwest Semitic Languages and Literatures, American Jewish University, Los Angeles, California.

INDEX